>>>>> THE <<<<<
WHYS
>>>>> OF A <<<<<
PHILOSOPHICAL
>> SCRIVENER <<

Also by Martin Gardner

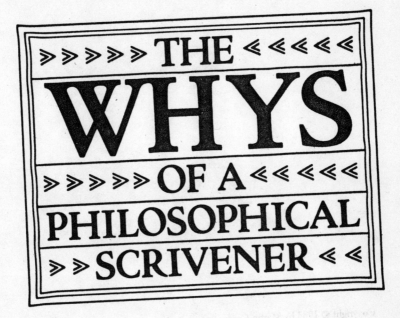

THE WHYS OF A PHILOSOPHICAL SCRIVENER

Martin Gardner

Quill
New York • 1983

Library of Congress Cataloging in Publication Data

Gardner, Martin, 1914–
  The whys of a philosophical scrivener.

  Includes index.
  1. Philosophy—Addresses, essays, lectures.
I. Title.
B29.G253 1983   191   83–5395
ISBN 0-688-02063-1
ISBN 0-688-02064-X (pbk.)

Printed in the United States of America

      6 7 8 9 10

BOOK DESIGN BY RICHARD ORIOLO

Why do I dedicate this book to Charlotte?

She knows.

CONTENTS

INTRODUCTION

This is a book of essays about what I believe and why.

—Martin Gardner

Philosophy is concerned with two matters:
soluble questions that are trivial, and crucial questions
that are insoluble.

—STEFAN KANFER, OPENING A REVIEW OF
A BOOK ABOUT HANNAH ARENDT,
Time, APRIL 19, 1982

1

THE WORLD:
Why I Am Not a Solipsist

Let me not look aloft and see my own
Feature and form upon the Judgment-throne.

—G. K. CHESTERTON

Solipsism is the insane belief that only one's self exists. All other parts of the universe, including other people, are unsubstantial figments in the mind of the single person who alone is truly real. It is almost the same as thinking one is God, and so far as I know, there has never been an authentic solipsist outside a mental institution or who in the past was not considered mad. Why, then, should I waste time beginning my confessional with a chapter on why I am not a solipsist?

One reason is that many philosophers have maintained that solipsism cannot be refuted in any rational way; that a belief in other people and in an outside world must rest on some kind of "animal faith," or perhaps it is no more than a posit one has to make to keep sane, or because it is convenient. In recent years there has been a renewed interest in opinions that, although far from solipsistic, are strongly tinged with solipsistic arguments. Curiously, such opinions are sometimes expressed by eminent physicists who are concerned with the philosophical implications of quantum mechanics. In this chapter I shall try to untangle some of the linguistic snarls in these old debates, and take a clear stand that is essential to all of my beliefs in the rest of the book.

Bertrand Russell enjoyed recalling a letter he once received from a respected logician, Mrs. Christine Ladd-Franklin, in which she professed to be a solipsist. The doctrine seemed to her so irrefutable, she added, that she couldn't understand why no other philosophers were solipsists! In a trivial sense, solipsism is indeed irrefutable. We are all trapped in what has been called our "egocentric predicament." Everything we know about the world is based on information received through our senses. This world of our experience—the totality of all we see, hear, taste, touch, feel, and smell—is sometimes called our "phenomenal world." Obviously there is no way to perceive anything except what can be perceived, to experience anything except what can be experienced. Charles S. Peirce invented a useful word for this phenomenal world. He called it the "phaneron."

What grounds do we have for believing that anything exists outside our private phaneron? Let us admit at once that there is no way to prove to a solipsist (in the unlikely event you ever meet one) that anything exists outside his or her phaneron, if by "prove" you mean the way you prove a theorem in logic or mathematics. The situation is even worse than that. As philosophers have often pointed out, there is no way a solipsist can demonstrate even to himself that he existed before yesterday. Perhaps he and his entire phenomenal world, including all his memories, jumped into reality last Tuesday. Nor can he prove that he and his phaneron will exist beyond next Thursday. Thus one is finally reduced to what has been called a "solipsism of the moment." One can be certain only that "I exist now," the starting point of Descartes's philosophy.

But wait! Even this is dubious. Perhaps, dear reader, you are only a figment in the dream of some god, as Sherlock Holmes was a figment in the mind of Sir Arthur Conan Doyle. There are Hindus who believe that the entire universe, including you and me, is a dream of Brahma. It will cease to be real as soon as Brahma awakes. Alice, behind the looking glass, thought she was dreaming about the Red King But the Red King sleeps through the story, and Alice is told that she is just a "sort of thing" in the Red King's dream. A student in one of Morris Cohen's philosophy classes once raised a hand to ask, "How do I know I exist?" Professor Cohen's reply was, "Who's asking?"[1]

Because all our knowledge of the world and other people derives from information that filters into our consciousness through our senses, there is no ironclad way to refute solipsism. By "ironclad" I mean in a strictly logical manner. There is no absolute way to refute anything outside of pure logic and mathematics, and even there refutation is always within a formal system with agreed-upon axioms and rules. Accept the axioms and rules of Euclidean geometry and you can indeed refute the statement that the sum of the interior angles of a triangle is more than 180 degrees. But this is not much different from refuting the statement that there are seven eggs in half a dozen. Nevertheless, in spite of its strict irrefutability, no sane philosopher has been a solipsist. Why?

It is difficult to discuss this question without approaching it historically. The reason is simple. Any fundamental view one can take toward any significant metaphysical question has been so well expressed and so expertly defended by great thinkers of the past that it is almost impossible to say anything new on the topic or to improve old arguments.

Aristotle held the commonsense opinion, an opinion held by almost everybody since—philosophers, scientists, and ordinary people—that behind the phaneron there is an independently existing world of "matter." No matter, now, what we mean by matter. It existed before human beings existed, and would continue to exist if all humans ceased to exist. It is this outside world that causes the inner world of our sensations, the world we perceive as our phaneron. Before Aristotle, Plato argued not only for the existence of such an external world (it produces the shadows in his famous allegory of the cave), he also argued for the independent existence, apart from both matter and human minds, of such universal ideas as cowness and the number three. For Aristotle, universals have no reality apart from the material universe, as the shape of a vase cannot exist apart from the vase. In the Middle Ages this debate usually took the form of nominalism versus Platonic realism, with complex terminological distinctions and subtle shades of opinion which need not concern us. The important point is that medieval Scholastics were "realists" in believing, as did Plato and Aristotle, that there is a vast world "out there," behind the world of appearance, that does not require our perceptions in order to exist.

The first great historical turn in Western philosophy on this question came in the early eighteenth century with the writings of Bishop George Berkeley, a devout Irish Anglican who spent several years in Newport, Rhode Island, in a vain attempt to establish a Christian college in Bermuda. I wonder how many students at the University of California, in Berkeley, know that the town was named for the bishop because, Russell tells us in his *History of Western Philosophy*, Berkeley had written the line, "Westward the course of empire takes its way." The bishop's last book was on the medicinal value of tar-water, a monograph that compares favorably with Aldous Huxley's treatise on how to cure eye refraction defects by wiggling your eyeballs.

It is easy to joke about Berkeley's philosophy, but he defended it with enormous skill, and I have read many later books on **God**-centered idealism that did little more than repeat Berkeley's arguments and not half so well. To understand those arguments it is best to say first a word about the bishop's distinguished predecessor, John Locke.

Locke, also a good Anglican, no more doubted than did earlier Christian philosophers that God had created a natural world which exists independently of human minds. As to the ultimate nature of matter, Locke readily admitted (as would Immanuel Kant) that it is transcendent and unknowable. As for the knowable part of matter, Locke divided its properties into two classes: primary and secondary. Primary properties are not dependent on perceptions. For example, a rock is solid whether anyone kicks it or not. But color, a secondary quality, depends on the complicated process of seeing. In the night all cats are gray, and in total darkness they are not even gray.

The distinction is still useful, but Berkeley saw clearly that there is a deeper sense in which all qualities are secondary. How do we know a rock is solid unless we feel or kick it? Indeed, all we can know about any material object is what we learn about it through our senses. Why assume a mysterious, unknowable substance behind our phaneron?

Now, one reason that Aristotle and the Schoolmen, as well as ordinary people and scientists, make such an assumption had been explained a thousand times before Berkeley was born. It is because it is the simplest hypothesis that accounts for the phaneron's peculiar regularities. Turn your back on a tree, then look at it again. It is still there. Go to sleep, wake up, and the room has the same furniture it had the day before. Moreover, our senses agree with one another. A cube not only looks like a cube, it feels like a cube. We can see, feel, smell, and taste an apple. Put the fruit in the refrigerator, remove it an hour later and take another bite. The apple looks, feels, smells, and tastes the same as before.

We, who of course are not solipsists, all believe that other people exist. Is it not an astonishing set of coincidences—astonishing, that is, to anyone who doubts an external world—that everybody sees essentially the same phaneron? We walk the same streets of the same cities. We find the same buildings at the same locations. Two people can see the same spiral galaxy through a telescope. Not only that, they see the same spiral structure. The hypothesis that there is an external world, not dependent on human minds, made of *something*, is so obviously useful and so strongly confirmed by experience down through the ages that we can say without exaggerating that it is better confirmed than any other empirical hypothesis. So useful is the posit that it is almost impossible for anyone except a madman or a professional metaphysician to comprehend a reason for doubting it.

Please observe that I have said nothing about the essential nature of the external world; only that *something* lurks behind the phaneron to preserve its complex regularities. Berkeley himself never doubted this. He only doubted that the "something" was material, by which he meant something more like pebbles than like thoughts. These doubts are strongly supported by modern physics. We now know that matter is not at all like pebbles. It is more like pure mathematics. Every particle can be viewed as a probability wave in an abstract multidimensional space. It is not observable directly, like a tree. Its properties are all inferred from complicated experiments. No one today knows what an electron is aside from its properties. All that Berkeley wanted to avoid was the idea that behind our perception of rocks, trees, and water is some sort of material substance similar to rocks, trees, and water—perhaps made of hard little pieces, as the Greek atomists maintained—and that this substance exists all by itself without the necessity of being perceived, even by a god. In addition, he saw no reason why God—Berkeley believed of course in the Old Testament Jehovah who created the heaven and the earth—would have to go through the unnecessary labor of first making matter, capable of existing all by itself, then endowing it with a special structure that would cause the phaneron.

At the heart of Berkeley's vision was a deep, emotional aversion to the notion that anything can exist without a mind to perceive it. It is an aversion that many people have—I myself can feel it—though not everyone. Let us try to understand it. Imagine a universe that consists of nothing, absolutely nothing, but a single pebble suspended in space-time. No minds of any sort exist, including the minds of gods. There is only that lonesome pebble. Would it not be pointless, ridiculous, absurd, meaningless, preposterous (substitute here any word you like that expresses your aversion) to suppose that such a stone exists? In Berkeley's phrase, unperceived matter is a "stupid, thoughtless some-what." And if this is true of one unperceived pebble, would it not also be true of unperceived stars and planets? I am persuaded that this vague but powerful emotion, rather than any rational argument, is the subtle secret behind Berkeley's philosophy. We find it expressed today in physicist John Wheeler's view that a universe without minds to perceive it is so "pointless" that we might as well say it doesn't exist.

Here is how Miguel de Unamuno expressed the same emotion in his *Tragic Sense of Life:*

> What would a universe be without any consciousness capable of reflecting it and knowing it? What would objectified reason be without will and feeling? For us it would be equivalent to nothing—a thousand times more dreadful than nothing. . . . It is not, therefore, rational necessity, but vital anguish that impels us to believe in God.[2]

"To be," said Berkeley in his most famous phrase, "is to be perceived." Grant this and the rest of his system follows smoothly. The bishop knew as well as Samuel Johnson that stones resist kicks, and as well as any materialist that there is *something* out there, independent of ourselves. For Berkeley, that something is the mind of God. Never mind what he meant by mind. The tree on the quad, as the old limerick goes, exists when no person perceives it because God perceives it. Concede God, and the entire world, with all its incredible patterns, is instantly restored. The only difference is that instead of saying that matter is behind the phaneron you say God is behind it. The Schoolmen and Locke had maintained that God first created matter (or perhaps gave form to a formless, preexisting primal matter), then used the matter to build the universe we inhabit and perceive. But why go around Robin Hood's barn? Is it not simpler, Berkeley asked, to rest our phaneron directly on God? In fact, Berkeley offered his philosophy as a new way of proving the existence of God.

All the objects and patterns and laws of the universe, for Berkeley, are timeless ideas in the mind of God. There is no need to interpose matter (in the sense of an "unthinking substance" with an absolute existence apart from God) between God and our minds. Berkeley was convinced that this view not only better accords with Scripture than any other epistemology, but that it also better accords with common sense. For do not ordinary people believe that what they perceive are the real objects, and not just the properties of some mysterious substratum—in modern terms, the structure of quantum wave systems—behind the things they see? If Berkeley were around today he would probably argue that quantum mechanics has reduced matter to pure mathematics, and that abstract mathematical ideas are more easily conceived as thoughts of God than as properties of empty space-time—that is, properties of nothing.

James Boswell fully understood, when he told how Johnson said "I refute it thus" and booted a large stone with such force that his foot rebounded, that Johnson had not in any way refuted Berkeley. For Berkeley, stones are as firm as they are in the universe of any atheist who puts a nonmental substance behind the phaneron. Berkeley's universe is as much "out there," beyond what Lord Dunsany liked to call "the fields we know," as the universe of Aristotle, Aquinas, or Locke. Go through the writings of these men and wherever they speak of matter or substance, change the word to "the mind of God" and you convert their epistemologies to Berkeley's.

Berkeley's linguistic trick of getting rid of matter by changing its name had an enormous influence on Kant and Hegel, and on all the post-Hegelian idealists in Germany and elsewhere. In my opinion there is no finer defense of God-centered objective idealism than lecture 11 of Josiah Royce's *Spirit of Modern Philosophy*. It is almost pure Berkeley. Like the bishop, Royce finds it absurd to imagine a substratum of matter capable of existing without being perceived. It is as absurd, he writes, as square circles, or two hills side by side with no valley between them, or the integral square root of 65. Then, in a passage of uncharacteristic confusion, he adds that substance without perception is the same kind of nonsense as "Snarks, Boojums and Jabberwocks." (Royce betrays no recognition that a Jabberwock is no more a contradiction than a unicorn or an ostrich.) Berkeley found unperceived matter repugnant and let it go at that. Royce tried to make it logically inconsistent. In this he surely failed. Nevertheless, the center of his argument is the same as Berkeley's. The regularities of our phaneron, and the existence of other persons, force us to believe in a reality behind our phenomenal world. Because nothing can exist without being perceived, we are forced to posit a divine mind or Absolute Self to perceive the universe.

This is not the place to discuss the thousand subtleties that distinguish the various languages fabricated by philosophers who call themselves idealists from those who call themselves realists. In my opinion the differences between the various schools are mostly verbal, with strong emotions supporting terminological preferences. The only point I want to stress here is that almost without exception the great philosophers of the past believed in a world independent of human minds. All agreed that the essence of this world is beyond our comprehension. What can we know, Kant asked, about any material object as a thing-in-itself apart from our perceptions of it? If we are atheists we can call the substratum "matter" or "substance" or "space-time events" or "pure mathematics." If we believe in some kind of deity we can also use such terms if we like or we can call the substratum "God," "the Absolute," "the Tao," "Brahman," or whatever poetic word we prefer as a name for the ultimate ground of being.

I myself am a theist (as some readers may be surprised to learn) but if you ask me to tell you anything about the nature of what lies beyond the phaneron—is it the mind of God, or pure mathematics, or some other kind of transcendent "stuff"?—my answer is "How should I know?" As I will be saying over and over again in this rambling volume, I am not dismayed by ultimate mysteries. What is the difference between something and nothing? Why is there something rather than nothing? Should the something of which the universe is fundamentally composed be regarded as like atoms or be regarded as more like a mind? Or is the substratum best thought of as something neutral: material when structured one way, mental when structured another way? I have no desire even to try to answer such questions. I find nothing absurd about the notion that the external world is the mind of God, nor do I find it repulsive to suppose that God can create a world of substance, utterly unlike ideas in God's mind or anybody's mind, that can exist whether God thinks about it or not. How can I, a mere mortal slightly above an ape in intelligence, know what it means to say that something is "created" by God, or "thought" by God? One can play endless metaphysical games with such phrases,[3] but I can no more grasp what is behind such questions than my cat can understand what is behind the clatter I make while I type this paragraph.

There are, however, some lower-order questions about these mysteries that can be answered. What kind of language, with what metaphors, is preferable for talking about the external world? And what do we mean by "preferable"? Before I give my opinions, let us consider another way of viewing "reality"—a third language, if you like, which was brilliantly defended by John Stuart Mill. It is a language curiously close to Bishop Berkeley's even though it abandons Berkeley's dictum that nothing can exist without being perceived. Change Berkeley's Christian God to an impersonal that-which-is, and you arrive at something not far from Mill's epistemology. Because it does not demand a personal deity, it has held a strong attraction for modern philosophers who call themselves pragmatists, positivists, and phenomenologists.

Mill's clearest defense of his epistemology is in Chapter 11 of his book on the philosophy of Sir William Hamilton. Accept the phaneron, said Mill, just as it is. Don't trouble yourself with what lies behind it. Simply *define* the external world as the set of all those "objects" in your phaneron that cannot be influenced by your will. Since these regularities, be they people or things, are what we all deem to be the outside world, the problem of a substratum never arises. It becomes a pseudoproblem. Matter, said Mill, is the "permanent possibility of sensation." There is no need to posit either a material substratum or a divine substratum. A tree is obviously outside us in the sense that it remains there whether we look at it or not. It continues to exist not because God perceives it but because it is that part of the phaneron that behaves that way. Why say more? To talk of a substratum, matter or mind, that causes the tree to exist is to add nothing to what we already know. There is no need to prove an external world because it is "there" by definition. The total collection of objects in our phaneron that exist independently of our experience of them is all we mean, and just what we mean, by "external world."

Mill summed it up this way:

> The belief in such permanent possibilities seems to me to include all that is essential or characteristic in the belief in substance. I believe that Calcutta exists, though I do not perceive it, and that it would still exist if every percipient inhabitant were suddenly to leave the place, or be struck dead. But when I analyse the belief, all I find in it is, that were these events to take place, the Permanent Possibility of Sensation which I call Calcutta would still remain; that if I were suddenly transported to the banks of the

Hoogly, I should still have the sensations which, if now present, would lead me to affirm that Calcutta exists here and now.[4]

Most philosophers, Mill admits, fancy there is some kind of material or spiritual substratum behind the phaneron. He sees nothing wrong with this belief; he just finds it superfluous. In modern terminology, to assert the existence of such a substratum is to add no surplus meaning to what can be stated in the language of phenomenalism.

As I have said, this point of view has strongly influenced philosophers of many schools. William James, in *Pragmatism* and in its sequel, *The Meaning of Truth*, often talked as if he held such a position. In my opinion this is a misreading of James's language, understandable in view of his many confusions and ambiguities. But space is limited and I content myself with quoting from a letter that James wrote in 1907, when controversy over pragmatism was at its height and critics were accusing James of denying that a mind-independent world exists.

James was shocked by this charge. "I am," he writes, "a natural realist," and he adds that he speaks also for his co-pragmatists F.C.S. Schiller and John Dewey. Imagine, James says, a handful of beans flung onto a table. Someone looks at them and notices various patterns. The recognition of these patterns is what James calls truth.

> Whatever he does, so long as he *takes account* of them [the beans], his account is neither false nor irrelevant. If neither, why not call it true? It *fits* the beans-*minus*-him, and *expresses* the *total* fact, of beans-*plus*-him. . . . All that Schiller and I contend for is that there is *no* "truth" without *some* interest, and that non-intellectual interests play a part as well as intellectual ones. Whereupon we are accused of denying the beans or denying being in any way constrained by them! It's too silly![5]

It seems to me that in this letter James spilled the beans about his epistemology. As we shall argue in the next chapter, his radical effort to redefine truth was essentially a linguistic program, not a basic change in the Aristotelian doctrine that truth is a correspondence of ideas with a structured outside world. As James's letter makes clear, he takes for granted that truth must fit the beans. In spite of pragmatism's novel language, James is not denying a world of objects independent of human minds.

As to the ultimate nature of such objects James is never clear (how could he be?), nor need this ambiguity concern us. In *The Meaning of Truth* he tells us that his critics often say that he admits the existence of objects outside human minds whereas Dewey and Schiller do not. Not so, James says. "We all three absolutely agree in admitting the transcendency of the objects. . . ." Again, he writes that Dewey's epistemology is meaningless unless one posits "independent entities." Dewey, James insists, "holds as firmly as I do to objects independent of judgments."

Does this mean that James and Dewey believed in a transcendent matter behind the "independent objects" of one's phaneron? Or did they, like Mill, define "independent objects" as regularities in the phaneron, as the permanent possibilities of sensation?

Dewey wrote often about this question, and with almost as much ambiguity as James. In *Logic: The Theory of Inquiry*, the most mature account of his epistemology, we read:

> That stones, stars, trees, cats and dogs, etc., exist independently of the particular processes of a knower at a given time is as groundedly established fact of knowledge as anything can well be. For as sets of connected existential distinctions, they have emerged and been tested over and over again in the inquiries of individuals and of the race. In most cases it would be a gratuitous waste of energy to repeat the operations by which they have been instituted and confirmed. For the individual knower to suppose that he constructed them in his immediate mental processes is as absurd as it would be for him to suppose that he created the streets and houses he sees as he travels through a city.[6]

There is, therefore, not the slightest doubt that the leading pragmatists, as did Mill, firmly believed in objects independent of human minds. What remains is a subtler question. To account for such objects is it necessary to put beans behind their patterns, or should we simply recognize the mind-independence of the patterns and let it go at that? My impression is that Dewey, unlike James, took the Millian view. In an earlier paper on the topic, in *Essays and Experimental Logic*, Dewey argues that the question is meaningless. It cannot even be posed, he claims, without assuming the very existence of the external world one is trying to prove.

I think it fair to summarize Dewey's position as follows: We are, in one of his most frequently intoned phrases, organisms interacting with an environment. The interaction is what Dewey calls experience. Within our experience we quickly learn as children the bifurcation between subjective and objective. We can easily imagine squashing an imaginary stone in our hand. We know we cannot do this with a "real" stone. The reality of objects in our environment is taken for granted because an organism cannot interact with something that doesn't exist. Because the assumption of an external world is implicit in the very concept of interaction, the task of proving the reality of an external world never arises.

In a footnote Dewey refers to a book by Hans Reichenbach, *Experience and Prediction*, in which the existence of an external world is treated as a philosophical conundrum. "According to my view," Dewey writes, "the problem is artificially generated by the kind of premises I call epistemological. When we *act* and find environing things in stubborn opposition to our desires and efforts, the externality of the environment to the *self* is a direct constituent of direct experience."[7]

This third approach, the view that it is meaningless to ask if there is a substratum behind the phaneron was also defended by several members of the Vienna Circle, notably by Rudolf Carnap. Carnap's first major work, *The Logical Structure of the World*, was an attempt to show that on the basis of a single primitive relation, similarity, one can construct a consistent solipsistic language in which it is possible to make any empirical statement about the world that can be made in a realist language. Because the two languages are two ways of saying the same thing, there is no surplus empirical content to the language of Aristotelian realism. The decision over which language to adopt is a practical one. Which is the most convenient? Carnap soon opted strongly for the "thing" language, the realist language of science and common sense, not because it is truer, but because it is the most efficient language for talking about experience.[8]

Similar views have been taken by philosophers who call themselves phenomenologists, but they disagree on so many details, and write with such uniform opacity, that someone better informed than I should be trusted for insight into their opinions. Some look upon the external world as somehow a cooperative creation of independent minds. You'll find this "collective solipsism" caricatured in George Orwell's *1984* where all "truth" about the world and its history is manufactured by the political party in power. Some anthropologists who are extreme cultural relativists have argued that the laws of science as well as all the theorems of mathematics have no reality apart from human cultures. Laws about gravity, and the fact that $2 + 3 = 5$, are not truths that transcend human minds. They are aspects of a culture's folkways, like its traffic laws or its rules of etiquette.[9]

Not all members of the Vienna Circle went along with Carnap's convenience-of-language approach. Herbert Feigl was the first leading heretic to argue that realism has firmer support than the mere efficiency of its language. For some twenty years he and Carnap debated this question, each modifying his views slightly but remaining unconvinced. Outside the Vienna Circle most philosophers of science sided with Feigl.

When I was an undergraduate philosophy student at the University of Chicago I attended a seminar given by Bertrand Russell. Carnap, then a professor at Chicago, went to these sessions and often engaged Russell in spirited debates which I only partly comprehended. On one occasion they got into a tangled argument over whether science should assert, as an ontological thesis, the reality of a world behind the phaneron. Carnap struggled to keep the argument technical, but Russell slyly turned it into a discussion of whether their respective wives (Russell's new wife was knitting and smiling in a back-row seat) existed in some ontologically real sense or should be regarded as mere logical fictions based on regularities in their husbands' phaneron.

The next day I happened to be in the campus post office, where faculty members came to pick up mail. Professor Charles Hartshorne, a whimsical philosopher from whom I was then taking a stimulating course, walked in, recognized me, and stopped to chat.

"Did you attend the Russell seminar yesterday?" he asked. "I was unable to go."

"Yes," I said. "It was exciting. Russell tried to persuade Carnap that his wife existed, but Carnap wouldn't admit it."

Hartshorne laughed. Then, by a quirk of fate, in walked Carnap to get his mail. Hartshorne introduced us (it was the first time I had met Carnap; years later we would collaborate on a book); then, to my profound embarrassment, Hartshorne said: "Mr. Gardner tells me that yesterday Russell tried to convince you your wife existed, but you wouldn't admit it."

Carnap did not smile. He glowered down at me and said, "But that was not the point at all."

Of course he was right. No sane philosopher doubts the existence of persons and objects outside his or her mind. One is fully justified, Carnap once wrote, in believing that the stars would continue on their courses if all minds disappeared. Philosophers differ only in what they mean when they say that the stars would so continue.

Carnap's final opinions can be found in his reply to critics in *The Philosophy of Rudolf Carnap*, a volume edited by Paul Schilpp. There Carnap explains why he rejects as meaningless such assertions as that the external world is "real," as well as the metaphysical claims of solipsism and numerous varieties of idealism and phenomenalism. Instead of taking metaphysical sides, Carnap sidesteps the controversies altogether by replacing them with questions about the usefulness of different languages in a specified context. If realism is taken as an ontological thesis, Carnap writes, he is not a realist. If realism is understood as a preference for a realistic language over a phenomenal one, in science, philosophy, and everyday speech, "then I am also a realist." The phenomenal language is rejected, not because it is false but because "it is an absolutely private language which can only be used for soliloquy, but not for common communication between two persons." Willard Van Orman Quine takes essentially the same position of metaphysical neutrality in his famous essay "On What There Is."

One of the most colorful arguments for a substratum behind the phaneron is Reichenbach's argument, alluded to briefly a few pages back. Taking a cue from Plato's cave, Reichenbach imagines that our universe consists entirely of a huge cubical box with translucent sides. Outside the box, birds are flying about, but all we can see are their shadows on the cube's top and sides. At first we think the shadows are the only realities. Eventually, after observing numerous regularities in the shifting shadow patterns, a Copernicus comes along to announce the bold hypothesis that the shadows are caused by objects—in this case, birds—that exist *outside* the box.

Imagine the cube shrinking until it becomes the skin of our body. We now have, says Reichenbach, a useful analogy with human experience. It is obvious that all we know about the world outside of us is what we infer from what is inside our skin, or rather inside our skull where the sensory inputs are interpreted. But the regularities of those inputs, such as the patterns of flying birds on our retinas, suggest the hypothesis that outside our eyes is a world independent of our inner experience. This hypothesis has enormous explanatory and predictive power. Moreover, it is a theory of extreme simplicity and therefore, by the principle of Occam's razor, preferable to more complex explanations. The hypothesis is confirmed empirically in the same way any other theory is confirmed. Indeed, it is *better* confirmed because all human beings, throughout all history, have confirmed it every minute of their waking life. We cannot say the hypothesis is absolutely certain, but surely it is as close to being certain as anything we have a right to believe.

It is not correct, Reichenbach goes on, to say that this hypothesis has no surplus value over a subjectivist view. In the first place it *means* something quite different to the person who affirms it. It is one thing to believe that the shadows of birds on the roof of Reichenbach's cube are all there is, quite another thing to believe they are shadows of something outside the cube, and still another thing to believe it meaningless to ask which point of view is true. We can never, of course, prove to a phenomenologist that outside birds generate the shadows. Even if we bore a hole in the roof, and through it see birds flapping about, he can still maintain that the birds are illusions caused by the shadows and therefore less real than the shadows. We can, however, assign to his theory a probability of being true that is indistinguishable from zero.

I am aware that the term "realism" has had so many different meanings in the history of philosophy that it has become almost useless unless it is defined with extreme precision. I am also aware that there have been many schools of realism, each with its preferred terminology for describing the complicated chain of causal events that go from an object "out there" to the object's perception by a mind.

Consider a familiar chain. You see on a television screen a lady wearing a red dress. Where is the color red? Obviously you can answer in a score of different ways, all correct, depending on how you define your terms. Even if you are in the studio, seeing the lady in the flesh, the causal chain is far from simple. Light shining on her dress is reflected in an intricate pattern of electromagnetic waves. The pattern is refracted by your corneas and eye lenses to produce an upside-down image on each of your retinas. These images are translated into electrical impulses which travel along optic nerves to both sides of your brain. Then, by a process nobody understands, the brain interprets this information and gives you the sensation of red. From one perspective, nature is a rich pattern of colors, sounds, and smells. From another perspective we can agree with Alfred North Whitehead:

> The poets are entirely mistaken. They should address their lyrics
> to themselves, and should turn them into odes of self-congratula-
> tion on the excellency of the human mind. Nature is a dull affair,
> soundless, scentless, colourless; merely the hurrying of material,
> endlessly, meaninglessly. [10]

The lady's dress is made of atoms, which in turn are made of protons, electrons, and neutrons. What are *they* made of? Physics necessarily reaches a point at which the nature of matter plunges into
darkness. Some particles may turn out to be made of quarks, but then
one can wonder what quarks are made of. A dog knows a tree's structure in part, but knows nothing about atoms. A modern physicist
knows a great deal about atoms, but there is always that cutoff point
beyond which the tree's "stuff" continues to elude understanding. Is
the ultimate nature of the stuff known to a god? Who can say? We
cannot even understand the question except in the mistiest way. There
may not even be an ultimate nature. For all we know, the structure of
matter may have infinite levels like an infinite set of Oriental boxes.

In this book I use the term "realism" in the broad sense of a belief in
the reality of something (the nature of which we leave in limbo) that is
behind the phaneron, and which generates the phaneron and its weird
regularities. This something is independent of human minds in the
sense that it existed before there were human minds, and would exist if
the human race vanished. I am not here concerned with realism as a
view opposed to idealism, or realism in the Platonic sense of a view
opposed to nominalism or conceptualism. As I shall use the word it is
clear that even Berkeley and Royce were realists. The term of contrast
is not "idealism" but "subjectivism." It is subjectivism either in the
strong sense of denying that there are beans behind the phaneron, or in
the weaker sense of regarding the bean question as meaningless and
therefore not worth asking.

Let me summarize three major reasons for affirming realism. The
first two can be accepted by a Deweyan or a Carnapian, but the third,
which introduces emotional meaning, would (I believe) have been rejected by both Dewey and Carnap. Of course they could have accepted
it in a sense, like accepting the fact that some persons prefer Mozart to
Wagner, but I think they would have said that feelings are insufficient
grounds for making what they would have considered a needless meta-

physical leap. My own view is that emotions are the only grounds for metaphysical leaps. In any case, it is the third reason that, for me, tips the scales toward realism as a justified ontological conviction

1. The convenience argument. The language of realism is necessary for communication between minds. It explains why realism has been preferred by almost all philosophers, theologians, and scientists, and by all ordinary people.

Most people are "naïve realists" who suppose that when they look at a stone they see the actual stone, and there are philosophers who defend this as a preferable language for realism. But it is not difficult to explain to a naïve realist something about modern theories of matter. After you have done so he or she will remain convinced that those waves and particles, out there and independent of our minds, are what make a stone look like a stone.

When G. E. Moore, in the course of a lecture, gave his famous "proof" of the external world by waving a hand and saying, "Here is one hand," then waving the other hand and saying, "Here is another," he was performing a symbolic act of common sense essentially the same as Johnson's kick of the stone. As Moore went on to say, the proof is just the same if you hold up a sock and say, "Here is a sock." To prove that objects existed in the past you need only add, "A moment ago I held up a sock." Moore was fully aware that he was not stating logical proofs. He was merely insisting, as was Johnson, that no sane person doubts the existence of rocks and socks as things independent of the mind.

If the big bang model of the universe is true, there is no way a mind (we leave aside the possibility of the bang being perceived by a god) could have witnessed the explosion. Note how needlessly complicated becomes the language of a subjectivist if he wants to explain why he believes that the universe existed three minutes after the bang. He is forced to say it existed because had there been a mind around somewhere, perhaps in a hyper-space-time, it could have observed the fireball. If he wants to explain why stars would continue to exist if all minds disappeared, he has to add that they would exist in the sense that if a mind existed it could see the stars. The subjectivist can say, "There is a penny in the box," only because he is sure that if the box is opened he will see the penny. He can say that the works inside a watch cause its hands to move, but only because he is sure that if he opened the watch he would see the wheels.

Philosophers call these "counterfactual statements." They lead into curious problems about the language of science that need not detain us. My point is simpler. The counterfactuals quoted above are needless complications. Ordinary people, even scientists and philosophers, do not hesitate to say the penny is in the box whether anyone opens it or not. Why scratch your left ear with your right hand? Not the least of the virtues of commonsense realism, from Aristotle to Karl Popper, is that it enables a philosopher who adopts it to converse about epistemology with ordinary people without mystifying and exasperating them.

2. The empirical argument. Realism is the simplest and best-confirmed hypothesis that accounts for the regularities of the phaneron.

Although Reichenbach opposed this argument to Carnap's metaphysical neutrality, Carnap was willing to accept it in a sense. Replying to critics in *The Philosophy of Rudolf Carnap*, he wrote:

> Later, Reichenbach gave to the thesis of realism an interpretation in scientific terms, as asserting the possibility of induction and prediction; a similar interpretation was proposed by Feigl. On the basis of these interpretations, the thesis is, of course, meaningful; in this version, it is a synthetic, empirical statement about a certain structural property of the world. I am doubtful, however, whether it is advisable to give to old theses and controversies a meaning by reinterpretation; I have similar doubts about Quine's reinterpretation of the term "nominalism."[11]

I take this to mean that Carnap had no quarrel with the claim that realism has a surplus value provided realism is taken as an empirical hypothesis rather than an ontological assertion. From Carnap's perspective, Reichenbach's cube argument simply strengthens the overwhelming convenience of the realist language. From Reichenbach's perspective, when convenience becomes that overwhelming, one has good grounds for an ontological leap. Now that we have photographed craters on the far side of the moon, no one hesitates to say that those craters exist. If the hypothesis that objects exist outside the phaneron is supported by even more convincing empirical evidence, why not embrace realism in an ontological sense?

3. The emotive argument. An ontological commitment to realism has a strong and salutary emotional effect on those who make it.

As I will stress in later chapters, I agree with William James that emotional meanings play fundamental roles in decisions about philosophical questions. I agree with James that in the absence of compelling counterarguments, emotions can be legitimate grounds for metaphysical jumps.

Realism, I am persuaded, reflects a healthy attitude toward oneself and others, and humility before the impenetrable mystery of being. Subjectivism reflects a narcissism which in extreme form can lead to madness. Let me speak plainly. There is a monstrous difference between thinking of another person as ontologically real, existing in his or her own right, and thinking of that person as a useful construct based on the patterns of your phaneron. There is almost as huge an emotional difference between the realist's belief and the pale gray view which sees no difference between the languages of realism and phenomenalism except one of efficiency. Even an authentic solipsist, if trained in philosophy, could accept the enormous convenience of the realist language. The convenience would simply underscore the incredible subtlety and complexity of his illusion.

It is easier to doubt matter, said James in his *Psychology*, than to doubt other minds. "We need them too much. . . . A psychic solipsism is too hideous a mockery of our wants. . . ." The belief that it is useful or convenient to assume that other people exist is, as Bertrand Russell wrote, "not enough to allay my sense of loneliness. . . . For what I desire is not that the belief in solipsism should be false in the pragmatic sense, but that other people should in fact exist."[12] Yet all the arguments about the lack of a need for a substratum behind our perceptions of stones apply with equal force to our perceptions of human beings.

Russell once spoke on solipsism at a meeting chaired by Whitehead. As Russell tells it in his autobiography, he said he could not believe he had written those parts of Whitehead's books which he (Russell) could not understand, although he could find no way to prove he hadn't. He meant, of course, no logical proof. But there are many things, indeed the most important things, that a living person of flesh and bone is compelled to believe for emotional reasons—call it animal instinct if you prefer. One of them is the existence of other persons on an ontological level, a level that goes beyond the patterns of the phaneron.

The point is worth stressing because we live at a time when there is an upsurge of public interest in the paranormal, sometimes joined to an interest in Hindu philosophies that regard the universe as maya, a set of illusions created by a god. Since our minds are at one with the Supreme Mind, it follows that we are partly responsible for the universe's existence and its structure. This sense of the physical world's unreality is embodied in several native religions (Christian Science for one) and in the popularity of such recent books as those by Carlos Castaneda about his imaginary guru Don Juan. In Richard Bach's *Jonathan Livingston Seagull* a bird raises its consciousness so high that it can fly right through a mountain as if it weren't there. In the movie *Close Encounters of the Third Kind* extraterrestrial spaceships flit back and forth through a mesa. A small number of eminent physicists, Eugene Wigner for example, believe that properties of the universe, perhaps its very existence, depend in some subtle way upon its perception by conscious minds. Since these opinions derive from certain technicalities in quantum mechanics, I will say no more about them here. [13]

Although there has never been a sane solipsist, the doctrine often haunts young minds. G. K. Chesterton is a case in point. In his autobiography he writes about a period in his youth during which the notion that maybe nothing existed except himself and his own phaneron had caused him considerable anguish. He later became a realist, and there are many places in his writings where he warns against the psychic dangers of solipsistic speculation. The epigraph heading this chapter is a couplet from his poem "The Mirror of Madmen." Another vivid defense of realism is "Wonder and the Wooden Post," an essay in Chesterton's posthumous book, *The Coloured Lands*. But nowhere did GK defend his realism with more passionate intensity than in a story called "The Crime of Gabriel Gale." It can be found in *The Poet and the Lunatics*, my favorite among GK's many collections of mystery stories about detectives other than Father Brown.

Since this book may be hard to come by, here is a brief summary of the story's plot. Gabriel Gale, poet, artist, and detective, is accused of a terrible crime. It seems that on a wild and stormy night Gale had thrown a rope around the neck of a young man who was preparing for the Anglican ministry. After dragging the poor fellow into a wood, Gale pinned him for the night against a tree by forcing the two prongs of a large pitchfork into the trunk on either side of the man's neck. After Gale is arrested for attempted murder, he suggests to the police that they obtain the opinion of his victim.

The surprising reply comes by telegraph: "Can never be sufficiently grateful to Gale for his great kindness which more than saved my life."

It turns out that the young man had been going through the same insane phase that had tormented GK in his youth. He was on the verge of believing that his phaneron did not depend on anything that was not entirely inside his head. Gabriel Gale, always sensitive to the psychoses of others (having felt most of them himself), had realized that the man's mind was near the snapping point. Gale's remedy was radical. By pinning the man to the tree he had convinced him, not by logic (no one is ever convinced by logic of anything important) but by an overpowering experience. He found himelf firmly bound to something that his mind could in no way modify.

"We are all tied to trees and pinned with pitchforks," Gale tells the half-comprehending police. "And as long as these are solid we know the stars will stand and the hills will not melt at our word. Can't you imagine the huge tide of healthy relief and thanks, like a hymn of praise from all nature, that went up from that captive nailed to the tree, when he had wrestled till the dawn and received at last the great and glorious news; the news that he was only a man?"

The story ends when the man, now a curate, remarks casually to an atheist, "God wants you to play the game."

"How do you know what God wants?" asks the atheist. "You never were God were you?"

"Yes," says the clergyman in a queer voice. "I was God once for about fourteen hours. But I gave it up. I found it was too much of a strain."[14]

2

TRUTH:
Why I Am Not a Pragmatist

I think pragmatism an amusing humbug.

—Justice Oliver Wendell Holmes, Jr.,
in a letter to Sir Frederick Pollock

Given the existence of a structured universe that is independent of our minds, and regardless of how we view its ontological status, there is an absurdly simple way to explain what is meant by saying that a statement or a belief (we will use these two words more or less interchangeably) about that world is true or false. It is called the correspondence theory of truth. Like the realist thesis defended in the previous chapter, the correspondence theory of truth has been held by almost all philosophers and scientists of the past, and it has always been taken for granted by every ordinary person who has not studied philosophy.

According to this theory an assertion or a belief is true if it corresponds with some aspect of the actual world. Sometimes the correspondence is said to be with a fact, taking "fact" in a much broader sense than we will give it in the next chapter. A geologist may say, for example: "Evolution is not just a theory. It is a fact." By this he means that he believes it has been confirmed to such a high degree that we can confidently say it is true. Thus we are involved in an obvious circularity. Truth is a correspondence of statements with facts, and a fact is an assertion we believe is true. Both correspondence and fact are fuzzy words, difficult to define, and there is a vast literature on the technicalities involved in trying to make them precise.

Correspondence clearly does not mean copying in the way a photograph or a painting copies nature. There is no way to put a statement over a part of the universe to see how well it fits. Sometimes the meaning of a statement is picturable in the mind, such as "The earth rotates on its axis," but this is not always the case. "There is life in the interior of Jupiter" is fairly clear in meaning, but because we do not know what the interior of Jupiter is like, or what a Jovian life-form would look like, any mental image of the meaning is necessarily vague. Albert Einstein conjectured that the space of our universe may be the surface of a four-dimensional sphere, finite in volume but unbounded. Here the correspondence is with an object that cannot be pictured in the mind, although it can be precisely defined by four-dimensional Euclidean geometry. Rather than get involved with the great technical problems of defining correspondence, we will consider some commonplace examples in which the term's meaning will become clear enough for our humble purposes.

Suppose a deck of fifty-two playing cards is shuffled, spread face down on a table, and someone withdraws a card by sliding it out of the spread without turning the card face up. Beside the card is placed a sheet of paper on which is written, "This is the queen of hearts." What does it mean to say that the sentence on the paper is true?

It is easy to guess how ordinary people answer. (If you have any doubts, try asking friends.) They will answer in the same way similar questions were answered by the ancient Greek philosophers. The statement is true if, in fact, the chosen card *is* the queen of hearts. As Aristotle put it: "To say of what is that it is not, or of what is not that it is, is false; while to say of what is that it is, and what is not that it is not, is true." Similar remarks are in the *Dialogues* of Plato.[1]

Now we must introduce an all-important distinction. The correspondence theory defines only what it *means* to say a sentence is true or false. It says nothing about how to *decide* whether a sentence is true or false, or (as in the case of most scientific assertions) to evaluate the probability of whether an assertion is true or false. In other words, the correspondence theory is not concerned with criteria for truth. It tells us nothing about the kinds of tests that can be made for truth. If our sentence about the card is true, this truth is not dependent on future testing. The truth or falsity of the statement is not something that springs into reality when we turn over the card to see its face.

Statements in number theory provide trivial instances of the time-independence of truths about abstract entities in pure mathematics. It was shown a few years ago that the integer formed by 317 repetitions of the digit 1 is a prime. Few people would want to say that this number became prime only after it was proved to be a prime. The sentence "the number formed by 317 repetitions of 1 is prime" was true in the days of Pythagoras. Only recently did mathematicians *know* it to be true.

Although the truth about this number is a truth in pure mathematics, like so much of pure mathematics it also tells us something about the physical world. A prime number of n pebbles, for example, cannot be divided evenly into equal sets of pebbles other than by forming n sets of one pebble each, or one set of n pebbles. Thus statements about primes can be translated into statements about physical objects that maintain their identities as units. To say of seven cows that there are a prime number of cows is as true a statement about the world as "Snow is white." Note that the statement's truth depends solely on the meaning of "prime number," not on the existence of algorithms for efficiently deciding whether a given number is prime or composite.

In our card experiment we are entitled to say that the statement on the paper has a probability of 1/52 of being true. The simplest way to know for certain is to turn over the card. There are more complicated ways of testing. For example, we could lift an index corner of the card and slip a mirror under it. Everyone agrees that such tests are the only ways of knowing whether the written sentence is true or false.

To those who accept the correspondence theory of truth, science is a search for statements that correspond to the world's structure. When Sir Isaac Newton concluded that gravity is a force that varies directly with the product of two masses and inversely with the square of the distance between them, he expressed a law which he believed corresponded with the dynamic structure of the actual world. We shall be unconcerned with the methods by which scientists test such hypotheses, sometimes confirming them, sometimes disconfirming, sometimes refining. We assume that science has no way of being certain that any of its statements is absolutely true, although many of them can approach extremely close to certainty. No astronomer now doubts that Saturn's largest moon, Titan, has an atmosphere. But there is no formal procedure by which precise probabilities—what Carnap called degrees of confirmation—can be assigned to scientific statements except in an extremely rough way. Where there are two rival hypotheses, the best a scientist can do is make vague statements such as that he thinks one is probably true and the other is probably false. If he thinks the evidence is about equal for each, he may tell you the odds are fifty-fifty but personally he likes one theory better than the other.

What does a scientist have in mind when he says, "I am convinced that general relativity is true"? If you ask him, it is unlikely he will launch into a technical discussion of experiments which confirm the theory. He is more likely to give an answer essentially the same as the ordinary person's answer when asked what it means to say the statement "This is the queen of hearts" is true. He will tell you that he believes general relativity is true because it expresses in mathematical form the way he thinks the universe "out there," the universe independent of human minds, actually behaves.

We can clarify the distinction between the meaning of truth and the criteria for truth by considering some statements to which truth values can be assigned but which are difficult or impossible to evaluate. Suppose our selected card is returned to the deck, without anyone having seen its face, and the deck is shuffled. We alter the sentence on the paper to "The selected card *was* the queen of hearts." Everybody will agree that this is either true or false, and that it is true if, and only if, the chosen card was in fact the queen of hearts. Testing the statement is now difficult but not impossible. If the deck is brand new, sliding the card over the surface of the table may have produced a faint smudge of dirt on the card's face. In taking the card from the spread, a corner may have become slightly bent. Fingerprints may be on the card. And so on. Such tests may not give as certain an answer as turning over the card before it was replaced, but they can establish the truth of the sentence with a high degree of probability. Scientific historians and criminal lawyers use just such tests to confirm or disconfirm conjectures about the past.

Suppose now that before the card of unseen face is replaced in the deck we take a photograph of its back. On the picture we write, "The card here photographed was the queen of hearts." The deck is then tossed into a furnace and destroyed. There is no longer any way to know what in fact the card was. Nevertheless most people, including most scientists and philosophers, would not hesitate to say that the untestable sentence is true if, and only if, the selected card was in fact the queen of hearts.

It is easy to think of scientific and historical statements for which truth is easily defined by Aristotle's correspondence theory even though it is unlikely they can ever be tested. "On a planet in the Andromeda galaxy there are ostriches." "At noon, on such-and-such a day, Shakespeare sneezed." Even though we may never learn the truth or falsity of either assertion, ordinary language puts no obstacle in the way of saying it is true or false. We need not be concerned here with statements about future events, such as Aristotle's famous example of a prediction that a sea battle will occur at a certain locale on a certain future date. Can such a statement be said *now* to be either true or false, or must one say it has no truth value until the assigned date arrives? Here the correspondence theory is inadequate unless, perhaps, one is a determinist who maintains that the statement corresponds to a state of the universe that inevitably will lead to the predicted sea battle or to its failure to take place.

The correspondence theory of truth has two traditional rivals: the coherence theory and the pragmatic theory. We will not discuss the first because, although it has its merits and its distinguished defenders, it has not been this century's major challenge to the correspondence theory. The major attack was launched by a group of philosophers who called themselves pragmatists. Their point of view dominated American philosophy during the first quarter of this century, and the school included three of our most eminent native thinkers: Charles Peirce, William James, and John Dewey. In England the movement's leader was F.C.S. Schiller, an interesting philosopher but one whose views were less influential. In any case, this chapter would be too long if we considered him.

The term "pragmatism" was first introduced by Peirce in an article in *Popular Science Monthly* on "How to Make Our Ideas Clear." The article's main point was what later became known as the pragmatic maxim for deciding what a concept or an assertion means. We simply ask what possible consequences in human behavior follow from the "idea" in question. If there are no consequences, the idea is meaningless. The sum total of all the consequences constitute the idea's full meaning.

What does "queen of hearts" mean? It denotes a card which our culture calls the queen of hearts. What does "This is the queen of hearts" mean? It means that if we look at the card's face and see that it is the face of a queen of hearts, we will call the sentence true. What does truth mean? Applying Peirce's maxim, it means the successful passing of whatever tests support the correspondence of the assertion with reality. Peirce did not abandon the notion of correspondence, he merely introduced a subtle shift in the way one talks about correspondence. Since only a process of verification can decide whether a statement is true or false, why not *define* truth as the passing of such tests?

William James, fascinated by this suggestion, initiated the pragmatic movement with a series of dazzling lectures that were published in 1907 as the book entitled *Pragmatism: A New Name for Some Old Ways of Thinking*. The subtitle was a good one. As James was fully aware, pragmatism did not introduce any radically new ideas. It offered only a radical way of talking about old ideas.

At the heart of James's pragmatism was the abandonment of the traditional definition of truth as a timeless correspondence of an assertion (or belief) with the real world regardless of whether it is verified or not. This was replaced by a definition based on Peirce's maxim. Truth is that which is confirmed by testing. It is that which "works" or, in one of James's more unfortunate phrases, that which "pays in cash value."

In our card experiment James would say that the sentence "This is the queen of hearts" is true if, and only if, when we turn the card over we see it is the queen of hearts. If the unseen card is returned to the deck and the deck destroyed, James would say that the sentence "The selected card was the queen of hearts" is true if, and only if, had the card been looked at before it was returned, we would have seen that it was the queen of hearts.[2]

James never discarded the notion of correspondence with reality. There are even passages in his writings in which he speaks of correspondence as something too obvious to require defense. The turning of the card verifies or falsifies the written statement, he would have readily admitted, depending on whether the selected card is or is not in fact the queen of hearts. And of course Aristotle would have agreed that the best way to decide if the sentence is true or false is to turn the card. The central issue here is one of linguistic preference. Is it best to preserve the language of the old correspondence theory, or is something gained by modifying it along the lines proposed by the pragmatists?

James lived at a time when Western philosophy was dominated by German metaphysics, by philosophers who insisted with boundless egoism that all sorts of timeless metaphysical truths could be established by rational arguments. During the same period, science was suggesting that all our ideas about the world are provisional, and can be established only with varying degrees of probability as they pass or fail empirical tests. It was James's belief that if the meaning of truth could be put more in harmony with scientific method—instead of saying a hypothesis works because it is true in some absolute sense, we turn the words around and say it is probably true because it works—this new way of talking about truth would inject enormous clarity into philosophical speculation and eliminate all sorts of metaphysical muddles.

James and Schiller introduced a second notion. In the absence of contrary evidence, if a belief satisfies a human desire, that too is a practical consequence and therefore a legitimate basis for calling certain beliefs true. If Moslem theology makes Moslems happier, the theology is for them true, and similarly for other metaphysical or theological "over-beliefs" (as James called them)—beliefs that cannot be established by reason or science but which do not conflict with reason or science, and which have psychological value for the believer.

Dewey did not accept this, but he did embrace the more fundamental tenet of pragmatism, the conviction that philosophy would be better served if it substituted for the ancient language of correspondence a new language in which statements become true only when they pass tests for truth. "The true means the verified and means nothing else . . ." was how Dewey crisply put it in the chapter on logic in his *Reconstruction in Philosophy*. In later years, to avoid misunderstanding, Dewey stopped using the word *truth* altogether. He preferred the phrase "warranted assertibility." It had for Dewey essentially the same meaning that "confirmation" had for Carnap and his friends.

James waxed so enthusiastic about the benefits he thought would follow from the pragmatic redefinition of truth that he made all sorts of extravagant statements which were easy to misinterpret. For example, if truth is no more than what is verified, then the statement "This is the queen of hearts" is not true or false until the card is turned. James did not hesitate to recommend this way of speaking. His *Pragmatism* abounds with eloquent passages about how truth is continually *made* by acts of verification. In ordinary language one would normally say this of only a very restricted class of statements. If I declare, "I will take a bath tonight," I can make the statement true by taking the bath. (Aristotle's sea battle!) But James made it sound as if he meant that science does not discover timeless facts, but somehow creates those facts by acts of verification. It seemed as if he meant that a statement such as "Saturn has rings" was not true in the days of Aristotle, but was made true by later astronomers when they first observed the planet's rings. James's ambiguous language, as well as the sometimes vague language of Dewey, lends itself easily to this kind of parody.

"The truth of an idea is not a stagnant property inherent in it. Truth *happens* to an idea. It *becomes* true, is *made* true by events. Its verity *is* in fact an event, a process: the process namely of its verifying itself. . . ."

"Truth is *made*, just as health, wealth and strength are made, in the course of experience."

Parodies? Alas, they are quotations from James's *Pragmatism*.

What James actually meant, however, is something utterly commonplace. He meant that as science keeps finding better and better reasons for calling certain assertions true (in the old correspondence sense), the process never reaches certainty. Science is forever changing and improving, but never incorrigible. For instance, astronomers keep altering their theories about how the solar system was formed, or about the chemical nature of the earth's core. Does this mean that as scientific opinions change about past events, those events change? Does it mean that as opinions change about the earth's core, the composition of the core changes? James certainly did not believe anything so ridiculous, but his language was so fuzzy and eccentric that it was easy for critics to suppose he meant such things. The classic instance of how preposterous James's *Pragmatism* seemed to British realists is G. E. Moore's essay "William James's *Pragmatism*" (you'll find it in Moore's *Philosophical Studies*). It is an amusing piece of polemics. By taking James's words at their face value it was easy for Moore to show how sharply they clashed with ordinary language, leading the reader to suppose James meant all sorts of absurd things he clearly did not mean.

James was so astounded by his failure to communicate in *Pragmatism* that he wrote an unintentionally funny sequel, *The Meaning of Truth*, in which he tried hard to clear up major misunderstandings. Unfortunately, the sequel contains so many of the same cloudy phrases that it only compounded the confusion. He repeats, for instance, his notorious passage from *Pragmatism:* "The true . . . is only the expedient in the way of our thinking, just as the right is only the expedient in the way of our behaving." Again, what James meant is commonplace: If an assertion passes certain tests for truth it is useful to assume it is true. If studies of the weather show it will probably rain, it is expedient to take an umbrella. But owing to James's novel language, with its refusal to talk of truth as a timeless relation, it was easy for his critics to suppose he meant that one could call any belief true if a person found the belief expedient at the time, and false if the belief had evil consequences. Sidney Hook once rebutted this charge by considering the statement on a label: "This bottle contains poison." If a person drinks the contents and dies, the label has been verified, although no pragmatist would suppose that this verification was useful to the person who made it.

Dewey was more cautious. As I have said, he found it less confusing to drop the word *truth* altogether. Nevertheless, his language, because it, too, departed so widely from common usage, also was widely misunderstood. Like James, Dewey fully realized that if an assertion passes tests for truth it is because the assertion corresponds with reality, but his way of speaking, like that of James, was easy to ridicule. Bertrand Russell, his most eminent antagonist, was both a realist in the sense of believing in a "stuff" behind the phaneron (whereas Dewey dismissed this belief as meaningless), and also a staunch defender of truth as a timeless correspondence with reality. The two men frequently attacked each other's view of truth, each presenting such a caricature of the other's opinions that it was easy to make them seem absurd. An entire book could be devoted to this battle of titans. I must here content myself with no more than giving my personal opinion of the debate.

I am persuaded that Russell and Dewey had no fundamental disagreement about truth, but only different ways of talking about it. I believe that any statement made by either man can be restated, when properly understood, in the language of the other. After all, both men were extremely intelligent, well acquainted with modern science as well as with the history of philosophy, and even in surprising agreement in their educational and political opinions. They had equally superficial differences about the nature of moral values. It seems unlikely that either man was quite the simpleton with respect to epistemology as the other made him out to be.

In my view the great controversy over truth was not much different from the old brain teaser (introduced by James in the second lecture of *Pragmatism*) about the man who circles a tree while a squirrel scrambles around the trunk so as always to keep the tree between itself and the man. After completing a circuit around the tree, has the man gone around the squirrel? It all depends, said James, on what is meant by "around." I find it surprising that James never seemed to comprehend that the storm aroused by his 1907 book was the result of using "truth" in a way that violated ordinary language. I find it equally amazing that philosophers by and large seem not to realize that similar arguments over linguistic preferences also account for the differences between Dewey and Russell in their historic clash over pragmatism.[3]

Russell and Dewey, if I am right, each accepted the basic notions of the other, but considered them too ordinary to be worth emphasizing. Dewey was always pointing out that his theory of truth included the idea of correspondence; indeed, he argued that his theory was the only one entitled to be called a correspondence theory! Because we know nothing about a reality behind the phenomenal world, the only meaningful correspondence is with that aspect of our experience which we call the external world. To put it plainly, Dewey's truth is a correspondence of two parts of our experience: assertions about the world and our success in validating those assertions.

How would Dewey have talked about our illustration of the selected playing card? I think he would have said the following. We are presented with a problem. Is the statement "This is the queen of hearts" a warranted assertion? To answer this question we must initiate an inquiry. This takes the form of turning over the card. If we see that it is the queen of hearts our doubts are dispelled. The problem has been solved. We have performed an act that establishes a correspondence between the sentence and the card. The process of inquiry has ended in the warranted assertion that the card is in fact the queen of hearts.

I see nothing in this description with which Russell could have quarreled. However, Russell and other nonpragmatists are allowed to say in their preferred language, that "This is the queen of hearts" is true even before making a test, if in fact the card *is* the queen of hearts. In their language, truth in this case is a time-independent relation between a statement and a fact, whether the statement is verified or not.

Nonpragmatists may even believe there is a final "absolute" truth about the world's structure, and combine this with what Peirce called "fallibilism," the doctrine that we have no sure way of knowing whether any belief about the world is absolutely true or not. Peirce liked to speak of the possibility that at some distant, perhaps infinitely distant, date the beliefs of scientists will finally converge on absolute truth. Dewey even quotes Peirce on this in a footnote to Chapter 17 of his *Logic*. "The best definition of truth known to me," writes Dewey (it is the only use of the word *truth* in his entire book!), is Peirce's statement: "The opinion which is fated to be ultimately agreed to by all who investigate . . ." Elsewhere Peirce phrased it this way: "Truth is that concordance of an abstract statement with the ideal limit towards which endless investigation would tend to bring scientific belief. . . ."

It is important to understand that Peirce is here speaking only of truth as we finite minds can know it. But Peirce was a thoroughgoing realist with respect both to the material world and to theorems of mathematics and logic. As a good disciple of Duns Scotus, Peirce never doubted that there are absolute timeless truths which are "out there," independent of you and me, and that science is a search for just such truth, even though it can never be certain it has found it.

In his *Collected Papers*, Peirce wrote that every person believes in timeless truth. "*That* truth consists in conformity to something *independent of his thinking it to be so*, or of any man's opinion on that subject" (Peirce's italics). For a pragmatist who thinks otherwise, "the only reality there could be would be conformity to the ultimate result of inquiry. But there would not be any course of inquiry possible except in the sense that it would be easier for him to interpret the phenomenon; and ultimately he would be forced to say that there was no reality at all except that he now at this instant finds a certain way of thinking easier than any other. But this violates the very idea of reality and of truth."[4] It would be hard to find a clearer statement of Peirce's reluctance to adopt the pragmatic language of James and Dewey.

One need not, of course, be a theist to believe in ultimate truth, the timeless ideal limit of knowledge. However, if one does believe in God, as Peirce did, presumably God knows all the facts about the universe and how it operates. This, too, combines easily with fallibilism since we, with our feeble minds and crude instruments of investigation, have no procedures other than fallible ones for getting at tiny portions of God's total knowledge.

But we are wandering from our present topic. Russell certainly would have taken for granted that to *know* whether the hypothesis that the card is the queen of hearts is true, one must turn over the card. For Russell this seemed too obvious to require stating. The center of the controversy is thus seen to be trivial. It is an argument over what the word *truth* should mean, perhaps also over what *mean* means. Each man thought his point of view included all that was essential in the other's. (Both views, incidentally, contain elements of the coherence theory of truth, but this is beside the point.) In brief, it is my contention that Dewey and Russell differed mainly, if not entirely, in the way they liked to talk about the same state of affairs. Their language preferences were grounded in their respective temperaments and backgrounds, perhaps also in their cultures. Their ways of speaking reflected what seemed to them most important in the process by which human beings acquire partial knowledge of the outside world.

The two men also differed in the way they talked about logic. This is strikingly brought out by the full title of Dewey's *Logic: The Theory of Inquiry*. As Carnap pointed out (in *Logical Foundations of Probability*), Dewey uses the word *logic* in a broad sense that has little to do with its traditional meaning. Instead of confining the term to formal reasoning within a deductive system, Dewey covers the entire process by which humans go about solving problems. As Carnap remarks, Dewey's book contains almost nothing about formal logic of the sort that interested himself and Russell. Even those sections where formal logic is briefly discussed seem out of place and unconnected with the rest of the book.

Dewey had little interest in formal logic and pure mathematics, or even in modern physics, where logic and mathematics play such essential roles. We must also keep in mind that in Dewey's overall philosophy there is no sharp distinction between subject and object, between the knower and the known. Dewey saw human history as a perpetual struggle of intelligent organisms to solve the problems created by their interaction with their environments. In this ongoing process, mathematics and formal logic are seen as useful tools, like plows and telescopes. Perhaps if Dewey had believed in a reality behind the phaneron, or in a God who constructed the phaneron, he would have been less eager to abandon the traditional ways of talking about logic and mathematics, and the timeless nature of truth.

If my assessment of the conflict between Dewey and Russell over truth is correct, as I think it is, another question at once arises. Which of the two languages, Russell's or Dewey's, is the most expedient? Here

I am on Russell's side. The ancient definition of truth as a timeless correspondence with reality is too useful to abandon. The linguistic reform attempted by the pragmatists turned out to be pragmatically unwise. It was unnecessary because everything the pragmatists wanted to say can be said just as well in the old language. Moreover, the attempted reform did in fact create more confusion than clarity.

Admirers of Lewis Carroll will recall Humpty Dumpty's notion that words can mean whatever one wants them to mean. Shortly after announcing this he fell off the wall and broke into so many pieces that he couldn't be put together again. Something like this happened to pragmatism. The pragmatists thought they could take *truth*, a respectable word which everybody understood in the Aristotelian sense, and redefine it to mean the passing of tests for truth. Their efforts lasted for a surprisingly brief time. Pragmatists were momentarily at the center of a storm in the United States and England until finally it dawned on philosophers that the pragmatists were not saying anything revolutionary at all. They were only saying the same old things in a bizarre way.

Nowhere is this more amusingly apparent than in a series of letters James exchanged with Charles A. Strong, a philosopher who shared his friend George Santayana's belief in old-fashioned realism and the correspondence theory of truth. Like everyone else, Strong had been mystified by passages in James's *Pragmatism* which seemed to deny the reality of objects independent of human minds. As the letters continue, James keeps stressing in stronger and stronger language that he is indeed a realist in the traditional sense, and that the utility of an idea lies precisely in its correspondence with a world that is independent of human experience.

Writing from Paris, Strong expresses enormous surprise:

Dear James:

. . . Santayana and I (he has just left for London this morning) have been greatly interested by your article on Pratt. We did not know you would acknowledge so roundly that truth is a relation between an idea and a reality beyond it, often quite separate from human experience, and it almost seems to us a complete change of face. We thought the pragmatist doctrine was that truth is a relation between the idea and *subsequent human experiences,*— that it "consists in the consequences" in this sense. Dewey certainly seems to teach that ideas are merely instrumental in resolving tangles in experienced situations, and that it is a fallacy to give them any other validity than that which they have as fulfilling this function. And as to the thoroughness of Schiller's idealism I have no further doubt after the discussions I have just had with him in the Engadine. He said he wasn't able to understand your article "A Word More about Truth"; which I think very likely. So I venture to predict that your developing realism will at once alarm your pragmatist colleagues and astonish those who have hitherto been your critics, who will think you are at last coming to your senses.

James reacts with amiable anger. He is furious, he says, to think he can be misunderstood so completely that anyone would imagine he had altered his views. "Epistemological realism," he insists, has always been the "permanent heart and center" of his thinking, and he reiterates his belief that this also is the case with Schiller and Dewey. At no time has he doubted that correspondence of ideas with reality is the reason for their utility. In a later letter to Strong he admits that some of his sentences may "squint toward idealism," and that he has been guilty of "groping," "fumbling," and "confusion," and has "probably made verbal slips."

When Strong writes to James a year later he has come to realize that he and James are in essential agreement but differ only in how they use words. Strong's finger rests squarely on the nub of their dispute. "I am forced to say that truth is a matter, and exclusively, of resembling or copying, and that what is addition to this is merely utility, and misnamed truth." James's reply, the final letter of the series, is disappointing. He simply points out the obvious. Truth is more than copying, he writes; otherwise one animal that resembled another animal would be "true" to it. Truth, he declares (as if anyone doubted), is a quality of human knowledge. It is here that correspondence comes in. Then James adds—who could disagree?—that the correspondence is "determinable only by the pragmatic method."[5]

It seems to me that there was a blindness on James's part, as well as on the part of Schiller and Dewey, to the kind of confusion that is inevitable whenever a philosopher, following Humpty, takes a useful word, with a commonly understood meaning, and gives it a new and novel meaning. Pragmatists believed, of course, that great benefits would flow from redefining truth as the meeting of tests for truth, but the actual results were decades of bewildering debate in which they wasted incredible amounts of time trying to explain to their opponents that they did not mean what their words, taken in the usual way, implied. They were guilty of violating what Peirce once called the "ethics of terminology," the moral obligation to respect the traditional meanings of entrenched philosophical terms.

Paul Edwards had a delightful way of making this point. Suppose, he wrote, a philosopher decides to redefine "shoe" as "footwear." The word now includes socks. This permits the philosopher to say that he habitually wears two shoes on each foot. The assertion may startle colleagues, and lead to curious arguments, but does it produce any fresh insights?[6] Many other philosophers, from Plato on, have warned against the perils of private definitions. Ironically, John Stuart Mill, who tried to redefine *matter* in a novel way, wrote one of the most eloquent pleas for terminology ethics.[7]

If I had to pick a single individual who, in my judgment, gave the egg of pragmatism the final push that toppled it off the wall, I would pick the Polish logician and mathematician Alfred Tarski. In the early thirties he published a historic paper on the semantic definition of truth, following it with articles that elaborated and popularized his results.[8] Using the tools of modern semantics and formal logic, Tarski found a precise, crystal-clear way of defining truth which he believed to be the same as Aristotle's. To oversimplify, Tarski posited an infinite hierarchy of formal languages in which every language is the "object language" of a "metalanguage" immediately above it. Only in a metalanguage can one speak of the truth or falsity of sentences in the object language below. If one wants to say that a statement about the physical world is true or false, one must assert this in a metalanguage. Tarski's favorite example is "'Snow is white' is true if and only if snow is white." Its counterpart for our card experiment is: The sentence "This card is the queen of hearts" is true if, and only if, this card is the queen of hearts. The truth of the metasentence in quotes must, of course, be tested by pragmatic means.

Tarski's semantic definition of truth has many merits. For one thing, it eliminates all the ancient semantic paradoxes that spring from allowing a language to talk about the truth or falsity of its own sentences. Forms of the liar paradox, such as "This statement is false," become nonstatements, without meaning. Another merit of Tarski's definition is that it applies to assertions in pure logic and mathematics as well as to scientific statements and ordinary speech. The meaning of truth is the same for all these languages; only the methods of testing are different. In logic and mathematics the correspondence is established by formal proofs, in science by empirical techniques.

Tarski's way of defining truth was enthusiastically endorsed by Russell and Carnap and Karl Popper, indeed by almost all philosophers of science outside the pragmatic school. Even the pragmatists could not fault Tarski's reasoning. They could only express dismay at his revival of a way of talking which they had hoped would become obsolete. All over the world, philosophers, troubled for decades by the pragmatic challenge, heaved a sigh of relief comparable to Strong's sigh in his letter when he finally realized that James agreed with him.

If you check the indexes of books on the philosophy of science published since 1950, you will find that the names of James, Schiller, and Dewey have almost vanished. This is not to say they were not influential thinkers or that their books are no longer worth reading. I myself admire Peirce and James more than any other American philosophers. Given the philosophical climate of the time, it is easy to understand James's enthusiasm for a radical redefinition of truth. The great debate that he and Peirce initiated was certainly stimulating, and we can expect many more historical studies that will trace the details of the debate and evaluate its good and bad influences.

Annoyed by James's excesses and distortions, Peirce changed his word to *pragmaticism*, adding that it was too ugly a word for anybody to "kidnap." He was right. Only students of Peirce know the word, and in ordinary discourse *pragmatism* has now degenerated into a synonym for practical. We say of a politician that he made a pragmatic decision. In this trivial sense everybody is a pragmatist. Even in the more technical sense of insisting that scientific hypotheses can be tested only in experience, every scientist and philosopher is a pragmatist. When I say I am not a pragmatist I mean only that I agree with most philosophers today in seeing no pragmatic reasons for adopting the epistemological language of pragmatism.

Let me put it this way: I believe that everything worthwhile that the pragmatists had to say about truth can be said better, with less ambiguity and misunderstanding, in a language that adopts the Aristotelian theory of truth as refined by Tarski. The notion that a statement can have an absolute, timeless correspondence with the world, whether verified or not, is too useful a notion. Abandon it and at once you have to invent another way to say the same thing.[9] Now that Tarski has established the pragmatic value of *truth* in its classic sense, why hesitate to use it? What harm is done by letting the word mean what it has always meant in ordinary discourse? Philosophers of science can then get on with the more important task of trying to understand and improve the methods by which human beings—Dewey's organisms interacting with environments—can decide when to call a statement about the world true or false, or how to assign to it a useful measure of credibility, albeit tentative, between one and zero.

3

SCIENCE:
Why I Am Not a Paranormalist

> No conceivable event, however extraordinary, is
> impossible; and, therefore, if by the term miracles we
> mean only "extremely wonderful events," there can be
> no just ground for denying the possibility of their
> occurrence.
>
> —THOMAS HENRY HUXLEY, Hume

Science is a search for reliable knowledge about the world: how the universe (including living things) is structured and how it operates. The search began when primitive minds first became aware of such obvious regularities as day and night, the beating of hearts, the falling of dropped objects. Slowly over the millennia the search was refined and systematized, first by better observations, then by making experiments and by inventing theories and new observing instruments.

In a rough way scientific information can be divided into three parts: facts, laws, and theories. No sharp lines separate these groupings, but if we did not give names to parts of continua we would be unable to talk. Day and night are useful terms in spite of—or, rather, because of—their fuzzy boundaries. If a lady tells you she dreamed about you last night, you are not likely to respond with, "Exactly what do you mean by night?"

For a typical fact let's take the statement "Mars has two moons." A typical law: Planets travel in elliptical orbits. A typical theory: general relativity. The first is a fact because it refers to a unique case. The second is a law because it generalizes from particular cases to all planets that go around single suns. The third is a theory because it deals with unobservable entities such as fields, and because it explains both facts and laws.

In all three areas—facts, laws, theories—scientific knowledge is never certain. Mars may have a third moon so small it hasn't yet been detected. Laws may be only crude first approximations. Theories may turn out to be mistaken. No statements about the world are absolutely certain, though some can be assigned a degree of credibility which everyone agrees is practically indistinguishable from certainty. Who would deny that elephants have trunks or that you who read this are not a cockroach?

Only in pure logic and mathematics can statements be deemed absolutely certain, but for this kind of truth a stupendous price is paid. The price is that such statements say nothing about the world. To apply abstract mathematics to physical things we have to make all sorts of assumptions which Rudolf Carnap called correspondence rules. Why do two elephants plus two elephants make four elephants? It is because we have strong empirical grounds for the correspondence rule which says that elephants combine like positive integers. But two drops of water plus two more drops can make one big drop. Applied mathematics is never absolutely certain because there is always the possibility, however remote, that a mathematical model is not absolutely accurate.

It does not follow from the vagueness of scientific method and the controversies surrounding it, that science does not genuinely advance. Nor does it follow that there is no rational basis for evaluating competing theories. Everyone agrees that science moves forward by a constant testing of new hypotheses, most of which have to be discarded. The process has been compared to that of organic evolution. Genetic mutations are copying errors that almost always lower the probability of a species' survival. Organisms with unfavorable mutations tend to die out; those with the rare favorable mutations tend to survive. In a similar way, the continual proposals of unorthodox theories, most of which turn out to be flawed, are essential to the progress of science. Establishment journals, contrary to what some people think, are crammed with just such offbeat speculations, and the surest road to fame is to advance a crazy theory that is eventually confirmed, often after intense resistance by skeptics. Such resistance is both understandable and necessary. Science would be total chaos if experts quickly embraced or even tried to disconfirm every eccentric theory that came along.[1]

Why do I stress such pedestrian views? Because, as a skeptic of paranormal claims, I am perpetually accused by parapsychologists of stubbornly denying the very possibility that psi forces such as ESP (telepathy, clairvoyance, precognition) and PK (psychokinesis) exist. It is a foolish accusation. No skeptic of psi known to me rules out the possibility of psi. Any law or theory is possible that is not logically inconsistent. It is possible that Wilhelm Reich discovered a hitherto unrecognized force, orgone energy. It is possible, as Scientologists contend, that a day-old human embryo records all words spoken to or by its mother. It is possible that you and I lived previous lives. It is possible that the sun stood still when Joshua commanded it, that Jesus walked on the water, turned water into wine, and raised people from the dead. It is possible that God made Eve from Adam's rib. It is possible that the earth is a hollow globe and we are living on the inside surface. All statements about the real world have varying degrees of credibility, with one and zero as unreachable limits, even though we can get within an infinitesimal distance from either end.

It is obvious, at least to me, that science has only begun to unravel the mysteries of the universe. If by paranormal you mean all the laws and theories not yet discovered, then all scientists believe in the paranormal. If we could somehow obtain a physics textbook of the twenty-fifth century, it is a good bet that it would contain information that no physicist now alive could guess or even understand. Every branch of science has frontiers on which it pushes outward into vast unexplored jungles that swarm with paranormal surprises. In this sense of paranormal I am a paranormalist of the most extreme sort. I firmly believe there are truths about existence as far beyond our minds as our present knowledge of nature is beyond the mind of a fish.

When I say I am not a paranormalist I use the word the way it is used today in ordinary discourse. We are living at a time of rising interest, on the part of an uninformed public, in wild beliefs which the entire science community considers close to zero in credibility. It is this vaguely defined body of crazy science that writers and television commentators mean when they use the term paranormal.

Need I summarize some of the things you are likely to see when a pseudodocumentary film explores the paranormal? UFOs bearing aliens from outer space; mysterious deadly forces in the Bermuda triangle; the power of the Great Pyramid's shape to preserve food and sharpen razor blades; the reality of demon possession, psychic surgery, dowsing, astrology, palmistry, numerology, biorhythm; the claims of Transcendental Meditators that one can learn to levitate, become invisible, and walk through walls; the human aura; out-of-body travel; poltergeists; Spiritualism; phone calls from the dead; statues of Mary that weep and bleed; the sensitivity of plants to thoughts; and (on a more credible level) ESP and PK.

In a competitive society such as ours the owners of the print and electronic media always pander to public taste, and there is much to be said for such pandering. If large numbers of people relish bad art, music, and literature, bad movies and television shows, and bogus science, who can say they should not be given the opportunity to read, hear, and see what they like? Any attempt at censorship, even of the most blatant porn, is always a risky business in an open society. No one who values liberty and democracy wants to see legislation on any government level, except in extreme cases, that tells the media what they cannot do.

There are, however (at least I so believe), many situations in which media officials face moral choices. Consider three examples. If NBC produced a documentary on the secret philandering of recent presidents, can anyone doubt that ratings would be fantastically high? Why is NBC unlikely to sponsor such a show? Not because laws prevent it, or because the facts would not be true, but because it would be in terrible taste. In the long run it would probably damage NBC's image.

Now a second thought experiment. A few scientists have recently claimed that blacks are slightly inferior to whites in genetic intelligence. NBC could produce a show that would permit the advocates of such opinions to present their case, unhampered by equal time for their opponents. After all, in a free society should not all viewpoints be aired, and would not millions of viewers be interested? Of course the film would start with a disclaimer stating that the opinions you are about to hear are not those of NBC, nor have they been accepted by most scientists.

Why does NBC not present such a show? It cannot be because ratings would be low, and I do not think that fear of damage to NBC's image, though it would no doubt be great, tells the entire story. Incredible as it may seem, I believe there are NBC executives who would consider such a documentary to be not only in bad taste but also morally wrong.

Our third example is, alas, not a thought experiment at all. It is a show that NBC actually sponsored in the fall of 1977, a ninety-minute special called *Exploring the Unknown* and featuring Burt Lancaster as narrator. The film opened with a fleeting voice-over pointing out that although the facts to be presented were believed true they had not been "conclusively proven"—a strange disclaimer because science never conclusively proves anything. No persons I spoke to who saw the show could recall the disclaimer. What they did remember was ninety minutes of dramatic glimpses into what Lancaster proclaimed to be great new frontiers of modern science.

They saw a French magician-turned-psychic bend an aluminum bar with the power of his mind. They saw a Japanese boy stare into a Polaroid camera, and when the film was developed, lo! there on the film was a photograph of the Eiffel Tower. A psychic bounced up and down on his back while a British paraphysicist solemnly concluded that the psychic had probably levitated. Psychic surgeons operated on patients without any instruments except their hands, although plenty of blood and tissue seemed to exude from the magic incisions. Someone moved a laser beam by PK. Another produced paintings under the guidance of long-dead artists. Ingenious inventions were displayed; then viewers were told that discarnate spirits had inspired them. Nothing in the film gave the slightest clue that everything being shown was considered rubbish by the entire science community.

In my opinion this atrocious film, and dozens of others like it that have been shown on television prime time during the past few years, was both in bad taste and morally reprehensible. It was wrong not just because it prompted some seriously ill viewers to fly to the Philippines for a worthless "operation" that could kill them if they neglected legitimate medical help, not just because it pandered to the public's hunger for the paranormal, but because it contributed to the growing inability of citizens to tell good science from bad.

Legislators and government officials, as ignorant of science as television producers and directors, reflect this trend. As a result, public funds are often diverted from worthy projects to worthless ones. In Samuel Goudsmit's book *ALSOS* (the code name for a secret project he headed to determine how far the Nazis had gone in atomic research during World War II) there is a sad scene in which Goudsmit confronts his old friend Werner Heisenberg, one of the few top German physicists who collaborated with Hitler. Germany had just been defeated, and Goudsmit listened patiently while Heisenberg spoke proudly about what he and his few assistants had achieved in the field of atomic explosives. Goudsmit could not then tell him how trivial it all was. It was trivial partly because knuckleheaded Nazi officials had squandered money on puerile projects, partly because great physicists had fled the Fatherland.[2]

The Nazi movement flourished at a time of enormous interest among the German people in the paranormal. Astrology boomed as never before. The public became obsessed with strange diet and health fads and bizarre pseudoscientific cults. A good case can be made for the view that this sprouting of crazy science in Germany made it easier for the populace to buy the crackpot anthropology that supported Hitler's "final solution." We are far behind Nazi Germany in such trends, but the similarities are glaring enough to be alarming.

As always with such manias, causes are multiple: the decline of traditional religious beliefs among the better educated,[3] the resurgence of Protestant fundamentalism, disenchantment with science for creating a technology that is damaging the environment and building horrendous war weapons, increasingly poor quality of science instruction on all levels of schooling, and many other factors. One factor, often overlooked in trying to explain recent mass enthusiasms, is the role of the media as feedback. This has always been true, but the fantastic power of television and motion pictures to influence opinion has made the feedback a force that now rapidly accelerates any trend. Producers of shows, like publishers of books and magazines, are correct in saying that they respond to public demand rather than initiate it. But just as mild porn stimulates a demand for pornier porn, and mild violence a demand for more violent violence, so does crazy science create a demand for crazier science.

Thirty years ago, in *Fads and Fallacies in the Name of Science*, I wrote about some of the outrageous parasciences of the fifties, just before the occult revolution got underway.[4] I have tried to cover part of the current scene in my recent anthology of articles and book reviews, *Science: Good, Bad and Bogus.*[5] Here I shall limit my remaining remarks to the milder claims of parapsychology.

As I made clear in *Fads and Fallacies*, I believe the claims of responsible parapsychologists deserve to be taken more seriously than any of the other topics listed above as prominent in the current occult explosion. Writers of shabby books about the paranormal usually make no distinction in worth between parapsychology and, say, astrology. Even leading parapsychologists have added to this confusion by contributing to periodicals, like *Fate* and *New Realities*, which they themselves regard with contempt. Clearly there is a rough continuum that runs from unorthodox but respectable science at one end to astrology at the other. Everyone agrees that there are no clear-cut criteria for distinguishing good science from bad. But rather than repeat what I and others have written elsewhere about the hazy guidelines for recognizing cranks,[6] I wish now to underscore a simpler point that I made earlier. The difficulty of drawing precise boundaries around portions of continua does not mean it is useless to distinguish widely separated portions of continua.

We can pin down the point with an extreme case. There are still flat-earth societies in parts of the world, including (where else?) California. If the leader of such a group is sincere, is there anyone not a flat-earther who would hesitate to call him a crank? The usefulness of the word is not impaired by the fact that crank science is at one end of a spectrum that fades into reputable science at the other. The situation is not unlike that in an old joke about a rich man who asked a woman if she would sleep with him for a million dollars. After she agreed, he offered five dollars. The woman was insulted. "What do you think I am, a whore?" "That's been settled," the man replied. "We are now haggling over the price."

No one can pretend that cranks, like prostitutes, do not exist, but trying to decide where to place a given maverick on the spectrum that runs from good science to crackpottery is a haggling over degree of credibility. There are no sharp criteria, and even a consensus among top scientists can reflect a wide range of cultural influences that distort judgments. Johannes Kepler is often cited as a great scientist whose views were mixed with astrology and eccentric speculations in contrast to the sounder views of Galileo. Yet even Galileo could not accept Kepler's correct theory of elliptical orbits or his claim that the moon causes tides. Today there are sophisticated techniques, unknown to Galileo and Kepler, for evaluating scientific theories, but they are still far from free of individual and cultural bias. There is always the possibility that a new point of view which seems outlandish to most scientists will eventually turn out to be right.

I am frequently criticized for having included a chapter on Joseph Banks Rhine in my *Fads and Fallacies*. Many who fault me for this do not recall that on the first page of that chapter, I wrote:

> It should be stated immediately that Rhine is clearly not a pseudo-scientist to a degree even remotely comparable to that of most of the men discussed in this book. He is an intensely sincere man, whose work has been undertaken with a care and competence that cannot be dismissed easily, and which deserves a far more serious treatment than this cursory study permits. He is discussed here only because of the great interest that centers around his findings as a challenging new "unorthodoxy" in modern psychology, and also because he is an excellent example of a borderline scientist whose work cannot be called crank, yet who is far on the outskirts of orthodox science.[7]

My opinion of Rhine's sincerity remains unchanged, though as more facts come to light about his early work, the less sure I am of his care and competence. My attitude is much the same toward other top parapsychologists. In my opinion they have not established their claims beyond a low degree of credibility, and at times I find them extraordinarily gullible, but I do not regard most of them as either fools or knaves. Let me do my best to make clear what I think of their work, and why I am not a paranormalist even in the limited sense of believing in psi.

The first point to emphasize is that the claims of parapsychology are scientific claims. They have no necessary connection with any religious or philosophical belief. I do not mean that they are not often connected in some way with such beliefs. For example, it is fashionable now to explain the healings of Jesus and the cures of faith healers as a form of psychic healing, and to find support for levitation in the biblical account of how Jesus ascended into the skies or the Catholic doctrine of the ascension of Mary. I mean only that the claims of parapsychology are set forth as resting on empirical evidence, and that one may hold any metaphysical or religious opinion and accept or reject psi solely on scientific grounds.

I am constantly amused by letters from well-meaning souls who assume that my skepticism about psi is a product of my atheism. It is true that I am one of the founders of The Committee for the Scientific Investigation of Claims of the Paranormal, first sponsored by the American Humanist Association, but I am not a humanist in their sense of the term. It also is true that the narrator of my novel, *The Flight of Peter Fromm*, is a secular humanist. But anyone who reads that curious novel carefully should realize that my purpose was to contrast the views of my narrator with the persistent theism of my young protagonist, and that my narrator's opinions no more reflect my own than the conservative political views of the narrator of *The Late George Apley* reflect the opinions of John Marquand, or the psychoses of the narrator of *Pale Fire* reflect the personality of Vladimir Nabokov. As I shall confess in later chapters, I am not only a theist but also, in a sense, a Platonic mystic. But what do God or the gods have to do with the question of whether PK can bend a spoon? Most of those I know who believe strongly in psi are atheists. Sigmund Freud and Mark Twain come to mind. Both believed in telepathy and both were atheists. And there have been and are a multitude of theists who are as skeptical as I of the claims of parapsychology. The question of whether psi forces exist is a scientific question. It should be as unaffected by philosophical and religious beliefs as the question of whether gravity waves exist.

Skeptics sometimes say that they don't believe in psychic forces but that the world would be more exciting if such forces did exist. Maybe. In some ways it would be exciting if, say, gravity could be suspended by mental effort, as leaders of Transcendental Meditation insist, but in other ways it would create enormous confusion. Jesus once remarked that no man by taking thought can add one cubit to his stature. It is amusing to read about how Alice grows and shrinks as she nibbles opposite sides of the blue caterpillar's mushroom, but in the real world such paranormal phenomena would not be so amusing.

I also value the privacy of my thoughts. I would not care to live in a world in which others had the telepathic power to know what I was secretly thinking, or the clairvoyant power to see what I was doing. It could be one of God's mercies that we mortals are able to communicate with one another only by willfully uttering words or making other kinds of signs. One of Emily Dickinson's unfinished poems begins with lines I have always liked:

A letter is a joy of Earth.
It is denied the gods.

Rhine once wrote about how ESP, if it ever became a reliable human capacity, would be a great force for peace and the control of crime:

> The consequences for world affairs would be literally colossal. War plans and crafty designs of any kind, anywhere in the world, could be watched and revealed. With such revelation it seems unlikely that war could ever occur again. There would be no advantage of surprise. Every secret weapon and scheming strategy would be subject to exposure. The nations could relax their suspicious fear of each other's secret machinations.
>
> Crime on any scale could hardly exist with its cloak of invisibility thus removed. Graft, exploitation, and suppression could not continue if the dark plots of wicked men were to be laid bare.[8]

It seems not to have occurred to Rhine that such awesome powers could be used just as easily by a police state. They would be tools with a far wider scope for repression and terror than the mere tapping of a phone, opening of a letter, or electronic eavesdropping.

Precognition? The advantages and disadvantages are so obvious that I will elaborate only by citing a Hindu myth and by telling another joke.

The myth: The Hindu god Shiva has a third eye, in the center of his forehead, with which he can see the future. His wife, Parvati, is perpetually and understandably annoyed by this ability because whenever they play a dice game, Shiva cheats by knowing the outcome of future dice rolls.

The joke: A devout Christian had become, like Samuel Johnson in his declining years, enormously worried over whether he was destined for heaven or hell. After he had prayed for insight, an angel appeared in the room. "I have," said the angel, "good and bad news. First the good news. You are going to heaven."

The man was overjoyed. "And the bad?"

"Next Tuesday."

PK opens up even more terrifying possibilities. I am not enthusiastic over the possibility that someone who dislikes me might have the power from a distance to cause me harm. The other side of white magic is black magic, whether it be the blackness of demons or the blackness of psychic power. A few years ago I attended a conference on psi at New York University. The lectures, by distinguished parapsychologists, were followed by question-and-answer periods. Several disturbed young ladies arose to say that they had enemies who were using PK to cause them terrible accidents. How could they prevent this? The speakers looked embarrassed, and I was impressed by the evasiveness of their replies.

Parapsychologists, eager to get research funds from the government, are correct in saying that if PK exists it could be used for sabotage. A psychic who can bend a key in someone's fist could surely use the same power to trip an explosive or damage computer circuitry. It is because of such fears—in my opinion groundless—that military forces in both Russia and the United States are funding secret research on psi. Again, could it be another of God's mercies that we do not have the ability to alter substances by taking thought?

Consider also the havoc PK would inject into science. Experiments often depend on the pointer readings of sensitive instruments. If an experimenter can unconsciously influence those instruments, causing them to favor strong hopes or fears, then tens of thousands of experiments become dubious. This injects cloudy elements even into parapsychology. Many eminent parapsychologists are convinced that PK can affect random number generators now widely used in psi testing. How can one be sure that an experiment, instead of measuring, say, the clairvoyant power of a subject, is not measuring the PK power of the experimenter, combined with precognition, over the randomizer used to select targets?

Paraphysicist Helmut Schmidt performed a famous experiment with cockroaches which seemed to prove that cockroaches had the paranormal ability to give themselves more electric shocks than chance allowed. Since cockroaches presumably want to avoid shocks, Schmidt suggested that, because he hated cockroaches, maybe it was *his* PK that influenced the randomizer![9] Parapsychologists often say that when skeptics observe an experiment, they inhibit psi. This could work the other way around. How can we be sure that the success of a psi experiment is not the result of PK influences by believers associated with the test rather than the psi ability of the subject?

Since it is easy to imagine how psi forces could be beneficial—psychic healing for instance—I have tried to balance the case by stressing some evils. My own feeling, as I have said, is neutral. I neither hope nor fear the reality of psi any more than I hope or fear the reality of quarks. The reason I do not believe in psi is that I find the evidence unconvincing.

Most people, brainwashed by a constant barrage of pro-psi rhetoric which they are not in position to evaluate, are astonished to learn that the great majority of psychologists, especially experimental psychologists, do not believe in psi. How can the public know that the number of full-time psi researchers in the country is exceedingly small? In 1978, Charles Tart, a widely respected parapsychologist, estimated the number to be about a dozen. Most of them, he added, are self-taught and poorly funded. Some are tireless propagandists. They churn out popular books, and appear on talk shows where they make excellent impressions as intelligent, open-minded scientists, bravely rowing against the currents of orthodoxy. Hack journalists pounce on their work to produce a constant avalanche of shabby potboilers that often earn fortunes for themselves and their conscienceless publishers.

How can the public know that for fifty years skeptical psychologists have been trying their best to replicate classic psi experiments, and with notable unsuccess? It is this fact more than any other that has led to parapsychology's perpetual stagnation. Positive evidence keeps flowing from a tiny group of enthusiasts, while negative evidence keeps coming from the much larger group of skeptics. William James, in *Memories and Studies*, expressed perplexity over having followed the literature of psychic research for a quarter-century and finding himself in the same state of doubt as at the beginning. More recently philosopher Antony Flew confessed similar sentiments. In 1953, in his *A New Approach to Psychical Research*, Flew argued that the evidence seemed too much to dismiss, yet there were no repeatable experiments that settled the matter. In 1976 he had this to say:

> It is most depressing to have to say that the general situation more than twenty-two years later still seems to me to be very much the same. An enormous amount of further work has been done. Perhaps more has been done in this latest period than in the whole previous history of the subject. Nevertheless, there is still no reliably repeatable phenomenon, no particular solid-rock positive cases. Yet there still is clearly too much there for us to dismiss the whole business. [10]

How do parapsychologists account for this? I have already mentioned a marvelous excuse which I call their Catch 22. If an experimenter is a skeptic, they maintain, even if skeptics are present only as observers, the skepticism inhibits the delicate operation of psi. (Because psi forces are said to be independent of distance and time, I'm surprised that parapsychologists have not yet attributed a replication failure to someone a thousand miles away who had doubted a week before that an experiment would be successful.) Catch 22 places the skeptic in a position unique in the annals of science. There is *no way* a skeptic can disconfirm ESP or PK to the satisfaction of a believer. Hence we face the dreary prospect that the next fifty years of psi research will be exactly like the last.

Catch 22 is only one of many excuses constantly invoked to account for replication failures. The subject had a headache or was emotionally upset, conditions in the laboratory were not sufficiently relaxed, there was a personality clash between subject and experimenter, apparatus for the test made a distracting noise, an experiment was too complicated, the weather was too cold, the weather was too hot, the subject (for some mysterious reason which occurs frequently) lost his or her previous abilities, and there are many others.

When I look over the vast literature of parapsychology I am overwhelmed by the absence of those strict controls that are essential for confirming extraordinary claims. If someone announces that he can clairvoyantly view a scene ten thousand miles away when given no more than the spot's map coordinates,[11] such a fantastic claim calls for far more stringent controls than are needed to determine whether he can juggle five balls or play "Dixie" by rapping his skull with his knuckles. Until parapsychologists can come up with experiments reliably repeatable by skeptics who are both capable and willing to impose extraordinary controls, their results will continue to have only the mildest influence on "establishment" psychology.

David Hume's essay on miracles (Section 10 of his *Enquiry Concerning Human Understanding*) should be required reading for anyone concerned with evaluating the wonders of psychic research. Hume writes mostly about biblical miracles, but if for them you substitute recent psychic miracles, everything in Hume's essay seems to have been written yesterday. "The knavery and folly of men are such common phenomena," he declares, "that I should rather believe the most extraordinary events to arise from their concurrence, than admit of so signal a violation of the laws of nature."

Of the many valuable commentaries on Hume's essay I particularly recommend the observations of Charles Peirce in the sixth volume of his *Collected Papers*, and Chapter 7 of Thomas Huxley's *Hume*, from which I took this chapter's epigraph. After the statement there quoted, and with which I fully concur, Huxley goes on to spell out what it means to say that extraordinary scientific claims demand extraordinary evidence:

> But when we turn from the question of the possibility of miracles, however they may be defined, in the abstract, to that respecting the grounds upon which we are justified in believing any particular miracle, Hume's arguments have a very different value, for they resolve themselves into a simple statement of the dictates of common sense—which may be expressed in this canon: the more a statement of fact conflicts with previous experience, the more complete must be the evidence which is to justify us in believing it. It is upon this principle that every one carries on the business of common life. If a man tells me he saw a piebald horse in Piccadilly, I believe him without hesitation. The thing itself is likely enough, and there is no imaginable motive for his deceiving me. But if the same person tells me he observed a zebra there, I might hesitate a little about accepting his testimony, unless I were well satisfied, not only as to his previous acquaintance with zebras, but as to his powers and opportunities of observation in the present case. If, however, my informant assured me that he beheld a centaur trotting down that famous thoroughfare, I should emphatically decline to credit his statement; and this even if he were the most saintly of men and ready to suffer martyrdom in support of his belief. In such a case, I could, of course, entertain no doubt of the good faith of the witness; it would be only his competency, which unfortunately has very little to do with good faith, or intensity of conviction, which I should presume to call in question.
>
> Indeed, I hardly know what testimony would satisfy me of the existence of a live centaur. To put an extreme case, suppose the late Johannes Müller, of Berlin, the greatest anatomist and physiologist among my contemporaries, had barely affirmed that he had seen a live centaur, I should certainly have been staggered by the weight of an assertion coming from such an authority. But I

could have got no further than a suspension of judgment. For, on the whole, it would have been more probable that even he had fallen into some error of interpretation of the facts which came under his observation, than that such an animal as a centaur really existed. And nothing short of a careful monograph, by a highly competent investigator, accompanied by figures and measurements of all the most important parts of a centaur, put forth under circumstances which could leave no doubt that falsification or misinterpretation would meet with immediate exposure, could possibly enable a man of science to feel that he acted conscientiously, in expressing his belief in the existence of a centaur on the evidence of testimony.

This hesitation about admitting the existence of such an animal as a centaur, be it observed, does not deserve reproach, as scepticism, but moderate praise, as mere scientific good faith. It need not imply, and it does not, so far as I am concerned, any *à priori* hypothesis that a centaur is an impossible animal; or, that his existence, if he did exist, would violate the laws of nature. Indubitably, the organisation of a centaur presents a variety of practical difficulties to an anatomist and physiologist; and a good many of those generalisations of our present experience, which we are pleased to call laws of nature, would be upset by the appearance of such an animal, so that we should have to frame new laws to cover our extended experience. Every wise man will admit that the possibilities of nature are infinite, and include centaurs; but he will not the less feel it his duty to hold fast, for the present, by the dictum of Lucretius, "Nam certe ex vivo Centauri non fit imago," and to cast the entire burthen of proof, that centaurs exist, on the shoulders of those who ask him to believe the statement.

Defenders of parascience often refer to its sensational discoveries as "white crows." It is a poor figure of speech because white crows are no more unusual than black swans or blue apples. Huxley's choice of a centaur is a much better metaphor. There is not much difference in degree of credibility between a centaur and the wee folk with gauzy wings that Conan Doyle believed had been photographed by two girls in an English glen. The Uri Geller metal-bending effect, the movements of objects by Nina Kulagina in Russia and Felicia Parise in the

United States, the claims by Harold Puthoff and Russell Targ that there is an easy way to use precognition for winning at casino roulette,[12] the "thoughtography" of Ted Serios, reports of UFO close encounters of the third kind, and a thousand other marvels that have excited not just the hack writers but many distinguished parapsychologists—these claims are much closer to ancient reports of centaurs than any reports of white crows.

Where in my opinion do parapsychologists go wrong? There is no single answer. In most cases I believe their results are the product of unintentional bias in designing experiments and analyzing raw data. In all types of research that depend heavily on statistics it is easy for experimenters to find what they passionately desire to find. It has often been pointed out that as Rhine learned more and more about controls, his results became less and less impressive. He never found a subject to rival Hubert Pearce, who once called twenty-five ESP cards in a row correctly. He never found another horse like Lady Wonder that could read his mind. Early issues of his journal are filled with papers revealing such trivial controls that if those same papers were submitted now to the same journal they would be rejected. It is no credit to today's parapsychologists that they continue to praise these early, strongly flawed experiments.

Another explanation of many classic psi tests is simply clever—sometimes not even clever—cheating on the part of subjects. As I have often said, electrons and gerbils don't cheat. People do. There is a type of individual, extremely common in the history of psychic research, who has no financial motive for cheating but does have a strong emotional drive to cheat. Such persons get their kicks from being considered psychic by their parents, by their friends, by parapsychologists, and by the public. Frequently they are young students who have the added incentive of wanting to please a teacher and to get good grades. In many cases they firmly believe they have paranormal powers. To reinforce and magnify what they think are authentic talents, they resort to cheating.

The history of Spiritualism swarms with mediums who had just such twisted personalities. Robert Browning's long poem "Mr. Sludge the Medium" is about one such man, D. D. Home. Handsome, intelligent, urbane, Home was the greatest medium of his day, perhaps of all time. I do not know what Home's private beliefs were about the dead, but I think Houdini described him accurately when he called him "a hypocrite of the deepest dye." Home even had the gall to write a book on methods by which other mediums cheated, carefully leaving out, of course, his own methods. But most of today's self-styled super-psychics live drab lives and have little talent for public entertainment. The only way they can get themselves noticed is by performing dull magic tricks and pretending they are not tricks. Some become consummate actors who play the role of simpleminded, sincere souls, utterly at a loss to comprehend their peculiar "gifts."

How often did Doyle and other Spiritualists declare that Mrs. So-and-So could not possibly have cheated when her trumpets floated about the darkened room because she is such a sweet, innocent grandmother who obviously knows nothing about magic. Sweet and innocent, my foot! The crafty old lady usually had behind her fifty years of sordid experience as a professional mountebank. No successful card hustler acts like a hustler when he is playing with strangers. No quack doctor talks or behaves like a quack. Psychic charlatans never talk or act like charlatans.

Finally, there are those rare cases when a parapsychologist himself cheats. A sad recent instance is the case of Walter J. Levy, Jr., the director of Rhine's laboratory who had been chosen by Rhine to be his successor. When *Time* devoted a cover article (March 4, 1974) to the occult explosion, its science editor, Leon Jaroff, told me that the most sensible letter of protest came from Levy. A few months later Levy was caught flagrantly cheating by pulling a plug on a counting device to make it register an abnormally high number of hits.[13] I have it on good authority that his crime was detected not because of careful controls in Rhine's laboratory, but because suspicious young staff members set a careful trap for him.

A more recently uncovered case of cheating, by a much more distinguished parapsychologist, is that of Samuel G. Soal. At first Soal was highly scornful of Rhine's work, especially the dice tests. Suddenly he began to get positive ESP results, and quickly became England's most famous psi experimenter. "Soal's work was a milestone in ESP research," said Rhine. "Entirely apart from the intrinsic value of his work, which is high, the manner in which his conclusion forced him to reverse his position on ESP has given it additional status." The evidence that Soal faked the data in one of his most widely respected tests is now overwhelming.[14]

To summarize, in my view there are three major sources of error in the classic psi experiments: unconscious experimenter bias, deliberate fraud on the part of subjects, and occasional fraud on the part of investigators. It is possible, of course, that the world is on the verge of a great new Copernican Revolution of the mind. I cannot say that psi forces do not exist. I do say that the evidence for them is feeble. Extraordinary claims demand much more extraordinary evidence than parapsychologists have been able to muster. When experiments can be reliably replicated by skeptics, when it is evident that controls are commensurate with the wildness of the claims, and when knowledgeable magicians participate in the designing and witnessing of such experiments, I will not hesitate to change my mind.

4

BEAUTY:
Why I Am Not
an Aesthetic Relativist

*The aesthetic principles are at bottom such axioms as
that a note sounds good with its third and fifth, or
that potatoes need salt.*

—WILLIAM JAMES, *Psychology*

When I say I am not a relativist with respect to beauty, or to use a more academic term, "aesthetic value," I mean that I believe there are standards of excellence in all the arts, fine or not so fine, that transcend both individual tastes and cultural norms. Before trying to clarify these utterly commonplace notions, let me put aside some problems I consider unimportant.

Words frequently have multiple meanings so wide-ranging that no single definition will capture them all. Ludwig Wittgenstein likened the meanings of such words to the resemblances of members of a family. A father may look like his son because they have similar chins, and the son may look like his mother because they have similar eyes, but this does not entail that the mother and father look alike. If you diagram the meanings of a family-type word with what mathematicians call Venn circles, circle A may overlap circle B (because they represent sets with some members in common), and circle *B* may overlap circle *C*, but *A* and *C* may not overlap at all. Wittgenstein offered the word *game* as an example. Does a game require at least two players? No, there are solitaire games. Must a game have winners and losers? No, consider a child bouncing a ball. And so on. No single definition of *game* includes all the ways the word is commonly used. The best we can do is what a dictionary does: list all the meanings that a given culture, at a given time, has bestowed on the word.

Aesthetic is such a family word. Some philosophers reduce it almost to meaninglessness by applying it to every kind of experience that gives immediate pleasure: gazing at a blue sky; listening to birds, wind, rain, and surf; breathing fresh air; smelling a flower; tasting a peach; enjoying the stillness of a snowy evening. Sneezing, scratching, and having an orgasm become aesthetic pleasures. The German Bauhaus pioneered in tactile sculpture designed to please the fingers. (I once had a short story in *Esquire* about a Chicago art school that made objects to be felt with the feet.) Every skilled card magician or card hustler will testify to the tactile delight of picking up a deck of cards and giving it a few false shuffles and false cuts. We speak of beautiful people. Should we not, therefore, regard seeing a beautiful woman, or a man or a child, as an aesthetic experience?

Other philosophers restrict *aesthetic* to the properties of humanly created objects of art: music, poetry, fiction, painting, sculpture, and mixed forms such as the song, dance, opera, play, and motion picture. Presumably these are objects (I will use the word in a broad sense to include all works of art) that have little or no utility beyond the giving of immediate pleasure. But even if we exclude such "practical" arts as architecture, interior decoration, the designing of wallpaper, fabrics, clothes, jewelry, cars, machines, tools, packages, store windows, and so on, we are trapped in a jungle of ambiguity. To give only one puzzling example: What about humor? Is laughing at a cartoon, a caricature, or a joke an aesthetic experience?

Aside from music and nonobjective art, most art objects are rich mixtures of many kinds of disparate values. Should we include all of them as components of aesthetic experience, or confine the term to what are often called the formal values of a work? By *formal* is meant the ways in which parts of the art object relate to one another. In music there are the patterns of beats and tones, in painting the harmony of shapes and colors, in poetry the interlocking of rhythms and sounds.

There is nothing wrong in limiting *aesthetic* to the formal aspect of a work, though at times it forces one to talk about art in unusual ways. For instance, a great realist painter could certainly produce a supremely beautiful (in the formal sense) picture of excrement. We probably would not care to hang it in our living room; nevertheless we would have to say it had superb aesthetic value.

Consider the mixture of values a novel can have: vicarious adventure, humor, eroticism, instruction, rhetoric (religious, political, moral), terror, sadness, sentimental recall, escape into fantasy, verisimilitude, insight into character, a beautiful style, the sheer pleasure of following a story and being surprised by what happens next, and many other things I haven't thought of. These values are all fused in a single object, although they are analytically separable and can be independently evaluated. A novel may tell a fine story but be written in an abominable style. Or vice versa. We can declare that a novel about, say, the oil industry has cardboard characters but gives an accurate picture of the industry and may also be effective rhetoric for an economic program. We can make scores of similar distinctions, rating the worth of any one value quite apart from the worth of any other.

Consider a chair. Is it beautiful to look at? Is it comfortable to sit on? The two values belong to the same object, but clearly they can vary independently. A vast literature is devoted to such dreary questions. There are, of course, endless subtle differences of emphasis, but it seems to me that the major schools of criticism, in all the arts, are little more than different languages for talking about a state of affairs that everybody fully understands. There is nothing wrong in critics taking on all the values of a work of art, and nothing wrong in concentrating on its purely formal aspects, or any other aspect that especially concerns a critic. All we can reasonably ask is that critics make clear how they are using their terms, and that they depart not too widely from customary usage.

The task of classifying the arts—defining precisely what is meant by such words as *poem, novel, painting, dance,* and so on—strikes me as equally trivial and unproductive. Hazy definitions will serve mundane purposes—bookstores divide stock into biography, fiction, science, poetry, health, and so on—but for every definition there are in-between things that elude classification. Even though *Moby Dick* contains long chapters of nonfiction, we still call it a novel because they are secondary to the story. But what is one to make of, say, H. G. Wells's *The*

World of William Clissold? It is always listed as one of Wells's novels, yet it consists of nonfictional essays loosely joined by the thinnest of narratives. Is Truman Capote's *In Cold Blood* fiction or nonfiction? A prose translation of Homer or Virgil is more like a novel than a poem. Are the poems of Stephen Crane genuine poems or just philosophical epigrams broken into short lines? Is a found piece of driftwood a work of sculpture? Is birdsong a form of music? I find debates over such questions so unprofitable that even now I am eager to press on to more interesting topics.

One danger of classification schemes is that they encourage critics to commit their most common sin: judging a work of art by standards that apply to something else. Criticism, G. K. Chesterton somewhere remarks, too often is like saying, "Of course I do not like green cheese; I am very fond of brown sherry." In his book on Robert Browning, Chesterton speaks of the absurdity of attacking *The Ring and the Book* because it is based on a sordid Italian murder case. Browning's specific intent was to write about good and evil as exhibited by a sordid murder case. It is ridiculous, says GK, to fault *Tristram Shandy* for its disheveled plot. Sterne's intent was to violate all the traditional rules for plots.

One could assemble—perhaps someone has—an amusing anthology of irrelevant criticism. Art critics are peculiarly prone to it. One will object to an abstraction because it doesn't resemble anything; another will object to a realistic painting because it does. I am typing this not long after the death of Norman Rockwell. Critics who for decades have lambasted the Philistines for confusing formal values with subject matter have been saying that Rockwell will have no place in the history of illustration, not because he lacked a sense of form and color, or displayed poor technique in his rather loose style of realism, but because they are offended by his subject matter.

Now there is nothing wrong with being offended by a picture's subject matter, provided you keep this emotion at arm's length from your perception of the picture's formal beauty. Is there not something strange about politically conservative art critics who perpetually downgrade the social art of the thirties for its sentimental political rhetoric, but are willing to overlook the sentimental religious rhetoric of Renaissance paintings of Jesus on the cross or Mary holding an infant God in her arms? There is as much propaganda in "The Last Supper" as in "Guernica." But critics don't like green cheese. It doesn't taste like brown sherry.

A third aspect of aesthetic theory that bores me even more are all those tiresome disputes, in book after book, about whether aesthetic values are subjective or objective. Here the situation is not quite the same as that of truth. In previous chapters I have argued that the least confusing way to talk about truth is to assume that the world and its structure are not mind-dependent. But beauty, so far as humanity is concerned (we will not consider what beauty may mean to birds or apes, to creatures on other planets, or to gods), obviously requires a human mind. Where is the red of an apple? As I have said, it is in the mind if by red we mean the sensation of red. It is on the apple if by red we mean the structure of a surface that reflects a pattern of visible light which causes a mental sensation of red.

I see no difference between this antique quibble and the question of whether beauty (however defined) is a property of an art object or a sensation in a brain. If by beauty you mean the pleasure aroused by a beautiful object, of course it is subjective. If by beauty you mean the structure of an object capable of arousing aesthetic pleasure, then the beauty is a part of the object. Or you may prefer a third approach and ground beauty in the combined dynamic structure produced by the interaction of an object and a mind. It is all such a weary waste of words. The last approach is the one taken by John Dewey in his influential book *Art as Experience*. Although I found fault with Dewey's attempt to redefine truth in pragmatic terms, I find his approach to aesthetics (essentially the same, by the way, as Aristotle's) a sensible way of speaking. Again, it is not a question of Dewey being right or wrong. It is a question of the most useful way to talk about aesthetic values.

Suppose someone writes a symphony that is played just once and recorded on tape. The tape is placed in a spacecraft and fired into outer space. No record of the music is kept. Eventually the composer and everyone who heard the symphony dies. Assume that the tape is never retrieved by extraterrestrials, but continues to orbit the galaxy without any mind ever hearing it. Is there musical beauty on the tape? The question is as inane as asking whether the hunter walked around the squirrel, or whether the falling tree makes a noise when no ear hears it. The answer is yes if we mean that on the tape is a structure which, properly transformed into sounds for a proper mind, would be considered beautiful. The answer is no if we mean the sensation of beauty in the mind of a listener.

A more stimulating question, the one with which this chapter is mainly concerned, is whether there are standards of judgment about beauty that transcend individual or group tastes. For a single person there clearly are standards; otherwise he or she would find all art objects equally pleasing. Some critics have actually maintained—it is the most extreme form of aesthetic relativism—that there are no standards beyond personal taste. Person A thinks Edgar Guest wrote the best poetry in English. B thinks Shakespeare did. To an extreme relativist, each is as right as the other and there are no grounds for arbitration.

I know of no way to argue against this view without assuming that individuals can, in some rough way, be ordered in a hierarchy based on their ability to appreciate aesthetic values. On each rung of the ladder the persons on that level are capable of experiencing all, or almost all, of the values experienced by those on lower rungs, but not vice versa.

At this point two questions should be kept separate. Does such a ladder exist? Do we know enough about aesthetic experience to draw up sharp criteria for distinguishing rungs that are near one another? I believe the answer to the first question is a qualified yes, to the second a thunderous no.

Young children are good examples of low-rung critics. A small child responds easily to the rhythms and harmonies of simple tunes, but cannot appreciate the complex values of a symphony. An adult who derives enormous pleasure from symphonic music is quite capable of enjoying a banal tune the way a child does. Young children like almost any kind of art in a storybook if they can tell what the picture represents, but are puzzled if they cannot recognize that a cow is a cow. A ten-year-old who loves comic books is likely to find a play by Shakespeare incomprehensible and boring. On the other hand, adults who enjoy abstract art and Shakespeare are quite capable of appreciating both the art and text of a good comic book.

Contrast a chess tyro with a grand master. The tyro may experience considerable satisfaction in checkmating another tyro, but to a grand master the mate is obvious at a glance and devoid of interest. If the tyro watches a game between two experts, he may not even understand why a certain move is called beautiful. The tyro simply does not have the skill to understand the elegance of high-level chess strategy. If you insist that tyros get as much pleasure out of their crude moves as grand masters get out of theirs, I have no objection. We are involved here in another ancient quibble similar to that of whether a baby or a pig can be said to be as happy as a happy adult. No one, of course, doubts that grand masters can easily defeat tyros in chess games. Alas, there is no comparable way to pit eminent critics against one another. At this point our chess analogy falls apart.

It would take too long to defend the right to say there are grand masters and tyros among both artists and critics, so I will give only a summary of my views. I believe that just as adult humans are superior to babies and baboons in their ability to create and enjoy art, so there are adults superior to other adults in the same respects. On the basis of this ranking we can assert that works of art enjoyed by those on the upper levels are superior to works of art enjoyed by those on the lower levels. In the two previous chapters I maintained that flimsy knowledge about the criteria of truth does not render futile the task of distinguishing good science from bad. Now I maintain that flimsy knowledge about the criteria of beauty does not render futile the task of distinguishing good from bad art.

The difficulties are, of course, immense—so much so that the relativist's position is as hard to refute as it is easy to comprehend. We know so little about how minds react to works of art. On the formal side there have been attempts by experimental psychologists to discover aesthetic laws, but the results have been disappointing. It isn't much help to be told that most people in a certain culture like a rectangle of one shape better than another, or that when someone views a painting the movements of his eyeballs prove that he looks longer at those parts of the picture that have for him the maximum interest. Will science ever fully understand the nature of aesthetic reactions? Emily Dickinson thought not:

> A color stands abroad
> On solitary fields
> That science cannot overtake
> But human nature feels.[1]

A contemporary American poet, X. J. Kennedy, in a clever quatrain titled "Ars Poetica," said it this way:

> The goose that laid the golden egg
> Died looking up its crotch
> To find out how its sphincter worked
> Would you lay well? Don't watch.[2]

I do not know whether these poets are right or wrong. In any case, there is no reason why experimental aesthetics should not continue, and one may hope that some day it will produce useful insights. What is gained by deciding in advance that beauty must always remain a mystery? Why resent the intrusion of science into any aspect of human behavior? If science can tell us why one person likes salt on potatoes and another doesn't, maybe it eventually can tell us why one person likes Brahms and another doesn't.

Aristotle, the first to do so many things, was the first to look empirically for aesthetic norms. He surveyed the major plays of his time and tried to state in his *Poetics* some of the rules for distinguishing good from bad tragedy. Innumerable similar attempts have since been made for all the arts, usually with thumping lack of success. The rules are too intricate, too variable, too deeply hidden in human minds. A computer will play grand-master chess, I am convinced, long before it will write a memorable poem or even compose a simple great tune, although the second task would seem to be little more than a problem in elementary combinatorial mathematics.

Relativists are on solid ground when they stress how widely aesthetic taste can vary. Let us count some ways.

1. Genetic differences. A color-blind person obviously cannot appreciate the full range of colors in a painting. A person of extremely low intelligence can hardly be expected to enjoy a complicated novel. Someone unable to recall a tune or tell one chord from another is not likely to be enthusiastic about Bach.

There is no question that innate differences influence aesthetic judgments, but our ignorance about such differences is profound. In some cases we may be able to rank genetic variations in ways that bear on the ladder of art critics; in other cases the variations are such that one cannot be put above or below another, any more than we can say a person with large feet wears "better" shoes than a person with small feet.

2. Acquired individual differences. Need I belabor the obvious? A person who has never been to sea without becoming violently seasick may not care for seascapes no matter how well painted. When I tried to read Joseph Conrad as a boy I found him dull. Then one day, having lived for two years on a destroyer escort in the North Atlantic, I found a grimy copy of *Lord Jim* in the ship's book locker and discovered to my surprise that I could read it with huge delight. It is easy to think of

hundreds of ways in which personal experiences can strongly condition one's capacity for enjoying a work of art.

3. Acquired cultural differences. Obviously no one can fully appreciate a good poem without understanding the language in which it is written as well as one understands one's native tongue. Perhaps some musicality comes through when you hear a poem recited in an unfamiliar language, but you miss all the sorcery—all the ways in which the sound patterns intensify the meanings conferred on the words by a culture, especially the overtones that spring from subtle associations of words with other words and phrases.

One of the saddest aspects of poetry is that as words slowly alter their meanings and pronunciations there is an inevitable erosion of a poem's beauty. Here for example is a stanza from Francis Thompson's "Daisy":

> Her beauty smoothed earth's furrowed face!
> She gave me tokens three:
> A look, a word of her winsome mouth,
> And a wild raspberry.

A few years ago, while reading a new edition of the collected poems of Dickinson, I came upon an unfinished poem in which she refers to a tiger's "mighty balls."[3] It took me several minutes to realize she meant his eyeballs, though here, perhaps, it was Emily's ignorance of uncouth slang rather than a change in language that turned the line into a joke.

In music it is extraordinarily difficult, without long training, to appreciate music based on a tone scale different from that to which one is accustomed. The literature of cultural anthropology swarms with papers on how a society influences, in ways that clearly cannot be ranked good or bad, one's judgments about beauty, not only in music but in all the arts.

Changes of fashion play obvious roles in conditioning one's sense of beauty. A person is strongly influenced by the opinions of peers, and they in turn go through inexplicable changes of taste. An artist can be lavishly praised by the top critics of one generation, only to be dismissed as mediocre by critics of the next. Decades later, influential critics rediscover the merits of the formerly maligned artist. Such changes of fashion are seldom abrupt, but over long periods of time the pendulum can make wide swings.[4]

One could fill a book with statements by famous critics that express opposite opinions of the same work. Creative artists are equally prone to differ about the competence of both predecessors and contemporaries. Is any artist so universally admired that you cannot find both critics and fellow artists who have low opinions of his or her work? *Lyrical Ballads*, which began the romantic movement in poetry (it contained Coleridge's "The Rime of the Ancient Mariner" and Wordsworth's "Lines Composed a Few Miles Above Tintern Abbey") had a miserable sale and was disliked by almost all readers. Coleridge himself greatly admired the work of the Reverend William Lisle Bowles, a poet no one reads today. The poet then most admired in England was Robert Southey. He is remembered today mainly because Lewis Carroll, in "You Are Old, Father William," parodied one of Southey's poems.

Few critics of the time recognized that *Moby Dick* and *The Adventures of Huckleberry Finn* were masterpieces. L. Frank Baum, our country's greatest writer of fantasy for children, was not discovered by critics (of course children discovered Oz at once) until half a century after his death. "Go back to any standard literature book of ten, or twenty, or thirty, or fifty years ago," wrote H. L. Mencken in an essay on George Ade, "and you will be amazed by its praise of shoddy mediocrities, long since fly-blown and forgotten." Check the contents page of Samuel Johnson's *Lives of the Poets* and you are struck by the number of unfamiliar names. William Cullen Bryant, himself now feebly admired, edited a mammoth anthology of what he considered the best of poems. It is chock-full of the unreadable work of unremembered rhymesters.

Wagner had a low opinion of almost all composers of his day except himself. Emerson disliked Jane Austen, Carlyle hated Keats, Ruskin despised Dickens and Thackeray, Samuel Johnson thought "Lycidas" worthless, Turgenev disliked Dostoevsky and Tolstoy, Henry James couldn't abide Poe (who did not win favor among American critics until after he became famous in France), and George Moore considered Conrad no good. I do not mean to suggest that these are all instances of cultural fashion; most of them reflect personal idiosyncrasies. But they do dramatize the enormous difficulties of defending standards that cut across individual and cultural boundaries.[5]

Another way in which a culture conditions artistic judgments is analyzed sardonically by Thorstein Veblen in a chapter on aesthetic taste in his *Theory of the Leisure Class.* We all know how beauty is universally imputed to jewels that are the most costly. Sapphires without flaws were once considered much more beautiful than flawed ones. Today a slightly flawed sapphire is more admired because it distinguishes it from a synthetic sapphire that is chemically identical.

Not many women would think a corsage of dandelions prettier than an orchid, yet one would be hard put to defend the superior beauty of an orchid on any ground other than what Veblen called conspicuous consumption. Leather shoes look best when polished, but (as Veblen reminded us) we deplore a shine on the seat of pants. Deformed feet were for centuries deemed beautiful in China because they indicated that ladies of high birth did not work. Even today in Western nations men are attracted to the shape of a female leg in heels so high that they make it difficult for the wearer to walk or run.

It is difficult not to impute great beauty to paintings that are the highest-priced, equally hard not to downgrade art that is cheap. Currier and Ives prints once sold to farmers for a dime. They reflected the tastes of rural purchasers just as Norman Rockwell's *Saturday Evening Post* covers reflected the tastes of middle-class *Post* readers. No art critics of the day had much to say about Currier and Ives. Now you'll find the originals, expensively framed, in the homes and offices of highbrows.

In spite of the many ways tastes can vary, I remain convinced that there are some universal standards in art even though we can specify them only in misty ways. Consider again the chair. There may be wide variations in personal taste about how comfortable it is, but because human bodies have roughly the same size and shape, we can say dogmatically that it is a poor chair in any country if it collapses under a weight of twenty pounds, or if its seat is covered with sharp spikes. It is in this trivial sense that we can speak of universal standards concerning the chair's value as a seat.

The aesthetic values of a painting are more difficult to evaluate, but the situation is similar. Those who view the picture do indeed differ more in their tastes than in the sizes and shapes of their bodies. But if they share a common human nature, with common needs, and if they can be ranked (albeit crudely) in their capacity for responding to art, we have a basis for believing in some universal standards even though we may not agree on exactly what they are. From this commonsense point of view the greatest works of art are (as has been said so often) those that give the most intense pleasure, for the longest period of time, to the most competent critics. Of course this is only a complicated way to state the obvious. Classics are those works of art that endure.

This may seem a dull point of view, but it has the merit of allowing us to be dogmatic about extremes in a way that is difficult for relativists. We can, for example, say dogmatically that the ceiling of the Sistine Chapel is greater, in a sense that transcends individual or group tastes, than an oil painting produced in ten minutes by a street-corner lightning artist who sells it with the paint still wet. At the same time it allows us to agree with relativists that on those broad, foggy fields where eminent critics play their games, we should refrain from loud cheering. We may have our own preferences, and make our own guesses about posterity, but we ought to be as tolerant of differences among respected critics as we are tolerant of the differences between those who prefer chocolate ice cream to strawberry and those who prefer strawberry to chocolate.

I spoke earlier of a ladder of critics. Now I withdraw the metaphor. It is far too clumsy to be useful except when contrasting art at the extreme ends of continua. A better image is that of a complicated, irregular lattice of constantly shifting points about which it is prudent not to be dogmatic as to which point, at any given time, is above or below another. The situation is even worse than that. A critic should not be represented by one point but by many. An art critic may be trustworthy in evaluating medieval tapestry, untrustworthy in evaluating modern sculpture. A ballet critic may be knowledgeable about choreography but have a poor ear for music. Now that I think about it more, the situation seems too chaotic to lend itself to *any* kind of network diagram. Of course all I say about critics, here and elsewhere, applies also to ordinary persons who make aesthetic judgments.

Since I am not a professional critic, and therefore have little to lose by taking risks, let me illustrate these complexities by confessing some of my own prejudices with respect to poetry.

I am unable to read Homer, Virgil, or Dante in their original languages; nevertheless I consider them the greatest of poets. Enough of their excellence comes through in translation (preferably in prose) that I find them great for me. I enjoy rereading the ending of the *Odyssey* more than seeing any western movie in which the good guy, against enormous odds, finally vanquishes all the bad guys who have seized control of a town. In English literature I have no doubt whatever about the greatness of Shakespeare, Milton, Keats, Byron, and a host of other poets all highly regarded by most critics and all of whom I can and do read with enormous pleasure.

The evidence that Goethe was a major poet is too strong for me to reject, even though I can get little from his work. Perhaps it would be different if I could read *Faust* in the original German. Among English writers I have no doubt that William Butler Yeats was a major poet, but because of some incompatibility between his mind and mine, it is difficult for me to admire his work. This is surely a defect on my part. As a youth I thought that all of Thomas Hardy's novels and poems were mediocre. A few years ago I found to my astonishment that I could read many of his poems with delight. How much this discovery was influenced by the current rise of critical interest in his poetry (not his novels) is hard to say. It was this trend that led me to check his poems again, but I hope my change reflected maturing taste, not just current fashion.

Lord Dunsany and Gilbert Chesterton both wrote large quantities of verse. Neither impresses me as a major poet—Dunsany in particular was a poor craftsman—but in both cases there are enough compatibilities between their ways of seeing things and mine to make it a pleasure to reread certain poems by them that I especially like. I have no doubt about the high quality of Emily Dickinson's work or my enthusiasm for it. Carl Sandburg, near whose celebrated goat farm I now reside, I consider a lesser poet than Emily, yet I enjoy reading him more than Walt Whitman. "Whitman was great, Sandburg is nothing," declared Jorge Luis Borges in an interview.[6] Much as I revere Borges (I wish I could read his poetry in Spanish), I am unable to share this harsh judgment.

Many poets currently regarded as great by large numbers of top critics, I find not only mediocre for me, but I also believe them to be mediocre in a more universal sense. Here I am betting that posterity will support my present taste, and that critics who now praise these poets will turn out to be as mistaken as the British critics who once heaped praise on poets whose works soon vanished from anthologies and who seem unlikely to be rediscovered.

With fear and trembling I confess that I have yet to find a poem by Ezra Pound or William Carlos Williams that I consider great, though I have done my best over the decades to read both men sympathetically.

I agree with Vladimir Nabokov that Ezra Pound was a "total fake." I much prefer T. S. Eliot (despised by Williams) to Pound (Williams's friend and mentor), but even Eliot seems to me overrated.

In my younger days it was almost impossible to pick up a "little magazine" that did not contain a poem by Williams. I always read it slowly, three or four times, hoping to find something of more value than undistinguished prose broken into lines, often so short that I wondered if the little magazines paid for poetry by the inch. Consider, for example, the following banal lines which I have concocted to parody one of Williams's most admired poems:

> *Your thighs are appletrees*
> *whose blossoms touch the sky.*
> *Which sky? The sky*
> *where Watteau hung a lady's*
> *slipper. Your knees*
> *are a southern breeze—or*
> *a gust of snow. Agh! what*
> *sort of man was Fragonard?*
> *—as if that answered*
> *anything.*

Now compare my crude efforts with this authentic poem by Williams, "The Red Wheelbarrow," which I quote in its entirety:

> *so much can be*
> *learned*
>
> *from a brown*
> *butterfly*
>
> *drenched with rain*
> *drops*
>
> *beside the red wheel*
> *barrow.*

Can you honestly say that you find something more worth reading in Williams's much-anthologized lyric than in my parody? It may be there, but it is not there for me. Perhaps it is not there. I do not know. Obviously I am losing my bet at the moment because Williams's reputation continues to be high. As recently as 1981 an 874-page biography of this New Jersey pediatrician-turned-poet, by Paul Mariani, called Williams "the single most important poet of the twentieth century," an opinion repeated by Gilbert Sorrentino when he praised the book on the first page of *The New York Times Book Review*.[7]

I record these biases for whimsical reasons. Long after I am dead, my readers (if I have any) will say either "How perceptive Gardner was" or "What peculiar blind spots he had."

Two strange categories of verse have always intrigued me, though they seem to hold no interest for most critics. One is the work of poets who were recognized by everyone (except themselves and maybe a few relatives and friends) as writers of doggerel, but whose work was so extremely worthless that it acquired an unintended value. It became funny. In America the best-known example is Julia Moore. She had such a genius for choosing the wrong word that she acquired a coterie of sophisticated admirers. There is even a collection of her verse, *The Sweet Singer of Michigan*, edited by the University of Chicago critic Walter Blair

In browsing through old bookshops I occasionally pick up privately printed volumes of verse sufficiently awful to be amusing. My most valuable treasure is Mrs. Miranda Kropp's *Complete Poetical Works*, published by Mrs. Kropp herself in Calicoon, New York, in 1905. The opening stanzas of her poem "A Drunkard (A True Story)" suggest her inimitable style:

> There was a man, David Church by name,
> He had a wife and family the same,
> He had genius, and a good trade,
> But drank up every cent he made.
>
> He owned a house, and a small farm,
> But he drank more as the day rolled on,
> Lower and lower, did he sink,
> Until he did nothing but drink, drink.

Of course even the best poets had their lapses. You'll find some of them in that surprising anthology of bad verse *The Stuffed Owl*, edited by D. B. Wyndham Lewis and Charles Lee,[8] but anyone can open the complete works of Shelley or Burns or any other famous poet with a large output, and find equally dismal specimens. None, however, achieved sufficient badness to make them as memorable as the effusions of Julia or Miranda.

Another strange subcategory of poetry—one so mystifying that I wish critics would try to unravel its secrets—catches those poets recognized by all critics as mediocre, but who were somehow inspired to produce a single poem which, although not great, continues to give so much delight to such large numbers of ordinary folk that it has become a classic of popular verse. Burton Stevenson called them "one-poem poets."9 It is easy to recall lines from "The Old Oaken Bucket" or "The Lost Chord," but can you remember who wrote them? Both poets were widely read in their day. Dickens thought so highly of Adelaide Anne Procter that he wrote an introduction to a collection of her verse. Sir Arthur Sullivan (of Gilbert and Sullivan fame) set her "Lost Chord" to music. It was often sung by Enrico Caruso, but it was not the song that made the poem famous; it was the other way around.

Clement Clarke Moore, a Greek and Oriental scholar in Manhattan, wrote poetry in the classical mode, all worthless, but one set of verses, scribbled carelessly to bemuse his children, became the immortal "A Visit from St. Nicholas." It even added substantially to this country's greatest native myth, the myth of Santa Claus. Ernest Lawrence Thayer, who studied philosophy under William James and was a friend of George Santayana, wrote dozens of humorous poems, but only one became famous. "Casey at the Bat" is doggerel, but surely great doggerel. Can anyone doubt that in one narrow corner of popular verse, humorous baseball verse, it has become a classic? I firmly believe that Thayer's ballad will outlast the entire poetic output of Ezra Pound.

All the above one-poem poets (there are scores of others) wrote more than one poem. Most of them, such as Sam Walter Foss, who penned the ever-popular "House by the Side of the Road," and Arthur Chapman, who wrote "Out Where the West Begins," published many books of verse. But what is one to make of the poet who has just *one* poem printed, no others, and it becomes so widely admired that it finds its way into collections of "best-loved poems," even into such ambitious anthologies as the ten-volume *Book of Poetry* edited and annotated by Edwin Markham?

I am thinking of "Evolution" ("When you were a tadpole and I was a fish, In the Paleozoic time . . .") by one Langdon Smith, a now-forgotten New York City newspaper reporter. Like "Casey" it has become a classic in a narrow genre—in this instance, popular verse about evolution and geology. It certainly ranks far below, say, "Ode on a

Grecian Urn," yet it has given me more pleasure over the years than any poem by Williams. I have no doubt that a century from now it will still be memorized and chanted.[10]

What I am suggesting is this: Even on the level of what Eliot—in the introduction to his selection of poems by Kipling—called popular verse, by which Eliot meant poems that can be totally understood and enjoyed after one reading, there are standards that rise above individual and group tastes. Such poems lack the richness of values that make for great poetry, but they can be good or bad in terms of what they are, as a cartoon or television commercial can be good or bad. Even on this humble level I am not a relativist. We know as little about the norms for pop verse, or any other kind of pop art, as we do for great art, yet I am persuaded that even in the lower nooks and crannies of art there are some universal standards.

No poem by Julia Moore or Miranda Kropp became a best-loved poem. "The Lost Chord" did. In these cases the differences in craft are obvious enough to elevate Procter above Moore and Kropp. I do not know how to compare the worth of "Gunga Din" with the worth of "The Shooting of Dan McGrew." I know even less about how to decide between the merits of Shakespeare and Dante, or Mozart and Bach, or Michelangelo and Rubens. It seems to me meaningless to say of such giants that one is superior to the other except in relation to a well-defined set of persons who experience their work, but of course defining such a set defeats what is intended when one tries to evaluate works in terms of universal standards. The fact is, when artists are on about the same level of excellence, human nature is much too variable to call upon it for settling arguments.

None of these admissions damages my main thesis. The lack of adequate ways to measure the worth of art objects does not mean there is not something "out there" to measure. The reality out there, independent of you and me, is an extraordinarily snarled process of interaction between minds and objects, an interaction that results in the kinds of satisfactions we call aesthetic. I see no reason why we cannot apply Alfred Tarski's semantic approach to truth and say: The sentence "*War and Peace* is a great novel" is true if, and only if, *War and Peace* is a great novel. And the same for all other arts. As in science we must, of course, carefully distinguish between the meaning of calling an aesthetic judgment true or false and the fallible criteria by which judgments are confirmed or disconfirmed by posterity.

Most aesthetic judgments, like those of science, are tentative bets made with varying estimates of probability about how those judgments will fare in the future. But at the extreme ends of spectra that run from good to bad in any art, the betting probabilities are close to certain, and one has every right to be dogmatic. I submit that it is justifiable to declare, in a stentorian voice, that Dante and Shakespeare were better poets than Ella Wheeler Wilcox, that Michelangelo was a greater painter than Jackson Pollock, and that Beethoven's music is superior to that of John Cage or a punk rock band. It is in this ancient and unremarkable sense that I prefer not to call myself an aesthetic relativist.

5

GOODNESS:
Why I Am Not an Ethical Relativist

*It is better to be rich and
healthy than to be poor and sick.*

—SIGN IN A RESTAURANT,
OKLAHOMA, CIRCA 1940

Are there standards in ethics, norms for right and wrong, that apply everywhere, at all times and places, because they derive from the needs of a common human nature? This question, clearly more important than the previous chapter's similar question about aesthetic standards, is intimately connected with difficult problems over which philosophers are as much divided today as they were in ancient times. Nevertheless, I believe the answer is yes, and that the yes can be defended in much the same way I tried to defend it for aesthetic values.

The most extreme ethical relativism is the belief that one person's moral standards are as good as any other's. Let us not waste time on such an imbecilic view. It is true that some thinkers and writers have defended it, but I doubt if many readers would be willing to say there is nothing wrong about the standards of a man who believes there is nothing wrong in raping and murdering little children. But there is a more sophisticated kind of relativism with which many readers may identify, especially if they are students of anthropology and sociology. This is the view that ethical standards do indeed transcend individual rules of conduct, but are no more than norms derived from the culture to which an individual belongs.

The word *culture* grows in vagueness as it is applied to larger and more diverse societies with many subcultures. Moral standards obviously vary as much from one subculture to another as from one society to another. More complications arise from the fact that many people belong to more than one subculture. Consider, for instance, a man who is active in a religious community, perhaps as a deacon of his church, and also active in a business community as the manager of a corporation that produces a worthless medicine. If he is philosophically inclined, conflicting ethical norms may trouble him at times; otherwise they rattle around harmlessly inside some cavity in his brain. Such refinements need not detain us. The point is this: For a cultural relativist it is perfectly proper to speak of good and bad behavior, of duties and crimes, provided all the underlying norms are culturally defined. It is never proper to say that the basic standards of culture A are better or worse than those of culture B. Ethical rules cannot cut across cultural boundaries. Cultures cannot be ranked in any sort of moral hierarchy. They are just different.

It is this version of relativism, a view vigorously championed by the Greek skeptics, that I wish to oppose. I shall maintain that human beings, for the period of recorded history and as far into the future as we can see, have a common human nature which makes it rational to believe in transcultural moral standards even though (as with standards for truth and beauty) it is not possible to know with certainty what those standards are. The skepticism about certainty would of course not be acceptable to philosophers who think they have a rational method for determining absolute ethical rules, or by those who believe that norms have been supplied by revelations from God or the gods. But the belief that universal standards are somehow "there," some of which we can know with a confidence approaching certainty, is a belief as old as humanity. It was taken for granted by Plato and Aristotle, and by most philosophers of later centuries. It is taken for granted by ordinary people. Today it is being defended by more and more behavioral scientists, even social scientists, as the pendulum swings away from the crude cultural relativism so loudly proclaimed by many social scientists in the early decades of this century.

Let me first clear away some verbal problems that I do not think deserve much attention. Are human needs (values), and the moral rules based on them, subjective or objective? My reply is the same as I gave about the whereabouts of red. We all know what the situation is. What do we gain by quibbling over the most efficient way to describe it?

Consider the need for water. Any society that intends to survive must make provisions for obtaining drinkable water. In any culture above the most primitive, this requires cooperative social action and obedience to rules of conduct. Suppose a tribal society has one community well. If someone poisoned the well (the reason need not concern us), the tribe would surely regard this as wicked. It is true that the ethical rule "It is wicked to poison the water" rests on one or more ulterior posits, such as the belief that it is good for the tribe to survive. Later I will take up the question of whether such fundamental posits are, in a recently fashionable terminology, cognitive or emotive. Our question now is whether need for water, and the moral rules relating to it, should be regarded as subjective or objective.

I can think of few questions in ethics that are more trivial. All human needs, and all moral norms, are subjective in some respects, objective in other respects. Thirst is subjective in the sense that it is a feeling inside a mind. It is objective in the sense that it involves a physical body and its interaction with a physical world. The rule "It is wicked to poison the well" is subjective in the sense that it is formulated by minds, and acted upon by mental decisions. It is objective in the sense that it derives from facts about the external world, namely that water is essential to life, and that poisoned water kills.

It is equally unprofitable to waste time on the question of whether ethical norms are absolute or relative. The two adjectives are as vague as objective and subjective. It has been said that cultural relativism was strengthened by Einstein's theory of relativity. Balderdash! Relativity theory introduced all sorts of new absolutes. Newton assumed that a piece of matter can travel at any speed relative to another piece, but relativity theory makes the speed of light an absolute limit. Newton assumed that the length of a moving object is absolute. In relativity theory the length depends on the observer's frame of reference, but that is only when the observer talks in the Euclidean language of three-dimensional space. If he talks in the non-Euclidean language of relativity's space-time, a spaceship preserves its absolute shape no matter how fast it moves. Indeed, one way of formulating general relativity is to say that it makes it possible for all observers, regardless of their frames of reference, to describe all the basic laws of the universe with exactly the same equations. Einstein originally considered calling relativity "invariant theory"! The theory may have had some mild psychological influence on social scientists who did not understand it, though I doubt even that. In any case, it furnishes no support for cultural relativism.

Ethical norms are clearly relative if all you mean is that they relate to human societies. A universe with no human life obviously would contain no human needs or moral rules. I suppose one could argue that such needs might exist as counterfactual abstractions, even in a universe devoid of life, in the sense that *if* intelligent creatures existed they would have needs, or that the needs can exist in the mind of a god capable of creating people or imagining them. Let philosophers and theologians worry over such conundrums.

Needs and norms are relative to human societies even if you believe, as I do, that some of them are common to all societies. It is equally trivial to point out that if human nature alters radically, either by natural evolution or by genetic engineering, needs and norms will also change. Less fundamental rules of conduct, what are sometimes called secondary moral rules as distinct from more primary ones, obviously are relative to circumstances that vary from time to time, place to place, and person to person. Consider the secondary rule that persons ought not to cohabit if they want to make sure there is no unwanted pregnancy. The rule is obviously affected by the availability of contraceptives, and by discoveries of new and better methods of birth control. Clearly the rule does not apply to homosexual sex or to persons who are sterile. In the light of such trivialities there is nothing wrong in speaking of hundreds of moral rules as relative.

On the other hand, given the nature of human beings and the laws of the physical world, there is nothing wrong in speaking of hundreds of rules as absolute. It is absolutely true that a society cannot flourish without adequate food and water. It is absolutely true that if a culture prohibits all childbearing, and all adoptions of new members from outside, that culture will not long remain on earth. In fact, eccentric religious communities have actually faded away for just this reason. Some philosophers speak of "relative absolutes" and call themselves "objective relativists." Since we all know exactly what the situation is, let us put this dull debate over terminology behind us.

Many ethical questions, not to be discussed in this chapter, are far from dull. Indeed they are among the darkest, deepest, and most controversial questions in philosophy. What, if anything, is meant by free will? What are the sources of egoism and altruism and how should the two impulses be reconciled? Assuming that happiness, whatever it means, should be maximized for a society or for the human race, what does "maximize" mean? What role, if any, does belief in God and/or immortality play in ethics? Can moral values be arranged in a hierarchy of importance? Is there a supreme value? And so on. Some of these questions will be considered in later chapters. For most of them I do not know the answers and will be able to give only cloudy personal opinions. In some cases I believe the answers exist although we may never know what they are.

In this chapter I am concerned only with defending the commonplace view that one is justified in saying, without help from intuition, metaphysics, revelation, or a faith in God or gods, that some ethical rules are universal in the sense that they apply to all societies. In modern philosophy this is usually called a "naturalistic ethics."

Is it possible for science and reason to construct such an ethics, or is it necessary to invoke desires that cannot be derived from science and reason? On this question, as on the meaning of truth, John Dewey often clashed with his perpetual British rival, Bertrand Russell. I am aware of the many subtle differences in the way philosophers have approached this problem, but by focusing once more on a historic conflict between two modern thinkers of enormous influence we can dramatize the two points of view that are dominant at the moment in secular philosophy. On the one side is Dewey, America's foremost champion of naturalistic ethics, insisting that reason and science are sufficient for grounding moral standards. On the other side is Russell, defending what has been called "emotive ethics"—an ethics in which science and reason are incapable of justifying moral standards unless aided by emotions.[1]

The use of the word "emotion" and its derivatives was perhaps unfortunate. It suggests that whatever your feelings tell you to do at a given moment, you are right to do it. "Noncognitive ethics" is a better phrase. A noncognitive ethics maintains that any system of ethics, like any formal system of logic and mathematics, rests on a set of unprovable axioms or posits. These posits cannot be justified by science or reason, or even the two combined, because they are expressions of human desires. Science can, of course, describe what people in various cultures do in fact desire, but this is descriptive, not normative, ethics. As has been said a thousand times, descriptive ethics tells us only what *is*, not what *ought* to be.

Ought here means the justification of an ultimate goal, not what should be done to reach an agreed-upon goal. In the latter sense, science and reason obviously provide norms. Moreover, science and reason can often decide what goals are possible or probable, and whether a particular set of goals are compatible. It is not possible, for example, to enjoy whatever benefits accrue from being married to just one person, and simultaneously enjoy whatever benefits follow from having seven spouses. It is possible to send astronauts to explore Mars, not possible to send them to explore the interior of the sun. It is possible for the world to achieve zero population growth, but improbable that this can be done before the year 2001. In the sense of specifying possible and probable goals, and telling what must or probably must be done to reach them, science and reason provide endless "oughts."

Most ethical decisions, as Dewey never tired of saying, involve long sequences of means and ends in which every end is a means to another end. At each step, reason and/or science may enter the decision process. We must improve space-travel technology if we want to land astronauts on Mars. We should send astronauts to Mars if we wish to know more about possible life on other planets. Knowledge of alien life will greatly increase our knowledge of earthly life. The more we know about earthly life the better we can solve problems involving genetics and human health. The better we solve our health problems the happier we all will be. The happier we are the more likely our race can avoid destroying itself by war. Now we come to an ultimate question: Why should humanity survive? Clearly the answer is beyond science and reason. The universe doesn't care. Maybe a god cares, but this is a matter of faith. Unless we have a trustworthy revelation in which a god details the ultimate goals of human history, a theist is no wiser about them than an atheist.

Nor is a scientist or philosopher wiser about ultimate goals than ordinary mortals. There is a useful analogy here with the way an operations-research expert goes about improving a corporation's efficiency. He cannot even begin his task until he first obtains from management a clear statement of the company's objectives in the order of their priority. Not until he knows exactly where a company wants to go can he give advice on how best to get there. Not until science is told where humanity wants to go can it give advice on how to get there.

There is nothing new about a noncognitive ethics. As with most philosophical positions, you find it anticipated in Plato's *Dialogues*, and David Hume defended it with thoroughness and ingenuity. Many logical empiricists such as Rudolf Carnap held an emotive view of ethics,[2] but it received its most systematic exposition in Charles L. Stevenson's *Ethics and Language*, and in his later writings. As already indicated, it was also the view of Russell, and it has been advocated by many other modern thinkers, such as Hans Reichenbach and George Santayana.[3] I would argue that the emotive view is sound but trivial, and that it does not differ in any significant way from the view advocated by Dewey and others of the naturalistic school.

Let me stress once more that noncognitive ethics does not deny that cognitive elements enter into all moral problems. "All my methods are rational," said Captain Ahab. "Only my ends are insane." In a complex industrial society the task of satisfying a population's need for drinking water is formidable, and no one disputes that reason and science play essential roles. On this, Dewey and Russell, and everybody else, agree. The rub comes when justifications for moral rules are traced back to the most basic posits. Here are some examples:

It is better to be alive than dead.

It is better to be healthy than sick.

It is better to be happy than miserable.

It is better for a culture to survive than perish.

It is better for the human race to survive than become extinct.

Can such posits be justified by reason and science? No, say the emotivists. They are not cognitive statements. They may indeed express desires common to humans everywhere, and scientists can take polls to establish this. They may even be, as today's sociobiologists maintain (echoing predecessors) in part genetically based. Even if there is little or no genetic base for the above posits, they may still be universal in the sense that all cultures are forced by their experience to make them. However, say the emotivists, the fact that all cultures desire something does not entail that what they desire is right in some larger sense. Dinosaurs no doubt had a strong urge to survive, but what can it mean to say they ought to have done so? Even if there is a God with long-range plans for the evolution of life in our solar system, or in the galaxy, how can we know that in those plans it is desirable that the human race survive?

Dewey was annoyingly vague about the justification of ultimate moral posits. In such works as *Theory of Valuation* and *The Quest for Certainty* he makes the familiar distinction between what is and what ought to be by distinguishing between what is desired by individuals and what is desirable in a larger sense that transcends individuals. Then just when you expect him to disclose how science can decide what is ultimately desirable, he veers off into less fundamental questions. Nevertheless I am persuaded that if you read Dewey carefully, you will find nothing in the preceding paragraph with which he would have disagreed. I believe that, like his battle with Russell over truth, Dewey's battle with Russell over the foundations of ethics is equally verbal, a matter of language choice and emphasis.

Dewey wrote at a time when he was fighting, alongside the positivists, against philosophical certitude. He saw all aspects of human life as a perpetual process of "inquiry," by which he meant the exercise of science and reason, and in this context his aim was to stress the similarity between the scientific search for knowledge and humanity's search for a rational ethics. When Dewey wrote about applying the experimental method to ethics, he wanted to emphasize that nothing is a priori or final about our choices of moral ends, that the ends are tentative hypotheses to be tested like scientific hypotheses. We must remember, however, that when Dewey talked about "ends" he usually meant subsidiary ends, not ultimate ones. He had in mind the solving of such problems as how best to provide medical care for the poor, not the answering of such metaphysical questions as "Is it better to be healthy than sick?" Dewey took for granted that there are fundamental human needs, common to all cultures, which it would be foolish to question. Because he took this for granted, he did not think it worth stressing, but the notion of a moral consensus, based on a common human nature, underlies all of Dewey's writings about ethics. Here are two explicit paragraphs from his essay, "Does Human Nature Change?":

By "needs" I mean the inherent demands that men make because of their constitution. Needs for food and drink and for moving about, for example, are so much a part of our being that we cannot imagine any condition under which they would cease to be. There are other things not so directly physical that seem to me equally engrained in human nature. I would mention as examples the need for some kind of companionship; the need for exhibiting energy, for bringing one's powers to bear upon surrounding conditions; the need for both coöperation with and emulation of one's fellows for mutual aid and combat alike; the need for some sort of aesthetic expression and satisfaction; the need to lead and to follow, etc.

Whether my particular examples are well chosen or not does not matter so much as does recognition of the fact that there are some tendencies so integral a part of human nature that the latter would not be human nature if they changed. These tendencies used to be called instincts. Psychologists are now more chary of using that word than they used to be. But the word by which the tendencies are called does not matter much in comparison to the fact that human nature has its own constitution.[4]

Russell, on the other hand, was struggling to introduce clarity into the languages of logic, mathematics, science, and philosophy. From his mathematically oriented perspective it was essential to distinguish the posits of ethics from the less fundamental norms based on them, just as in logic and mathematics it is necessary to distinguish the axioms of a formal system from the system's theorems, and in science to distinguish the posits of a theory from the theory's testable consequences. As for Dewey's insistence that reason and science should be brought to bear on the process of determining the best means for reaching agreed-upon ethical goals, and that this process is as uncertain and risky as science itself, Russell (and those who shared his ethical views) were surely in complete agreement.

Let me put it this way: Suppose a nihilist wants to trigger a nuclear holocaust that will destroy humanity. You try to reason with him. He insists that the human race is not worth preserving, that it should go the way of the dinosaurs, that the universe would be better off if the human race were to vanish. Is it not obvious that there is no way to confront him with scientific evidence that will refute his belief, or with any rational arguments he will find persuasive? In this sense the emotivists are clearly right. A disciple of Dewey can only insist that anyone holding a belief so contrary to human nature must be mad. I cannot see how Russell, Carnap, Reichenbach, or Santayana could have disagreed.

It is one thing to believe that ethical standards can be based on posits common to all societies, quite another thing to express those standards precisely and dogmatically. The difficulties are not much different from those of specifying criteria for truth and beauty. We have good reasons to believe that the universe has a structure independent of human minds even though we cannot be certain exactly what that structure is. We have equally good reasons to believe in standards of excellence in the arts and standards of goodness in ethics even though we cannot be certain exactly what those standards are. The best we can do is to look at ethics the way we look at science, as an ongoing process, a search for truths we can believe are "there," independent of individual persons and cultures, even though we can never be absolutely sure we have captured them. "It is better for the human race to survive than become extinct" is true if, and only if, it is better for the human race to survive than become extinct. But is it true? I do not know how to answer this question except emotionally.

As with truth and beauty, the case for universal standards is best made by considering extremes. Anthropologists have found tribal societies that do such a poor job of meeting basic needs that it takes a peculiar type of mind to insist that, by some obscure magic of compensation, every culture does as good a job as any other. One thinks of the Yanamanos, with their vicious male dominance, the Iks of Northern Uganda, the Dobuans discussed in Ruth Benedict's *Patterns of Culture*, or the Alorees described in *The People of Alor*, by Cora du Bois. Dewey, in the essay cited above, put it like this:

> The existence of almost every conceivable kind of social institution at some time and place in the history of the world is evidence of the plasticity of human nature. This fact does not prove that all these different social systems are of equal value, materially, morally, and culturally. The slightest observation shows that such is not the case.

Is it not curious that anthropologists who claim to be cultural relativists seldom hesitate to pass strong moral judgments on aspects of their own culture which they find distasteful? As with Hume, their skepticism about universal values vanishes as soon as they leave their workrooms. Ruth Benedict, for instance, argues for moral relativism in her *Patterns of Culture*, yet the same book passionately condemns those American cultural traits that she identifies with capitalism. William Graham Sumner, the Yale sociologist who defined those valuable terms *folkways* and *mores*, took an opposite tack. Although a cultural relativist, he fumed against the steady creep of socialism in America, and devoted much of his energies to public agitation against trade unions, child-labor laws, the eight-hour day, and anything else he thought interfered with the natural laws of the market place.

No doubt Sumner and Benedict would have maintained that they were doing no more than argue from their own culturally determined perspectives. Benedict's mentor, Franz Boas, was disarmingly frank about this: "My ideals have developed because I am what I am and have lived where I lived; and it is my purpose to work for those ideals, because I am by nature active and because the conditions in our culture that run counter to my ideals stimulate me to action."[5] But if you ponder the ringing animadversions of most cultural relativists you are struck by how much they sound as if they are moralizing from some universal point of view. If so, on what podium are they standing?

And what about the idea of progress? If one is a consistent cultural relativist it is not easy to see how any culture could advance. For every gain there must be a compensating loss; otherwise the culture would become better than it was before, but "better" implies standards external to the culture, and that is just what a cultural relativist cannot grant. For the same reason, no culture can get worse. I find these beliefs as fantastic as the superstitions of any primitive tribe.

Of course a cultural relativist may concede that, given a culture's ethical posits, it can find better or worse methods of meeting them. For example, two cultures may have identical posits about the desirability of maximizing, in some vague sense, the happiness and well-being of its members, but have disagreements on how best to do this which spring from disagreements over empirically known facts. If one culture moves faster than the other in solving and acting upon the relevant scientific questions, I suppose most cultural relativists would permit themselves to say that the culture is making faster progress toward its own entrenched goals.

The outstanding historical example of this kind of progress is the slow, painful discovery by most of the civilized world that persons are not born to be slaves. Even the most ardent admirers of Aristotle admit today that one of the master's gravest errors was his conviction that some people are born with slavish natures. Greek society took this for granted, and of course Aristotle was not in possession of enough knowledge about human nature to know that the slavishness of slaves was a product of conditioning. Not until recently has science provided convincing evidence that there are no naturally born slaves. A hundred years ago, millions of good Christians in our nation and elsewhere devoutly believed that blacks were inferior to whites and therefore destined by the Creator to be slaves. Here is how Mark Twain described his mother's views:

> Yet, kind-hearted and compassionate as she was, she was not conscious that slavery was a bald, grotesque, and unwarrantable usurpation. She had never heard it assailed in any pulpit but had heard it defended and sanctified in a thousand; her ears were familiar with Bible texts that approved it but if there were any that disapproved it they had not been quoted by her pastors; as far as her experience went, the wise and the good and the holy were unanimous in the conviction that slavery was right, righteous, sacred, the peculiar pet of the Deity and a condition which the slave himself ought to be daily and nightly thankful for. Manifestly, training and association can accomplish strange miracles.[6]

After Huckleberry Finn has lied to Aunt Sally about being on a riverboat that blew a cylinder-head, she asks if anyone has been hurt. "No'm," replies Huck. "Killed a nigger."

To which Aunt Sally responds: "Well, it's lucky; because sometimes people do get hurt."

Later in the novel, Huck is so convinced that his desire to rescue Jim, a runaway slave, is wicked that he even tries to pray for strength to resist. When Tom Sawyer offers to help, his respect for Tom goes down.

Cultural relativists have a point in insisting that we ought not to condemn morally those who truly believed in natural-born slavishness. They cannot, however, deny that once it becomes apparent there are no natural slaves, a society that alters its attitude toward slavery thereby acquires a better way to meet its own posits about equality and freedom. But does this not give the game away? If a culture abandons slavery as a result, or partly as a result, of more accurate knowledge about human nature, is not one entitled to say that the culture has improved? And will not the same argument apply to two contemporary cultures, one enlightened about slavery, the other not?

A similar example of slow progress is provided by the history of changing cultural attitudes toward women. The belief that woman are by nature intellectually inferior to men did not start to decline until about the time of John Stuart Mill's famous essay on women's rights. Here again there was agreement in democratic nations on the posit that all persons are entitled to equal opportunities for happiness, but factual disagreement over the natural differences between the minds of men and women. It is a disagreement now settled by science. If society A treats its women as born slaves, and society B treats them as equal to men, it seems foolish not to admit that in this respect society B is better than A, or to admit that if a society that once regarded women as inferior to men has learned to regard them as equal, that society has made genuine progress. Of course the progress presupposes the rule "It is better to be free than a slave," but even societies that practiced slavery agreed on that.

As I said, progress of this sort, based on better scientific knowledge, does not imply that a society has made moral progress. If witches truly exist, C. S. Lewis observes, perhaps they ought to be executed. "It may be a great advance in *knowledge* not to believe in witches: There's no moral advance in not executing them when you don't think they are there! You wouldn't call a man humane for ceasing to set mouse-traps if he did so because he believed there were no mice in the house."[7] It is a good point. We have no right to feel morally superior to the ancient Greeks or the southern plantation owners, or to cultures past and present in which women were and are considered inferior to men. We do have a right to think that science has given us a better understanding of human nature, and that this in turn has improved a society's ability to meet universal needs.

Cultural relativists performed a valuable service in disclosing the enormously varied ways in which societies meet human needs, but they carried their value-free perspective to such extremes that it became self-refuting. Many critics of cultural relativism have called attention to its central paradox. Since relativism developed within the subculture of modern anthropology, how can an anthropologist who holds such views say it is any better than a contrary view, held by other subcultures, without appealing to the very universal standards he denies? "If all is relative," Hilary Putnam somewhere remarks, "then the relative is relative too." A cultural relativist cannot even say that one culture is as good as another, because he has no objective criteria for defining what is meant by "as good as."

In his book *Man and His Works: The Science of Cultural Anthropology*, Melville J. Herskovits praised cultural relativism for its tolerance of all ethical norms.[8] But some cultures do not respect tolerance. Why did Herskovits assume tolerance to be more admirable than intolerance? He closes his book by saying that cultural relativism "puts man yet another step on his quest for what ought to be." What ought to be? If humanity ought to be other than it is, by what standards did Herskovits make this assertion?

Because I believe there are universal posits based on a common human nature—a human *telos*, if you like—and because I am certain that reason, aided by science, can formulate ethical rules that fulfill those posits with differing degrees of success, I agree with those philosophers who defend a naturalistic ethics. This does not deny the monumental difficulty of constructing such an ethics. We know far too little about human needs, the extent to which they may or may not have a genetic basis, and the best ways to go about satisfying them. We do not even know, except in the crudest way, how to distinguish normal from neurotic behavior in ways that cross cultural boundaries.

We do know, thanks to early anthropology, how widely cultures can differ in moral standards. The new task of anthropology is to search for deeper ways in which cultures are alike. There is nothing wrong, I suppose, in social scientists trying to keep their work as value-free as possible, restricting it to investigating what is, not what ought to be. But if this is their only goal, they should not at the same time pretend to be philosophers, or to belabor philosophers for their efforts to construct a rational morality based on data provided by descriptive social science. And what, may I ask, is there to prevent a social scientist from combining descriptive science with philosophical speculation?

I cannot pretend to know whether the nuclear family, with its monogamous base, is rooted in genetics or cultural conditioning, nor do I know (regardless of its roots) whether it is the most desirable way to meet human needs. I do not know what patterns of family life are best, or even if there is a best. So far as I know, there may be different but equally good ways to organize families and to bring up children. If sociobiologist Edward O. Wilson is right, a diversity of cultures, meeting primary needs in wildly different ways, may in the long run contribute to the survival of the species. Experiments in cultural conditioning may be nature's way—God's way, if you are a theist—of improving human life.

Do not ask me how to decide between just and unjust wars. I have no strongly held opinions on how best to prevent crime or how to treat criminals. I possess no magic formulas by which primitive cultures, or the great cultures of the past and present, can be ranked in terms of their overall moral worth. Biologists may soon learn how to alter human nature and direct its future evolution. Moral decisions will then have to be made that are staggering to contemplate and for which humanity is almost totally unprepared. I have no light to throw on these rapidly approaching and terrible questions.

My claims are less grandiose. I believe that a person can be well adjusted to a culture and strongly maladjusted as a human being. I believe that Hitler and Stalin were not only mentally sick but also morally evil. I believe that those in Germany who opposed the Nazi subculture, and those in the Soviet Union who opposed the Stalinist subculture, were morally superior in their obedience to higher laws. I believe that a leader of organized crime who sells lethal drugs to slum children, corrupts labor unions, and executes his enemies is morally depraved no matter how carefully he obeys the rules of his criminal class, or how much he loves his family and is loyal to his friends, or how much money he gives to his church.

Let me summarize. Although ethical knowledge is weak and uncertain, I believe that goodness is firmly grounded in the nature of the human species. Because the human race is as much a part of the universe as atoms and galaxies, moral laws are as independent of you and me, and of whatever cultures helped shape our character and ethical convictions, as the laws of truth and beauty.

6

FREE WILL:
Why I Am Not a Determinist or Haphazardist

"There is a lot to be said for destiny," said Jorkens,
"but you can't ignore free will."
"What do you mean?" said one of the philosophers.

—LORD DUNSANY, "JORKENS
CONSULTS A PROPHET"

We all know what destiny is, but what do we mean by free will?

A famous section at the close of Ludwig Wittgenstein's *Tractatus Logico-Philosophicus* asserts that when an answer cannot be put into words, neither can the question; that if a question can be framed at all, it is possible to answer it; and that what we cannot speak about we should consign to silence.

The thesis of this chapter, although extremely simple and therefore annoying to most contemporary thinkers, is that the free-will problem cannot be solved because we do not know exactly how to put the question. I do not mean that the question is meaningless, unless one adopts an empiricist's narrow definition of what "meaning" means. Many questions in philosophy are not meaningless in a wide sense, yet are unanswerable nonetheless. Why is there something rather than nothing? What is space? What is time? We have ways to measure time, but no way to explain it without introducing the notion of change, which presupposes time.

Is there anyone without an intense intuitive belief that his or her will is free? "Sir, we *know* our will is free," said Samuel Johnson, "and *there's* an end on't."[1] Just about everyone feels the same. Who considers himself an automaton, like Tiktok of Oz, who does only what he is wound up to do—or, in today's computer language, what he is programmed to do? We all know in our bones what L. Frank Baum meant when he said that Tiktok could think, speak, act, and do everything but live. Yet when we try to put it into words, to define human consciousness and its incredible ability to make free choices, we come up against one of Immanuel Kant's most notorious antinomies. Our attempt to capture the essence of that freedom either slides off into determinism, another name for destiny, or it tumbles over to the side of pure caprice. Neither definition gives us what we desperately want *free will* to mean.

William James, in his essay on "The Dilemma of Determinism," tried to persuade readers that determinism forces one into a dilemma, both horns of which are abominable. Although I share the sentiments of James's impassioned attack, his essay sidesteps the deeper dilemma, the Kantian dilemma which James himself recognized in other writings but failed to bring out in his celebrated essay. This deeper dilemma is the dilemma of will itself. When we try to define it within a context of determinism it becomes a delusion, something we think we have but really don't. When we try to define it within a context of indeterminism it becomes equally delusory, a choice made by some obscure randomizer in the brain which functions like the flip of a coin. It is here, I am convinced, that we run into a transcendent mystery—a mystery bound up, how we do not know, with the transcendent mystery of time.

A free-will act cannot be fully predetermined. Nor can it be the outcome of pure chance. Somehow it is both. Somehow it is neither. The question, as H. L. Mencken once put it, "is dark, puzzling, and not a little terrifying."[2] My own view, which is Kant's, is that there is no way to go between the horns. The best we can do (we who are not gods) is, Kant wrote, comprehend its incomprehensibility. As we now know, some mathematical problems can be "solved" only by showing them to be unsolvable. I believe this is also true of many, if not most, of the great traditional questions of philosophy. In what follows I shall try to convince you that the only solution to the problem of free will is to admit that we cannot know the solution. I do not mean it has *no* solution; only that if it has one, you and I cannot know it. We do not even know exactly how to put the question. Maybe God knows. Maybe God doesn't. Whereof one cannot speak, one had best keep silent.

Let us start our metaphysical excursion by considering the case for determinism with respect to human actions. We know that the human body, including its brain, is an incredibly complex organization of molecules. It is part of nature and subject to nature's laws. As a thought experiment, imagine a superbeing, perhaps a god, who knows all the laws of the universe and is capable of obtaining complete information about both a person's brain and the environment with which that person interacts. The determinist thesis is that such a being could in principle predict, under all circumstances, how the person would behave.

We must assume that our hypothetical predictor is not interacting with the person; otherwise we get into contradictions that have been explored in many recent papers dealing with what are called prediction paradoxes. Obviously if a predictor tells you that you will take a bath tonight, you can falsify the prediction by not taking a bath. And there are amusing logic paradoxes that arise whenever a predictor's behavior, while predicting, is part of the predicted event.

For example, suppose I put on the table two cards, one bearing the word *yes*, the other bearing the word *no*. I can now describe an event that will or will not take place in the room in the next five minutes, and bet a million dollars against your dime that you cannot predict correctly whether the event will or will not occur by touching the *yes* or *no* card. The event is: "You will make your prediction by touching the *no* card." This traps you in a variant of the liar paradox. If you touch the *no* card you will be wrong because the event will have taken place. And if you touch the *yes* card you will be wrong because the event will not have taken place.[3]

Such paradoxes need not detain us, because we are not concerned with the accuracy of predictions that interact with human behavior, only with whether there is a sense in which human behavior, given the total state of a person and his or her environment, must always be just what it is. The same point can be made by considering past decisions. Suppose that last Monday you decided to take a bath. Given the total state of the world, including the state of your brain, could you have decided other than the way you did?

Before quantum mechanics, in which pure chance is built into the theory's formalism, many scientists and philosophers regarded the universe as one vast machine which could not change in any way other than the way it did. In the eighteenth century Pierre de Laplace (in his _Mécanique Céleste_) gave the classic expression of this point of view:

> An intelligence knowing at a given instant of time all forces acting in nature as well as the momentary positions of all things . . . would be able to comprehend the motions of the largest bodies of the universe and those of the lightest atoms in one single formula, provided his intellect were powerful enough to subject all data to analysis; to him nothing would be uncertain, both past and future would be present to his eyes.

Here is how Samuel Taylor Coleridge, in his _Biographia Literaria_, colorfully phrased it:

> Thus the whole universe cooperates to produce the minutest stroke of every letter, save that I myself, and I alone, have nothing to do with it, but am merely the causeless and effectless beholding of it when it is done. Yet scarcely can it be called a beholding; for it is neither an act nor an effect; but an impossible creation of a _something-nothing_ out of its very contrary! It is the mere quicksilver plating behind the looking-glass; and in this alone consists the poor worthless I!

The feeling of free will has been called an "epiphenomenon," a psychological by-product of events that has no more influence on the universe, as it goes its predetermined way, than a rainbow has on the sun or on falling drops of rain. This view is as consistent with theism, pantheism, or polytheism as it is with atheism. Greek mythology had its three Fates, and the notion that there is no escape from destiny was central to Greek tragedy. Most of the great Christian theologians of the past, Protestant as well as Catholic, believed that God, in his omniscience, knows every future event. Glinda of Oz has a magic book that records all important events in Oz the instant they take place, but it cannot predict the future. The Koran speaks of a book in heaven in which all events, future as well as past, are recorded.

No person is truly free, Spinoza taught, until he or she realizes that free will is a delusion. If a falling stone were conscious, Spinoza wrote in a letter, it would believe it was falling of its own free will. I mention Spinoza because he was one of the greatest of secular philosophers to stress total determinism, and also because of the influence of his pantheism on Einstein. "Honestly," Einstein once remarked, "I cannot understand what people mean when they talk about freedom of the human will." Not only did Einstein believe that human behavior was completely determined by causal laws, he also refused to accept the chance aspect of quantum theory. He could not believe that God, Spinoza's God, would play dice with the universe. Until his death, he hoped and believed that some day quantum mechanics would be replaced by a deeper theory in which determinism on the microlevel would be restored.

At this point it is useful to introduce James's distinction between what he called hard and soft determinism. The hard determinist, said James, is one who does not "shrink from such words as fatality, bondage of the will, necessitation, and the like. Nowadays, we have a *soft* determinism which abhors harsh words, and, repudiating fatality, necessity, and even predetermination, says that its real name is freedom; for freedom is only necessity understood, and bondage to the highest is identical with true freedom." One of his colleagues, James wrote with amazement, even calls himself a "free-will determinist."[4]

Among the hard determinists, those who do not hesitate to call free will a delusion, one thinks first of Spinoza, but also of Leibniz, Nietzsche, Schopenhauer, Marx, Santayana, and scores of other philosophers. Among eminent lawyers in the United States, no one more effectively used determinism in the defense of criminals than Clarence Darrow. "I am firmly convinced," Darrow once said in a debate on free will, "that a man has no more to do with his own conduct than a wooden Indian. A wooden Indian has a little advantage for he does not even think he is free."[5] Among today's psychologists, B. F. Skinner is the most outspoken in expressing similar views. Man is a machine—a computer made of meat, as Marvin Minsky once said—acting in a way that is fully determined by its hereditary structure and the modifications introduced by that structure's interaction with the world.

It is hard to draw a sharp line between hard and soft determinism, especially since it is so much a matter of word choice and emphasis. The soft determinist usually does not like a language without the term *free will*, because abandoning it implies that human beings are automatons and this makes it difficult, if not impossible, to defend the use of such ordinary words as *right* and *wrong*, *praise* and *blame*. To restore morality, he redefines *free will* as acting in such a way that one's behavior is not compelled by external forces. If my hands are tied behind my back, I am not free to scratch my nose. Untie the hands and now I am free to do so. It is certainly true that ordinary language distinguishes between the unfreedom of a prisoner and his freedom when released. But if one continues to believe that decisions inside the brain, made in a way not coerced by outside forces, are the inevitable outcome of inner forces, it is hard to see how soft determinism differs from hard except in its ways of using language.

Consider a mechanical turtle that crawls across the floor in obedience to internal mechanisms. It moves here and there, seemingly at random. Contrast this with a toy turtle that a child pulls with a string. The toy is compelled by outside forces to move as it does, whereas the mechanical turtle is under no extraneous compulsion. Does anyone want to maintain that the mechanical turtle has free will? Yet is not the soft determinist doing exactly this when he speaks of a person's free will? It is easy to convert anyone to theism by redefining God as everything that exists. It is easy to convert anyone to a belief in free will by redefining it so that it means no more than acting from internal causes.

I wish I had space to discuss the curious history of this attempt to save determinism and simultaneously find a meaning for free will and moral responsibility. It was brilliantly argued by John Stuart Mill in a way that is indistinguishable from later arguments by Bertrand Russell, John Dewey, and Vienna Circle members and their admirers. Similar arguments are in the writings of Leibniz, Hobbes, Locke, Freud, Marx, Engels, Hegel and his followers, and hundreds of other thinkers. Charles Peirce and his friend James, both candid indeterminists, had little patience with such rhetoric. It seems "scarcely defensive for a thoroughgoing determinist," wrote Peirce (chiding Paul Carus for his arguments), ". . . to fly the flag of Free Will."[6] For James, soft determinism "is a quagmire of evasion under which the real issue of fact has been entirely smothered."

As G. K. Chesterton observed, a determinist has the very real problem of explaining why he says "Thank you" to anyone who passes him the mustard. "For how could he be praised for passing the mustard, if he could not be blamed for not passing the mustard?"[7] Raymond Chandler somewhere describes private detectives as having the moral stature of stop-and-go signs. If our activities are internally compelled by mechanisms inside the brain, there is only a difference in complexity between a person and a stop-and-go sign. Soft determinism doesn't eliminate compulsion; it only shifts the compulsion from outside fo inside the brain.

Karl Marx and Friedrich Engels were determinists, but this did not prevent them from passionately exhorting humanity to do one thing and not another. Stalin did not hesitate to kill millions because they disagreed with him, or he thought they did, even though his philosophy required him to believe that those whom he murdered could not have behaved otherwise. The ancient Greeks were fully aware of this paradox at the heart of determinism, and it has been discussed endlessly since. If a person must do whatever he or she does, where is the basis for moral judgment? There is no "ought," said Kant, without a "can." In recent times Jean Paul Sartre and his fellow existentialists have tried to escape the trap by emphasizing the reality of human freedom, even though they fail (in my opinion) to give an adequate account of what they mean by freedom.

If determinism implies fatalism, as I believe it does, can anything be gained by trying to make a free act an indeterminate act? Alas, as all determinists know, it cannot. The indeterminist position, with respect to human behavior, can only mean there are moments when the brain decides, perhaps by choosing which of two or more paths a nerve impulse will take, in a way that is not the outcome of prior causes. But if this is the case, the decision degenerates into one of pure chance. Surely this is even further from what we want "free will" to mean than a decision that is somehow internally caused. If we cannot praise or blame persons for decisions they could not have made otherwise, even less can we praise or blame them for decisions made by dice rattling inside their skulls!

Quantum mechanics is no help to the indeterminist except in the sense that if indeterminism exists on the microlevel, it may remove a mental block against believing that indeterminism can, in some incomprehensible way, also be involved in human behavior. Indeed, this was the main argument of such scientists as Sir Arthur Stanley Eddington and Arthur Holly Compton. Quantum mechanics, they said, does not explain free will; it just makes it easier to believe in free will.

I have no objection to this ploy if it is joined to a realization that quantum mechanics tells us nothing about the nature of free will. Suppose a decision in the brain is triggered by a random quantum jump or, as Epicurus phrased it, by a random "swerve" of a fundamental particle. Since the jump is the result of pure chance (assuming quantum mechanics is indeed correct), clearly this in no way satisfies what we intuitively feel "free will" to be. It merely transforms the decision from a causal one to a haphazard one, like deciding between possible courses of action by spinning a roulette wheel. There is certainly nothing creative about such a decision. In my opinion quantum mechanics sheds no light on the understanding of free will.

Pierce and James, and later Alfred North Whitehead, Charles Hartshorne, and others, became strong opponents of determinism, although few of them were or are as fully aware as was Kant of the free-will problem's intrinsic unsolvability.[8] Perhaps this is not quite fair. There are few indeterminists who do not, in unguarded moments, catch glimpses of the central mystery. Peirce once likened the problem of defining free will to that of trying to write down the entire decimal expansion of pi. Obviously pi is a limit "to which no numerical expression can be perfectly true. If our hope is vain; if in respect to some question—say that of the freedom of the will—no matter how long the discussion goes on, no matter how scientific our methods may become, there never will be a time when we can fully satisfy ourselves either that the question has no meaning, or that one answer or the other explains the facts, then in regard to that question there certainly is no *truth.*"[9] Peirce meant, of course, truth in the pragmatic sense. He immediately followed this remark by pointing out that to say there is no "true" answer to such a question (no way to confirm an answer by testing) does not mean there is no "reality" that answers the question.

James comes the closest to restating Kant's position in the third chapter of his *Pragmatism*:

> So both free-will and determinism have been inveighed against and called absurd, because each, in the eyes of its enemies, has seemed to prevent the "imputability" of good or bad deeds to their authors. Queer antinomy this! Free-will means novelty, the grafting on to the past of something not involved therein. If our acts were predetermined, if we merely transmitted the push of the whole past, the free-willists say, how could we be praised or blamed for anything? We should be "agents" only, not "principals," and where then would be our precious imputability and responsibility?
>
> But where would it be if we *had* free-will? rejoin the determi-

nists. If a "free" act be a sheer novelty, that comes not *from* me, the previous me, but *ex nihilo*, and simply tacks itself on to me, how can *I* the previous I, be responsible? How can I have any permanent *character* that will stand still long enough for praise or blame to be awarded? The chaplet of my days tumbles into a cast of disconnected beads as soon as the thread of inner necessity is drawn out by the preposterous indeterminist doctrine. [10]

It has always puzzled me that James, although he recognized that free will posed a "queer antinomy," could not bring himself to say, with Kant, that once the antinomy is recognized, there is no more to be said. James was enormously effective in arguing that determinism leaves no room for morality, and that only free wills can inject creative novelty into history, yet he was curiously reluctant to take that final step of putting the nature of will beyond the comprehension of finite minds.

Among this century's physicists, the most vigorous champion of Kant's attitude toward will was Niels Bohr. It provided one of his favorite applications to human life of what he called the "complementarity principle" of quantum mechanics. The psychologist, acting as a scientist, must regard all human behavior as fully determined. On the other hand, our sense of morality makes it equally imperative to believe that our behavior is not entirely determined. We must approach human behavior from both points of view, but we can no more reconcile them than we can perform an experiment in which we simultaneously measure the position and the momentum of an electron. "A great truth," Bohr liked to say, "is a truth whose opposite is also a great truth."[11] It is no surprise to learn that Bohr was so taken by the yin-yang symbol of the Orient that he put it at the center of his coat-of-arms.

Determinists sometimes argue that the chance aspect of quantum mechanics has no relevance for human history because all physical objects of the macroworld, including brains, contain so many billions upon billons of particles that quantum uncertainty on the microlevel becomes negligible. In other words, determinism holds, in a statistical sense, with a probability indistinguishable from certainty. This may be true in general, but there is a dramatic thought experiment (I do not know who first proposed it; it goes back to the early days of quantum mechanics) which proves that chance on the particle level can easily be magnified until it is capable, in a microsecond, of unleashing forces that radically alter history in ways that are unpredictable in principle.

Imagine a plane flying at supersonic speed over a continent. It carries a hydrogen bomb that is dropped by a mechanism triggered by the click of a Geiger counter. If quantum mechanics is correct, the timing of this click is purely random. Hence absolute chance determines where the bomb falls, and thereby decides between many alternate, equally possible courses of history. I mention this thought experiment only as an aside. It proves that if indeterminism rules on the microlevel, then strict determinism can be radically violated on the macrolevel. All of this, in my opinion, has no bearing whatever on the mystery of will.

Nor does religious belief have any bearing. In all great religious traditions the nature of will is as incomprehensible as it is in secular philosophy, and the secular viewpoints and arguments all have their counterparts in religious discourse. If the God of Judaism, Christianity, or Islam is omniscient, will he not know every detail of the future? But if God has such knowledge, how can our wills be free? And if our wills are not free, how can God treat us as morally responsible? On the other hand, if our actions are in principle unpredictable, then God cannot be all-knowing. Moreover, if our decisions are uncaused random events, we are as morally irresponsible as if they were totally determined. Rewards and punishments in another life seem monstrously unjust if we cannot behave other than the way we do, and equally unjust if all our actions result from dice throws.

The traditional Judaic-Christian attempt to solve these old conundrums was proposed by Maimonides and Augustine, and later adopted by Thomas Aquinas and all the great Scholastics, as well as by leading Muslim theologians. It rests on the assumption that God is outside of time. As a consequence he sees all history from the standpoint of eternity. He sees the future as well as the past, but (the argument continues) from our time-bound perspective we make genuine choices. Roman Catholic thinkers of the Middle Ages differed in the degree to which they were bothered by what seems here to be a sharp contradiction. If an omniscient God can know our future, is there not a sense in which that future exists even now, and if so, how can our decisions be truly free? The argument seems to turn history into something like a motion picture film. While it is being projected, the shadow actors on the screen make real choices about what they say and do, even though everything is permanently recorded. Some Scholastics were untroubled by this doctrine. Others regarded it as a disturbing paradox, the resolution of which is known only to God.

The Christian doctrine of predestination, that every person is foreordained to be saved or unsaved, is a natural corollary of believing that God knows the future timelessly. The leading Protestant theologians who stressed this doctrine—Martin Luther, John Calvin, Jonathan Edwards, Karl Barth, to mention a few—followed their Catholic predecessors in finding support for predestination in remarks by Paul (Romans 9: 18–21):

> Therefore hath he mercy on whom he will have mercy, and whom he will he hardeneth.
> Thou wilt say then unto me, Why doth he yet find fault? For who hath resisted his will?
> Nay but, O man, who art thou that repliest against God? Shall the thing formed say to him that formed it, Why hast thou made me thus?
> Hath not the potter power over the clay, of the same lump to make one vessel unto honour, and another unto dishonour?

Thomas Paine, a deist who believed in both God and immortality (though not in Christianity) attacked Paul's reasoning in a characteristic way. "Nay, but who art thou, presumptuous Paul, that puttest thyself in God's place?" To compare man with a clay pot, said Paine, is a "wretched metaphor" because it implies that human beings are no more than lifeless lumps of clay. "If Paul believed that God made man after His own image, he dishonors it by making that image and a brickbat to be alike."[12]

Christian leaders have quarreled interminably over predestination. Evangelists like John Wesley saw little point in exhorting sinners to repent if it was already decided in heaven who would and would not be saved. Yet there was always, even for the foes of predestination, the nagging problem of how persons could be genuinely free without limiting the power of God to know the future. Some predestination sects, like the Two-Seed-in-the-Spirit Predestination Baptists of the southern United States, openly opposed evangelism on the plausible ground that the question of who is or is not saved is already settled.

Leibniz exchanged letters with Samuel Clarke over this difficulty. As someone said, if they had hit their heads together it would have produced more light. "That which happens is assured," wrote Leibniz, "but it is not therefore necessary, and if anyone did the contrary, he would do nothing impossible in itself, although it is impossible . . . that that other happen."

Here is René Descartes making similar comments: ". . . We will be free from these embarrassments if we recollect that our mind is limited while the power of God, by which he not only knew from all eternity what is or can be, but also willed and preordained it, is infinite. It thus happens that we possess sufficient intelligence to know clearly and distinctly that this power is in God, but not enough to comprehend how he leaves the free actions of men indeterminate. . . . "13

In Milton's *Paradise Lost* (Book 3) God recalls his creation of Adam and Eve, and how their disobedience resulted from free will even though he knew how they would decide:

> . . . *They themselves decreed*
> *Their own revolt, not I. If I foreknew,*
> *Foreknowledge had no influence on their fault*
> *Which had no less proved certain unforeknown.*

Peirce saw nothing wrong in this medieval way of harmonizing free will with divine foreknowledge, even though it seems "to most persons flatly self-contradictory." The contradiction arises, Peirce continued, only if we think of God's knowledge as existing, like ours, in time. "But it is a degraded conception to conceive God as subject to Time, which is rather one of His creatures. Literal foreknowledge is certainly contradictory to literal freedom. But if we say that though God knows (using the word *knows* in a trans-temporal sense) he never did know, does not know, and never will know, then his knowledge in no wise interferes with freedom."14 Thus did Peirce defend his doctrine of "tychism," a belief that the future is in part undertermined, without regarding it as in conflict with the view of Aquinas and Kant that God, being outside time, knows the future in a timeless way.

Here is C. S. Lewis saying the same thing in his own clear language:

> But suppose God is outside and above the Time-line. In that case, what we call "tomorrow" is visible to Him *in just the same way* as what we call "today." All the days are "Now" for Him. He doesn't *remember* you doing things yesterday; He simply *sees* you doing them, because, though you've lost yesterday, He has not. He doesn't *foresee* you doing things tomorrow, He simply *sees* you doing them: because, though tomorrow is not yet there for you, it

is for Him. You never supposed that your actions at this moment were any less free because God knows what you are doing. Well, He knows your tomorrow's actions in just the same way—because He is already in tomorrow and can simply watch you. In a sense, He doesn't know your action till you've done it: but then the moment at which you have done it is already "Now" for Him.

This idea has helped me a lot. If it doesn't help you, leave it alone. It is a "Christian idea" in the sense that great and wise Christians have held it and there is nothing in it contrary to Christianity. But it is not in the Bible or any of the creeds. You can be a perfectly good Christian without accepting it, or indeed without thinking of the matter at all. [15]

Another way to avoid the paradox is to regard God as omniscient only in the sense that he knows all that can be known, allowing for parts of the future to be in principle unknowable. The Scholastics stressed the fact that God cannot do logically impossible things, such as alter the past or construct a square triangle. Perhaps there are aspects of the future that God, in a similar way, is powerless to know because God is not outside of time, and the future is not completely determined.

In one of James's picturesque metaphors, God is playing a vast game of superchess with the universe. Because God made up the rules and can play a perfect game, the outcome is certain even though God allows the universe to make some moves that even he cannot anticipate. Put another way, God's providence is only an overall plan. It allows for many different ways of winning, depending on how the universe moves. Our wills constitute part of the freedom God has permitted his universe to have to make the game interesting. He has made us in his own image by giving us genuine creativity. Free will, as Charles Hartshorne likes to say, is the "glory" of our very being. This notion of a "finite God," suggested by Hume and championed by Mill, has strongly appealed to many later thinkers. Even H. G. Wells was once so taken by the concept of a finite God that he wrote an entire book about it, *God the Invisible King*. (Later, Wells decided he was an atheist.)

There are, then, two essentially different ways of harmonizing free will with divine foreknowledge. One is to put God outside of time and see no contradiction between his timeless knowledge of the future and our free choices. The other is to model God as in some sort of time, his omniscience limited to what can be known, allowing room for contingent events that not even God can unerringly predict. Which view is right? I can give my opinion at once. I don't know. Do not ask *me*! As a theist I see nothing inconsistent about either view, or any reason why the truth may not be a third view which we are incapable of formulating or understanding. Who am I to know how to answer such questions?

I do know this. I cannot conceive of myself as existing without a body in both space and time, or without a brain that has free will. I agree with Samuel Johnson that "All theory is against the freedom of the will; all experience for it."[16] I cannot comprehend how the dilemma can be resolved, but I am no more troubled by this than by the fact that I cannot understand time, being, consciousness, or the nature of God. Indeed, it was with a feeling of enormous relief that I concluded, long ago, that free will is an unfathomable mystery.

Listen to Raymond Smullyan. The speaker in his dialogue is God:

> Why the idea that I could possibly have created you without free will! You acted as if this were a genuine possibility, and wondered why I did not choose it! It never occurred to you that a sentient being without free will is no more conceivable than a physical object which exerts no gravitational attraction. (There is, incidentally, more analogy than you realize between a physical object exerting gravitational attraction and a sentient being exerting free will!) Can you honestly even imagine a conscious being without free will? What on earth could it be like? I think that one thing in your life that has so misled you is your having been told that I gave man the *gift* of free will. As if I first created man, and then as an afterthought endowed him with the extra property of free will. Maybe you think I have some sort of "paint brush" with which I daub some creatures with free will, and not others. No, free will is not an "extra"; it is part and parcel of the very essence of consciousness. A conscious being without free will is simply a metaphysical absurdity.[17]

I do not wish to imply that we have souls that are somehow distinct from the pattern of our molecular structure, even though I grant that this may be the case. I do not want to suggest that free will is limited to human organisms, not possessed in lower degrees by humbler creatures. Nor am I a panpsychic who thinks that all things, including plants and stones, possess some degree of will. I believe that a stone or a plant has no will at all, and that in a butterfly's brain, although there may be a low degree of will, the amount is so minute as to be negligible. I cannot say it is impossible for humanity some day to build a computer or a robot of sufficient complexity that a threshold will be crossed and the computer or robot will acquire self-consciousness and free will. These are profound questions about which I have no fixed opinions.

Thomas Henry Huxley, in an unguarded moment, wrote: "I protest that if some great Power would agree to make me always think what is true and do what is right, on condition of being turned into a sort of clock and wound up every morning before I got out of bed, I should instantly close with the offer. The only freedom I care about is the freedom to do right; the freedom to do wrong I am ready to part with on the cheapest terms to any one who will take it from me."[18] Much as I admire Huxley, I find this statement monstrous. To be turned into a Tiktok would mean ceasing to be human. Sara Teasdale said it this way in her poem "Mastery":

> I would not have a god come in
> To shield me suddenly from sin,
> And set my house of life to rights;
> Nor angels with bright burning wings
> Ordering my earthly thoughts and things;
> Rather my own frail guttering lights
> Wind blown and nearly beaten out;
> Rather the terror of the nights
> And long, sick groping after doubt;
> Rather be lost than let my soul
> Slip vaguely from my own control—
> Of my own spirit let me be
> In sole though feeble mastery.

I am persuaded that somehow, in a way utterly beyond our ken, you and I possess that incomprehensible power we call free will. I am content to let theologians worry over whether God could, if he liked, create a person who always wills to do right. Such a person, to be a person, may be as self-contradictory as a square triangle. Or it may be otherwise.

You and I—this I know—are not such creatures. But I have no insight into the nature of the transcendental magic that operates inside our skulls. I believe that the magic is neither fate nor chance, yet how it escapes those two categories is beyond my grasp. Like time, with which it is linked, free will is best left—indeed, I believe we cannot do otherwise—an impenetrable mystery. Ask not how it works because no one on earth can tell you.

7

THE STATE:
Why I Am Not an Anarchist

> *There were no poor people in the Land of Oz,*
> *because there was no such thing as money, and all*
> *property of every sort belonged to the Ruler. The*
> *people were her children, and she cared for them.*
> *Each person was given freely by his neighbors*
> *whatever he required for his use, which is as much as*
> *any one may reasonably desire.*
>
> —L. Frank Baum, *The Emerald City Of Oz*

The economic and political structure of Oz, as befits a fairyland, is a whimsical mix of anarchism and monarchism. Citizens are free to live as they please, no matter how eccentric their appearance and behavior. Since almost all are kind and unselfish, there is no need for money, police, law courts, or prisons. On the other hand, the country's beautiful girl ruler, Ozma, is a benevolent dictator of awesome power, thanks to her strong magic and the even stronger magic of friends like Glinda, the good witch of the South. Ozma's magic picture enables her to see anything happening anywhere in the world. Glinda's huge *Book of Records* prints a running account of every significant event in Oz the instant it occurs. Big Sisters are watching you!

Although Baum was only playing with utopian ideas, most of the early writings of anarchists and socialists seem to me on a level not much higher than the third chapter of *The Emerald City of Oz*, where the Royal Historian gives the fullest report on how Oz is governed. In this and the next two chapters I shall try to explain why I think a modern industrial nation must avoid Ozzy extremes, and why I call myself a democratic socialist—that is, why I consider myself a conservative.

After some preliminaries about democracy and socialism, the chapter you are now reading is largely about anarchism and libertarianism. The next chapter will deal mostly with the free-market obsessions of those I call the Smithians. The third will report briefly on Karl Marx and several other things. There will be considerable overlapping of topics in these three chapters, but I found it hopeless to organize them better. Perhaps their chaotic character reflects the chaotic state of my own thinking about economics as well as the chaotic state of modern economic theory.

When I called myself a conservative, I said it partly in jest. I am aware that words such as *liberal, radical, conservative, socialist,* even *democratic,* have been used with so many meanings that they are as ambiguous as *idealist* and *realist.* There is always a temptation to define an ideology so broadly that it converts everyone by definition. Thus Garry Wills, in his *Confessions of a Conservative,* follows the common practice of defining a conservative as one who wants to conserve the wisdom of the past, or what Gilbert Chesterton called the "democracy of the dead." At the same time, naturally, a good conservative is always open to wise and cautious change. Wills quotes a passage in which GK compares humanity with Perseus, unable to see "the Gorgon of the future except in the mirror of the past. . . . Among the dead I have living rivals. In the future all my rivals are dead because they are unborn."[1] This way of defining conservatism makes everybody a conservative. Who wishes to abandon the wisdom of the past? Certainly no Christian, for whom the appearance of God on earth was the greatest event of history. But now we have a new linguistic problem. We must invent new terms to distinguish William F. Buckley's way of evaluating the wisdom of the past from John Kenneth Galbraith's way.

Margaret Cole, in her article on socialism in *The Encyclopedia of Philosophy,* employs the same dodge to convert everybody to socialism. According to Mrs. Cole, if you believe existing governments are unjust, and that they ought to be more just, you are a socialist. This makes Buckley one of our country's leading socialists.

Compounding the confusion is the old propaganda technique of stealing an adversary's buzzword. Jacques Maritain liked to call Roman Catholicism the true humanism, and humanist John Dewey, in *A Common Faith*, explains how an atheist can in good conscience speak of faith and God. Communist states call themselves people's democracies and deplore the absence of freedoms in capitalist countries. Friedrich von Hayek, in his classic defense of free markets, *The Constitution of Liberty*, heads a postscript: "Why I Am Not a Conservative." Members of the Chicago School of economics, widely hailed as ultraconservative, prefer to call themselves true liberals, taking the word in its nineteenth-century sense. When Milton Friedman, the school's chief choreographer, was asked in 1978 if he was conservative, he responded with: "Good God, don't call me that. The conservatives are the New Dealers like Galbraith who want to keep things the way they are."[2]

I respect Friedman's point. Is anything in recent history more obvious than the steady creep of central planning into the world's democracies? All are now mixed economies in which free markets flourish side by side with big corporations that are either government-owned or government-dominated. In spite of recent backslides, such as the election of Margaret Thatcher in England and Ronald Reagan in the United States, the trend is so deeply entrenched that it seems a misuse of language to call persons conservative if they want to reverse it, or radical if they want to preserve or accelerate it.

There was understandable jubilation among native conservatives when Reagan won the 1980 election, especially since their man Barry Goldwater had earlier failed to make it. "I really think this is the watershed moment," said William Rusher, publisher of Reagan's favorite magazine, *The National Review*. "Conservatism is at the crossroads. And incidentally, our old enemy liberalism has died."[3]

Ideologues like to speak in hyperboles, and if you take the pronouncements of conservatives seriously, you might suppose that socialism also is dead or dying. "The most important event in the recent history of ideas is the demise of the socialist dream." So reads the first sentence of George Gilder's paean to supply-side economics, *Wealth and Poverty*. As the rest of his paragraph makes clear, Gilder sees no essential difference between the withering of socialist ideals in Russia and mild modifications of democratic socialism in Sweden.[4]

This refusal to distinguish democratic socialism from totalitarian socialism is characteristic of conservative scriveners. Here is a typical snatch of purple prose from William F. Buckley, Jr.: "The objective failure of socialism is as manifest as the brightness of the sun, the aridity of the deserts, the whiteness of the snows."[5]

While I type, democratic socialism is on the upswing in Europe and England. It has captured the Greek government under Andreas Papandreou, the French government under François Mitterand, and the Spanish government under Felipe González, a socialist sufficiently enlightened to declare himself not a Marxist. "Her majesty's new opposition" in Britain is the newly formed Social Democratic Party, the first significant new party in England in half a century. The radical socialism of the Labour Party may indeed be dying, but democratic socialism of the sort I prefer—democratic freedoms combined with the most desirable mix of government controls and free enterprise—is making a strong bid for British power as Margaret Thatcher holds fast to her Tory "root canal" effort to cure England's economic ills. In spite of rightward swings in West Germany, the Netherlands, Denmark, Norway, and Belgium, democratic socialism is still thriving, thank you, in other countries. In 1982, Olof Palme and his Social Democrats won a decisive victory in Sweden, ending six years of "conservative" rule. I put the word in quotes because conservative parties in Europe support many goals that Gilder and Buckley consider socialist.

From my perspective, words like *conservatism*, *liberalism*, perhaps even *socialism*, though not exactly dying, are fast fading into vagueness. If by "socialism" Gilder and Buckley have in mind the progressive decline of classical free markets as big corporations and big governments get bigger, I fear they are in for continual disappointment. There simply is no way an advanced industrial state can cope with technological complexities, can minimize waste and misery and the danger of revolutions, without strong government controls. Because regulation is necessary to "conserve" both capitalism and freedom, the conservative question is not how to get rid of government controls but how to improve them, how to preserve what Galbraith calls the consensus in today's democratic societies. But before going into more details about this task, let me put aside two beliefs I take for granted.

Democracy, I assume, is a good thing. By this term, also far from precise, I mean democracy in the modern sense of a constitutional, representative government, a political system in which leaders can be voted in and out of office by a secret ballot that offers genuine alternatives. As John Dewey once compressed it, democracy is the recognition "that no man or limited set of men is wise enough or good enough to rule others without their consent." I assume we agree also on the merits of universal suffrage—that the franchise is not to be withheld from any citizen because of sex, race, religion, or economic status.

Please do not remind me of Athenian democracy. It was not democracy in the above sense, but an aristocracy in which voting was a way of resolving differences within an elite. Two thirds of the Athenians were slaves who could not vote, not to mention the disenfranchised women of the elite who were almost slaves. Plato in his *Republic* made a stab at defending women's rights, but who took him seriously? Aristotle never questioned that slaves were born with slavish natures, and that women were intellectually inferior to men. Can you think of any strong arguments for women's rights in the long stretch of male-dominated centuries between Plato's *Republic* and John Stuart Mill's essay "The Subjugation of Women"?

Democracy clearly functions best to the degree that voters are intelligent and well informed, which means, of course, that the efficiency of democracy is strongly tied to education. When I consider that women in the United States did not vote until after I was born, and that blacks could not vote in significant numbers until even later, I am not pessimistic about our great experiment in extending education and the franchise to every citizen. It is hard to imagine how such a monumental task could be undertaken without a temporary decline in the standards of schools and colleges, hence in the wisdom of the electorate. But considering how recently the effort began, how huge a cultural wrench it is, I am surprised by how well we are doing.

The greatest danger—it was raised in Mill's *Representational Government*, emphasized by Alexis de Tocqueville's *Democracy in America*, and colorfully delineated in José Ortega y Gasset's *Revolt of the Masses*—is that education may not keep pace with extensions of the franchise, that ignorant voting will substitute a rule by boobs for a rule by the wise. Uneducated masses, Thomas Hobbes reminded us, are as easily influenced by the flummery and flattery of politicians as any ruler is influenced by similar tactics on the part of advisors.

On July 18, 1967, *The New York Times* reported that the four thousand good citizens of the coastal town of Picoaza, Ecuador, had elected a foot powder as mayor. A company making a toes deodorant had advertised: "Vote for any candidate, but if you want well-being and hygiene, vote for Pulvapies." On election eve the firm distributed leaflets saying: "For mayor, honorable Pulvapies." The town elected Pulvapies by a comfortable majority. How H. L. Mencken would have guffawed over this confirmation of his low opinion of mass voting. "I do not believe in democracy," Mencken once confessed, "but I am perfectly willing to admit that it provides the only really amusing form of government ever endured by mankind."

Plato feared democracy precisely because of the dangers of rule by an ignorant majority. The people, said Alexander Hamilton, is a great beast. One thinks of the mob terror that followed the French Revolution, of the lynchings of blacks in the South by local white majorities. At the moment, some states with large Protestant fundamentalist constituencies have almost succeeded in passing laws that forbid state-supported colleges to teach evolution. Of course the power of the popular vote in the United States is severely limited by the Constitution and the Bill of Rights, and by the Supreme Court. Nevertheless there remain vast areas in which no one yet knows, aside from improving education, how best to prevent a "tyranny of the majority."

Other deep dilemmas of democracy are far from resolved. In deciding who has the right to vote we do not know exactly where to draw lines that separate children from adults, the mentally competent from the incompetent, the criminal from the noncriminal. We do not know how the powers of government are best dispersed through states and cities. We do not know whether elected representatives should vote for what they think is best for the world or for their country or for their constituents, or whether they should vote for what they think their constituents think is best for one or another of those objectives.

In brief, we all know that democracies have their flaws. We all know there is no consensus among political scientists on what form of representative democracy works best. There may not even be a best. As Kenneth Arrow and others have shown, if we make certain reasonable posits about the goals of a voting system, the posits can at times be contradictory. In a sense there *is* no perfect system. The democracies of the world are still evolving, still experimenting, and (one may hope) still improving.

Looking back on the last few centuries of world history I am impressed by how recently we have disposed of the divine right of kings and the absolute monarchist views of Hobbes. (One fine morning England will decide that the preservation of even a symbolic monarchy is not worth all the cost, flimflam, and anachronistic social implications.) The recent rise of constitutional democracy seems to me, as to most political philosophers and historians, the single most significant way progress has been made in the art of government. Regardless of its flaws and terrible blunders, regardless of how you guess the future, I assume we agree that constitutional democracy is superior to any system in which there are either no elections, or voting is, as in communist countries, a bogus ritual.

Another belief I take for granted is that the recent worldwide awareness that humanity has the power to control its own destiny, to minimize (if not eliminate) war, poverty, and other needless suffering—the power to shape a better world—is also a good thing. (Not everyone believes this. Millions of Protestant fundamentalists expect the world to get worse and worse until, any day now, history ends with the appearance of the Antichrist, followed by his ignominious defeat and the Second Coming.) Like democracy, the idea is as old as the ancient Greeks, but only in recent times has it become sufficiently widespread to be a force for change.

H. G. Wells had a phrase for it that I have always liked. He called it the Open Conspiracy. "Open" was intended to distinguish it from such closed, clandestine conspiracies as anarchism and communism. It is a movement that operates in daylight, not in darkness. Wells saw the Open Conspiracy as a broad, formless, ill-defined process of mass education correlated with slow, nonviolent changes made cautiously, by democratic means, within open societies such as Wells's England and our own. "The ceaseless whisper of the more permanent ideals," wrote William James, "the steady tug of truth and justice, give them but time, *must* warp the world in their direction."[6]

Democratic socialists, at least those I admire, share with libertarians a fear of the "unintended consequences" of abrupt social alterations. Just as most biological mutations are detrimental to an organism's survival, or to the survival of its species, so most sudden changes in a society are similarly catastrophic. Moving slowly toward a social goal is usually the fastest way to get there. "No prophecy is safer," wrote Herbert Spencer, "than that the results anticipated from a law will be greatly exceeded in amount by results not anticipated. Even simple physical actions might suggest to us this conclusion. Let us contemplate one."

You see that this wrought-iron plate is not quite flat: it sticks up a little here towards the left— "cockles," as we say. How shall we flatten it? Obviously, you reply, by hitting down on the part that is prominent. Well, here is a hammer, and I give the plate a blow as you advise. Harder, you say. Still no effect. Another stroke? Well, there is one, and another, and another. The prominence remains, you see: the evil is as great as ever—greater, indeed. But this is not all. Look at the warp which the plate has got near the opposite edge. Where it was flat before it is now curved. A pretty bungle we have made of it. Instead of curing the original defect, we have produced a second. Had we asked an artizan practised in "planishing," as it is called, he would have told us that no good was to be done, but only mischief, by hitting down on the projecting part. He would have taught us how to give variously-directed and specially-adjusted blows with a hammer elsewhere: so attacking the evil not by direct but by indirect actions. The required process is less simple than you thought. Even a sheet of metal is not to be successfully dealt with after those common-sense methods in which you have so much confidence. What, then, shall we say about a society? "Do you think I am easier to be played on than a pipe?" asks Hamlet. Is humanity more readily straightened than an iron plate?[7]

What sort of gentle poundings are the most effective in improving the world's shape? Following the sage advice of the Cheshire Cat, that you can't find the best road to take unless you know where you want to go, is it not obvious that any Open Conspirator must have in mind, if only dimly, the shape of what Plato called the City in the Skies?

Two extremes are no longer seriously debated among mature Open Conspirators. One is the extreme anarchism in which everyone does his or her own thing, and the state is replaced by uncompelled cooperation among free individuals or among small autonomous groups. The other is the extreme socialism in which a government owns everything, except maybe a citizen's clothes and a few other personal belongings, and everybody is forced to do whatever the government wants them to do.

First, a look at the anarchist end of the spectrum. As things are, there simply is no way a modern industrial society can flourish without a strong government to enforce the law. This means, of course, a system of police, courts, lawyers, judges, jails, and, given the absence of a world community, a military establishment. You cannot even enjoy your humblest possessions unless a government supports a vast system that prevents thieves from taking them. Regardless of whether altruism is genetically based (as anarchists like Prince Peter Kropotkin argued and some modern biologists believe), or entirely acquired after birth, there is not the slightest reason to suppose that humanity can, in the foreseeable future, eliminate what Christians call original sin.

It is not just the necessity of a state to preserve law and order that makes the extreme anarchist dream so hopeless. Even if small communities of like-minded visionaries found a way to police themselves, there is no way they could maintain, let alone establish, an industrial society. Small self-governing groups are incapable of building reservoirs to bring them clean water, or roads to connect cities, or dynamos to supply electricity, or cars, or printing presses, or modern hospitals, or anything else that is a product of an advanced technology. Big tasks can be done only by big corporations that are either state-owned or state-controlled, or that operate as vast independent oligarchies within the state. Old-fashioned anarchism might work in a preindustrial society modeled, say, on the tribes of American Indians before the white man came. But if we want to enjoy the benefits of science and technology, the ideals of anarchism are as irrelevant as the ideals of the Sermon on the Mount.

Although the anarchist dream still plays a mythic role in Marxist communism, there is not a whiff of evidence that the state in Russia or China or Cuba or any other country that calls itself Marxist is withering away or even planning to wither away. Now and then novelists like Tolstoy and Aldous Huxley, poets like Karl Shapiro and Paul Goodman, or some third-rate philosopher will take up anarchism as one takes up a harmless fad. During the sixties there were small groups of ignorant children such as the Weathermen who uttered loud Bakunin-like burps, and even made some infantile attempts at what the ungentle anarchists of earlier times called the propaganda of the deed. They had less influence on the nation's politics than Jehovah's Witnesses.

The entire counterculture scene of the sixties, with its weird mixture of kinky sex, pot, rock, zen, astrology, obscene language, and fusty anarchist theory, always struck me as a prime example of how quickly angry rebels turn into other-directed conformists of the most extreme sort. After telling everybody over thirty that each person has a right to do his or her own thing, millions of youngsters proceeded to do identical things. Boys let their hair grow to their shoulders. Little girls learned how to shock their grandmothers with four-letter words. Boys and girls alike bought the same records, worshiped the same rock stars. The radicals among them loudly proclaimed their devotion to "participatory democracy," simultaneously praising Hanoi and plastering their rooms with photos of Fidel Castro and Che Guevara. They even began, you know, to talk alike. A few became so mentally disturbed that they bombed and murdered those who wanted to do their own but different things. Who conforms more than adolescent nonconformists?

As soon as the winds began to change, leaders of the new left discovered it was less fun to fly the black flag and blow themselves up than to cast horoscopes, take up an Eastern religion, join a consciousness-raising cult, peddle cocaine, take a job on Wall Street, or marry someone rich. Aside from a few threadbare pockets of anarchism around the world, it is as dead as any political ideology can get.[8] How could it be otherwise? A successful revolution requires authority, discipline, agreement on a plan, and considerable self-sacrifice—demands not easily met by a ragtag army of naïve narcissists who want to be left alone to behave as they please. As the Royal Historian put it, anarchist ideals are not "practical with us," though Dorothy assured him they work quite well in Oz.

At the other end of the spectrum is extreme socialism. Unlike anarchism, it collaborates easily with modern technology. "I saw the future," I can imagine the shade of Lincoln Steffens now saying, "and, alas, it works." But at what a price! A state that owns and runs almost everything cannot maintain its power without becoming a monstrous tyranny in which all the freedoms of Western democracy evaporate while the culture takes on the character of a termite colony. Although the word *socialism* has been stolen by Marxist and fascist movements that ended in dictatorships, I know of no democratic socialist today who favors a state in which all private business is abolished and all free competition suppressed. Even aside from losses of freedom and massive violations of human rights, who would prefer the dull uniformity of goods, services, art, and ideas that characterize dictatorships, over the variety and multiplicity of choices available in democracies with mixed economies?

Certainly every democratic nation today, whether it calls itself cap-

italist or socialist, is a blend of free markets and government-owned or
-regulated corporations. As the platform of the German Social Democratic Party phrased it in 1959 when it made its historic break with
Marxism, "as much competition as possible, as much planning as necessary." In a sense, even the economies of Russia and China are
mixed. No economy of a large nation can be *totally* controlled. But
the Russian and Chinese economies are so close to extreme socialism
that it seems misleading to call them mixed.

The belief that a mixed economy can be a lasting middle way between unregulated capitalism and tyrannical socialism was strongly rejected by the two great Austrian fathers of modern libertarianism,
Ludwig von Mises and Friedrich von Hayek. This incredible notion is
suggested in the very title of Hayek's most popular book, *The Road to
Serfdom*, a work of the mid-forties that still supplies all the essential
passion and rhetoric for modern libertarianism. Any move toward socialism, the two vons argued, is a move toward what Hilaire Belloc
called the servile state.

This view is echoed by Milton Friedman and his wife, Rose, in their
Capitalism and Freedom, or, as some detractors call it, *Capitalism
and Friedman*. Their most recent book, *Free to Choose*, perpetuates
the same bogus either/or. Nowhere does the book use the phrase
"mixed economy." The United States is now at that fork in the road,
the Friedmans warn, at which we must choose either to move "toward
greater freedom and limited government in the spirit of Smith and
Jefferson or toward an omnipotent monolithic government in the spirit
of Marx and Mao." To me this is like saying that in religious faith we
must choose between moving toward Roman Catholicism or toward
atheism. And of course the Friedmans do not often remind us that
earlier this century three capitalist nations—Germany, Italy, Spain—
became dictatorships, not to mention the pro-capitalist dictators of
Latin America. Not even Joseph Schumpeter, who loathed socialism,
thought it incompatible with democracy. Surely the achievements of
democratic mixed economies around the world, all more socialistic
than ours, refute the shallow prophecy that democratic socialism must
lead to serfdom.

Although communist countries show no signs of a democratic drift,
elements of economic decentralization and capitalist incentives are
starting to seep into their marketplaces as stealthily as socialism seeps
into the cracks of capitalism. Yugoslavia's creeping capitalism began in

the sixties. Hungary moves sluggishly and Poland catastrophically in the same direction. The new leaders of China are now talking about the values of competitive markets (who knows how long this talk will last or what will come of it?) and even Castro has been stimulating production in Cuba by offering profit incentives to workers who exceed quotas. In my view the two extremes that Mises and Hayek thought inevitable are precisely the two systems that are the least stable.

How much of a democratic mixed economy should the government own? How much planning and regulation is necessary for the private sector? Does the United States need more planning than it has now, or just shifts in the kinds of planning—shifts that would leave the balance between planning and free enterprise essentially the same? It is over these questions that top economists clash. Before discussing their battles, however, let us review the broad area of their agreement.

Consider the three best-known U.S. economists: Galbraith (democratic socialist), Friedman (libertarian), and Paul Samuelson (an eclectic neo-Keynesian somewhere in the middle). All three are intelligent, well-informed, honorable men. All agree on the virtues of democracy and its freedoms. All reject the extremes of anarchism and near-total socialism. All favor a mixed economy. All are Open Conspirators. All believe that humanity, by joining reason and knowledge to a sense of justice (whatever the source of that sense), can eventually eliminate large-scale suffering and maximize the happiness of everybody.

I trust the reader knows I know how fuzzy are the phrases in the last part of the preceding sentence. Utilitarianism, with its slogan "the greatest good for the greatest number," never succeeded in making clear the meaning of that slogan, and most political philosophers today agree that any form of utilitarianism tacitly assumes a theory of justice that is not easy to formulate. We have no adequate way to measure happiness, no way to measure what is meant by greatest good. There is not even agreement on what those terms mean. Even if we could agree on the meaning of happiness, and had ways to measure it, there would still be the intractable problem of deciding what is meant by saying it should be maximized.

Is it better to have everyone mildly happy or an elite extremely happy in a sea of unhappy people? Jeremy Bentham's "hedon," the quantum of happiness that underpinned his "felicific calculus," turned out to be as useless as phlogiston. The notion that human values can be quantified and economic problems solved like equations in physics reached towering heights of absurdity in the "mathematical psychics" of Francis Ysidro Edgeworth. For Edgeworth, every man, woman, and child is a "pleasure machine" that always behaves so as to maximize its satisfactions. Game theory, decision theory, utility theory, and other modern mathematical tools now being applied to human behavior are of some help, but not much. They presuppose goals the tools cannot supply, and over which economists squabble as much as ever. [9]

One fundamental question on which there is little agreement is this: How far should an ideal government go in trying to alleviate extreme forms of suffering, both inside a nation and in other countries? A fashionable phrase at the moment for such direct action is "redistributive justice." Put bluntly, it means using taxes to get money for welfare programs. Democratic socialists obviously believe in redistributive justice. One of the strongest recent arguments for it is John Rawls's celebrated book, A Theory of Justice. For Rawls, the state has a moral obligation to redistribute justice, not for utilitarian reasons (to maximize hedons) but because it would be morally wrong, in an absolute Kantian sense, to do otherwise. The abolition of slavery, and the civil rights victories of the sixties, were instances of redistributive justice initiated by federal action and enforced against the violent opposition of state and local governments. The Social Security program, and other "safety nets" for the poor, are forms of redistributive justice that not many conservatives would care to abandon completely.

There is an old joke about the boy scout who came home with a black eye. When his mother asked what happened he said he had tried to help an elderly lady cross a street but she didn't want to go. The Robin Hood state, taking seriously Jesus' command to the rich young man to sell all he owned and give the money to the poor, compels the rich to go partway along this road. Naturally they don't want to go. Need I remind the reader that at every past step along this road an enormous hue and cry has gone up from all those who stood to gain if a proposed welfare measure had not been carried out?

There was a time in England and America when parents could force their children to spend almost their entire waking life at dreary, unhealthy labor in a factory. In the mid-1800s it was a great advance for American socialism when laws made it a crime for children under twelve to work more than ten hours a day. Both nations finally decided that child labor was immoral, that children should be in school instead, and of course public schooling meant higher taxes. The first child-labor laws were strenuously opposed by both parents and factory owners, in England even by the Anglican Church. How dare the state, thundered newspaper editorials, tell mothers and fathers what to do with their progeny![10]

A famous New Yorker cartoon by James Thurber showed a man and woman seated at a table and the woman asking: "Whatever became of the Socialist Party?" Well, one thing that surely hastened its decline in this country was the New Deal. Again, a great groan of agony came from the business community as Congress adopted plank after plank in the Socialist Party's 1928 platform.[11] Surely this weakened the party as much as its dogmatism and shallow optimism, or Norman Thomas's unwise decision to allow Trotskyists to join the ranks, or Thomas's initial opposition (springing from his lifelong hatred of war) to America's involvement in World War II.

Since the New Deal, government controls over the economy have steadily tightened. We have antidiscrimination laws about race, sex, and many other things. A federal agency does its best to prevent the sale of dangerous or worthless foods and drugs. There are laws against deceptive advertising. The government subsidizes large sectors of the economy, sometimes even helping big corporations out of financial straits. It funds scientific research and space exploration on a massive scale. It assists private universities. It promotes the arts. Can you imagine a conservative today who would like to see the government withdraw its insurance of his bank accounts? Yet when such insurance was first proposed, conservatives denounced it as unworkable socialism.

Although libertarians quarrel among themselves as much as democratic socialists, most of them agree that big government is bad and small government is beautiful. It is not that they disagree with socialists over what is evil—everyone assumes that starvation, sickness, poverty, unemployment, racial and sexual discrimination, and so on are evils—but that they are convinced that most federal efforts to combat such evils are worse than the disease. If big government will only trim its powers, stop needling business, stop telling free citizens what they must choose, the invisible hand of Adam Smith will work its sorcery and bring about the best possible form of justice. In brief, libertarians believe that social evils are more likely to diminish in the long run if Washington abandons its "overload" and stops trying to improve society.

One of the most widely discussed recent defenses of extreme libertarianism is a 1974 book called *Anarchy, State, and Utopia,* by Robert Nozick, a Harvard philosopher. Ironically, his office then adjoined that of Rawls, for whom Nozick professes unbounded admiration but with whom he vigorously disagrees. Reading Nozick's book has been for me a mystifying experience. Not the least of its idiosyncrasies is that a philosopher has managed to write a large book on political theory without mentioning Aristotle!

Although Nozick is far from a traditional anarchist, he recommends a state so feeble in powers, so close to the minimal state of Spencer, that it makes Friedman look like a socialist. The sole purpose of Nozick's night-watchman state is, as it was for his mentors Locke and Spencer, to prevent persons from infringing on the basic rights of others. In Nozick's words, it is "limited to the functions of protecting all its citizens against violence, theft, and fraud, and to the enforcement of contracts, and so on." If it goes beyond those aims, especially by forcing citizens to pay for welfare programs, it is immoral. In opposition to extreme anarchists, Nozick argues that the night-watchman state is just. In opposition to modern conservatives, liberals, and socialists, he argues that all "patterned" structures of compulsory redistribution are unjust. His vision of utopia is a nation that contains many small communities of variegated economic and political structures, including communities in which wealth *is* redistributed provided no one is compelled to participate in the redistribution.

Nozick's "entitlement theory," as he calls it, rests on a whopping metaphysical posit: that the right to acquire and keep money and property is one of the most inviolable of all human rights. Those who acquire wealth legally, he insists, without harming others, may do with it whatever they please. They may spend it, give it to anyone (including their children), gamble it away, or destroy it. It is immoral for the state to tax this wealth for any purposes except those of the minimal state.

Most anarchists regarded property, obtained by any means other than honest toil, as the primary source of social evils. "Property," said Pierre Proudhon, "is theft." For Nozick it is state taxation for welfare purposes that is theft. The state has no moral obligation to redistribute wealth. It is unjust to compel anyone to help the needy. All charity should be voluntary. If the poor cannot persuade the rich to take care of them, so be it. Nozick is blunt: "There is no justified sacrifice of some of us for others." If a ten-cent tax per year on the wealthy could be used to alleviate a small bit of human misery, he has said, the tax would be immoral.[12]

Nothing is easier than to make contrary posits about human rights. If, for example, the rights to adequate food and medical care are considered more fundamental than property rights, a welfare state that taxes and redistributes incomes to guarantee such rights would be more just than Nozick's minimal state. But Nozick will have none of this. He seems to say that if a nation is unable to prevent some of its citizens' starving to death without taxing others, it would be morally right to let them die rather than impose a tax and collect it by force. However, Nozick has an escape hatch. It may be necessary at times to violate property rights, he says casually in a footnote on page 30, "to avoid catastrophic moral horror," but he adds that he does not care to go into such complexities. Because Nozick ignores such details, it is hard to know what he means by horror. As Samuel Scheffler asks, in a persuasive attack on Nozick, "How many cripples and orphans would have to die in order to constitute a 'catastrophic moral horror'?"[13]

Libertarians constantly accuse liberals and socialists of wanting to do not the things that are really best for the poor, especially in the long run, but only those things that make them (in Irving Kristol's italicized words) "*feel* good and *look* good while doing good." Judging by Nozick's book, liberal do-gooders have a sound basis for their familiar counteraccusation. Libertarians often seem icily indifferent to human misery. They are content to allow large amounts of temporary suffering in the belief that, if their programs of noninterference with the free market are sound, great benefits ultimately will trickle down to the poor, and the injustices of society are more likely to vanish in the long run.

In the short run, unfortunately, people can perish. The great wave of Irish immigration to America in the early 1850s was the result of a potato blight that struck Ireland in the late 1840s. How did the leaders of Ireland meet this crisis? Instead of rationing wheat, or supplying free wheat to the starving, the price of wheat was allowed to float to normal free-market levels. The sellers of wheat made lots of money and those who could afford to buy it remained well fed, but a million poor people, unfree to choose and unable to persuade the rich to feed them, simply died. Another million left Ireland. The hand of Smith proved to be a clenched fist with brass knuckles.

Reviewers of Nozick's book (which, by the way, won a National Book Award) noticed that although Nozick expresses little compassion for the millions around the world who die needlessly every year from lack of food, he devotes many pages to the suffering of animals. Nozick is a confirmed vegetarian. Although his section on animal rights raises more questions than it answers, it gives a strong impression that Nozick feels it is morally wrong to eat any animal (including fish?). At the same time he is against a state promoting the health of its citizens by taxation. No one can doubt Nozick's brilliance, originality, and ebullience, but (as one of his critics has said) there is something "creepy" about his philosophy. Some of his fans have touted his entitlement theory as a new Kuhnian paradigm in political philosophy. Maybe so, but my guess is that he will turn out to be one of those philosophers who achieve temporary fame by adroitly defending a point of view that everybody else thinks outrageous. His nimble arguments may provoke learned critiques in academic journals, but they are not likely to have much influence, if for no other reason than that ordinary people and politicians will not be able to understand them.

Nozick likes to write long paragraphs that consist entirely of questions. Let me imitate it by asking some obvious questions about rights. Does a citizen have a right to_____? In the blank space we can put such things as a job, protection of savings, protection from poisonous foods and drugs, minimal education, adequate food, adequate medical care, old-age assistance, protection against hazards on a job, free libraries and parks, free fire protection, free vaccinations, clean air and water, and so on. Do residents of a city have a right to government aid if the city is destroyed by an earthquake?

Nozick obviously considers all or most of these rights desirable, but if I read him correctly, none are as fundamental as the right, stressed by John Locke, to keep money and property and to do with them whatever one pleases. As a consequence, the ideal state should not tax its citizens for any kind of public welfare, not even for schools. There may be suffering in the short run, but in the long run, Smith's invisible hand will do more for the poor than any government program financed by taxes.

Nozick's libertarianism has much in common with the philosophy of the Russian-born American writer Ayn Rand. Rand's cult of "objectivism," combining free-market libertarianism with a moral code based on "rational selfishness," made its biggest splash on college campuses around the turn of the fifties to the sixties. Its fading during the seventies was due mainly, I suspect, to its strident atheism, and its loathing of all forms of altruism and self-sacrifice. There is no mystery about why Roman Catholic conservatives, and Protestant fundamentalists of the new right, have little use for a hybrid produced by mating Milton Friedman with Madalyn Murray O'Hair. Nevertheless it is a sobering thought that Alan Greenspan, who was President Ford's top economic advisor, started his career as an avowed Randian.

Rand died in 1982. William Buckley, who couldn't abide her, wrote an amusing obituary in which he described his first meeting with the lady. Her opening icebreaker was: "You ahrr too intelligent to believe in Gott." Buckley quotes from a review that Whittaker Chambers wrote of one of Rand's books: "Out of a lifetime of reading, I can recall no other book in which the tone of overriding arrogance was so implacably sustained. Its shrillness is without reprieve, its dogmatism without appeal." [14]

I concur with those sentiments, though I cannot agree with Buckley when he calls Rand "an eloquent and persuasive anti-statist." I found her political views as simplistic as her ethics and metaphysics. She even looked favorably on the use of dynamite to make a point. Her best-known novel, *The Fountainhead*, ends when Howard Roark, a self-centered architect said to have been modeled on Frank Lloyd Wright, is acquitted by a jury. His crime, you may recall, had been to blow up his own housing project because its builders had altered his sacred architectural plans. Gary Cooper played Roark in a forgettable 1949 movie based on this absurd plot.

Less extreme than the libertarianism of Rand and Nozick, though pushing in the same direction—the direction of anarchism—are the views of a motley crew of writers and economists in the United States who, in spite of sharp differences, share a common enthusiasm for Adam Smith and a common disrespect for socialism and Lord Keynes. I refer to Milton Friedman and his monetarist followers, to activists in the Libertarian Party, to the supply-siders who once captured the mind of Reagan, conservatives who admire Buckley and Russell Kirk, and neoconservatives who look to Irving Kristol and Norman Podhoretz for pearls of wisdom. The next chapter will give my reasons for thinking that these Smithians (the best word I can think of that catches them all) are defending a cause as hopeless as the restoration of the Holy Roman Empire.

8

THE STATE:
Why I Am Not a Smithian

It has been well said: "If Milton Friedman had never existed, it would have been necessary to invent him."

—Paul Samuelson

To avoid business depressions, to stimulate economic growth, John Maynard Keynes stressed government efforts to maintain an adequate consumer demand. Today's supply-side economists, who in 1980 captured the mind and heart of Ronald Reagan, turn this around.[1] The United States and other democratic countries, they believe, have gone much too far in the direction of socialism and welfarism. The only way to revive the stagflating American dream is to stimulate the economy's supply side. Lower taxes on corporations and the wealthy, abolish minimum-wage laws, reduce welfare handouts, and get the government off the backs of business. Not until after-tax profits are sufficiently high, as they were in the golden past, will entrepreneurs find it worthwhile to take those risks so essential to a vigorous, expanding technology.

To dramatize the importance of lowering taxes, the supply-siders draw the "Laffer curve," a curve said to have been sketched on a cocktail napkin by California's economist Arthur B. Laffer when he explained his supply-side views to an official of the Ford administration. If federal taxes are zero, obviously the government gets no money at all. If taxes are 100 percent, it is just as obvious that nobody will work (the country would revert to a secret barter economy), and again the government would get nothing. So you draw a mysterious bell-shaped curve, the Laffer curve, that plots tax rates against government revenue; then you find on it the point E where revenues are maximized.

There is a big catch. Nobody knows what a Laffer curve looks like. George Gilder,[2] whose rousing defense of supply-side theory, *Wealth and Poverty*, sold so well in 1981 that he began to look for tax shelters, has a Norwegian elkhound named Laffer. Gilder calls the dog's tail a Laffer curve. It is not a bad model. The curve may symbolize the ancient and incontrovertible fact that when taxes are too high they are counterproductive, but otherwise it is about as much use to economists as an elkhound's tail.

There is another catch. Even if we knew what a Laffer curve looked like, we wouldn't know where along it to put the economy. Irving Kristol, defending supply-side in *Commentary*, admits he can't prove it, but he agrees with Laffer that we are "too far up" on the Laffer curve. He applauds Reagan's plan to slide down the curve by across-the-board tax cuts, arguing that if the rich were taxed less they would abandon unproductive tax-evasion schemes, and the government would get more money than it does now.[3] In the long run, as Gilder exclaims, "Regressive taxes help the poor!" Talk about the Laffer curve sounds impressive until you realize that it is just a trivial application of Aristotle's golden mean. Taxes are best when neither too low nor too high.[4]

But when are they neither too low nor too high? This is not easy to answer. Will lowering marginal tax rates on corporations increase employment enough to justify Reagan's welfare cuts? Maybe big corporations will use their tax savings for research and development, but maybe not. Maybe they will just use the money to buy other corporations, or to expand overseas where labor is cheap. Will lowering marginal taxes on the rich and middle class really cause them to save and invest more, or will they just spend more on conspicuous waste? Will broad tax cuts cause people to work harder, or will they work less because they can afford more leisure? As Galbraith has observed, the assumption that executives will experience a burst of creative energy if they have less taxes to pay implies widespread malingering on their part which simply is not supported by any evidence.

Even if Reagan's program stimulates production, will it hold inflation to an acceptable rate once the economy starts growing again? The phenomenon of stagflation is enormously complex and poorly understood. Surely it is obvious that big firms and big unions are not going to hold prices and wages down voluntarily, no matter how passionately a president jawbones, unless the country is near to collapse. A corporation or a union has too much to gain by disobeying, especially if some others obey. It could be that the only way to quench inflation without simultaneously increasing unemployment is by carefully applied federal controls on selected industries and unions. This, of course, is creeping socialism still so abhorrent to the American psyche that such controls may not be politically possible except in extreme emergencies.

To many ill-informed citizens, the notion of wage and price controls raises a specter of a mammoth bureaucracy to determine and enforce them, and the rise of criminal black markets. This, of course, is rubbish. Advocates of wage and price controls have in mind only controls on big corporations, big labor, and big farming, sectors where prices already are controlled, and where federal standards can easily be enforced. Nobody is suggesting price controls on the retail level where good old-fashioned Smithian competition still flourishes.

The sad truth is that economists don't know the best way to halt inflation. Empirical evidence is too thin. Few economists predicted stagflation, which today afflicts most of the world's mixed economies, and there is no consensus on either the causes of inflation or ways to cure it without producing social misery.

As to how Reagonomics will fare in the years ahead, economists can only guess. I am writing this soon after Reagan, with the help of his enemies in Congress and to the vast dismay of his conservative friends, has pushed through tax increases to partly offset the earlier cuts. But Reagan's economic program continues to be the same jumble of supply-side theory, monetarism, industry deregulation, and strange mumblings about the gold standard, a flat tax, a constitutional amendment requiring a balanced budget, and other fantasies. It is still what Kevin Phillips describes as a Rube Goldberg machine in which each triggering step has to work perfectly or the contraption fails.[5] It is still an effort, based on dream theory, to move America back to the days of Calvin Coolidge.

If Reaganomics has not worked by 1984, you can be sure that not a single supply-sider will blame supply-side theory, just as no monetarist will blame monetary theory. The failure will be blamed on such things as past administrations, Congress, David Stockman, Milton Friedman, unforeseen events, the liberal media, Reagan's unwillingness or inability to avoid compromises, insufficient time for tax cuts to stimulate growth, and other parameters.

Shortly before Reagan's election, Laffer was asked how it was possible for cuts in taxes to have an instantaneous explosive effect on the economy. Would it not take at least three years for the incentives to work? Laffer replied: "How long does it take you to reach over and pick up a fifty-dollar bill in a crowd?" After the economy had responded to Reagan's tax cuts by moving into a recession, Laffer told *The Wall Street Journal* that he really meant the incentive would *start* to act at once, but that the cuts would not pay for themselves until two to four years later.[6] In a long interview in *Barron's*, Laffer blamed the recession on the postponement of tax cuts, which he in turn blamed on David Stockman, the budget director. "Once we are in '83 and '84," he predicted, "we are going to be in a great economy. . . . There is no question of that in my mind. I couldn't be more certain of a proposition than I am of that." Asked what he saw as the greatest threat to this prophecy, he replied with one word: "Stockman."[7] The two had been good friends before Stockman broke the faith.

Monetarist Beryl Sprinkel, the Treasury Undersecretary, is equally optimistic. On *Wall Street Week* (November 5, 1982) he spoke with pride about how the Dow was rising, inflation steadying at 5 percent, interest rates plunging to single digits, and so on. The unfortunate but necessary recession, he said, had ended. The economy would soon be booming, and by the end of 1983 everybody would agree that Reaganomics had been a whopping success.

From my perspective, Reagan's attempt to free America from its bondage to big government resembles nothing so much as the plan devised by Tom Sawyer, at the close of *Huckleberry Finn*, to free Jim from slavery. Huck's commonsense advice was much too dull for Tom's romantic impulses. Here is how Tom reacted to Huck's plan:

> "*Work?* Why, cert'nly it would work, like rats a-fighting. But it's too blame' simple; there ain't nothing *to* it. What's the good of a plan that ain't no more trouble than that? It's as mild as goose-

milk. Why, Huck, it wouldn't make no more talk than breaking into a soap factory."

I never said nothing, because I warn't expecting nothing different; but I knowed mighty well that whenever he got *his* plan ready it wouldn't have none of them objections to it.

And it didn't. He told me what it was, and I see in a minute it was worth fifteen of mine for style, and would make Jim just as free a man as mine would, and maybe get us all killed besides. So I was satisfied, and said we would waltz in on it. I needn't tell what it was here, because I knowed it wouldn't stay the way it was. I knowed he would be changing it around every which way as we went along, and heaving in new bullinesses wherever he got a chance. And that is what he done.

For me it is as difficult to believe in the present powers of Smith's invisible hand as to believe in the magic of Glinda. Lacking today's federal controls, our economy periodically got so out of kilter that in the thirties, had the government not intervened with massive welfare programs, there would have been suffering and chaos of the sort that often leads to tyranny. It is easy to forget that before the crash of 1929, few economists believed that government had any responsibility at all for managing the economy. The concept of the gross national product was then unknown. Had it been known, economists would not have known how to compute it. (Even today they don't agree on how to compute the GNP.) The most a government can do about depressions, said Herbert Hoover, is let them "blow themselves out."

Milton Friedman's views are not that extreme, but almost. He thinks the government should cushion depressions, but only by manipulating the money supply. The Big Depression of the thirties, he is persuaded, can in no way be blamed on a failure of free-market capitalism. It occurred because the Fed failed to regulate money properly. Only a sound monetary policy, he is convinced, can prevent depressions and hold down inflation.

You might suppose that the supply-siders, who share Friedman's enthusiasm for Adam Smith, would be sympathetic to Friedman's monetary views—essentially a demand for a slow, steady, predictable growth of the money supply, keyed to a growth of GNP. This is not the case. Jude Wanniski, in his popular defense of Lafferism modestly titled *The Way the World Works*, has as low an opinion of Freidman as he has of Marx and Keynes.[8] None of the leading economic models, Wanniski believes, is accurate enough to explain the crash of 1929. He reminds us that Irving Fischer, the godfather of monetarism, issued almost daily statements in late October 1929 telling investors the economy was sound and to keep buying. "Stock prices have reached what looks like a permanently high plateau," Fischer declared just before losing about $9 million of his own money. Wanniski blames the monetarists for making the Depression worse than it would have been if the Fed had not listened to them.

What *did* cause the crash? Every economist who has written a book on this question is wrong. Wanniski, all by himself, has found the answer. "The stock market Crash of 1929 and the Great Depression ensued because of"—so help me, I quote verbatim from Chapter 7— "the passage of the Smoot-Hawley Tariff Act of 1929."

Jack Kemp, a former quarterback for the Buffalo Bills who is now the most vocal Lafferite in Congress, assures us (in his book, *An Amer ican Renaissance*) that Wanniski has "demonstrated beyond any rea sonable doubt" the truth of his remarkable discovery. (This statement is less surprising when you learn that Wanniski helped Kemp write his book.) Irving Kristol, who should know better, has hailed Wanniski's volume as "the greatest economic primer since Adam Smith." Laffer, on whose screwball theories the book is based, is less restrained. "In all honesty," he is quoted on the cover of the paperback edition, "I believe it is the best book on economics ever written."

Some Smithians, like some monetarists, believe that the best way to lower inflation is by letting a severe recession blow prices down. This is exactly what has happened under Reagan, whether intended or not, and it remains to be seen how far the administration will allow unemployment to increase before it tells the Fed to loosen the money supply. Kristol is to be applauded for taking a dim view of such a cure. A government might get away with it in pre-welfare days, he argues in his *Commentary* article, but no party can expect to stay in power if it permits a long, deep recession. We shall soon see if England's Iron Lady can survive the social costs of having taken this road. We shall soon see how Reagan and his party will fare if unemployment continues to be high in 1984.

Though he calls himself a neoconservative, Kristol's acceptance of federal controls to prevent needless suffering—welfarism but not paternalism is how Kristol likes to put it (yes, Virginia and North Carolina, this means that A meets with B to decide what C gives to D)—brings him so near to the kind of democratic socialism favored by his friend Daniel Bell that a strong shove could conceivably (though not likely) propel Kristol back into a neosocialist camp. This is even more true of Paul Samuelson, who describes himself as a "post-Keynesian eclectic." When Samuelson speaks of "structural changes" in the economy that are necessary to ease inflation, he may mean such an increase in government planning (preserving of course the welfare state and traditional liberties) that one could call him a closet socialist. Like Galbraith he sees the democratic mixed economies of the world as adopting the same basic strategies regardless of whether they are called socialist or capitalist. Both words, as I have said, are becoming so fuzzy as to be almost useless. There are countries in which groups calling themselves "radical socialists" actually want less government tinkering with the economy than some American political leaders who, under no circumstances, would call themselves socialists.

We who openly call ourselves democratic socialists, for want of a better phrase, believe as much as any Smithian in an untrammeled free market in every area where untrammelism actually works. We, too, oppose government overloads, if by this is meant attempts by the state to do more than it can do adequately. We socialists—perhaps now I should speak only for myself—recognize that citizens have the mysterious power of free will. (Economists seldom use such a metaphysical term; they prefer to hide it under such euphemisms as "capriciousness of expectations" and "mood management.") We, too, are aware of the impossibility in principle of transforming economics into a science with the predictive power of physics. Atoms, planets, and bees obey unalterable laws. Human societies don't.

That much we share with Smithians. But unlike most Smithians we are overwhelmed by a modern phenomenon which Smith could only dimly foresee. For Smith, a factory could consist of no more than a dozen people. Since his time, capitalism has seen the inexorable rise, as Marx correctly predicted, of mammoth corporations and multinationals that employ hundreds of thousands, and that behave like independent nondemocratic socialist states more powerful than small nations. In the United States, if you add the assets of Exxon and AT&T they just about equal the total assets of firms owned by single persons. About 80 percent of all sales are made by the five hundred largest firms. "General Motors," remarked Ralph Nader, "could buy

Delaware if Du Pont would sell it." Free of government regulations, oligopolies have the power to administer prices in ways that have little respect for the short-run fluctuations of a free market. What should an ideal state do about these behemoths?

Suppose a giant oil company, one of the Seven Sisters, gobbles up a dozen small independent producers. Is not competition drastically curtailed? The Seven Sisters, as we all know, collaborate for their mutual benefit by sharing pipelines, agreeing on prices, and in many other ways. Let us admit at once that the exploration, production, refining, transporting, and marketing of oil and gas is much more efficient if only one company, or a small number of companies, dominates the scene. Nothing is more wasteful than fifty companies extracting oil from one large pool as rapidly as they can, unshackled by laws regulating the spacing of wells and the speed with which they pump. The oil industry is a natural monopoly. The bigger the companies, the smaller their number, the less waste.

What policy should Smithians take toward such giant firms? Should the government try to break them up to restore competition and market-set prices, ignoring the waste that would result? Should it regulate the Seven Sisters to prevent abuses of their power, or take them over? Are the evils of private ownership of big oil less or greater than the evils of government ownership? If state ownership of natural monopolies and oligopolies is ultimately best, then attempts to break them up, even if possible, would not be desirable. Leave them alone, some socialists have argued (and many conservatives have feared!) to make the eventual paper transfers easier! After Mitterand nationalized France's strongly controlled banks and big industries, were there any visible differences in the way the managers behaved? It is a great irony that some conservatives who plead for a federal "hands off" policy toward megacorporations may actually be hastening the day when a strong government will take them over.

You will look in vain through Robert Nozick's *Anarchy, State, and Utopia* for light on these thorny questions. We are told that a state should not prohibit "capitalist acts between consenting adults." A clever phrase, but what does it mean? Does it mean that the state should not prohibit the formation of companies so powerful that they interfere with free markets? Nozick's book is not so much a defense of specific economic programs as it is a book offering no economic programs. With his central theme—that an ideal state should not be too small to do what it ought to do, or so large that it does what it ought not to do—who could disagree? It is as vapid as the statement that taxes should not be too high or too low, or the declaration of the German social democrats that government interference with competition should be neither too much nor too little. Evil is a bad thing.

On the practical level at which Friedman argues with Samuelson, and Samuelson argues with Galbraith, and Galbraith argues with Friedman, Nozick's pronouncements are either too lofty or too extreme to be relevant. His book is fun to read, filled as it is with amusing asides and bizarre arguments based on game theory, but it comes straight out of Oz. Behind its fantasy is a "me generation" approach to economics that differs little from Ayn Rand's. Leave me alone! Don't take any of *my* money. Don't trouble my conscience about corpses on the roadsides of Africa, or the unemployed, or the aged, or the sick who live where the only doctors are chiropractors and veterinarians. Don't worry over the possibility that if the poor get too miserable and too numerous they might burn down Boston, and Harvard Yard along with it. The poor will be taken care of, in the sweet by-and-by, by the prestidigitation of Smith's nimble fingers.

Although today's Smithians are more sophisticated than the early anarchist dreamers, they share with those dreamers a fervent hatred of big government, and for this reason their writings often reflect more sympathy for anarchism than for democratic socialism. Pierre Proudhon called his French anarchist periodical *La Liberté*, and in America, Benjamin Tucker called his similar magazine *Liberty*.[9] *Liberty* has always been the top buzzword for both anarchism and libertarianism. It is not surprising to find Nozick quoting Proudhon's famous tirade against the state, to learn that Friedman's son David, an economist at the University of California, Los Angeles, is an anarchist whose book, *The Machinery of Freedom: Guide to a Radical Capitalism* is much admired by his father. It is not surprising to find libertarians getting misty-eyed when they write about the Wobblies.

Capitalism versus socialism! The conflict, it seems to me, is almost obsolete. The burning question is not one of either/or. It is over the most desirable blend of free enterprise and state controls. In my view this is an open question involving both technical knowledge and moral assumptions. There may not even be a best mix, just as there may be no best system of voting or best city or best house or best spouse. The best mix may be so interwoven with cultural habits as to make it impossible to compare, say, Japan's best mix with ours. Variety itself can be a good. A world in which all economies were alike could be as dull and undesirable as a world in which all cities were alike, or a city in which all houses were alike.

To underscore the room here for legitimate debate, let me dredge up some memories of the time when I was an undergraduate at the University of Chicago, and Frank H. Knight and Jacob Viner were leaders of the "Chicago School" of economics. One of Knight's disciples and colleagues was a troubled young man named Henry C. Simons. His monetary views would later have a strong influence on Friedman, the man destined to become Simons's most eminent student. At that time the campus hangout was a bar on Fifty-fifth Street called Hanley's. It stayed open illegally after closing hours, and could be entered only by walking through an adjoining all-night restaurant, knocking on a back door, and being inspected through a small window. If you looked like a student or a faculty member, you were let in. Every night Professor Simons, who suffered from insomnia, would be there, sitting at a back table and mulling over the bulldog edition of the *Chicago Tribune*. In 1946, aged forty-six and in ill health, Simons died from an overdose of sleeping pills.

In 1934 the University of Chicago Press published a pamphlet by Simons entitled A *Positive Program for Laissez-Faire*.[10] It blew up a storm in academic circles, and is still cited as a basic reference on the Chicago School. When the pamphlet came out, I bought a copy and read it with mounting bewilderment. Simons, like Adam Smith, did not like monopolies. They were "malignant cancers," said Simons, to be "stamped out" as soon as possible. He recognized that they were inevitable in areas where competition would be wasteful, but since they provide no support for laissez-faire, and because it would damage the economy to break them up, he believed the state should own them outright rather than try to muzzle them. Accordingly, his pamphlet recommended that the government gradually take over such key industries as the railroads, public utilities, and "all other industries in which it is impossible to maintain effectively competitive conditions." Where free markets are possible, Simons wanted competition to be encouraged and enforced by regulations of the most extreme sort.

I could hardly believe it. Here was Simons, hailed as the prophet of a new laissez-faire, urging a policy of socialization so radical that Norman Thomas considered it premature! Thomas used to say that one of his recurring nightmares was dreaming that the government had seized the railroads. (Today, railroad passenger service has in effect been nationalized by a whopping federal subsidy to Amtrak, and a good portion of freight service has been nationalized under Conrail, not to mention the less visible subsidies to airlines and buses.) Thomas believed that a long period of education, and improvement in federal skills and morality, should precede such an extreme move. Otherwise would not a corrupt bureaucracy mismanage the railroads even more than their private owners? Not only did Simons recommend federal ownership of natural monopolies, he also favored extending government welfare services and tightening federal controls over advertising. After all, he argued, how can a consumer make a free and rational choice if he or she is brainwashed by Madison Avenue?

Can anyone except Milton Friedman and employees of advertising agencies seriously believe that the millions spent every year on huckstering cars, soap, cigarettes, beer, aspirin, deodorants, stomach-relief pills, hemorrhoid preparations, and so on, operate for the benefit of the consumers? Or the billion dollars that was spent in 1981 on nonproduct advertising by big companies just to improve their public image? ITT and sixteen other firms spent $10 million each. ITT's main concern was to combat a poll's finding that 60 percent of the public thought they were AT&T.[11]

Simons's views on monopoly may be embarrassing to today's Smithians; nevertheless there is as much disagreement among them over the structure of the best mix for an economy as there is among democratic socialists. Most native conservatives favor a variety of welfare programs as well as strong police forces and a large military establishment. Some—Kristol for instance—would like to see laws against pornography. Their disagreements, like those of the democratic socialists, are mostly over questions of degree and timing. What controls should be added, what dropped, what altered, and when is the best time to make a change? The line between democratic socialism and managed capitalism is not easy to draw. To me this gray "best mix" question is largely empirical. In the absence of a better phrase, I call myself a democratic socialist because, adding up the pluses and minuses, I believe our government should move circumspectly, always preserving democratic freedoms, toward a mixed economy in which there is more and better central planning than we have now.

As for the business community, how can it possibly agree on what government controls are best when the controls desirable for one company are undesirable for another? If a regulation helps A and injures B, obviously the managers of A will favor it and managers of B will oppose it. Have you ever met a businessman (or labor leader) capable of saying: "I know that federal law x will decrease my company's (union's) profits but I support it nonetheless because x is good for the nation"? Or a business manager (or labor leader) capable of saying: "Law x would greatly benefit my firm (union) but I oppose it on the grounds that it would be bad for my country"?

Eugene V. Rostow, the eminent Yale professor and frequent government official, is a highly paid consultant to AT&T. In 1980 Ma Bell gave him $180,000. Is it thinkable that Rostow would favor antitrust action against AT&T? In 1975 he wrote an article for *The New York Times* titled "Keeping Ma Bell in One Piece." The belief that what is good for company B is good for the country is a universal syndrome among those who work for B, whether it be Ma Bell, Bell's hardware store, or Dr. Bell, a dentist who has incorporated to save taxes.

Can you imagine an executive of Chrysler or Braniff, even though an admirer of Friedman, opposing government aid to his firm because he believes that when a big firm goes broke in a free economy it should be allowed to disappear? The fact is, some of the most regulated industries in the United States *want* to be regulated. It all depends, naturally, on whether the regulations help or hurt. [12]

At the time I write, certain car manufacturers would like to see federal action stem the flow of cars from Japan because the flow decreases their sales. But General Motors and Chrysler, which import cars, have a contrary view. Big banks want to be deregulated; small banks need regulations to survive. Big truckers and the Teamsters union want trucking regulated; small truckers don't. Big booze stores would like deregulation; mom-and-pop liquor stores fear it. Big TV stations deplore controls that hamper their freedom, but they want controls that discourage new stations and cable systems. Big gas wants federal help because without it Alaska's natural-gas pipeline could not be completed. The big airlines wanted deregulation until they found themselves in a destructive price war. Now they would like some regulations back. We are the only nation on earth that permits its airlines to be privately owned.

Jesse Helms, North Carolina's extreme rightist senator, is gung ho for unfettered free markets except when it comes to federal support of the tobacco and peanut growers of North Carolina. Tennessee senator Howard Baker is eager to get government off the backs of business except when it comes to federal aid for Tennessee's Clinch River breeder reactor. Have you ever heard of a congressman, Democrat or Republican, who breathed a word against federal subsidies and helpful regulations on the back of any major industry in his or her home state?

My father was a small independent oil producer, sometimes called a wildcatter, in Tulsa. One of our neighbors was a vice-president of Gulf. Both men were ultraconservative. When I was a child listening to them talk, it was apparent that my father heartily favored all federal regulations that helped the independents, and objected to all regulations that helped Gulf. Our neighbor had the reverse opinion. On these questions the gulf between Gulf and Gardner was unbridgeable.

"Get the government off the back of the oil industry" is a vacuous demand unless you specify which part of the industry you mean, and exactly what controls you want lifted. Take away all controls from the finding and production of oil and what happens? Does the hand of Smith take over? It does not. The hands of the Seven Sisters take over. And it is much the same with other major industries. Remove certain federal controls and the oligopolies grow fatter, the small competitive firms (and hence the free market) grow weaker. Remove other controls and it works the other way.

In 1981 the FCC lifted old regulations on AT&T, allowing it to enter the exploding market for computer data processing. AT&T is naturally delighted by this deregulation, but IBM, GTE, Xerox, and a hundred smaller firms who will be hurt by Ma Bell's power to eliminate competition, through its monopoly on long-distance telephone lines and its ownership of Western Electric, would much prefer to have the old regulations back. Is the free market served by the FCC's action? The answer depends on what business manager you ask.

Most economists and journalists who call themselves conservative are understandably vague on what to do about ways in which the megacorporations hinder competition. Sometimes they pretend that the giant firms are not there. At other times they pretend that they are just large versions of small businesses; in Galbraith's words, "Mobil is just the corner store grown up." Because the big corporations are not going to vanish—what they do can be done only by big corporations—what should the government do about them? Leave them alone and let them get bigger? Take them over? Try to regulate them so as to maximize competition? If the last option is chosen, the option favored by Kristol, then the task is not to abandon controls but to improve them. Here there are no simple guidelines for either Smithians or socialists because the issues are too snarled and technical.

If all the world's economists were stretched end to end—so goes a one-liner usually attributed to George Bernard Shaw—they still would not reach a conclusion. In 1980, on Larry King's radio talk show, I heard King ask Friedman why he and his colleagues so often quarreled. This, said Friedman, is a myth. Economics is a science. Economists agree on all basic issues. You mean, said the surprised King, that you and Galbraith have no fundamental differences? "Oh," said Friedman, "I thought you asked me about economists."[13]

Sidney Weintraub, coeditor of *The Journal of Post Keynesian Economics*, described Friedman's recommendations in 1980 to the government as a "surefire recipe for disastrous stagflation."[14] This, as we all know, is just what happened when Margaret Thatcher tried to follow Friedman's monetary strategy in England, but Friedman is predictably (and correctly) complaining that the lady failed to follow his advice. No doubt Friedman considers Weintraub not an economist. In mid-1982 Friedman began to complain (again correctly) that Reagan was not following his advice when he agreed to compromise with Congress on raising taxes. In his latest book, *Free to Choose*, Friedman not only never mentions Galbraith, he also never mentions Samuelson. Maybe he considers Samuelson also not an economist.

On November 1, 1981, I heard Friedman and Walter Heller interviewed on television by Louis Rukeyser. Friedman gave Reagan "high marks" for his tax cuts, budget cuts, and deregulations. (The tax cuts are welcomed by Friedman mainly because they force budget cuts.) His advice to Reagan was to hold firmly on course, and never, under any circumstances, at any time, agree to tax increases. Heller disagreed. He compared the conflict between Friedman monetarism and Laffer supply-side to "two scorpions in a bottle," and urged Reagan to boost taxes as soon as feasible to avert disaster.[15] The following month Herbert Stein declared: "If the captain of the ship sets out from New York harbor with a plan of sailing north to Miami, 'Steady as you go!' will not be a sustainable policy, and that will be clear before the icebergs are sighted." I assume that Friedman doesn't think Heller or Stein are economists.

At least Uncle Miltie is candid and consistent, and as invulnerable in debate as a fundamentalist preacher. Instead of shouting like Herbert Armstrong, "Wake up, America, and blow the dust off your Bible!" Friedman is shouting, "Wake up, America, and blow the dust off *The Wealth of Nations!*" Some of his views are anathema to business leaders and opposed even by many economists who call themselves conservative. He is for unrestricted free trade, and believes that a unilateral lifting of all tariffs would do more to combat administered prices by corporations than any kind of trust busting. If the Japanese can make better and cheaper cars than we can, we should all buy Japanese. Not a penny should go to Chrysler, or to Lockheed or Braniff or any other company that stumbles in the market place. He wants to replace all welfare programs by a negative income tax—a novel plan also favored, by the way, by such liberals as Samuelson and James Tobin, and advocated by the three Presidents who preceded Reagan. (It has about as much chance of becoming law as the "flat tax" now being touted.) He recommends a voucher system that would give parents the freedom to choose between public and private schools.

Most of Friedman's opinions spring from an intense devotion to Smith's invisible hand, and a firm conviction that almost all efforts by government to improve the economy or aid the poor, here or anywhere else, are less effective in the long run than doing nothing. In the eleventh revised edition of his celebrated textbook *Economics*, Samuelson suggests that before you read one of Friedman's persuasive books you should ask yourself if it is possible today for a professional economist to be against the following:

1. Social security
2. Flood relief
3. Farm legislation
4. Pure food and drug regulation
5. Compulsory licensing and qualifying of doctors
6. Compulsory licensing and qualifying of car drivers
7. Foreign aid
8. Public utility and SEC regulation
9. Post office monopoly
10. Minimum wage
11. Peacetime drafts
12. Wage and price controls

13. Anticyclical fiscal and monetary policies
14. Auto-safety standards
15. Compulsory and free public schools
16. Prohibition of heroin sales
17. Stricter federal and state standards for migrant workers
18. Minimum interest-rate ceilings on usurious lenders
19. Truth-in-lending laws
20. Government planning
21. Pope Paul VI's encyclical naming central economic planning the key to economic growth[16]

Go through Friedman's books and his *Newsweek* columns, Samuelson comments, and you will find him opposing every one of the above features of our mixed economy. Although you may agree with some of these negations, Samuelson adds, you must admit that to argue relentlessly for all of them is a startling indication of how far Friedman pushes his Smithism.

Friedman is as down on the American Medical Association as he is on the Pure Food and Drug Administration. Both block the freedom of Americans to choose their own doctors, even if they are quacks, and the freedom to choose their own remedies, even if they are worthless or harmful. Better an occasional thalidomide tragedy, better to have worthless drugs on the market (and greater profits to the drug hucksters), than to have an agency which, in Friedman's opinion, blocks the introduction of new medicines in its zeal to protect consumers. The FDA, he declares flatly, "has done more harm by retarding progress in the production and distribution of valuable drugs than it has done good by preventing the distribution of harmful or ineffective drugs." Friedman would like to abolish the FDA totally, not reform it. Naturally he is opposed to all forms of socialized medicine.

On some issues I find myself more in agreement with Friedman than with his antagonists. In the absence of a public sufficiently informed and motivated to support democratic socialism, political compromises and halfway measures that involve federal tinkering with the economy can indeed be worse than doing nothing, or doing something so trivial that it allows free markets to solve a problem better than bureaucrats can solve it. (There is a wise old chess adage: When in doubt, push a pawn.) Our health system is a case in point. No other industrialized democracy has such a shoddy way of meeting the health needs of its citizens. As Michael Harrington has put it, "The American system combines the worst of capitalism with the worst of socialism." On the whole, however, I see Friedman as a witty and doctrinaire radical who is fighting for a mystical vision that had much to recommend it in the days of Herbert Spencer, but today is as simplistic as, say, Say's law, or Laffer's curve, or Von Thünen's marvelous square-root formula for the wage every worker ought to get.

Friedman is one of those economists—he has his doubles in all economic schools—who seems to me similar in many ways to a chiropractor. Suppose you suffer from a lower-back pain. You go to a reputable M.D. and what happens? He is too busy to listen to all your complaints, and seems to have no precise idea of just what is wrong. Instead of a diagnosis, he proposes numerous laboratory tests, all costly and time consuming. But if you go to a chiropractor, he will diagnose your trouble in ten minutes. It is a subluxation of a certain vertebra, and he assures you it will clear up after a few inexpensive spinal rubs. He listens patiently to all your troubles, and replies with unbounded confidence and authority. Indeed, he talks more like a doctor than a real doctor. Of course the reason the real doctor is vague is because he knows too much. He knows that a lower-back pain can have a hundred different causes, and that he would be a fool to commit himself until he has sufficient facts. Given the current state of affairs in medical science and practice, and the public's medical ignorance, if chiropractors didn't exist, our society would have to invent them.

I once heard Norman Thomas deliver a ringing sermon in the University of Chicago Chapel, where his old friend Charles Gilkey was the dean. At the finish the congregation did something unprecedented. It stood up and applauded. The sermon's theme couldn't have been simpler or more fundamental. It was on the right of children and older people not to die by the millions from lack of food in a world capable of eliminating hunger.

It is a sobering thought that with all our vaunted science and technology we are still far from refuting the dismal prophecies of the Reverend Thomas Malthus, though for reasons Malthus did not anticipate. An agricultural technology for feeding a world population many times its present size is already here; only social and political barriers keep the food from getting to the starving.

I know that accurate statistics about world hunger are unavailable. I am aware that estimates of world population can be off by hundreds of millions, and that malnutrition is the fuzziest of concepts. From my perspective, both the optimists and doomsdayists who write popular books about world hunger have a distressing lack of humility in extrapolating to the future on the basis of shaky information, imprecise terminology, complex parameters, and vast uncertainties about social and political change.

The point I wish to make, however, is as undeniable as it is depressing. Even though there may be grounds for long-range optimism, the short-range problem of hunger remains a terrible reminder of how far social progress lags behind the progress of science. "Gigantic inevitable famine," as Malthus called it— "the last, the most dreadful resource of nature" for checking population growth when it outruns food supply—still stalks the world. The number of hungry people around the globe is certainly increasing in absolute numbers, and may even be increasing at the moment (because of inflation) as a percentage. It takes a lot of blind faith, and a peculiar insensitivity to suffering, to believe that Smith's hand is the best way to give millions of starving children the right to live.

Norman Thomas may have been weak in his knowledge of philosophy and economic theory but he was strong in love and compassion. Consider one small instance. During World War II our government herded 110,000 persons of Japanese ancestry (75,000 of them American citizens, all but 5,000 citizens by birth) into ten concentration camps where they were kept for three to four years. They had commited no crimes. It is no good to say that this monstrous violation of civil liberties was necessary to prevent sabotage or spying, or to preserve their safety. No comparable program was even suggested for Americans of German or Italian descent. No Japanese were interned in Hawaii.

Who protested? Not the communists or their lobotomized fellow-travelers. After all, one must show no mercy to possible enemies of the Soviet Union! Not the conservatives or the liberals. Except for some ineffective church groups and a few independent thinkers such as Eugene Rostow, they were all caught up in a racism bred by war hysteria. President Roosevelt ordered the internment; Congress approved; the Supreme Court validated.

Earl Warren actively supported the evacuation, as did other liberals: Francis Biddle, William Douglas, Tom Clark, Carey McWilliams, Walter Lippmann, Hugo Black, Henry Stimson, Abe Fortas . . . the list is endless. (Some of them later regretted their words and actions.) No college students demonstrated. Even the national office of the American Civil Liberties Union, in spite of divided opinion among members, remained officially silent. Only one notable American cried shame: Norman Thomas. From left, right, and center, the only vigorous protests came from Thomas and his democratic socialists. Here is how Thomas expressed himself in a magazine article:

> In an experience of nearly three decades I have never found it harder to arouse the American public on any important issue than on this. Men and women who know nothing of the facts (except possibly the rose-colored version which appears in the public press) hotly deny that there are concentration camps. Apparently that is a term to be used only if the guards speak German and carry a whip as well as a rifle.[17]

American liberals still feel twinges of guilt about the Red "witch hunt" that came later. Comic and reprehensible though it was, it was trivial beside the suffering inflicted so senselessly upon, and endured so patiently by, our Japanese minority. Yes, their suffering was mild compared to that of the millions of Jews murdered by Hitler, and the even larger number of victims killed by Stalin without regard to race, color, or creed.[18] I am also aware that the incarcerated Japanese were eventually compensated in part for financial losses.

As for the victims of Hitler and Stalin, it is good to remember that American liberal and conservative leaders were as quiet about these crimes as they were about our Japanese concentration camps. Thomas's efforts to persuade Roosevelt to open America to German Jews fell on uncomprehending ears. When Thomas, John Dewey, Sidney Hook, and other democratic socialists spoke out about the Russian purges and death camps, they were roundly denounced by fellow-travelers and ill-informed liberals as reactionary, red-baiting, pro-fascists, as little to be trusted as the editorials and stories about Russian famines that were appearing in the Hearst papers, and which happened, by the way, to be true.

Few liberals read or cared to read the 800-page report, *Not Guilty*, issued in 1938 by a committee chaired by Dewey that was formed to investigate the Moscow trials. Corliss Lamont, than whom no fellow-traveler ever more consistently fellow-traveled, regarded Dewey and his friends as "completely discredited enacters, conscious or unconscious, of Hitler's well recognized strategy of sowing misunderstanding, suspicion and hostility between Russia and Western democracies . . . you are all . . . simply an ignominious spot of mud whirling down the great sewer hole of history." [19]

A depressing anthology ought to be assembled some day of quotations from leading liberals and intellectuals of England, America, and Europe who steadfastly refused to listen to what leaders on the noncommunist left tried to tell them about Stalin. To me the incident that best highlights this sordid tale was Vice-President Henry Wallace's visit to Magadan in 1944. Magadan was the capital of the Kolyma slave-labor system in the gold-mining area of northern Siberia. Although it was well known to be one of the most notorious of the labor camps, Wallace toured the region without once suspecting that Magadan was anything but a happy, thriving pioneer town!

Elinor Lipper, who was there as a prisoner, has a chapter about Wallace's visit in her book *Eleven Years in a Soviet Prison Camp*. The scene was high comedy. Wallace and his party, which included Owen Lattimore, were easily gulled by taking down all the guard towers, keeping the prisoners out of sight, and dressing pretty office girls as swineherds. The ladies had difficulty with some of Wallace's knowledgeable questions about pigs (asked through John Hazard, his interpreter), but poor Wallace suspected nothing. He described Magadan in glowing terms in his book *Soviet Asia Mission*, and Lattimore did the same in an article in *National Geographic* (December 1944). "There has probably never been a more orderly phase of pioneering than the opening up of Russia's Far North under the Soviet," wrote Lattimore. To which Elinor Lipper replied: "This is absolutely true. What other government would send hundreds of thousands of its own citizens every year to forced labor in new territories?"

When Lipper's chapter on the Wallace visit ran in the *New York Post* (June 11, 1951), Wallace sent the *Post* an incredible letter which it published on June 20. "It was not until long afterward," said Wallace, "that I knew that slave labor camps existed. The testimony of those who have escaped from the camps indicates that Communist Russia treats political dissidents in much the same way as czarist Russia but on the whole less humanely."

This prompted me to make a comment which the *Post* ran on June 24. I listed six excellent books in English about the labor camps, all published before 1943, and pointed out that under the czars the number of prisoners never exceeded 50,000.[20] Only a small fraction of this number were political prisoners. That a man of Wallace's stature could have written a book about Russia without bothering to read anything critical of Stalinism is now hard to believe, yet such was the temper of the times. I recall lending a copy of David Dallin's *Forced Labor in Soviet Russia* to a liberal friend, only to have him return it unread on the grounds that Dallin had been a Menshevik and therefore couldn't be trusted. In France, Albert Camus tried to convince his former friend Jean Paul Sartre about the horrors of Russian slave labor, only to be held up to ridicule in Simone de Beauvoir's novel *The Mandarins.*

Wallace was sufficiently enlightened by 1952 to call the Soviet system "something utterly evil," but it took him a long time to learn what Norman Thomas and his friends had tried to teach him for twenty years. In 1948, when Wallace ran for President as a Progressive, the American Communist Party, which then controlled the Progressive Party, bamboozled Wallace with as little difficulty as did the fake lady hog farmers in Magadan. I agree with Dwight Macdonald's characterization of Wallace (in his book *Henry Wallace: The Man and the Myth*) as the "most boring and humorless egomaniac on the American political scene since William Jennings Bryan."

Much as I deplored the know-nothing antics of Senator Joseph McCarthy and his friends, who, as Thomas once said, didn't know the difference between communism, socialism, and rheumatism, it must be admitted that the blindness of American liberals and intellectuals to the evils of the Soviet system was a major cause of the slow swing to the right that is still with us. If you think *blindness* is too strong a word, I recommend the following painful experiment: Go to a large library and read the accounts of Stalin's purge trials in *The New Republic, The Nation,* and in Walter Duranty's dispatches to *The New York Times.*

I know of no political leader in American history, other than Thomas, who so consistently raised a booming voice of indignation whenever and wherever injustice was being done. Who knows when we shall see his like again? On Park Avenue, in Manhattan, there is a Norman Thomas High School. I would be surprised if any high school were named after Milton Friedman or any other contemporary Smithian. I doubt if anyone will ever refer to Friedman, or to Buckley or Kristol or President Reagan, as the "conscience of America."

9

LIBERTY:
Why I Am Not a Marxist

*How can I accept the doctrine which sets up as its
bible, above and beyond criticism, an obsolete
textbook [Das Kapital] which I know not only to be
scientifically erroneous but without interest or
application to the modern world?*

—JOHN MAYNARD KEYNES

"Liberal" is an even cloudier conception than "socialist," but I think
one thing that separates most of us who call ourselves democratic socialists from most of those who prefer the liberal label is a keener perception of flaws in the economic and political structures of modern
democracies. No one is more aware than a democratic socialist of the
low caliber of most U.S. Presidents and congressmen, of the similarity
(rhetoric apart) of Republicans and Democrats, and of our crazy system of campaigning and voting which can permit the election of can-
didates considered incompetent by a majority of the electorate. There
are voting systems much superior to ours which work quite well in
other countries.[1] We even vote for politicians and judges whose very
names are unknown to us until we enter a voting booth.

No one is more amused than a democratic socialist by the gaudy
vulgarity of a party presidential convention, with its carefully rehearsed
"spontaneous" demonstrations and the bellowing of ignoramuses who

have few goals beyond getting elected or reelected. Politicians of both parties frequently do not believe and sometimes do not even understand the remarks supplied by their speech writers and public relations advisers. What is worse, melodramatic phrases in the speeches of both liberal and conservative politicians are often empty of all content. A hilariously supreme moment in the campaign of Senator Ted Kennedy, when he ran against Jimmy Carter for the 1980 presidential nomination, was when he shouted that there are three ways to cure unemployment—more jobs, more jobs, more jobs![2] Yes, and there are three sure cures for inflation—stop prices from rising, stop prices from rising, stop prices from rising! No one saw more clearly than most democratic socialists, in contrast to most liberals, the pious lying and blatant hypocrisies of John Kennedy's Camelot.

No one is more aware than a democratic socialist of the repressive aspects of big labor: the racism of some craft unions, the "invisible handshake" with big business in boosting inflation, unashamed cooperation with organized crime, and crude delaying tactics against computerized technologies that would enormously benefit consumers. When all is said and done, is labor's opposition to robotics really much different from Frédéric Bastiat's cynical proposal that woodchoppers in France be required by law to use blunt axes to make their tasks last longer and thereby provide more jobs? One would be hard put to prove that the aims of the Teamsters Union have more in common with the ideals of democratic socialism than, say, the aims of the American Medical Association or the National Association of Manufacturers.

No one is more aware than a democratic socialist of the creaking machinery that seems permanently locked into our economy: the madness of the stock market, tax systems that steadily grow more baroque and incomprehensible, the inefficiencies of government bureaus, the venality of bureaucrats, the corruption of welfare programs. You don't have to remind us that if unemployment benefits exceed the wages a person could get on a job, that person will prefer to stay on welfare and will conceal secretly earned income. Irving Kristol is telling us nothing we don't know when he says, "Dependency tends to corrupt and absolute dependency corrupts absolutely."

We cheer as loudly as any Smithite when a local group finds a way to deliver city mail faster and at lower cost than the archaic post office. At the same time we are aware of comparable inefficiencies in privately owned companies. Megacorporations can become as snarled in red tape and clumsy decision procedures as any government bureau. It is sometimes as hard for a big firm to get rid of an incompetent manager as it is for a government agency. Do bureaucrats really waste more money and time than the managers of Exxon? Did any state-owned manufacturer of cars around the world make as many bad judgments as Chrysler? Americans are still so frightened by domestic socialism that in 1980 the stockholders of American Motors actually voted to let the company be taken over by Renault, a firm nationalized by Charles de Gaulle and now owned by the French socialist government!

The problem of government inefficiency is not much different from the same problem in corporate management. To a large extent it is a problem in social science for which there are no clear answers. The task is not how to get rid of big business or big government, since neither is possible. The task is how to improve big business and big government. Clearly, the road to an efficient democratic socialism is as long and agonizing as the road to an efficient free-market economy must seem to those who call themselves conservatives.

The reader surely knows by now that I believe Karl Marx is of no help in smoothing any of the economic roads that are open to us. I agree with the statement made by Keynes in 1931 that provides this chapter's epigraph. Marx's towering influence on history resulted primarily from his rhetoric—his passionate attacks on the evils of unregulated capitalism and his apocalyptic visions of the future. His whopping conceptual errors, his colossal egotism, his angry intolerance, his male chauvinism, his wildly inaccurate prophecies, his ponderous Hegelian baggage, his simpleminded materialism, all added up to so many excrescences that H. G. Wells once likened them to Marx's enormous beard. Wells saw that beard everywhere, on busts, portraits, and statues, when he made a trip to Moscow in 1920, a trip he described in an unjustly forgotten little book called *Russia in the Shadows:*

> About two-thirds of the face of Marx is beard, a vast solemn woolly uneventful beard that must have made all normal exercise impossible. It is not the sort of beard that happens to a man, it is a beard cultivated, cherished, and thrust patriarchally upon the world. It is exactly like *Das Kapital* in its inane abundance, and the human part of the face looks over it owlishly as if it looked to see how the growth impressed mankind. I found the omnipresent

images of that beard more and more irritating. A gnawing desire grew upon me to see Karl Marx shaved. Some day, if I am spared, I will take up shears and a razor against *Das Kapital*; I will write *The Shaving of Karl Marx*.[3]

The trouble is this: Once Marx is shaved of irrelevancies, what remains looks so little like Marx (what *did* the fellow look like under all that brush?) that calling it Marxism seems to me another glaring misuse of ordinary language.

The same thing happens, by the way, when Freud is shaved. Take away the fantasies and errors of psychoanalysis, and what is left is so close to the common heritage of pre-Freudian psychiatry that there is no need to keep calling it Freudian. It is astonishing how few people realize that Freud was no more the first to discover the role of unconscious motives than Marx was the first to discover the role of profit motives. Just as I do not look favorably on the recent revival of Marxism in democratic countries, especially among young scholars,[4] so I would be similarly appalled if a revival of interest in psychoanalysis took place, as it no doubt will, among young psychiatrists. Going over newly discovered documents by Marx and Freud, to find out what those garrulous gurus *really* believed and at what time in their lives, may provide challenges for historians, but they strike me as having as little relevance to modern problems as examining ancient Hebrew documents to find out exactly what Jehovah meant when he talked to the Prophets. Marx and Freud have had their day. Let them find their appropriate niches in history.

A modern physicist does not call himself a Newtonian or an Einsteinian or a Bohrian. A modern biologist has no compulsion to call himself a Darwinian or a Mendelian. Why should democratic socialists call themselves Marxists, especially in America and Canada where so much prejudice exists against the word? Why damage a socialist program by calling it Marxist even though you may be convinced that in his heart Marx believed in democracy? In my opinion, the sooner democratic socialists, abroad as well as here, stop calling themselves Marxists the better. They have nothing to lose except rusty ideological chains. Our own doyen of democratic socialism, Michael Harrington, has become a much more effective heir to Norman Thomas since he stopped feeling obligated periodically to intone Marx's name.[5]

As for the form Marxism has taken in Russia, China, and other countries that call themselves communist, the failure of those countries to escape from a tyranny indistinguishable from fascism except in its mythology has long been apparent to everyone who is not a victim of what a friend likes to call *cerebral dormitosis*. In view of this fact, Susan Sontag's famous *mea culpa* speech in 1982 at Town Hall in Manhattan, in which she announced her stunning discovery that communism is a bad thing, struck me as the funniest event on the radical front since Eldridge Cleaver discovered Jesus.

It was funny on two levels. Here was Miss Sontag, an intelligent woman approaching fifty, professing to be suddenly aware of something Mary McCarthy knew when she was eighteen. Even funnier were the boos and hisses that greeted her speech, and the tortured replies that surfaced in *The Nation*, *The Village Voice*, and other publications.

Sontag was, of course, exactly right when she said that anyone reading *Reader's Digest* during the fifties and sixties would have learned more truth about the Soviet Union than someone reading only the *The Nation* or *The New Statesman*. It would have been even more to the point had she cited the thirties and forties, and nice if she had mentioned a few democratic socialist periodicals, not just a mass-circulation lowbrow magazine that hired some anticommunist ex-leftists like Max Eastman to write about Russia. Even so, it is good to know that Sontag considers herself a democratic socialist, and one must applaud her courage in saying plainly, to many who obviously did not want to listen, that for half a century large numbers of American liberals and radicals have been had.[6]

They were had not because their hearts were evil, but because they were ignorant and gullible. Their flimflammability is easier to understand than the opinion, still held by many radicals, that Marx continues to have something of significance to say about the problems of today's economics. The truth is that Marx is now as irrelevant as Smith. The great capitalist barons of the past have no counterparts today. The real owners of our giant corporations, the millions of stockholders, play no roles in managing these oligopolies.[7] The big firms are in the hands of professional managers and technical experts whose names most stockholders would not recognize if they heard them. Although on top levels the pay of some executives may be large (in 1981 more than fifty U.S. executives had annual salaries above $1 million, some in excess of $5 million), their principal motive is to keep the company alive and growing. They maximize profits not for themselves but for stockholders, for those whom Galbraith describes as the "unknown, anonymous and powerless persons who do not have the slightest notion of whether their profits are, in fact, being maximized."[8]

There is no way to eliminate these impersonal behemoths unless you also wish to eliminate such things as cars, telephones, television, airplanes, and modern weapons of war. And there is no way that the technostructure, to use Galbraith's term, can function without managing prices well enough to avoid the chaotic short-term effects of numerous parameters that are inescapable aspects of the real world. Yes, monopoly competition of a sort still prevails—aluminum versus steel, wood and glass versus plastics, and so on, and classical competition is still vigorous on lower levels of the economy—but within the technostructure the picture is a far cry from the simple free-market capitalism of Adam Smith.

The classical and neoclassical models, as some economists like to say, ignore "real time." They assume that money changes hands immediately, but of course it doesn't. There are innumerable delays. Big business has to make "forward contracts" with labor, shelling out higher wages long before it makes and sells the products the workers will be paid to make. In setting prices, big firms must try to anticipate the effects of decisions not only by labor, but by other firms, by branches of the government, by governments of other nations where they have interests. They must try to guess future public moods. Will consumers want big or little cars three years from now? A bad guess by General Motors could mean a loss of millions.

In the simple Eden of free markets, unemployment ought to lower wages. But in the real world, wages tend to go only one way. Unions may grudgingly accept wage freezes, as some are doing now, but a reduction? Never! As a result, wages stick like a wheel that can turn only clockwise because of a ratchet. Moreover, workers are afflicted by what Keynes called a "money illusion." They naïvely suppose that all wage increases are real; then, when they find prices also going up, they feel cheated even though there may actually have been a modest increase in their real income. Hence their constant demand for still higher wages, which in turn push prices further upward.

In an idealized free-market economy, workers who lose their jobs will sell their house, pack up their possessions, and move with their families to another region where jobs are available. If trained for skill

x, and the new job requires skill y, they will learn skill y. In the real world it is not easy to sell a house, pull up roots, and move to another town. It is not easy to abandon a trade in which one is experienced and learn a new one. A few individuals may be capable of changing their abode and way of life quickly, but for most workers it takes time; so much time, in fact, that after a worker has mastered a new skill and moved to another spot, the economy may have altered so radically that nothing was gained by the change.

No one denies that in the long run the laws of supply and demand influence the wages and prices set by the technostructure. We don't need Milton Friedman to tell us that. The point is that labor unions, government regulations, government subsidies, the power of oligopolies to administer prices, and many other things all play havoc with free-market mechanisms. Eventually the market will "clear," but it may take years for prices to spiral around what economists call the "cobwebs" on their charts before they settle into equilibrium, and by that time the parameters usually have thrown the prices into other spirals. Conservatives see these time lags as brief and the waste they produce, perhaps even social distress, as small. Liberals and socialists see the lags as long and the waste enormous.

In any case, there is no way to force classical free-market mechanisms into the technostructure, not to mention the excessive amount of government control that would be required to keep them there. Laws against monopoly, for example, may prevent the titans from overt collusion, but they manage prices just as well by tacit understanding that is as impossible to prevent as clandestine signaling in bridge tournaments when the stakes are high.

The old trust-busting of Teddy Roosevelt has become a futile exercise in nostalgia, kept alive by small groups of sentimental liberals and conservatives, and by the stratospheric fees of lawyers. In early 1982, after thirteen years of costly litigation, the Justice Department dropped its antitrust action against IBM. As an encore, it abandoned nine years of unsuccessful efforts to break up the oligopoly of the Big Three breakfast cereal companies: Kellogg, General Mills, and General Foods. Curiously, these were decisions that produced unified applause from many liberals, conservatives, socialists, and even Friedman! "What sense does it make," asked Lester Thurow, "to consume so much time and talent to debate whether people are spending a tenth of a cent too much for Kellogg's corn flakes?"[9]

As for AT&T, which the Justice Department supposedly busted with so much fanfare at the same time it dropped its other antitrust actions, it was not really much of a bust. The Bell System was indeed ordered to sell its twenty-two local-service companies, but these were the troubled, unprofitable "railroads" of the Bell System. The regulations of a 1956 consent decree were lifted, allowing Ma Bell to give birth to "Baby Bell," a subsidiary called American Bell that will soon be invading the exploding electronic fields of cable television, computer communications, data processing, computer terminal equipment, and other aspects of the coming Information Age. By retaining Western Electric, Bell Labs (one of the world's finest research centers), and its monopoly on long-distance lines, AT&T may soon be providing homes with news and advertising on screens connected to telephone lines, perhaps even on newspapers printed by a telephone attachment. As a result of the government's actions, Ma Bell is likely to grow even fatter, and the competition between local phone companies may only produce inefficiency and higher prices than otherwise would have prevailed.

There is no way to stop the steady march of technology into awesome, unknown territory. Our nation now faces increasingly fierce competition from the thriving economy of West Germany and the rhythmic, clean, steely efficiency of Japan's manless factories where tireless robots work around the clock—some of them making other robots—with no person around at night except a lonely watchman. The surest way to lose the race for cheaper cars and smaller, more powerful computers would be to break up General Motors and IBM, and chop government funding for basic research. Small may sometimes be beautiful, but if a small and beautiful nation like Japan thinks a big, computerized, robotized technology is beautiful, the international hand of Adam Smith is likely to slap down any economy that pins its hope on the domestic hand to regulate its technostructure.

At the time I write (1982) the country is being swept by a wave of corporate mergers. Not only does Reagan not object, but (surprise!) neither do many liberals. Even big labor does not seem to mind. "It's saving the jobs of workers," said Douglas Fraser, president of the United Auto Workers. "I'm for mergers particularly where you can strengthen the companies. . . . In the short pull for Chrysler, and the long run for Ford, it's almost a necessity. You would get economies of scale and more profitability, which would enhance the security of the workers. . . . You don't have to break up General Motors; they've got all they can handle from foreign competition. Even if GM would gobble up Chrysler and Ford now, the competition is so stiff from the Japanese that it wouldn't be a tragedy anymore."[10] The handshake between big labor and big business is becoming less invisible!

To argue the other side, big companies can reach a point at which additional increase in bulk may not increase efficiency. It may just increase bureaucratic fumbling, and induce a complacency that discourages innovation. Most of all it increases the concentration of political clout in the hands of fewer and fewer decision makers. The pros and cons are enormously tangled, and knowledge of the probable consequences of the new takeovers hard to come by. The truth is, there is little consensus among top economists, of all political shades, on the best approach to take toward the goliaths which are steadily growing wider and taller.

Of one thing we can be sure. Smith and Marx have little to say that will help us know what is best to do. A government takeover of the giants is no solution, even if it were politically possible. Conservatives are surely right in warning that such a revolution at this time, in the United States, would lead to corruption, economic stagnation, and political tyranny. Nor is there any way to break up the giants and restore old-fashioned Smithian individualism. How can a government that wants to survive bust half the American economy? It could be done only if some sort of grotesque revolution put the nation in the hands of a regime of radical Smithites capable of fracturing the big corporations and multinational conglomerates into small competing firms, and with the strength to keep the giants from regrouping. Paradoxically, both tasks would require an enormous increase in the size and power of the federal government. How to handle this inescapable trade-off between oligopoly and free competition is as difficult a problem for democratic socialism as it is for democratic capitalism, or any other ism that wants to preserve a mixed economy.

Since the Supreme Court broke up Standard Oil, the elephants of American business have grown more elephantine. Ironically, as Galbraith points out, the government's feeble efforts at trust busting have not only left the elephants undamaged, they have at the same time prevented the ants from collaborating to get bigger. How can it contribute to free-market competition when the government forbids two small companies in industry *x* from merging to form a larger company that could genuinely compete with the biggies of industry *x*?

Conglomerates are growing by leaps and bounds. ITT (International This and That) owns Wonder Bread, Hostess Twinkies, Burpee Seeds, Scott's lawn products, the Sheraton hotel chain, and hundreds of other businesses (car rentals, insurance companies, mutual funds, publishing houses, to name a few) that have nothing to do with telephones or telegraphs. Did you know that Armour and Company is now owned by Greyhound? That Gulf & Western owns Madison Square Garden, Simon & Schuster, and firms that make movies, cigars, clothing, pulp, steel, and a few score other things? That Coca Cola recently bought Columbia Pictures? That 7-Up, now advertising that its product is healthier than soft drinks like Pepsi-Cola which contain caffein, is owned by Philip Morris? [11] No person thinks that nicotine is better for you than caffein, but let's not forget that Philip Morris is not a person.

It is pleasant to see Smithians sporting neckties with Smith's profile on them to remind us all of the free market's indispensable role in any democratic mixed economy. At least Smith's face is less vulgar than the silver dollar signs that Ayn Rand's "objectivists" liked to wear. But any conservative who imagines that Exxon and General Motors behave like rugged individualists, and that classical competition can be extended throughout the technostructure, is living in a fantasy world.

Today's most pressing economic questions involve complexities—subtle shades along endless continua—that were unknown to Smith and Marx. Consider one such question: To what degree should the group decisions of megacorporations be free of government interference? "Spending by government must be limited to those functions which are the proper province of government," Reagan told Congress in 1981. Thank you, Mr. President, for this enlightening remark! The real debate, of course, is over what functions are proper. And this is a technical question with no easy answer in any country, including the Soviet Union.

Most of the planning in Russia is by the state, with growing efforts to stimulate incentives by enlarging the autonomy of corporations. Here in the United States the major planning is still by big corporations, but subject to increasing government control. Although the U.S. and the U.S.S.R. show no signs of converging in their political systems or in their respect for human rights, they do seem to be converging in the way their technostructures operate. It is not a convergence toward free-market practices so much as a convergence toward committee plan-

ning by relatively independent giant corporations. The United States
and Japan may also be growing more alike as old antagonisms here
between management and labor grow weaker, and individualism in
Japan grows stronger. At any rate, in democratic societies with advanced technologies, the line between decision making by private corporations and decision making by the state is steadily blurring. Here is
how Galbraith puts it in *The New Industrial State*:

> Were it not so celebrated in ideology, it would long since have
> been agreed that the line that now divides the public from
> so-called private organization in military procurement, space ex-
> ploration and atomic energy is so indistinct as to be nearly im-
> perceptible. Men move easily across the line. On retirement,
> admirals and generals, as well as high civil servants, go more or
> less automatically to the more closely associated industries. One
> experienced observer has already called these firms the "semi-
> nationalized" branch of the economy. . . . Increasingly it will be
> recognized that the mature corporation, as it develops; becomes
> part of the larger administrative complex associated with the state.
> In time the line between the two will disappear. Men will look
> back in amusement at the pretense that once caused people to
> refer to General Dynamics and North American Aviation and
> A.T.&T. as *private* business.

If by economic socialism you mean something like the present Soviet economy, in which the technostructure is completely state-owned
and all basic decisions are made by the state, then I certainly am not a
socialist. If you mean a mixed economy and a welfare state such as
ours, half free-enterprise for small business, half dominated by monster corporations that are semi-autonomous but increasingly under
state regulation, then I am a democratic socialist.

I am not happy with the term, but I can't think of a more honest
one. Because I favor a mixed economy, I could call myself a democratic capitalist, but that would imply that I want less state planning,
not more. Tom Hayden and his wife, Jane Fonda, call their present
program "economic democracy." Hayden insists that this is not socialism, because it stresses the roles of consumers and workers in government planning. Okay, so I'm an economic democrat. I could also call
myself a social democrat, a conservative radical, a radical conservative,
a libertarian socialist, a progressive, a neo-liberal, a neo-capitalist, a

neo-Keynesian, a post Keynesian, a humanistic economist,[12] or a dozen other equally confusing and almost meaningless labels now floating about.

Perhaps I like the word *socialism* for sentimental reasons. Of course I am only a writer. If I were running for a political post I might find it expedient to abandon the word. Perhaps the word does not deserve to survive. Maybe the point of view I hold would benefit enormously from a name not yet invented. It is hard to say. At the moment I am hoping the word can be revitalized in such a way that it will preserve its continuity with democratic socialists of the past, and at the same time broaden and deepen in meaning to reflect new economic knowledge and the complexities of modern technology.[13]

Whatever it is called, there is no way our economy, with its mammoth industries and awesome war-making power, can return to those earlier Smithy days when the entire economy could actually be regulated, after a fashion, by free-market mechanisms. Exactly how future planning will be made, by what groups and for what moral ends, I do not pretend to know. As I never tire of saying, there may be no best way. There may be many ways, equally good, for balancing government controls with the free decisions of big corporations and small businesses. And of course the entire process is interfused and shaped by moral ends that lie outside economic questions altogether. There is no way an ideology can escape the human conflict between egoism and altruism. For a Smithian, especially a Roman Catholic Smithian, original sin is too deeply ingrained in human nature to be significantly modified by new social structures. For the democratic socialist there is hope for some modification. The truth is, we don't know yet the extent to which egoism can be curbed by education and other environmental forces. What we do know is this: Society is poorly served by a government that leaves business entirely alone, and even more poorly served by a government that takes all business over.

I see our country, like its sister democracies, bewildered by conflicting religious faiths and a multiplicity of moral standards, held back by inadequate knowledge in the social sciences, yet engaged in a vast, bumbling attempt to advance the Open Conspiracy as best it can. The ongoing debate over the nature of the best economic system is essential to this attempt. It is sad we are not moving faster, but in the perspective of world history I am surprised we have moved so fast and come so far. With the usual caveats about a nuclear holocaust and the threats of overpopulation, what can we lose by being hopeful?

The steel mill sky is alive.
The fire breaks white and zigzag
shot on a gun-metal gloaming.
Man is a long time coming.
Man will yet win.
Brother may yet line up with brother:

This old anvil laughs at many broken hammers.
There are men who can't be bought.
The fireborn are at home in fire.
The stars make no noise.
You can't hinder the wind from blowing.
Time is a great teacher.
Who can live without hope?

In the darkness with a great bundle of grief
the people march.
In the night, and overhead a shovel of stars for
keeps, the people march:
"Where to? what next?"

Forgive me, admirers of Pound and Eliot, for taking familiar lines from a popular poet instead of from a poet whose stanzas can be understood only by professors.[14] I do not know where we are going or what is next. "It is very difficult to predict," said Niels Bohr, "especially the future." Like Wells's, my moods alternate between optimism and despair, but with optimism dominant. "While there is a chance of the world getting through its troubles," said Wells (in his novel, *Apropos of Dolores*), "I hold that a reasonable man has to behave as though he was sure of it. If at the end your cheerfulness is not justified, at any rate you will have been cheerful." Let me close by quoting Wells again in one of his cheerful moods. It is the final paragraph of his *Open Conspiracy:*

The Open Conspiracy is the awaking of mankind from a nightmare, an infantile nightmare, of the struggle for existence and the inevitability of war. The light of day thrusts between our eyelids, and the multitudinous sounds of morning clamour in our ears. A time will come when men will sit with history before them or with some old newspaper before them and ask incredulously, "Was there ever such a world?"[15]

10

THE GODS:
Why I Am Not a Polytheist

Sometimes we'd have that whole river all to ourselves
for the longest time. Yonder was the banks and the
islands, across the water; and maybe a spark—which
was a candle in a cabin window; and sometimes on
the water you could see a spark or two—on a raft or a
scow, you know; and maybe you could hear a fiddle or
a song coming over from one of them crafts. It's lovely
to live on a raft. We had the sky up there, all speckled
with stars, and we used to lay on our backs and look
up at them, and discuss about whether they was made
or only just happened. Jim he allowed they was made,
but I allowed they happened; I judged it would have
took too long to make so many.

—Mark Twain, *The Adventures of Huckleberry*
Finn

We are all, as commentators on *Huckleberry Finn* like to remind us,
living on a raft, on the old rickety earth, drifting down the long river of
dark time. Above our heads, day and night, are the almost countless
stars, emblems of an almost measureless universe. Was our universe in
some sense, a sense we can convey only by a crude metaphor, "made"
or did it "just happen"? It has been said that all philosophers can be
divided into two categories: those who divide philosophers into two
categories and those who don't. I belong to the first. I believe that the
dichotomy between those who believe in a creator God and those who
do not is the deepest, most fundamental of all divisions among the
attitudes one can take toward the mystery of being.

In line with the practice I have tried to follow throughout this book,
I take the word *God* to mean what I believe it means and has always
meant to most philosophers and theologians in the history of Western
thought, as well as to almost all ordinary people. As I use the term,

God is a God who is in some way outside our universe, who in some manner created the universe, who has some kind of plan for humanity and for every person, a God to whom we can pray, above all a God who sustains our hope for immortality. A personal God. Yes, the God of Christianity, but not only of Christianity. The God of Judaism, of Islam, and hundreds of smaller faiths. The God of Plato (yes, Plato!) and Kant and Charles Peirce and Miguel de Unamuno and a thousand other eminent philosophers and writers who were theists unshackled by the doctrines of any organized religious institution.

I take for granted that we cannot "know" anything about God's existence or nature in the way we can know the truth of a logical or mathematical theorem, or in the way we can know, with varying degrees of assurance, the truth of a scientific fact or law or theory. Nevertheless, every person who has even the weakest impulse to think occasionally about existence must build some sort of model, held together by filmy metaphors, that expresses his preferred way of approaching the ultimate mystery. To an atheist the model is an intricate, perhaps infinitely complex, structure that has either always existed or "just happened" to emerge, slowly or explosively, from the void, possessing nothing resembling a mind, as uncaring about the destinies of you and me as are the planets in our solar system or the molecules within our toenails. As Chesterton says, in an essay on Shelley, to an atheist the universe is "the most exquisite masterpiece ever constructed by nobody."[1]

Let us not waste time distinguishing the atheist's model from the agnostic's. It is trivially true that there is no way to prove God's nonexistence. Someone says: "I don't believe in God, but of course I can't be absolutely certain there is no God. Therefore I call myself an agnostic." Is not that person taking a position indistinguishable from the vast majority of thinkers who have called themselves atheists? Is there any significant difference between not believing in God and believing there is no God, or not believing in an afterlife and believing there is no afterlife?

On the other hand there may be individuals with so little metaphysical curiosity that they really don't know whether to believe in God or not. I have never met such a person. Perhaps they exist, but I would be as surprised to come upon one as I would be to find a playing card that had fallen on the floor and remained balanced on one edge, or a Buridan's ass that had starved to death between two piles of hay.

There are cosmologists who are unsure of the reality of black holes, and who have no opinion about life on Titan—indeed, I myself am an agnostic with respect to both those conjectures—but the question of God's existence is too charged with emotion to permit this sort of neutrality.[2] I would not know what to say to a genuine theological agnostic. How can you talk about music to persons so tone-deaf that they tell you, in complete honesty, that they cannot decide whether music is worth listening to or not? "There is no greater fool," Bismarck is said to have said, "than he who says 'there is no God,' unless it be one who says he does not know whether there is one or not."

For those who decide they are not atheists or agnostics, a variety of God models are available. There is a continuum, or rather many continua, that stretch from the personal God of traditional theism, the creator God, to the impersonal God of pantheism. But before explaining (in the next chapter) why I prefer the traditional model to the pantheistic, we must consider a curious question that no longer seems to trouble Western thinkers. Why *one* God? Why not a multiplicity?

I share with William James—see the Postscript to his *Varieties of Religious Experience*—a belief that this is not a frivolous question. After all, millions of intelligent people have been and are comfortable with a pantheon of deities. Speaking for myself, I cannot see how one can read Plato's dialogues or Cicero's *Treatise on the Gods* and continue to regard Greek mythology as on a level of superstition far below the Christian mythology of the Middle Ages and the Renaissance. It is always easy to see alien myths as inferior to familiar ones. A Roman Catholic may be unable to imagine how a devout Greek could suppose that bright-eyed Athena would actually help Achilles defeat Hector. As for archangel Michael helping Joan of Arc, that of course is a different matter! An alien myth tells how a god dropped a garment from the sky. Can anything be more absurd? A medieval myth tells how Mary dropped her girdle from the sky to reassure doubting Thomas when he was again having misgivings about his faith.

"Who today takes such medieval legends literally?" an enlightened Catholic asks. Well, it depends on what legends you have in mind. The assumption of Mary's body? Jesus walking on the water or turning water into wine? God commanding Abraham to murder his son? It is true that no Christian today takes literally such colorful nonbiblical myths as the legend of the Wandering Jew, but neither do educated Hindus take literally similar legends in their own traditions. Nor did Plato or Cicero. Plato, remember, wanted to keep Homer out of the hands of school children because he regarded Homeric mythology as blasphemy against the gods. It is hardly fair to interpret bizarre Judaic-Christian myths as symbolic of deep truths, then compare this practice with the literal beliefs of ignorant people in modern India or in ancient Greece and Rome.

There are, it seems to me, two strong reasons for the popularity of polytheism in so many cultures. One surely is that it is difficult for many people to feel a close personal bond with a god so mysterious and transcendent that the god can be approached only with fear and trembling. One longs for the warmth of some humbler deity, a god with a nature closer to our own. It is the great secret of the popularity of the Christian doctrine of the Incarnation. The other reason is that if a single deity is modeled as a person, if there are no other gods, how can one escape the feeling that God must be exceedingly lonesome? We know that no human child can grow up to be a person without having complex interactions with other human beings. If we apply the single-person model to God, how can we avoid the notion that God must somehow participate in a society of equals?

Both these impulses, I believe, lie behind the polytheism of Christianity. Polytheism? Well, let's look at the facts. First of all, many passages in the Old Testament clearly indicate that the ancient Hebrews believed Jehovah to be the most powerful of many gods. More than one famous theologian of the early Christian church did not deny the existence even of Greek and Roman gods. Pagan deities were for them the personifications of Christian demons.

The Christian Trinity consists of God the Father, God the Son, and God the Holy Ghost. The Son actually walked the earth as a man, and more completely a man than any Greek deity who impersonated a mortal. Nor must we overlook the countless angels, including Satan and his minions. For Catholics, Mary has been elevated to the rank of a sinless woman who miraculously gave birth to God, and who did not die a natural death. In the very first sentence of the Bible the word for God is *Elohim*, a plural word that could have been translated as "the gods," although paradoxically, as Jorge Luis Borges somewhere points out, the verb "created" is singular in the original Hebrew.

Does this passage not suggest, I can hear a Christian responding, the mystery of the Trinity—three persons incomprehensibly united in One? Yes, but there are similar mysteries uniting One and Many in religions more polytheistic than Christianity. Paul Tillich was often accused of being an atheist. Cannot he also be accused of being a quaternarian? Did he not speak of the "God above the God" of orthodox Christianity, an ultimate "ground of being" indistinguishable from the Gnostic God above the creator; or Brahman, who manifested itself in the great Hindu trinity of Brahma, Vishnu, and Shiva? In the eleventh canto of *Don Juan*, Byron refers to an argument that:

> . . . *at once established the whole Trinity*
> *On so uncontrovertible a level*
> *That I devoutly wished the three were four,*
> *On purpose to believe so much the more.*

I am not suggesting that there are no significant differences between the Christian Trinity and the four gods of Hinduism; only that Christianity satisfies more of the polytheistic impulse than, say, Islam or the theology of late Judaism. It is with ill grace that Christians belittle tales about gods who once were, or still are, worshiped and loved in traditions other than their own.

The impulse toward polytheism springs up in unexpected places. Edgar Allan Poe, in his prophetic essay on cosmology, "Eureka" (it defends an oscillating universe), proposes that each galaxy has its special god. Deist Benjamin Franklin wonders in his autobiography if our solar system is in the hands of a local god. Lord Dunsany often expressed sorrow over the passing of the Greek gods and told how he filled this void by creating a polytheism of his own—the great gods of Pegāna.

One thinks also of James Branch Cabell and the gods who look down on Poictesme. There is a marvelous scene in *Jurgen* where we learn how Koshchei, busy with other cares, forgot about the earth until he learned from Jurgen's grandmother about the millions of pious souls who lived and died believing in the Christian Heaven and Hell.[3] Koshchei, "who made things as they are," obtains a copy of the Bible and carefully studies the book of Revelation. "I see," says Koshchei. "The idea is a little garish. Still—!" And so Koshchei, moved by the grandmother's strange ability to love, creates not only a Heaven and a Hell, exactly as he found it described, he also creates the biblical God, and God's angels, causing them all "to have been here always, since the beginning of time, because that, too, was in the book." Yet even Koshchei, who made things as they are, may be the "butt of some larger jest."

Why must we assume, asks Philo, in the fifth part of David Hume's *Dialogues Concerning Natural Religion*, that a single deity made heaven and earth?

> A great number of men join in building a house or ship, in rearing a city, in framing a commonwealth: why may not several deities combine in contriving and framing a world? This is only so much greater similarity to human affairs? By sharing the work among several, we may so much further limit the attributes of each, and get rid of that extensive power and knowledge, which must be supposed in one deity, and which, according to you, can only serve to weaken the proof of his existence. And if such foolish, such vicious creatures as man can yet often unite in framing and executing one plan; how much more those deities or demons, whom we may suppose several degrees more perfect?

No natural phenomenon, Philo continues, suggests by analogy that the creator must be a single god. We see one side of a balance scale go up. If the other side is hidden, how can we know whether there rests upon it a single weight or a set of weights? And if the weight required on the concealed pan exceeds anything in our experience, the hypothesis of a single weight becomes even more dubious.

As you see, dear brothers and sisters, I share with Dunsany a wistful sadness over the deaths of the beautiful gods of ancient pagan cultures, the deities in whom no one now believes. And I am not alone in this emotion. Only a few years ago David L. Miller, a professor of religion at Syracuse University, wrote a fascinating little book called *The New Polytheism: Rebirth of the Gods and Goddesses*. Miller actually recommends reviving Greek mythology—not of course as tales to be taken historically, but as gorgeous parables which he thinks have more to say to our "pluralistic sensibilities" and our tolerance for diversified religious faiths than the pallid monotheistic myths of the Bible.

In view of these sentiments why do I avoid calling myself a polytheist? Let me confess at once that in the strictest sense I do not know—how could anyone know?—whether God is One or Many. Concepts of the Divine obviously are vague projections of our experience onto the wall of eternity. Who are we to trace sharp outlines? That which is totally beyond our comprehension can be modeled only in familiar symbols, and like the mystery of free will it may be that God is best modeled by what seems to us are conflicting symbols. Nevertheless, let me try to explain why I find the monotheistic model preferable to the polytheistic one.

My wife and I own a cat we call Eureka, after Dorothy's cat in the fourth Oz book. In Eureka's dim mind she must be a kind of polytheist, fed as she is by the two of us, and by neighbors when we take a trip; surrounded on all sides by giant creatures who move about on their hind legs to do things utterly beyond her ken. But we who are her gods have a power of speculation far greater than that of her tiny feline brain. We can, as she cannot, wonder why we exist. If someday we receive messages from another planet, from minds as much above our own as our minds are above those of our pets, or if earth is ever visited by such superbeings, we would certainly not conclude that they made the universe any more than we did. We are thus caught up emotionally (not rationally!) in an infinite regress of higher and higher intelligences similar to the hierarchy of angels about which medieval Schoolmen professed to know so much. There is an unavoidable longing, at least for me, to "go to the limit," as William James once expressed it—to apply a singular term to the ultimate mystery.

What are the sources of this desire? First of all, and obviously, there is Occam's razor, a preference for the simplest hypothesis that does all we want it to do. This is not to deny that God, in some unfathomable way, may be a plurality. But since we have no way of knowing this, indeed we have no way of even knowing what it means to say God is One or Many, there is a pragmatic convenience in using the simpler term.[4] Those who feel a need to imagine God as a society can adopt the Christian paradox of asserting a plurality that, in some unthinkable way, is also a unity. Viewed in this manner, I see the Trinity as a profound and satisfying metaphor, though no more so than the quaternity of Hinduism or the multiplicity of Greek and Roman mythology.

Here is Chesterton defending the Trinity with characteristic Chestertonian flourishes:

> The God who is a mere awful unity is not only a king but an eastern king. . . . For to us Trinitarians (if I may say it with reverence)—to us God Himself is a society. It is indeed a fathomless mystery of theology, and even if I were theologian enough to deal with it directly, it would not be relevant to do so here. Suffice it to say here that this triple enigma is as comforting as wine and open as an English fireside; that this thing that bewilders the intel-

lect utterly quiets the heart: but out of the desert, from the dry places and the dreadful suns, come the cruel children of the lonely God; the real Unitarians who with scimitar in hand have laid waste the world. For it is not well for God to be alone.[5]

Although I cannot fault the sentiment behind these lurid lines, I suspect that GK would have been reluctant to grant the same depth of mystery to the Hindu foursome or the Greek multiplicity, and that his disrespect for Islamic monotheism did not extend to the monotheism of Moses. Three persons also can be lonely. Of course there are all those bright angels surrounding the throne of the Christian God, but we must remember that even the highest-ranking angels are separated from God by a qualitative difference far greater than the difference between apes and us. Life would be rather desolate for three human beings who lived in a society consisting entirely of monkeys.

Because I do not know if God is One or Many, or even what it means to say God is One or Many, I am quite content to leave this unanswerable question unanswered. Because I have no preference for the number three over four, or over seven or forty-seven or any other number, because I do not know if any number means anything when applied to God, I find it adequate for my needs to think of God as a Unity. We see this impulse toward monotheism operating even in the great polytheisms of the past. There are many gods, but almost always One among them towers over all the others.

There is, however, much more to the impulse than the convenience of simplicity. To split God into many gods is to slide our model in the direction of an ugly anthropomorphism. Just as we cannot conceive of a human society except one in which individuals differ in their personalities, desires, and abilities, so we cannot conceive of a plurality of gods without assuming that they, too, have individualities and limitations. What would be the point in distinguishing between Venus and Diana, or between Vishnu and Shiva, if they were in every respect identical? If there were just two equal gods, Thomas Aquinas sensibly argued, one would necessarily have some trait the other lacked; hence neither could be perfect.

In a later chapter I will return to this notion of an imperfect, "finite god," but now I wish only to speak of how the many-gods model creates for the man or woman of faith a disturbing problem. To whom should one pray? If God is a society, perhaps its members, like the gods of Greece, are in conflict with one another. A Greek warrior could pray to Athena, but there was always the possibility that her wishes might be countermanded by Apollo or some other deity. Of course one may assume, as does Christianity, that God is a small family, completely united with respect to all plans and decisions for humanity. "I and the Father are one," Jesus is reported to have said. But to assume this is to move away from threeness toward oneness, and it is precisely this longing for an ultimate God, at least in our Western traditions, that overrides the need for an unlonely god. One desires communion with a God who has no rivals, with a God who provides escape from the anxiety of trying to imagine a plurality of gods or an infinite ladder of unequal gods.

William James summarized the argument with his usual felicity: "Unless there be one all-inclusive God, our guarantee of security is left imperfect. . . . If there be different gods, each caring for his part, some portion of some of us might not be covered with divine protection, and our religious consolation would thus fail to be complete."[6]

James himself seemed to prefer, at least in the Postscript of his *Varieties* from which I have just quoted, a pluralistic view. "Thus would a sort of polytheism return upon us. . . ." I am not sure how serious he was; the view is not stressed elsewhere in his writings. It certainly is not the view of ordinary people, or of most philosophers and theologians, in cultures that stress God's unity. Even in polytheistic cultures there have been great philosophers, such as Plato and Aristotle, who went beyond the mythology of their time to the concept of a supreme deity.

My own preference—and this book is little more than a slovenly summary of my preferences—is for the monotheistic model. I have no desire to worship a god, or a set of gods, who are not God. At the same time I confess I can no more answer the question of One versus Many, when I speak of God, than I can say whether God is male or female, tall or short, thin or fat, or has one, two, or ten thousand eyes. Because we cannot know what such attributes mean when applied to God, if they mean anything at all, what is gained by treating them as questions worthy of prolonged debate?

Having said this I must say one thing more. I believe with Sören Kierkegaard that a primitive polytheist, praying with honesty and passion to one wooden idol among many, is closer to God, expressing a truer religious emotion, than a philosophical monotheist who tries to pray, or who cannot pray, to an abstract impersonal deity of the sort I shall consider in the next chapter.[7]

11

THE ALL:
Why I Am Not a Pantheist

> "In the name of God, what is this! Are we going to
> believe out of hand that the highest Being has in fact
> no motion or life or soul or intelligence—a thing that
> neither lives nor thinks, but remains forever fixed in
> solemn, holy, unconscious vacuity?"
>
> —THE STRANGER, IN PLATO'S Sophist

The many meanings of *pantheism*, one of philosophy's most protean words, fall on a rough spectrum that stretches from the personal God of theism to a hazy view that is almost indistinguishable from atheism. Usually the word means a belief in something midway between atheism and theism, a god remote from the personal model, coeternal with the universe rather than a creator, more immanent than transcendent, and unconcerned about human history. It is not easy to pray to a pantheistic deity. It is not easy for a pantheist to hope for immortality.

I earlier spoke of the rhetorical dodge, often practiced by philosophers who like to play language games and send up verbal smoke screens, of purloining an enemy's terminology and redefining its important words. It is hard to understand, but outspoken atheists sometimes like to talk as if they believe in God. In his book *A Common Faith*, John Dewey suggests that *God* be redefined to stand for all those forces in nature and society that work to bring about the ethical ideals of humanity.

> It is this *active* relation between ideal and actual to which I would give the name "God." I would not insist that the name *must* be given. There are those who hold that the associations of the term with the supernatural are so numerous and close that any use of the word "God" is sure to give rise to misconception and be taken as a concession to traditional ideas. [1]

Nevertheless, Dewey hoped that the use of the word could protect the atheist's emotions "from a sense of isolation and from consequent despair or defiance." Humanism, for Dewey, was the "common faith" of the world, destined to replace archaic theisms. We can best escape despair not by faith in God and hope for another life, but by joining H. G. Wells's Open Conspiracy, by collaborating with one another to make a better world. Like Wells at a youthful stage of his career, Dewey saw no objection to humanists appropriating *God* and using the word in the Pickwickian sense he suggested.

In an earlier chapter we saw how the pragmatists' effort to redefine truth has faded from the philosophic scene. My impression is that humanist suggestions for redefining God and religion failed at the out-set to gain many adherents. Wells quickly saw the semantic dishonesty of his own redefinition and went back to calling himself an atheist. Even Dewey's good friend and disciple Sidney Hook could not engage in such transparent flimflam. "By taking over the word 'God' as the religious humanists do," he wrote, "the waters of thought, feeling, and faith are muddied, the issues blurred, the 'word' itself becomes the object of interest and not what it signifies." [2]

More curious even than Dewey's willingness to use the word *God* is its use by many modern theologians who call themselves Protestants. Consider Shailer Mathews, who was dean of the University of Chicago's Divinity School and a leading exponent of what used to be called the "social gospel." For Mathews, God is a name for the "personality-producing forces" of the universe. Such forces obviously exist, as our presence on earth testifies; therefore everybody is automatically converted by definition to a belief in God.

The "theology" of Paul Tillich is a more complicated case in point. Tillich defended his metaphysics with such infuriating vagueness that it is often impossible to know exactly what he meant, but I side with those who find it hard to distinguish Tillich's God from what atheists mean when they talk about all that is. It sounds as if Tillich is saying something deep when he speaks of the "ground of being," "being-as-such," and the "transcendent unconditioned," but what these terms finally come down to mean is simply that which is, taken in its incomprehensible totality.[3] Is there not a touch of deception when a man who professes to be a Protestant theologian calls the "ground of being" God, then discards as unworthy all those aspects of the person model that were stressed not only by the Reformers but by Jesus himself?

It is not Tillich's pantheism that most puts me off—after all, it is a respectable metaphysical way to look at things. I am put off by the hypocrisy of parading such pantheism as the culmination of Protestant theology. There is a point beyond which it seems unfair to go in trying to reform a religious tradition. Better abandon it altogether than struggle to change it so radically that its founders would no longer recognize it as their own. Can you imagine the reaction of Luther or Calvin (or Jesus!) to a concept of God so lacking in the attributes of a person as to be almost identical with Brahman, or the Tao, or the All of Buddhism, or the Absolute of Hegel and the post-Hegelian pantheists?[4]

If God is merely another name for Being, or an impersonal ground of being, then only the terminology distinguishes pantheism from atheism. On the other hand, because we experience such a minute portion of the Whole, there is a sense in which the nature of Everything transcends our comprehension. Approach the mystery of Everything with humility, with such human emotions as love, hope, awe, terror, and so on, and your attitude can move extremely close to that of a theist toward a personal God. At this end of the pantheist spectrum a pantheist may think of the All as containing something, or being something, similar to a human mind. We are caught here in a welter of conflicting languages, with their respective ways of manipulating symbols, and with varying emphases that spring from different emotional attitudes. The result is that the great pantheistic gods of the past, in the systems of Plotinus, Spinoza, Fichte, Schelling, Hegel, Royce, Emerson, Whitehead, and so many other thinkers and religious movements of both East and West, become extremely difficult to distinguish from one another. To make matters worse, many great religions have combined pantheism and polytheism, displaying a plurality of gods that are all manifestations of an ultimate impersonal and transcendent ground of being.

One variant of pantheism lies a bit off the mainstream. This is the view that God is a World Soul, or *Anima Mundi*, a consciousness that arises from the structure of the universe in a way analogous to the way our consciousness arises from the molecular structure of our body, or that an anthill or beehive takes on the traits of a living individual organism. The God of Samuel Alexander, for instance, is a world consciousness slowly emerging as the universe evolves. In Alexander's vision this development is unending, the World Soul becoming more and more powerful and Godlike but never reaching final perfection.[5]

Modern science fiction has given a new twist to this vision by imagining that computers grow more and more intelligent until they become creator gods or God. Thus, in Frederic Brown's short-short "Answer," when a mammoth brain (formed by the linking of 96 billion planetary computers) is asked "Is there a God?" it replies, "Yes, now there is. . . ."

Isaac Asimov's "The Last Question" is the classic expression of this theme. As entropy slowly, relentlessly pushes the universe toward its ultimate "heat death," computers steadily improve. But each time a computer is asked how the death of the universe can be circumvented, it replies, "Insufficient evidence for a meaningful answer." Billions of years later, all independent consciousnesses have been fused into one universal consciousness, a supercomputer known as AC that operates in a hyperspace. After the universe dies, AC broods over the chaos for a timeless interval. Suddenly the data is sufficient:

> *And AC said, "LET THERE BE LIGHT!"*
> *And there was light—*[6]

Although pantheism comes in many trappings, I think it fair to say that because it identifies God with Nature, or with some aspect of Nature, the pantheist God tends to be abstract and impersonal. Spinoza's God, for example, is a universal Mind with an infinity of attributes about which we can know nothing. Like the God of theism, Spinoza's God is both transcendent and analogous to a human mind, but it is not a God to whom one can relate in the way one relates to a father or a mother or to any other loved person. It is not a God who created the world, for God and the universe are coeternal. It is not a God to whom one can pray, for how can anything be other than it is, or become other than what it must become? It is not a God to whom one can look for fulfillment of hope for a life beyond the grave. From one point of view Spinoza, with his strong sense of the mystery of existence, could be called "God intoxicated." From the point of view of a theist, Spinoza was an atheist. "Pantheism is said, and rightly said," wrote Miguel de Unamuno, "to be merely atheism disguised; and, in my opinion, undisguised. And they were right in calling Spinoza an atheist. . . ."[7]

In evaluating any variety of pantheism it is always useful to go behind the rhetoric, which often resembles the rhetoric of theism, to find how a pantheist God functions in the life of an actual believer. If the relationship is what Martin Buber called one of I and It rather than one of I and Thou, then God is little more than an icy abstraction, so unconcerned about paltry human affairs that the term *God* seems inappropriate.[8] Shelley began his notorious essay on "The Necessity of Atheism" with this honest heading: "There is no God." But he immediately added: "This negation must be understood solely to affect a creative deity. The hypothesis of a pervading Spirit coeternal with the universe remains unshaken."

Of course it is mainly a weary worrying over words. But if we hope to be understood, to avoid needless confusion, we should do our best—it is one of this book's major themes—to respect the way words are commonly understood. It seems to me that by and large the great pantheists of the past have been more guilty than theists or atheists of using language in obfuscatory ways. (Were they unconsciously trying to make their systems seem more profound than they really were?) Two pantheists may sound very much alike in their ways of talking about God, but beneath the language there can be astonishingly different visions. Josiah Royce, for instance, I would place near the theist end of the pantheist spectrum. Unlike F. H. Bradley's Absolute, Royce's Universal Mind is both responsive to prayer and a provider of immortality. Although historians of philosophy usually classify Bradley and Royce as post-Hegelian pantheists, when you look behind their surface similarities you find beliefs that are poles apart.

Let us not waste time trying to untangle the subtle differences between pantheistic models. The theistic model, the model I prefer for emotional reasons (there are no others), requires a God to whom one can pray, and who offers hope for immortality. A God who is both "wholly other," yet who pervades every aspect of the universe and who dwells inside our hearts. A God who is utterly beyond our understanding, yet must be modeled by those human attributes without which the concept of God plays no role in meeting our desires.[9]

The Schoolmen had a phrase, *via negativa*, for a way of speaking that emphasized God's transcendence. The negative way is to say not what God is but what God is not. He is not a created being. He is not made of molecules. He does not change. And so on. We cannot even say, some medieval theologians maintained, that God "exists" if we mean *exist* in the same way the sun exists or we exist. God is, yes, but in a manner we cannot and perhaps will never comprehend.

God's superexistence, as it has been called, can be distinguished from the existence of the universe, including us, by many metaphors. One of them, deriving from geometry, is to place God outside our space-time, in a higher continuum, perhaps in a space of four or some higher number of dimensions, perhaps even an infinite number. Consider Flatlanders living on the surface of a sphere. They are unable to conceive of three-dimensional space, though they might guess their surface to be curved in 3-space if they discovered that by moving far enough, in any direction along the straightest possible path, they would eventually return to where they started.

We who live in 3-space can see every point of Flatland. We can do more. We can reach out and touch every point of the Flatlander's world without passing a finger through any part of their space. In the same way a god in 4-space could look "down" on our three-dimensional universe, which could be, as Einstein conjectured, the hypersurface of a four-dimensional hypersphere. Such a hyperbeing could see every point in our universe without looking through our space. The being could stretch out a finger and touch every point in our world, and the finger would not pass through any part of our space. The being would be utterly beyond us, yet closer to us than our breathing, or (as the Koran has it) closer than the jugular vein in our neck.

This use of higher space-time as a model of how God can be both transcendent and immanent was a popular one in the last century, after the discovery of N-dimensional geometries, and many books were written with this as the central theme. Karl Barth often used the metaphor by speaking of God's actions as entering human history from a higher dimension. Karl Heim, another German theologian who was one of Barth's contemporaries, used the metaphor even more explicitly.[10] It is, of course, no more than a metaphor—an elaboration in modern geometrical theory of Plato's great comparison of our world with the shadows on the wall of a cave. "When I get to heaven," wrote Charles Peirce, "which will be four-dimensional, of course . . ."[11]

A more literary metaphor for transcendence, a favorite of Unamuno's, is to think of God as beyond us in a manner similar to the way a novelist is beyond his characters. There is a curious sense in which Don Quixote seems more real than Cervantes, Sherlock Holmes more real than Conan Doyle, yet we know they were only figments in the mind of their creators.[12] The universe, said Poe in "Eureka," is a "plot of God." In Unamuno's greatest novel, *Mist*, the protagonist visits the author to protest his death—a death Unamuno has deemed necessary for the novel's plot—and to remind Unamuno that he too is a misty character who is acting out a dream in the mind of God. In *The French Lieutenant's Woman*, the author, John Fowles, enters the novel to sit opposite his imaginary character Charles Smithson, while Smithson dozes in a Victorian railway compartment. Watching Smithson sleep, and wondering how to end his novel, Fowles thinks of two equally plausible alternatives, one happy, one sad, then flips a florin to decide which to give first. This toss of a coin symbolizes, as Fowles makes clear in his last chapter, the random mutations by which Nature chooses between possible forking paths in the great epic of evolution. One could compile a long list of novels, plays, stories, poems, and myths in which beautiful variations are played on this life-as-plot metaphor.

When the stress on God's transcendence goes to such extremes that nothing at all can be said about God, even metaphorically, then God becomes, as Schopenhauer liked to say, free of content and therefore almost indistinguishable from nothing. Not that God is nothing—God may be Everything—but that there is nothing to say about so distant a deity. All one can say about Brahman is *neti neti*, not this, not that. We might as well use Herbert Spencer's impersonal term and call such a God the Unknowable. The Unknowable may not be nothing, but if we cannot talk about it even with our poor human symbols, how can it be of any use or comfort to us? If God is to play a role in our lives, is it not obvious that at least *some* attributes of a person must be applied, even though we cannot know how they apply?

The reason God must be modeled as a person is simple. It is the highest model we have of Something to whom we can relate in an I-Thou way. You can worship, love, thank, confess to, seek forgiveness from, make requests of, a person. You cannot do any of these things with a potato or a galaxy or with a God who is (as a bit of graffito, circa 1967, had it) a 6,000-foot-tall jelly bean. You can hope that a God powerful enough to make a universe ("make" in the human sense of making a watch) is powerful enough to make a life for you after death, but you would hardly suspect this of a God who was no more than a super dog or cat, or even a super chimpanzee. How can we model a God except in our own image? God, if there is a God, surely is not less intelligent than such clever people as you and me!

In almost every profession there is a pleasant practice, especially at funerals, of speaking of the dead as having been called out of this world by the Great Musician, or the Great Mathematician, or the Great Artist, and so on. To sailors, God is the Great Pilot. To actors, God is the Great Stage Manager. To conjurors, God is the Great Magician. We model God in our own images because they are the best images we have.

On my office wall is a color photograph of a large oil painting by a Canadian friend, Pat Patterson, that seems at first glance to be a copy of Leonardo da Vinci's "Last Supper." Closer inspection reveals that Jesus has just finished performing what magicians know as the ancient cups-and-balls trick. For the climax, Jesus has turned over the three cups to disclose three baby chicks. The twelve apostles are in their familiar thunderstruck attitudes, but instead of asking "Is it I?" they are asking, "How did he do it?"

Even if I were a Christian I would not consider this painting blasphemous. Was not the biblical Jesus a Great Magician? He turned water into wine. He multiplied loaves and fishes. And is not the miraculous production of baby chickens a beautiful symbol of the creation of life? I have observed a curious fact about how visitors react to this picture. Devout Roman Catholics laugh as hard as any unbeliever. The picture seems to offend most those liberal Protestants who still go to church but long ago stopped believing Jesus ever performed a miracle.

God is the Great Magician. Anthropomorphic? Of course! C. S. Lewis once pointed out that pantheists who object to anthropomorphic images of God seldom realize that they substitute for them images far more ludicrous, indeed more blasphemous, than images deriving from human attributes:

"I don't believe in a personal God," says one, "but I do believe in a great spiritual force." What he has not noticed is that the word "force" has let in all sorts of images about winds and tides and electricity and gravitation. "I don't believe in a personal God," says another, "but I do believe we are all parts of one great Being which moves and works through us all"—not noticing that he has merely exchanged the image of a fatherly and royal-looking man for the image of some widely extended gas or fluid. A girl I knew was brought up by "higher thinking" parents to regard God as a perfect "substance"; in later life she realised that this had actually led her to think of Him as something like a vast tapioca pudding. (To make matters worse, she disliked tapioca.) We may feel ourselves quite safe from this degree of absurdity, but we are mistaken. If a man watches his own mind, I believe he will find that what profess to be specially advanced or philosophic conceptions of God are, in his thinking, always accompanied by vague images which, if inspected, would turn out to be even more absurd than the man-like images aroused by Christian theology. For man, after all, is the highest of the things we meet in sensuous experience. He has, at least, conquered the globe, honoured (though not followed) virtue, achieved knowledge, made poetry, music and art. If God exists at all it is not unreasonable to suppose that we are less unlike Him than anything else we know. No doubt we are unspeakably different from Him; to that extent all man-like images are false. But those images of shapeless mists and irrational forces which, unacknowledged, haunt the mind when we think we are rising to the conception of impersonal and absolute Being, must be very much more so. For images, of the one kind or of the other, will come; we cannot jump off our own shadow.[13]

Some religious monotheisms, such as Islam and Judaism, object to pictures showing God in human form. The sentiment behind this is easy to understand because we have not the slightest notion of what God looks like, or indeed if there is any meaning in saying God can be "seen." Nevertheless, most religions have allowed artists to meet the desires of believers for symbolic pictures of gods or God, and I for one am not offended. God certainly has nothing resembling my index finger; or perhaps I should say I have no reason to suppose God has. Yet I believe the universe we inhabit for so brief a time was in some sense the work of God, and when I see Michelangelo's painting of God and Adam touching fingertips I find it a striking symbol of the creative process by which God brought into existence such preposterous mammals as you and me. If there are intelligent creatures on another planet who are shaped like doughnuts, I have no doubt that their God, if they have a God, is depicted in their art, if they have an art, as a large doughnut. Nor am I in the least annoyed by Hindu statues that model, say, Shiva with four arms. They convey the obvious truth that any God worthy of worship has a greater power to manipulate things than any two-armed earthling.

This impulse to enlarge human traits to a kind of limit clearly underlies such traditional beliefs as that God is omnipotent, omniscient, omnipresent, and so on. We know some things; God knows all things. We can do some things; God can do all things. We are somewhere; God is everywhere. We are in time; God is in eternity. Our love, goodness, and mercy are intermittent and feeble. God's love, mercy, and goodness are perpetual and infinite. Of course when we push such traits to the ultimate we must always keep in mind what the Schoolmen, and especially Aquinas, called the doctrine of "analogical predication." We have no way, absolutely no way, of knowing what it means to push the personal attributes of God to the ultimate. Every human trait applied to God has a unique meaning for God, utterly beyond our understanding. At the same time, we believe—in my view only by faith—that there is some sort of likeness, the nature of which is necessarily vague.

A number of theologians have made interesting comparisons of God's relation to us with our relation to lower animals. An ape has a low-grade intelligence, perhaps greater than formerly thought, and seems also to be aware of its own identity. Yet think of the vast and complex regions of experience open to us of which the smartest ape has no comprehension. How much greater must be the distance between us and God!

We can understand fairly well what a chimpanzee does and thinks and feels. When we see a chimp who has been taught in sign language to ask for a banana, we know that it wants a banana because it likes to eat bananas, and that it is making the sign because it has learned that when it does, it is likely to be given a banana. In analogous fashion, so goes the argument, God understands all our thoughts and behavior even though we cannot understand what God thinks and does. Between our mind and the mind of a cow the gulf is infinitesimal compared to the gulf between our mind and God's. All this is implicit in the Thomist doctrine of analogical predication.

We can go even further in the direction of theological positivism. I do not know whether our traits, the admirable ones of course, reach an infinite limit in God, because I do not know what it means to speak of such attributes as infinite. I am not saying that God's perfections are not infinite, only that I don't know what it means to say they are. Even in mathematics infinity is a complex and spooky concept, as Georg Cantor's wondrous hierarchy of alephs testifies. Nevertheless, pushing human attributes to a limit in God is a natural way of expressing the hugeness of the gulf that separates us from God. I see no reason why, in our stammering symbolic forms of religious discourse, we cannot speak—indeed we can hardly avoid speaking—of God as all-wise, all-seeing, all-merciful, and so on. If we keep constantly in mind how little we comprehend such terms, they serve the purpose of reminding us of the mystery of God's nature. At the same time they preserve the person model without which a transcendent God is too unapproachable to be of value to us.

I share William James's conviction that reason is powerless to establish any of the traditional attributes of a personal God. It cannot even prove that such a God exists. Nevertheless, I think James went too far in the tenth lecture of his *Varieties*, where he heaps scorn on all attempts to think about God's nature. Applying Peirce's pragmatic test of meaning, James considers first such metaphysical attributes as God's simplicity, immateriality, indivisibility, self-sufficiency, and other traits over which the Schoolmen so tirelessly debated. He concludes that it would make not the slightest difference to a believer if any of them were true or false.

"Pray, what specific act can I perform in order to adapt myself the better to God's simplicity?" James asks. "Or how does it assist me to plan my behavior, to know that his happiness is anyhow absolutely complete?" James likens the dogmatic, systematic theologians to "closet naturalists" who study only stuffed birds, never troubling to observe them alive in the fields:

What is their deduction of metaphysical attributes but a shuffling and matching of pedantic dictionary-adjectives, aloof from morals, aloof from human needs, something that might be worked out from the mere word "God" by one of those logical machines of wood and brass which recent ingenuity has contrived as well as by a man of flesh and blood. They have the trail of the serpent over them. One feels that in the theologians' hands, they are only a set of titles obtained by a mechanical manipulation of synonyms; verbality has stepped into the place of vision, professionalism into that of life. Instead of bread we have a stone; instead of a fish, a serpent. Did such a conglomeration of abstract terms give really the gist of our knowledge of the deity, schools of theology might indeed continue to flourish, but religion, vital religion, would have taken its flight from this world. What keeps religion going is something else than abstract definitions and systems of concatenated adjectives, and something different from faculties of theology and their professors. All these things are aftereffects, secondary accretions upon those phenomena of vital conversation with the unseen divine, of which I have shown you so many instances, renewing themselves *in sæcula sæculorum* in the lives of humble private men.

So far I share James's sentiments, but now he goes on to consider attributes of God that *do* relate to our lives: holiness, omnipotence, omniscience, justice, unchangingness, love, and so on. These, too, are rejected as useless. As a fideist I agree with James that none of these traits can be proved by reason, but James does not see even a pragmatic value in employing such terms analogically. He wants only a God or gods who are sufficiently above us to provide some vague basis for religious experience.

I think we can trace James's reluctance to model God as a person, to push human traits analogically to their limits, to the fact that his own religious emotions seem to have played only a small role in his life. He never made the leap to a personal God with whom he could establish an I-Thou relation. The best he could do, as he put it in a 1901 letter, was believe that "Something, not our immediate self, does act on our life!" He described the Something as "a sphere of life larger and more powerful than our usual consciousness, with which the latter is nevertheless continuous."

In a 1904 letter James wrote: "I have no living sense of commerce with a God. I envy those who have. . . ." One of his answers that year on a religious questionnaire was: "I can't possibly pray—I feel foolish and artificial." From a letter of 1907: "I doubt whether you will find any great harm in the God I patronize—the poor thing is so largely an ideal possibility."[14] There was thus considerable justification for

George Santayana's remark that there is ". . . no sense of security, no joy, in James's apology for personal religion. He did not really believe; he merely believed in the right of believing that you might be right if you believed."[15]

James's "poor thing" of a God reminds me of the tendency of modern atheists, who are into occultism and psychic phenomena, to replace God with extraterrestrial intelligences from other galaxies or from higher space-times, or shapeless cosmic minds with which one can establish subliminal contact. Perhaps it is not an accident that James's weak sense of God combined with a strong interest in the investigation of psychic phenomena.

The great danger of all person models of God, it goes without saying, is that human metaphors, when elaborated and made too explicit, can turn a theology into crass anthropomorphism. Humans have a sense of humor, and presumably this is a desirable trait. Does God have a sense of humor? Is he the Great Comedian? Does the Almighty ever shake in some incomprehensible way with incomprehensible mirth? There are just four references in the Bible to God laughing, and in every case it is Jehovah laughing over the fate of the wicked—hardly a case for God's appreciation of a subtle joke. With Chesterton, who ended his *Orthodoxy* by imagining that when God became Jesus he concealed his mirth, I like to think that God has something akin to our sense of humor, and I enjoy fantastic tales about the laughter of God or the gods. But how can we know? Since I stand aloof from any Revelation that sheds light on such curious questions, I find it best to leave the nature of God's humor enveloped in mystery.

One of the crudest forms of anthropomorphism is involved in the question, stirred up in recent years by leaders of the women's liberation movement, of whether our model of God should be masculine, feminine, or neither. Let me state at once that I am in complete sympathy with all those feminists, in or out of Christian traditions, who are appalled by the male symbolism that dominates the mythology of Judaism, Islam, and Christianity, and who are writing explosive books about it. It is true that no important theologian of any of those three faiths, so far as I know, maintained that God has a male anatomy, but to say this is not to say much. The Bible, like the Koran, is saturated from beginning to end with masculine images of God.[16]

In the New Testament, the older image of a male Jehovah is strongly reinforced by Jesus' constant references to God as our Heavenly Father, and by the doctrine that Jesus is God's Son. A Christian may justify Jesus' use of "Father" as a concession to the language of male dominance in old Judea, but how can a Christian escape the implications of knowing that when God chose to walk the earth and die for our sins he became a man instead of a woman? I am unimpressed by the familiar rejoinder that it was necessary for God to become one or the other, and given the cultural context, the preferred choice was inevitable. Were I a Christian, male or female, I would be enormously perplexed over what to make of the inescapable maleness of the Incarnation.

There are other male chauvinist attitudes in basic Christian doctrines that go much deeper than just the lack of neuter pronouns in ancient Hebrew and later languages. God created Eve, we are told, as a sort of afterthought, to provide Adam with a companion and servant; constructing her not in the dignified way he constructed Adam and the animals but by shaping her from one of Adam's minor bones. Could anything be more insulting? It was Eve who first sinned, precipitating the Fall. In Hebrew sacred literature God is pictured as the husband, Israel as the wife. In the New Testament the Church is the "bride" of Christ. The twelve disciples were all men. Even the Devil is masculine.

Nor is there any good way to escape from the all-too-explicit views of Saint Paul about the subservient roles of women. "For a man . . . is the image and glory of God: but the woman is the glory of the man. For the man is not of the woman; but the woman of the man. Neither was the man created for the woman: but the woman for the man." (I Corinthians 11:7–9) In this typical passage Paul is struggling to explain why it is shameful for a man to pray or to prophesy in church with his head covered, and equally shameful for a woman to pray or to prophesy with her head exposed. It is all tied up with God having endowed women with long and beautiful hair. "Doth not even nature itself teach you, that if a man have long hair, it is a shame unto him?" (11:14). Paul would not have cared much for the way Jesus was destined to be portrayed in Christian art!

It is refreshing to learn from Elaine Pagels's book on the newly discovered Gnostic documents that the earliest Christians sometimes applied to God both male and female symbols.[17] One dares to hope that as the liberation of women advances, Christians will somehow find their way back to these early symbols that for so long have been deemed heretical. There is no reason why singular pronouns, sexless in implication, cannot come into widespread use in theological discourse, but it is hard to see how the Incarnation could be purged of maleness without altering the heart of orthodoxy. A sexless God is easy to accept, but an androgynous Savior? Catholicism has partly compensated for Christianity's masculine bias by elevating Mary above all other mortals, but there is no way around the fact that Mary is not God the Mother, but the mother of a male incarnation of God. Nor is it much help to brandish Gnostic gospels in which Jesus is said to have had a special love for Mary Magdalene.

In the canonical gospel of John, Jesus is portrayed as having a special love for John, a love described in such a way that it has become the cornerstone of a considerable literature (most of it untranslated from European languages) suggesting that Jesus was homosexual. Indeed, this is the firm opinion of many gay Christians, including ministers and priests, though it is still too taboo a topic to be discussed openly in the United States.[18]

A year or so ago I had what was, at least for me, an amusing conversation with a gay Episcopalian priest who made no secret of his lifestyle, openly sharing as he did an apartment with his lover. He was violently opposed to the ordination of female priests on the familiar ground (recently upheld by Pope John Paul II) that priests are symbols of Jesus, who, though God, was also truly a man. It seems to me that traditional Christian theology is so deeply interfused with male dominance that it will be a long time, with slow doctrinal changes that now can only be guessed, before a truly emancipated woman, or a man who shares her views, will find himself or herself (how one longs for that neuter pronoun!) comfortable with Christianity. Of course the same can be said of Jewish and Islamic faiths.

The controversy over God's sex underscores the dangers of shaping the person model of God so anthropomorphically that it becomes offensive. Nevertheless, if God is to have a meaning at all in human lives, God must be modeled somehow. I have argued that the person model, with anthropomorphism held in check by the doctrine of analogical predication, is the best, indeed the only, model we have if we wish to escape from a pantheism in which God evaporates into a watery cloud of so little emotional value that one might as well chuck the God symbol altogether. And why not? In the next two chapters I shall explore what I think are the wrong and right reasons for believing in a personal God.

12

THE PROOFS:
Why I Do Not Believe God's Existence Can Be Demonstrated

You remind me of the farmer who said to his bishop, after a sermon proving the existence of God, "It is a very fine sermon, but I believe there be a God after all."

—WILLIAM JAMES, IN A LETTER OF 1897

If God spoke to us audibly, as Jehovah does so often in Old Testament tales, we might (unless we thought ourselves mad) believe in God's existence for much the same reasons we believe in the existence of other persons. If God demonstrated his power by stupendous miracles, such as turning someone into a pillar of salt, there would be other good empirical grounds for believing. If we could perform experiments that supported, even indirectly, the hypothesis "God exists," we would believe in God for the same reasons we believe in gravity. I do not think God reveals himself, or has ever done so, in such crude ways.

Are there purely logical arguments for God, arguments so convincing that if an intelligent atheist understood them he or she would become a theist? There are no such arguments. In Lecture 18 of his *Varieties of Religious Experience*, William James summed up the situation in a few sentences that could have been written last week:

The arguments for God's existence have stood for hundreds of years with the waves of unbelieving criticism breaking against them, never totally discrediting them in the ears of the faithful, but on the whole slowly and surely washing out the mortar from between their joints. If you have a God already whom you believe in, these arguments confirm you. If you are atheistic, they fail to set you right.

A long line of distinguished thinkers, fully capable of understanding the arguments yet remaining unconvinced, is testimony to the flabbiness of those "proofs." But, you may respond, is there not also a long line of equally distinguished theists who firmly believed God's existence *could* be established by unaided reason?

Yes, and now I must explain why I qualified "logical" by saying there are no "purely" logical arguments. There indeed are partly logical arguments. If you make certain posits, posits unsupported by logic or science, the traditional proofs do make a kind of sense. From my fideist perspective, the posits required to confer validity on the proofs are not rational but emotional. They are made in response to deeply felt needs. Grant these emotive posits and the proofs become compelling, but the posits themselves are from the heart, not the head.

Logical and mathematical systems also require posits, but they are not posits based on passions. We believe in the truth of the Pythagorean theorem, for example, because we can prove it within the formal system of Euclidean geometry and because its truth can be empirically confirmed with physical models. If we could draw a triangle and find that the sum of its interior angles was 90 degrees, our trust in the theorems of Euclidean geometry would be shaken, but of course we cannot draw such a triangle any more than we can produce five pebbles by adding two pebbles to two pebbles. Given the formal system of Euclidean geometry, it follows with iron logic that the angles of every triangle must have a sum of 180 degrees, just as it follows from the formal system of arithmetic that the sum of two and two must be four. Even in the interior of a sun, Bertrand Russell once said, there are three feet in a yard.

The posits that confer plausibility on the traditional proofs of God are of an altogether different sort. Consider the familiar argument from first cause. If every event has a prior cause, we seem to be faced with either believing in a first cause (Aristotle's unmoved mover) that is self-caused or uncaused, or accepting chains of causes that go back forever in time.

Now whenever Thomas Aquinas encountered an infinite regress in one of his proofs of God he simply dismissed it as absurd. But why absurd? This is precisely the spot at which a subliminal emotion stealthily slips into the argument. An endless regress is absurd only to someone who finds it ugly or disturbing. There is nothing *logically* absurd about an infinite regress. We may feel uncomfortable with the infinite set of integers, but who wants to deny that the sequence goes to infinity in both positive and negative directions? Fractions in the sequence ½, ⅓, ¼, ⅕ . . . get smaller and smaller but the sequence never ends with a smallest fraction. The proof by first cause may be emotionally satisfying in its escape from the anxiety generated by an infinite regress, but clearly it is logically flawed.

The same applies to a closely related variant of the argument. We allow the universe to be infinite in time, but insist that the entire sequence of events cannot be uncaused or self-caused. Again, it is emotionally satisfying to many people, perhaps to most people, to hang a beginningless universe on a higher peg, but without this emotion the argument proves nothing. If God, the transcendent peg, is declared to be self-caused or uncaused, we are merely evading the mystery of being, not solving it. Would it not be simpler, as David Hume suggested, to allow the entire universe to be uncaused or self-caused, like one of Saul Steinberg's cartoons that show a man, pen in hand, drawing himself on the page? For many people it is impossible to think of the universe doing this, but the difficulty springs from an emotion, not from reason. There is nothing irrational about the thought. Every person, Bertrand Russell somewhere says, has a mother. This doesn't entail that the human race had a mother. Every integer has a predecessor. This doesn't entail that the infinite sequence of negative integers had a predecessor.

The teleological argument, or argument from design—that patterns in nature imply a Patternmaker—has been and still is the most popular of all traditional proofs of God. Before Darwin it was constantly invoked with reference to the marvelously adapted parts of living things. We all know how those arguments have been weakened by evolution. It is no longer possible to think of the wondrous structure of a human eye, or even the patterns of such lifeless things as galaxies and solar systems, as having histories analogous to the making of a watch.

This does not, of course, deny that most people, when they contemplate the grandeur of the starry heavens or the humbler patterns of flowers and snow crystals, may experience a strong feeling that behind such marvelous order there must be something like a human intelligence. Even Immanuel Kant, who demolished the logical force of the design argument in his *Critique of Pure Reason*, granted the proof's strong emotional power:

> This proof always deserves to be mentioned with respect. It is the oldest, the clearest, and the most accordant with the common reason of mankind. It enlivens the study of nature, just as it itself derives its existence and gains ever new vigour from that source. It suggests ends and purposes, where our observation would not have detected them by itself, and extends our knowledge of nature by means of the guiding-concept of a special unity, the principle of which is outside nature. This knowledge again reacts on its cause, namely, upon the idea which has led to it, and so strengthens the belief in a supreme Author [of nature] that the belief acquires the force of an irresistible conviction.
>
> It would therefore not only be uncomforting but utterly vain to attempt to diminish in any way the authority of this argument. Reason, constantly upheld by this ever-increasing evidence, which, though empirical, is yet so powerful, cannot be so depressed through doubts suggested by subtle and abstruse speculation, that it is not at once aroused from the indecision of all melancholy reflection, as from a dream, by one glance at the wonders of nature and the majesty of the universe—ascending from height to height up to the all-highest, from the conditioned to its conditions, up to the supreme and unconditioned Author [of all conditioned being].

One could easily fill a book with colorful extracts from writers who have testified to the persuasiveness of the proof by design. Here, for instance, are the thoughts of Charlotte Brontë's Jane Eyre, alone on the moor:

> Night was come, and her planets were risen: a safe, still night; too serene for the companionship of fear. We know that God is everywhere; but certainly we feel His presence most when His works are on the grandest scale spread before us: and it is in the un-

clouded night-sky, where His worlds wheel their silent course, that we read clearest His infinitude, His omnipotence, His omnipresence. I had risen to my knees to pray for Mr. Rochester. Looking up, I, with tear-dimmed eyes, saw the mighty Milkyway. Remembering what it was—what countless systems there swept space like a soft trace of light—I felt the might and strength of God. Sure was I of His efficiency to save what He had made: convinced I grew that neither earth should perish, nor one of the souls it treasured. I turned my prayer to thanksgiving: the Source of Life was also the Savior of spirits. Mr. Rochester was safe: he was God's and by God would he be guarded. I again nestled to the breast of the hill; and ere long, in sleep, forgot sorrow.

Listen to Sir Isaac Newton, speaking iambic pentameters in Alfred Noyes's *Watchers of the Sky*:

Was the eye contrived by blindly moving atoms,
Or the still-listening ear fulfilled with music
By forces without knowledge of sweet sounds?
Are nerves and brain so sensitively fashioned
That they convey these pictures of the world
Into the very substance of our life,
While That from which we came, the Power that made us,
Is drowned in blank unconsciousness of all?

Whittaker Chambers's *Witness* provides a final example, one that might have come straight from the pen of the eighteenth-century English theologian William Paley:

But I date my break [with the Communist Party] from a very casual happening. I was sitting in our apartment on St. Paul Street in Baltimore. It was shortly before we moved to Alger Hiss's apartment in Washington. My daughter was in her high chair. I was watching her eat. She was the most miraculous thing that had ever happened in my life. I liked to watch her even when she smeared porridge on her face or dropped it meditatively on the floor. My eye came to rest on the delicate convolutions of her ear—those intricate, perfect ears. The thought passed through my mind: "No, those ears were not created by any chance coming together of atoms in nature (the Communist view). They could have been created only by immense design." The thought was involuntary and unwanted. I crowded it out of my mind. But I never wholly forgot it or the occasion. I had to crowd it out of my mind. If I had completed it, I should have had to say: Design presupposes God. I did not then know that, at that moment, the finger of God was first laid upon my forehead.[1]

I find nothing in this passage to ridicule. Why should not the ear of a loved child be as good an example of God's design as anything in the universe? The inner ear is no less complex than the eye. Both are far more intricate than the watch Paley used in his famous proof. The argument's emotive force is not in the least diminished by the truth of evolution. In fact it is augmented. Cosmic evolution implies that the elementary particles that came into existence during the first few minutes of the big bang had mathematical properties that would permit them, billions of years later, to form microscopic eggs which would grow to become you and me.[2] I cannot imagine anyone reading *Witness* without being impressed by the authenticity of Chambers's religious experience.

Since the development of organic chemistry, a new version of the argument from the design of living things has been advanced by a number of scientists and thinkers who have no quarrel with biological evolution. The argument focuses instead on the probability that life could arise spontaneously in earth's primeval seas. Presumably life began several billion years ago when carbon-based molecules, shuffling for millions of years in an organic soup, happened to form a self-replicating microorganism. The probability of this occurring by blind chance, so goes the reasoning, is so incredibly low that intervention by a deity is needed to explain how life started.

Pierre Lecomte du Noüy gave this argument in two of his widely read books of the forties. More recently, Sir Fred Hoyle and his associate N. Chandra Wickramasinghe have refined the argument in their book *Evolution from Space*. They estimate the odds against blind chance producing a single self-replicating microorganism to be 10 to the power of 40,000 (1 followed by 40,000 zeros) to 1. Unable to make the leap to a God outside the universe, Hoyle and his friend (who was raised a Buddhist) settle for what they call an "intelligence" within the universe that is constantly fabricating microorganisms in interstellar gas. These tiny life-forms are pushed around the cosmos by the pressure of starlight. Comets carry them to the planets, where they flourish and evolve if conditions are suitable.[3]

Few scientists take Hoyle's new science-fiction theology seriously. Its weakest point is that there are no compelling reasons for assuming that when organic molecules shuffle together, either in organic soups or in outer space, they combine by blind chance alone. Rather they combine by what Isaac Asimov once called "unblind chance"—chance constrained by natural laws about which we as yet know nothing. Because of our vast ignorance, there are no ways to make reasonable probability estimates.

A more subtle recent variant of the design argument centers on the nature of the big bang. Physicists see no reason why this explosion could not have produced a universe in which certain basic constants, such as Planck's constant or the fine-structure constant or the rate of the universe's expansion, would have been other than what they are. But let some of these constants deviate ever so slightly from what they are and we get a possible universe in which not even stars could congeal, let alone planets and microorganisms. Therefore . . .

I find this argument for God as logically fragile as the old design arguments before Darwin. For all we know, as physicist John Wheeler has taught us, billions of big bangs may be constantly taking place in hyperspace and throughout eternity, explosions that manufacture universes in which all possible combinations of constants occur. As the old song goes, "We're here because we're here because we're here because we're here." The argument that God had to fine-tune the fireball to create a cosmos capable of producing intelligent life is compelling only to those who shrink from contemplating an infinity of lifeless universes, who find it more comforting to suppose that a superior intelligence guided our big bang to form just the universe it did.

Note that Wheeler's vision provides the atheist with a way of escaping Hoyle's probability estimate even if we grant that organic molecules combine by blind chance. The odds against life in any one universe may be low, but there is no limit to the number of universes that can live and die if time and space are endless. No matter how low the odds, eventually there will be a universe in which the rare event occurs, and so here we are!

My remarks are not intended to disparage what cosmologists call the "anthropic principle." According to this principle we can "explain" certain properties of the earth, solar system, galaxy, universe, even the original fireball, by asking what sort of conditions are necessary to account for the existence now of cosmologists. Only the name of the principle is new. To chess problemists it is no more than the application to cosmology of "retrograde analysis." Given a position on the chessboard with, say, one piece removed, you can sometimes deduce the nature of the missing piece by reasoning backward through the game.[4]

The principle appeals to physicists with solipsistic urges because it seems to say, though of course it does not, that somehow our consciousness makes the universe what it is. "We have found a strange footprint on the shores of the unknown," wrote Sir Arthur Stanley Eddington in the often-quoted last paragraph of his *Space, Time and Gravitation*. (By "strange footprint" he meant the strange way our universe is put together.) "We have devised profound theories . . . to account for its origin. At last, we have succeeded in reconstructing the creature that made the footprint. And Lo! it is our own."[5]

This may seem profound, but when expressed with less poetry and ambiguity it becomes trivial. "Imagine an ensemble of universes of all sorts," say Robert Dicke and P.J.E. Peebles in their contribution to *General Relativity: An Einstein Centenary Survey*. "It should be no surprise that ours is not an 'average' one, for conditions on the average may well be hostile. We could only be present in a universe that happens to supply our needs."

Dicke and Peebles describe a game of Russian roulette played by thousands of persons. From a large supply of guns each player randomly selects a gun that may or may not be loaded. At the end of the game a statistician makes a retrograde analysis and concludes "that there is a high probability of the randomly selected unloaded guns being drawn by the survivors of the game."[6]

The Russian roulette analogy surely demolishes any effort to invoke the anthropic principle as an argument for God. Of course you may assume, if you like, that a Creator carefully selected our particular unloaded-gun universe in preference to loaded ones, but an assumption is not a proof. Roger Penrose, in the book cited above, imagines God looking over a large map on which each point represents the plan for a possible world, then sticking a pin in the map to cause a universe to explode into reality. Maybe only one such universe is chosen. Maybe God creates millions of universes by stabbing the map in many spots, perhaps even stabbing at random, or stabbing simultaneously with a billion hands. It is a celestial game in which the Creator entertains himself (and others?) by experimenting with myriads of possible worlds to see how each works out.

Whatever the scenario, the argument from the fine-tuning of the fireball to the existence of a Great Tuner seems to me no different in essence from the early arguments based on design in nature, and which today sound like Irish bulls. If water did not expand when it freezes, ice would form from the bottom up in lakes, thus killing all fish. If the earth's axis did not tilt at just the angle it does, our seasons would be either too mild or too severe for life (see Dante's *Paradiso*, Canto 10). If the earth's orbit were closer to or farther from the sun, its surface would be too hot or too cold to support life. Meteors would destroy our cities if they were not burned out by the earth's atmosphere. James, in Lecture 20 of *Varieties*, cites dozens of other amusing examples from theological rhetoric. Even the youthful Kant was not immune to such reasoning. In his monograph *On the Only Demonstrative Proof of the Existence of God* (which he later repudiated), Kant extolls the earth's atmosphere for (among other things) producing twilight, a slow transition to darkness that is easy on the eyes. Presumably if daylight went out like a snuffed candle we would have less reason to believe in God.

Such arguments have been interminably caricatured by skeptics. Dr. Pangloss, in Voltaire's *Candide*, observes how carefully the nose is made to support spectacles. Freud, in his witty book on wit, quotes Jules Michelet: "How beautifully everything is arranged in nature. As soon as the child comes into the world, it finds a mother who is ready to care for it."[7] How providential that polar wastes are in regions where nobody lives! How pleasant that Washington and Lincoln were born on holidays!

The old argument from common consent—that because so many people have believed in God the belief must be true—obviously is not logically convincing, though it does have a crude kind of merit. The fact that so many persons, especially persons of towering intellect, have believed in God should at least give an atheist pause, just as a tone-deaf person might suspect there is something of value in music because so many admirable people profess to enjoy it. But this, too, is clearly an emotive argument. It does no more than demonstrate what all atheists know, that for large numbers of people a belief in God or gods satisfies deep longings.

It is easy to turn the design proof upside down and argue that the chaos and evil in the world suggest the nonexistence of God—an old argument that C. S. Lewis once called the "argument from undesign." It is particularly forceful when applied to natural evils which beset human life, such as earthquakes and plagues, but it applies to lower forms of life as well. Long before Darwin it was apparent that an anatomical design of great benefit to one species could hardly be called beneficial to the species it preyed upon.

"To the grub under the bark," wrote James in *Pragmatism*, "the exquisite fitness of the woodpecker's organism to extract him would certainly argue a diabolical designer." In 1964 a pair of ants in Johnny Hart's comic strip *B.C.* made the same point. "It's wonderful to be alive, to exist! What magnificent purpose has put me here? Is it to elevate the species? Is it to discover the secret of creation? Am I here to inspire my kind? Am I king? Prince? Prophet?" Says the other ant: "Try anteater food!"

In later chapters we will look more closely at the argument from undesign. Here I add only the old thought that even if one finds the argument from design valid, it offers no assurance that the Designer had anything more in mind than to design a plaything. Every now and then some whimsical mechanic constructs a large, intricate piece of machinery with thousands of gears, levers, pulleys, chains, shafts, lights, and so on, designed only to run, not to *do* anything.[8] Perhaps the entire universe is just such a joke, a vast cosmic jest fabricated by a god who had no motive except to amuse himself and his friends. It could even be a diabolical joke perpetrated by a demon god. Part of the joke is to place intelligent beings in a universe designed to arouse in them false hopes that they are in the hands of a benevolent God who will reward them with a future life.

The proof of God that I find the least defensible is Saint Anselm's famous ontological argument. C. S. Lewis, in his poem "Abecedarium Philosophicum," summed up Descartes's version this way:

D *for Descartes who said "God couldn't be*
So complete if he weren't. So he is. Q.E.D." [9]

The proof does indeed establish that if we form a concept of God as the most supreme being we can imagine, we cannot avoid adding existence to the concept. Clearly an existing God is superior to one who doesn't exist. But I agree with those critics who fail to see how we are logically compelled to make the ontological leap from a concept of an existing God to the assurance that the concept represents something outside our mind. I am aware that the argument continues to have distinguished advocates who defend it tirelessly and, to my mind, tiresomely: Norman Malcolm, Richard Campbell, my former teacher Charles Hartshorne, and several others. I can only say that I have never found the argument expressed in such a way that I could not find at some juncture a gap crossable only by an emotive jump.[10]

Kant saw the fallacy of the proof quite clearly, but because he expressed it in a terminology easily misunderstood, he has often been unfairly belabored. When Kant said existence is not a predicate, and that a hundred real thalers contain not a thaler more than a hundred possible thalers, he meant only that the *concept* of a hundred thalers is not altered by one's belief, or by the discovery through experience, that thalers actually exist.

Suppose I express my idea of a blue apple by painting a picture of five blue apples. I point to it and say, "This represents five blue apples." If I later learn that blue apples actually exist I can point to the same picture and say, "This represents five real blue apples." Even if I fail to discover that blue apples exist I can point to the picture and say, "This represents five imaginary blue apples." In all three cases the picture remains the same. The concept of five real apples contains not an apple more than the concept of five possible apples. The idea of a unicorn does not acquire additional horns if real unicorns exist. In Kant's terminology you do not add a new property to a concept by expressing your belief that the concept corresponds to an actual object outside your brain.

Of course it is all a matter of words. In other epistemological languages it is quite acceptable to say that existence is a predicate. But to suppose that Kant did not realize it is better to have real money in your pocket than imaginary money is to suppose Kant to have been a moron, which he wasn't. "My financial position," Kant wrote, "is, however, affected very differently by a hundred real thalers than it is by the mere concept of them." When you think you have found a statement by a great philosopher that is obviously absurd, it is a good bet you have not understood the statement. A surprising recent example of such a failure to do homework occurs in Mortimer Adler's *How to Think About God*. Adler chastises Kant severely for falling into a childish blunder:

> Is not a hundred dollars in my pocket better than an imaginary hundred dollars by virtue of its enabling me to buy things with it? Is not a really existent umbrella or raincoat better than an imaginary one so far as protection from the rain is concerned?[11]

As a lifelong champion of the Great Books—his friend Robert Hutchins liked to call him the Great Bookie—Adler above all should not have supposed that Kant was unaware of the value of real money and real umbrellas.

I shall waste no time on trivial variants of the ontological argument that reduce it to such tautologies as that Being must exist, or that if there is a necessarily existing perfect Being, that Being must necessarily exist. Nor do I wish to deny that in thinking through various forms of the ontological argument, a believer in God is led to *feel* that the highest possible Being must exist, but of course the proof claims to be more than that. It claims that the sentence "There is no God" is as self-contradictory as "A triangle has four sides." Not even Aquinas could accept this, and although the argument still mesmerizes a few metaphysicians, I agree with the vast majority of thinkers who see the proof as no more than linguistic sleight-of-hand. There is no existing thing, said Hume, including the entire cosmos, whose nonexistence entails logical contradiction. The thought that everything would be much simpler if nothing existed at all may stab us with anxiety, but there is nothing logically inconsistent in the thought.

Karl Barth wrote a cantankerous and (to me) funny book about Anselm's proof. The book has the following thesis: The ontological argument proves nothing, but it serves to deepen a believer's understanding of God.[12] Some medieval Schoolmen, Bonaventure in particular, said much the same thing, and although I cannot fault this thesis, it certainly is not what Anselm or most later defenders of his proof intended the proof to say. We can rephrase Barth's thesis as follows. For believers in God it is emotionally intolerable that their concept of a perfect God, so sublime and so satisfying, does not include belief in the actual existence of God. Hermann Lotze in his *Microcosmos* (Book 9, Chapter 4) put it crisply: "We *feel* the impossibility of God's nonexistence." (Italics mine.)

When Barth's book on Anselm appeared in an English translation in 1962 it was reviewed by John Updike, a great admirer of Barth and a former Barthian. I agree with Updike that Barth wrote more about his own theology than about Anselm's. As you inch your way through Barth's curious monograph, Updike writes, you anticipate "the gigantic leap that lies ahead, from existence as a concept to existence as a fact—from *esse in intellectu* to *esse in re*. Then a strange thing happens. Anselm takes the leap, and Barth does not, yet he goes on talking as if he had never left Anselm's side."[13]

Indeed, Barth ends by accepting the traditional criticisms of the proof, but admiring it nonetheless because it shows, as Updike puts it, "we cannot pray to or believe in a God whom we recognize as a figment of our own imaginations." In Barth's words: "God is the One who manifests himself in the command not to imagine a greater than he." Is this all that Anselm meant? Updike does not think so, nor do I, nor did Étienne Gilson, who criticized Barth's book along similar lines.

I repress the urge to devote more pages to the classic proofs of God, and to their refutations by Hume, Kant, Mill, and many others. Let me capsule my own view: In every proof I find an explicit or implicit emotional leap that springs from a desire or a fear or both, a leap that occurs at some point between the proof's links. As fully rational arguments, instances of what Kant called pure reason, the proofs are invalid. As partly rational, given certain emotional posits, they express deeply felt convictions in persuasive, reasonable ways, and for this reason they continue to flourish. Actually, this view is not far from that of many Schoolmen who maintained that without special illumination from God, a special grace, it is not possible to find the proofs convincing. Given prior faith, the proofs dramatize the intensity of our hunger for God. They deepen and strengthen our belief in God.

A curious position held by a few Christian thinkers is that although no logically flawless demonstration of God's existence has yet been formulated, one may believe by faith that such a formulation is possible. The scriptural authority for this, quoted endlessly by medieval theologians, is Saint Paul's statement: "For the invisible things of him from the creation of the world are clearly seen, being understood by the things that are made, even his eternal power and Godhead. . . ." (Romans 1:20) "It may be that there are true demonstrations," wrote Blaise Pascal in his *Pensées*, "but it is not certain. Thus this proves nothing but that it is not certain that all is uncertain, to the glory of skepticism." Kant, near the end of his *Critique of Pure Reason*, attributes the hope for a perfect proof to "certain excellent and thoughtful men," including his Swiss contemporary, the philosopher Johann Georg Sulzer, who wrote mainly about aesthetics. Kant adds, "I am certain that this will never happen."

In spite of Pascal's doubts and Kant's certainty, the hope for a valid proof of God, not yet devised, continues to haunt Mortimer Adler. Back in the thirties, when Adler was teaching at the University of Chicago, he believed so firmly in all five of Aquinas's proofs of God that he made strenuous efforts to persuade his students to accept them. Then he began to have doubts. They were first expressed in technical detail in an article on "The Demonstration of God's Existence" in a *Festschrift* issue of *The Thomist* (January 1943) honoring his friend Jacques Maritain. In this paper Adler argued that all five proofs are seriously flawed. He tried to outline a valid proof that had the form: If things exist, God exists; things exist, therefore God exists. Kant put it this way in his *Critique of Pure Reason:* "If anything exists, an absolutely necessary being must also exist. Now I, at least, exist. Therefore an absolutely necessary being exists."

Unfortunately, as Adler says in his autobiography, "The demonstration, I admitted, left a number of difficulties still to be resolved. This amounted to saying that although God's existence might be demonstrated in the future, it had not yet been accomplished. . . ."[14]

Adler's criticism of Aquinas provoked vigorous adverse reactions among Thomists. "My greatest disappointment," Adler tells us, "occurred when I learned that I had even failed to make any headway in changing Maritain's mind on the subject." Indeed, in his book *Approaches to God*, Maritain warns against Adler's viewpoint.

Adler is still searching for the elusive proof. In *How to Think About God* he repeats the usual objections to the traditional arguments, finding all the arguments invalid. Then in Chapter 14 he defends what he calls a "truly cosmological argument" that goes as follows. If the cosmos as a whole needs to be explained, and if it can't be explained by natural causes, then God must have caused it. The second *if* is the troublesome one. In his next chapter Adler argues that the second premise is the same as saying it is impossible for the cosmos to cease to exist and be replaced by nothingness. According to Adler, our cosmos is one of many possible worlds; hence it is possible for it not to exist. Because it does exist, we must assume either that God created it out of nothing (in which case God exists) or that the world has always existed. In the latter case Adler gives his reasons for believing that the continued existence of the cosmos requires God as a "preservative cause." He admits his argument does not furnish certitude that God exists, but he thinks it establishes God's existence either "beyond a reasonable doubt," or at least it shows that there is a "preponderance of reasons" for believing God exists.

The God that Adler thinks he has established as probable is, Adler recognizes, only an impersonal abstraction, not a God to whom one can pray. The argument tells us nothing about whether God cares about us, or will provide us with life after death. These are among those beliefs that demand, Adler says, the leap of faith.

I find it depressing that Adler's long "dogmatic slumber," as Kant described his own earlier thinking about the proofs before Hume awakened him, and his admiration for Étienne Gilson (to whose memory *How to Think About God* is dedicated), still hold Adler back from the simple step to fideism that would dissolve his difficulties.[15] Even among Roman Catholic thinkers, increasing numbers no longer feel obliged to establish God's existence even by probable reasoning, or to hope that some day a flawless proof will come to light.

For Kierkegaard, whose fideism so strongly influenced Barth and Unamuno and Heidegger, the desire to find rational evidence for God betrays a weakness of faith. In his *Concluding Unscientific Postscript*, Kierkegaard draws a parallel with a young woman who is so unsure of her love for a man that she keeps trying to find remarkable traits in him that will revive her fading emotion. Is it not an insult to God, Kierkegaard asks, to try to prove him? Is it not like standing in the presence of a mighty king and demanding irrefutable evidence that he exists?

Atheists will, of course, find all this absurd. But those who make the leap of faith are not only certain of God's existence, they see all Nature as a manifestation of God even though God remains invisible. They "prove" God inwardly, writes Kierkegaard, through worship and prayer and submission to God's will. To all those who demand logical proofs or physical wonders, God "craftily" hides himself. "A poor wretch of an author, whom a later investigator drags out of the obscurity of oblivion may indeed be very glad that the investigator succeeds in proving his existence—but an omnipresent being can only by a thinker's pious blundering be brought to this ridiculous embarrassment." The most interesting references in the bibliography at the back of Adler's book are the books not there. Apparently he has been totally uninfluenced by any of the great Jewish, Christian, or philosophical fideists.

The hope for a valid proof of God strikes me as strangely similar to Bertrand Russell's youthful hope that someday he, or someone else, would discover a logical justification for induction. In his last great book, *Human Knowledge, Its Scope and Limits*, Russell abandoned this hope for the view that induction can be justified only by making certain posits about the structure of the external world. Put simply, induction works because the world is what it is. John Stuart Mill said essentially the same thing. Induction works because nature is orderly. Naturally we learn about the world's order only by induction, but Russell finally concluded that this is not a vicious circle, and he tried to go beyond Mill by specifying a minimum set of posits about nature's structure that would permit induction to work as well as it obviously does.

To my way of thinking, the hope for a logical justification of God's existence is as futile as the hope for a logical justification of induction. With respect to both questions, I believe only pragmatic answers can be given. Is it not the height of human pride and folly to suppose that our finite little brains can construct a proof that the world must be built just the way it is, or a proof that there must be a God who built it?

One way of justifying induction pragmatically was put forth by Hans Reichenbach. If there is any way at all to learn something about the structure of the world, that way is by induction; hence induction is justified. One could similarly argue that if there is a God who has chosen to be indemonstratable by either reason or science, then if we are to know God at all, it can only be through faith.

Please do not suppose from these remarks that I wish to defend an argument, often employed by theists, that a scientist's belief in an ordered world is comparable to a believer's faith in God. The popular American Baptist preacher Harry Emerson Fosdick put it this way:

> I am sure that the faith by which one thus orders and unifies his spiritual world, although it is more difficult of demonstration, is essentially the same kind of faith as that by which the scientist in his realm is conquering chaos.[16]

The same point has been elaborated by innumerable philosophers. Josiah Royce, for instance:

> To make the parallel a little clearer, we may say that science postulates the truth of the description of the world that, among all the possible descriptions, at once includes the given phenomena and attains the greatest simplicity; while religion assumes the truth of the description of the world that, without falsifying the given facts, arouses the highest moral interest and satisfies the highest moral needs.

All this has often been said, but it has not always been clearly enough joined with the practical suggestion that if one gives up one of these two faiths, he ought consistently to give up the other. If one is weary of the religious postulates, let him by all means throw them aside. But if he does this, why does he not throw aside the scientific postulates, and give up insisting upon it that the world is and must be rational?[17]

In his article on faith in the *Encyclopedia Britannica* (fourteenth edition), the Cambridge philosopher Frederick Robert Tennant draws the same parallel between the faith of a theist and the faith of a scientist. Induction, he writes, rests on "human hope, sanguine expectation, faith in the unseen. . . . Our very rationality of the world, which science would read and expound, is at bottom an idea of faith." Tennant puts it even more preposterously in his masterwork, *Philosophical Theology:* "The electron and God are equally ideal positings of faith-venture, rationally indemonstrable, invisible; and the 'verifications' of the one idea, and of the other, follow lines essentially identical. . . ."[18] Even William James, in his essay on "The Sentiment of Rationality," favors the same inept analogy.

Is not the flaw obvious? There may well be no purely rational demonstration that induction must always work, but the patterns we find in nature are so strongly confirmed that we cannot disregard them without risking our lives. The quickest way to get from a high floor to the street is to jump out a window, but our "faith" in the laws of gravity and the fragility of our bodies make this an irrational act for anyone who cares to stay alive. On the other hand, an atheist gets along quite well, thank you, without believing in God. It only obscures the nature of faith to liken it to the inescapable necessity of believing in causal laws.

We know what it means to say induction works. What does it mean to say that belief in God works? To fideists it can mean only this—that belief in God is so emotionally rewarding, and the contrary belief so desolate, they cannot not believe. Beneath the *credo quia absurdum*, as Unamuno said, is the *credo quia consolans*. I believe because it consoles me. The true water of life, says our Spanish brother, is that which assuages our thirst. The true bread is that which satisfies our hunger. And this leads to another mystery, the mystery of faith.

13

FAITH:
Why I Am Not an Atheist

*"If you listen to your heart," said the Philosopher,
"you will learn every good thing, for the heart is the
fountain of wisdom, tossing its thoughts up to the
brain which gives them form."*

—JAMES STEPHENS, *The Crock of Gold*

Whenever I speak of religious faith it will mean a belief, unsupported by logic or science, in both God and an afterlife. Bertrand Russell once defined faith, in a broader way, as "a firm belief in something for which there is no evidence." If "evidence" means the kind of support provided by reason and science, there is no evidence for God and immortality, and Russell's definition seems to me concise and admirable.

Faith of this pure sort, uncontaminated by evidence, is easily caricatured. In "The Will to Believe" William James quotes a schoolboy remark: "Faith is when you believe something you know ain't true." No fideist accepts this, of course, but if we alter it to "Faith is when you believe something you don't know is true," it is not a bad definition.

In the Christian tradition, *faith* has two related but distinct meanings. One is that of nonrational belief, the sense adopted here; the other is that of trust. Trust in God presupposes faith in the belief sense. You can't trust a person unless you think that person exists. Throughout both Testaments of the Bible, faith almost always means trust. It has often been observed that nowhere does the Bible give arguments for God. You will look in vain for them in the preaching of Jesus. God's reality is taken for granted, never defended. In this and the book's remaining chapters I will not be concerned with faith as trust, only with faith as belief.

The author of the Epistle to the Hebrews opens his famous chapter on faith, Chapter 11, with a familiar definition that Edgar J. Goodspeed translates as follows: "Faith means the assurance of what we hope for; it is our conviction about things we cannot see." To a philosophical theist this is a superb definition of faith as belief, even though the chapter goes on to catalog instances of faith which are more examples of blind trust than belief, and which no non-Christian theist can accept as historical or even praiseworthy.

I do not, for example, believe that God ever drowned all men, women, and children on the earth (not to mention innocent animals) except Noah and his family. Even as a myth it is hard to admire the "faith" of a man capable of supposing God could be that vindictive and unforgiving. I do not believe that God asked Abraham to murder his only legitimate son as a blood offering. I know how Abraham's obedience has been justified, and I have read Kierkegaard's little book about it, *Fear and Trembling*, but unlike Kierkegaard and the author of Hebrews I am under no obligation to find anything beautiful or profound in this abominable story. To those outside the Judaic-Christian tradition, Abraham appears not as a man of faith, but as a man of insane fanaticism. He would have done better to have supposed that he was listening to the voice of Satan.[1]

Jephthah, also mentioned in the eleventh chapter of Hebrews as a man of faith and uprightness, is even harder to admire. Since only orthodox Jews and Protestant fundamentalists now read the Old Testament thoroughly, let me urge you, if you are a liberal Christian, to look up Judges, also Chapter 11, and see what you can make of this horror tale. Read how Jephthah made a rash vow that if he won a military victory over the Ammonites he would sacrifice whatsoever first came out of his house to greet him when he returned. That turned out to be his only child. The virgin girl so loved her father that she met him dancing and shaking tambourines. Read how the poor girl, upheld by her great "faith," cooperated with the demented judge and warrior. "O Jephthah, judge of Israel," exclaims Shakespeare's Hamlet, "what a treasure hadst thou!"[2]

The Old Testament God, and many who had great "faith" in him, are alike portrayed in the Bible as monsters of incredible cruelty. A philosophical theist, standing outside any religious tradition, can construct better models of God than Jehovah. Nevertheless, Hebrews 11:1, especially in the familiar phrasing of the King James Bible, remains a beautiful way of saying how faith, as a form of belief, is distinct from hope and knowledge.

I have spoken of God and immortality as twin objects of faith, and later will return to this linkage. Now let me say only that when I use the word *God* it means a God who has provided for our survival after death. When I use the word *immortality* it means survival in whatever manner God has provided. Following such fideists as Immanuel Kant and Miguel de Unamuno, and in line with the overwhelming majority of theists past and present, I will assume that the two beliefs go hand in hand and are mutually reenforcing.

Not that they can't be separated. Many thinkers have professed faith in God while denying an afterlife, but in almost every case the God involved is a pantheistic deity. A God more or less synonymous with Being or Nature obviously need not be concerned over whether we mortals live again, but such a God is the God of Spinoza, or the impersonal Absolute of Hegel and F. H. Bradley, not a God modeled on human personality. A personal God who did not provide for immortality would be a God less just and merciful than you and I. The whole point of the person model is to elevate human attributes, not lower them.

It is easier, perhaps, to hope for or even believe in an afterlife without faith in a personal God. One simply regards survival as part of the nature of things.[3] This point of view is sometimes taken by atheists and pantheists who believe in reincarnation. Among modern philosophers, John Ellis McTaggart of Cambridge University, and the French-born American, Curt John Ducasse, were notable in combining nonbelief in God with a belief in the preexistence and the afterlife of human souls. Robert Ingersoll, the famous American infidel, never hesitated to denounce any kind of deity, yet he was curiously open-minded about life after death. One may, of course, hope for immortality and at the same time estimate the odds against it as high, as one may hope to win a sweepstakes without believing the win is likely.

Although it is possible to believe in a personal God without believing in immortality, and vice versa, both views are extremely rare, and in any case they play no role in what follows. I agree with Unamuno that for almost all theists God is essentially the provider of immortality. Did any religious leader ever emphasize this more than Jesus? In the first chapter of *The Tragic Sense of Life*, Unamuno tells of suggesting to a peasant that there might be a God who governs heaven and earth, but that we may not be immortal in the traditional sense. The peasant responded, "Then wherefore God?"

Let us now inquire as to the sources of this faith. What prompts some men and women and not others to make that quixotic somersault of the soul, what Kierkegaard called the "leap of faith"? What enables them to turn themselves around, like Dante's rotation at the center of the earth when he began his climb from hell to purgatory, and believe in God and immortality even though both beliefs are unsupported by reason or science; even though both are plainly counterindicated by persuasive arguments?

Most people never worry about why they believe any religious doctrine. They just absorb their beliefs, often conflicting, from parents, relatives, friends, and surrounding cultures. But insofar as one is capable of deciding whether to believe or not believe in God and immortality, or at least to reflect about such a decision, what can be said to justify this leap?

Perhaps there is built into human nature a natural tendency toward faith, something comparable to a natural thirst for water. This is, of course, an ancient notion. In modern terms, is there a genetic basis for faith? Some sociobiologists have raised this possibility. Maybe it is balanced by a genetic predisposition toward atheism, like conflicting genetic impulses toward egoism and altruism. Maybe the relative strengths of the two tendencies vary with individuals, and vary statistically with cultures. I do not know the answers to these questions.

Assume there is no genetic basis for either atheism or altruism. The same questions return on an environmental basis. It is obvious that most cultures within recorded history have been dominated by religious systems. Can we say that in a reasonably healthy society, one that does a good job of meeting human needs, the healthier members of that society make leaps of faith? Even Freud, for whom religion was a neurosis, considered the possibility that all cultures need such illusions to remain happy and secure.

Soviet philosophy is officially atheist, and for decades we have watched a remarkable religious experiment taking place in Russia—an attempt by the government to stamp out religious faith among its citizens. How successful has this been? Even among Soviet officials, are the majority genuine atheists or are they closet believers? Is the great Russian campaign for atheism influencing Russia for good or ill? Is there a direct or inverse correlation in Russia, or for that matter anywhere else, between mental health and faith? I do not know the answers to these questions.

There is, however, one fact about which both atheists and theists can agree. For many people, perhaps most people, there is a deep, ineradicable desire not to cease to exist. Perhaps this desire, this fear of falling into what Lord Dunsany once called the "unreverberate blackness of the abyss," is no more than an expression of genetic mechanisms for avoiding death. Or is it more? It is easy to understand why any person would think death final—everything in our experience indicates it—but I share with Unamuno a vast incredulity when I meet individuals, seemingly well adjusted and happy, who solemnly assure me they have absolutely no desire to live again. Do they really mean it? Or are they wearing a mask which they suppose fashionable while deep inside their hearts, in the middle of the night and in moments of agony, they secretly hope to be surprised some day by the existence and mercy of God?

That the leap of faith springs from passionate hope and longing or, to say the same thing, from passionate despair and fear, is readily admitted by most fideists, certainly by me and by the fideists I admire. Faith is an expression of feeling, of emotion, not of reason. But, you may say, does not this lower faith? Is not man the only rational animal? No. Emotion more than reason, certainly as much as reason, distinguishes us from the beasts. "More often I have seen a cat reason," wrote Unamuno, in that marvelous chapter to which I referred a moment ago, "than laugh or weep." Yes, and I have watched my desk calculator reason more often than laugh or weep.

Freud thought of faith as little more than a desire to obtain in one's adult life the warmth, security, and comfort of the child who is cared for by loving parents. Of course! What else? Friedrich Schleiermacher said it all when he spoke of faith as springing from our feeling of "creaturehood," our dependence on outside help for our survival.

The true fideist grants it all. He may—in my opinion, should—go even another step, the ultimate step, in conceding points to the atheist Not only are there no compelling proofs of God or an afterlife, but our experience strongly tells us that Nature does not care a fig about the fate of the entire human race, that death plunges each of us back into the nothingness that preceded our birth. Is there need to elaborate the obvious? Thousands of good people are killed by an earthquake. Where is God? Not only is there no God, said Woody Allen, but try getting a plumber on weekends. So dependent is the mind on the material structure of the brain that genetic damage, drugs, injuries, diseases, operations, and senility can severely alter one's personality and ability to think and act normally. Even ordinary sleep can wipe out consciousness. If there is a soul capable of existing apart from that gray lump of tissue inside every skull, it is as hidden from us as God is hidden.

I agree with Pierre Bayle and with Unamuno that when cold reason contemplates the world it finds not only an absence of God, but good reasons for supposing there is no God at all. From this perspective, from what Unamuno called the "tragic sense of life," from this despair, faith comes to the rescue, not only as something nonrational but in a sense irrational. For Unamuno the great symbol of a person of faith was his Spanish hero Don Quixote. Faith is indeed quixotic. It is absurd. Let us admit it. Let us concede everything! To a rational mind the world *looks* like a world without God. It *looks* like a world with no hope for another life. To think otherwise, to believe in spite of appearances, is surely a kind of madness. The atheist sees clearly that windmills are in fact only windmills, that Dulcinea is just a poor country bumpkin with a homely face and an unpleasant smell. The atheist is Sarah, justifiably laughing in her old age at Abraham's belief that God will give them a son.

What can be said in reply? How can a fideist admit that faith is a kind of madness, a dream fed by passionate desire, and yet maintain that one is not mad to make the leap?

Persons of strong faith sometimes say they have a direct awareness of God, a knowledge of the sort that philosophers have called "knowledge by acquaintance." Mystics claim to have perceived God in a manner analogous to looking at the sun. We shall not linger over these claims. They carry no weight with anyone who has not had such an experience. No empirical tests can confirm that a person who professes such contact with God is actually in such contact. In many cases of persons who claimed such visions there is good evidence that they were experiencing delusions.

A subtler argument was made famous by Kant. Pure reason, said Kant, can prove neither God nor immortality, nor can it show them to be impossible. But we do not live by pure reason alone. We also live by what Kant called practical reason, by what a modern Kantian could call pragmatic reason. Everyone, said Kant, has a sense of duty, a conscience (Freud's superego). It tells us there is a difference between right and wrong, that it is our duty to be as good as we can and thereby promote the *summum bonum*, the highest good for humanity. This "moral law" within us is so powerful and awesome, as awesome as the spectacle of the starry heavens,[4] that we cannot escape believing that the highest good will someday be realized.

But look around. You see virtuous people, often children, suffering and dying for no apparent reason. At the same time you see wicked persons living healthy, happy, and prosperous lives until they die peacefully of old age. Where is the justice in such a scene? It can be just, said Kant, only if we assume another life, a life in which good is rewarded and wickedness punished. Not only that, but the perfection of goodness, for every individual, demands unlimited time in which to grow and profit from experience. Our life is cut off when we have just started to learn how to live. If there is no afterlife, no future in which virtue and happiness can be correlated, then our sense of morality becomes a sham. It arouses in us a passionate hope that can never be fulfilled.

Kant did not regard these arguments as proofs in the sense that one can prove a theorem in mathematics or establish a fact or law of science with high probability. We cannot "know" there is an afterlife. All Kant insists on is this. If we take seriously our hope that justice will be done with respect to our lives, we must posit an afterlife. And if there is an afterlife there must be a God who is good enough and powerful enough to provide it. It is not our *duty* to believe in God and immortality. Our duty is only to be good, and many atheists (Kant singled out Spinoza) can be very good. But if we want to make our beliefs consistent with the demands of our moral nature, we must posit God and immortality. And if we have faith, we do more than recognize them as posits. We also believe them to be true.

What should a modern fideist make of this? I think there is much to be said for Kant's arguments, and I will return to them again, but I agree with Unamuno that behind the complicated language of Kant's *Critique of Practical Reason* is one simple fact which Kant did not fully admit even to himself. As a man of flesh and bone, to use one of Unamuno's favorite expressions, Kant passionately desired God and immortality. He may have thought he posited God to make sense of morality; actually he posited God because he needed God in order to live. But let us listen to Unamuno himself, as he writes about Kant in the first chapter of *The Tragic Sense of Life:*

> Take Kant, the man Immanuel Kant, who was born and lived at Königsberg, in the latter part of the eighteenth century and the beginning of the nineteenth. In the philosophy of this man Kant, a man of heart and head—that is to say, a man—there is a significant somersault, as Kierkegaard, another man—and what a man!—would have said, the somersault from the *Critique of Pure Reason* to the *Critique of Practical Reason*. He reconstructs in the latter what he destroyed in the former, in spite of what those may say who do not see the man himself. . . .
>
> Kant reconstructed with the heart that which with the head he had overthrown. And we know, from the testimony of those who knew him and from his testimony in his letters and private declarations, that the man Kant, the more or less selfish old bachelor who professed philosophy at Königsberg at the end of the century of the Encyclopedia and the goddess of Reason, was a man much preoccupied with the problem—I mean with the only real vital problem, the problem that strikes at the very root of our being, the problem of our individual and personal destiny, of the immortality of the soul. The man Kant was not resigned to die utterly. And because he was not resigned to die utterly he made that leap, that immortal somersault, from the one Critique to the other.
>
> Whosoever reads the *Critique of Practical Reason* carefully and without blinkers will see that, in strict fact, the existence of God is therein deduced from the immortality of the soul, and not the immortality of the soul from the existence of God. The categorical imperative leads us to a moral postulate which necessitates in its turn, in the teleological or rather eschatological order, the immortality of the soul, and in order to sustain this immortality God is introduced. All the rest is the jugglery of the professional of philosophy.

Kant argued that it was necessary to posit God to satisfy a universal human desire for moral justice. Unamuno did not disagree. He simply saw more clearly than Kant, or perhaps more clearly than Kant was willing to admit, that the desire for moral justice flows from a deeper passion. For Unamuno, for all those who do not want to die, who do not want those whom they love to die, God is a necessary posit to escape from unbearable anguish. It is easy to say with the head that God does not exist, but to say it with the heart? "Not to believe that there is a God or to believe that there is not a God," wrote Unamuno, "is one thing; to resign oneself to there not being a God is another thing, and it is a terrible and inhuman thing; but not to wish that there be a God exceeds every other moral monstrosity; although, as a matter of fact, those who deny God deny Him because of their despair at not finding Him."[5]

Psalm 14:1, Unamuno liked to remind his readers, does not say, "The fool hath said in his *head*, There is no God."

There is another way to approach the task of justifying faith. I like to view it as a generalization of Blaise Pascal's famous "wager," but first let us see how Pascal himself presented it. Pascal was a Roman Catholic, and like all Catholics of his day he believed that every human soul had one of two destinies: eternal happiness in heaven or eternal misery in hell. Moreover, he believed that the soul's future state depended on accepting or rejecting Catholic doctrine. A person knowing of the Church's claim is thus faced with two alternatives. He may accept or reject the Church. In either case, the Church's doctrines may be true or false. Suppose he accepts. The payoff is infinite happiness if the Church is right; at the most a finite loss if it is wrong. Suppose he rejects. The payoff is at most a finite gain if the Church is wrong, but infinite misery if the Church is right. In view of these possibilities, said Pascal, is not joining the Church clearly the best bet?[6]

It is hard to imagine a reader of this book being impressed by Pascal's argument. As numerous critics have pointed out, even in Pascal's time the Muslim religion offered the same monstrous alternatives to potential converts. But if you wagered on immortality in the Islamic heaven you ran the risk of misery in the Christian hell. Who could genuinely convert to all religions that offered similar alternatives? Nevertheless, behind Pascal's wager there is a broader notion that can be applied to belief in God and immortality quite apart from the salvation doctrines of any organized church. This generalized Pascalian wager is suggested as far back as Plato's *Phaedo*, where Socrates, before drinking hemlock, speaks of belief in another life as a worthy risk because "fair is the prize and the hope great." In recent times the generalized wager has found its classic defense in William James's "The Will to Believe," an essay to which I now turn.

James argued his case with more care than he is usually credited with. First he makes a distinction, essential to all that follows, between what he calls a live option and a dead or trivial option. A live option is a choice between two alternatives that meets three provisos:

1. The alternatives must be plausible enough so that you are truly capable of deciding either way. Should you believe the earth flat or round? This was once a live option. Today it is dead, except perhaps for a handful of ignorant Protestant fundamentalists. Should you believe or not believe that the Reverend Sun Myung Moon is the new Messiah? This is a live option for some naïve young people, but for most people it is not. Should you spend your next vacation in Indianapolis? This is not a live option if you have no reason or desire to go there.

2. The choice must be forced. It must be what Kierkegaard liked to call an either/or. James gives the humble counterexample of choosing between going out with or without an umbrella. You can avoid the choice by not going out at all. Should you become a Scientologist or a Moonie? Clearly you need not join either cult. But the choice between voting for candidate X or not voting for candidate X is an either/or.

3. The alternatives must be momentous, not trivial. Should you have an egg for breakfast? This meets the first two criteria, but it is not a live option because the alternatives are too unimportant. Should you marry a certain person? Now the question is not so trivial.

James's thesis can be put simply. When we are confronted with live options, and when there are insufficient grounds for deciding rationally, we have no other way to decide except emotionally, by what James called our "passional nature." Who can deny that when a momentous decision is thrust upon us, and the head cannot decide, the heart must take over? But James is saying more than that. He is saying that there is nothing irrational or absurd about letting the heart take over.

The question "Does God exist?" confronts many people, perhaps most people, as a live option. The choice is forced in the sense that one must either believe or not believe. The agnostic may not insist there is no God, but he has exercised his option not to believe. Elsewhere, James likens the agnostic to a person who refuses to stop a murder, or to bail water from a sinking ship, or to save one's life by leaping across a chasm. The metaphors are overdramatic and pejorative but the basic point is sound. To avoid making an emotional decision about a live option (when there are no other grounds for a decision) is itself an emotional decision, and one that can have momentous consequences. Like Kierkegaard, James spoke of faith as a "leap in the dark." A leap across a precipice is made at our peril. Of course one would be foolish to make such a leap for no reason at all, but if there are no reasons, then it is not a live option. The decision to believe or not believe in God, James maintained, is for many persons a live option because it makes a difference in how they feel and how they live.

The leap of faith is made at our peril, yes, but so is the decision not to leap. James expressed it polytheistically. A man who shuts "himself up in snarling logicality," and demands that "the gods extort his recognition willy-nilly, or not get it at all," may be cutting "himself off forever from his only opportunity of making the gods' acquaintance."

James closes his essay with a passage from Fitz James Stephens:

> We stand on a mountain pass in the midst of whirling snow and blinding mist, through which we get glimpses now and then of paths which may be deceptive. If we stand still we shall be frozen to death. If we take the wrong road we shall be dashed to pieces. We do not certainly know whether there is any right one. What must we do? "Be strong and of a good courage." Act for the best, hope for the best, and take what comes. . . . If death ends all, we cannot meet death better.

The resemblance to Pascal's wager is obvious, and in other writings, especially in his essay on "The Sentiment of Rationality," James makes the parallel even stronger. In substance this is what he says: Belief in God and immortality are unsupported by logic or science, but because they are live options we cannot avoid an emotional decision. If for you the leap of faith makes you happier, then for you faith is the best bet. You have much to gain and little to lose. You have a *right* to believe. (In later years James said he should have called his essay "The Right to Believe.") I think James would have liked the way Count

Manuel, in James Branch Cabell's *Figures of Earth*, formulates the wager:

> "That may very well be, sir, but it is much more comfortable to live with than your opinion, and living is my occupation just now. Dying I shall attend to in its due turn, and, of the two, my opinion is the more pleasant to die with. And thereafter, if your opinion be right, I shall never even know that my opinion was wrong: so that I have everything to gain, in the way of pleasurable anticipations anyhow, and nothing whatever to lose, by clinging to the foolish fond old faith which my fathers had before me," said Manuel, as sturdily as ever.[7]

It was characteristic of James, as we saw in earlier chapters, to indulge at times in rhetoric that made his views easy to ridicule. His many examples of how "faith in a fact can help create the fact"—such as belief in one's career, or in winning a battle or a football game—surely have no relevance to faith in God. As if somehow believing in God could help make God a reality! George Santayana, in his marvelous essay on James,[8] is right in attacking James for these excesses (a product, in my opinion, of James's enthusiasm coupled with a confused epistemology), but Bertrand Russell's attack (in the chapter on James in his *History of Western Philosophy*) is as wide of the mark as his attack on Dewey in the chapter that follows. Russell actually suggests that James's arguments would establish the truth of "Santa Claus exists" as readily as "God exists," although it should have been clear to Russell that the Santa Claus hypothesis is not a live option for anyone except a young child. James might well have argued that under certain conditions a child is justified in believing in Santa Claus, but as soon as the child matures enough to understand the evidence against the hypothesis, the belief tips the other way.

On the other hand, I think Russell is right in saying that James often wrote as if he were concerned only with the pragmatic consequences of thinking and acting as if God exists, not with the question of whether God actually does exist. In my opinion James did not regard faith in such a superficial way. In any case it is not how most fideists regard faith.

It should be obvious that anyone who manages the leap of faith does not say to himself or herself: "I really don't know whether God exists or not, or whether there is another life, but because I find these beliefs comforting I shall pretend they are true." Perhaps some philosophers have been capable of this crazy "as if" approach to faith, but I have never met a theist who thought that way. Quite the contrary! For a person of faith, belief in God's reality is usually stronger than belief in any scientific hypothesis.

This was true even of Kant. It surely is a mistake to accuse Kant of the *als ob* perversion that some of his followers proclaimed in Germany. True, belief in God is not knowledge, but Kant, as he himself said, denied knowledge in order to make room for faith. For Kant, as for Plato, the phenomenal world, the phaneron open to exploration by science, is less real than the transcendent world of which the phaneron is but a shadow. It is our transcendent self, momentarily trapped in space-time, that believes by faith in a transcendent God. Not only does Kant avoid the notion of God as an "as if" posit less real than the universe, he argues the exact opposite.

Let me speak personally. By the grace of God I managed the leap when I was in my teens. For me it was then bound up with an ugly Protestant fundamentalism. I outgrew this slowly, and eventually decided I could not even call myself a Christian without using language deceptively, but faith in God and immortality remained. Much of my novel, *The Flight of Peter Fromm*, reflects these painful changes. The original leap was not a sharp transition. For most believers there is not even a transition. They simply grow up accepting the religion of their parents, whatever it is. For others, as we all know, belief can come suddenly, in an explosive conversion experience as startling as a thunderclap.

James applied the term "over-beliefs" to beliefs supported only by the heart. This does not mean they are not genuine beliefs. It only means they are beliefs of a special and peculiar sort. Why do I believe in the Pythagorean theorem? Because I can follow a deductive proof that rests on the posits of Euclidean geometry, and because the theorem is confirmed by experience. But this is not a choice about a live option. In a sense, belief in the formal truth of the theorem is a trivial, empty belief. It tells me only that if I accept certain posits, and rules for manipulating certain symbols, I am allowed to form a chain of those symbols that can be interpreted as the Pythagorean theorem. I believe in the formal truth of the theorem for much the same reason that I believe no bachelor is married.

Mathematical theorems are useful because they apply to the physical world, but (as I have said earlier) the applications require what Rudolf Carnap called correspondence rules, such as identifying the number 1 with a pebble or a star, or a straight line with a ray of light. As soon as we move from pure mathematics to applied mathematics, we move to a realm where hypotheses become uncertain, where the best we can do is weight them with varying degrees of credibility. Naturally we believe most strongly in those assertions of science that seem to us the best confirmed, but belief in God can carry with it a certitude, springing from the heart, that is stronger than any belief about the world. It is easier for me to believe that any fact or law of science is no more than a momentary illusion, produced by the Great Magician and subject to change whenever the Great Magician decides to modify his Act, than to believe that the Great Magician doesn't exist.[9] But this certainty is not knowledge of the kind we have in mathematics or science. It is trivially true that we believe what we know, or think we know. To believe what we do not know, what we hope for but cannot see—this is the very essence of faith.

I am quite content to confess with Unamuno that I have no basis whatever for my belief in God other than a passionate longing that God exist and that I and others will not cease to exist. Because I believe with my heart that God upholds all things, it follows that I believe that my leap of faith, in a way beyond my comprehension, is God outside of me asking and wanting me to believe, and God within me responding. This has been said thousands of times before by theists. Let us listen to how Unamuno says it:

> Wishing that God may exist, and acting and feeling as if He did exist. And desiring God's existence and acting conformably with this desire, is the means whereby we create God—that is, whereby God creates Himself in us, manifests Himself to us, opens and reveals Himself to us. For God goes out to meet him who seeks Him with love and by love, and hides Himself from him who searches for Him with the cold and loveless reason. God wills that the heart should have rest, but not the head, reversing the order of the physical life in which the head sleeps and rests at times while the heart wakes and works unceasingly. And thus knowledge without love leads us away from God; and love, even without knowledge, and perhaps better without it, leads us to God, and through God to wisdom. Blessed are the pure in heart, for they shall see God![10]

No more can be said. The leap of faith, in its inner nature, remains opaque. I understand it as little as I understand the essence of a photon. Any of the elements I listed earlier as possible causes of belief, along with others I failed to list, may be involved in God's way of prompting the leap. I do not know, I do not know! At the beginning of the leap, as at the beginning of all decisions, is the mystery of free will, a mystery which for me is inseparable from the mysteries of time and causality, and the mystery of the will of God.

14

PRAYER:
Why I Do Not Think It Foolish

> *Scientists will tell you that they have never seen the*
> *sequence of cause and effect interrupted at the*
> *instance of prayer or of divine reward or retribution.*
> *Do they think, the fools, that their powers of*
> *observation are cleverer than the devices of a god?*
>
> —THORNTON WILDER, *The Cabala*

Active members of organized religions obviously behave in ways atheists do not—their mere going to church for instance—but what about
philosophical theists who are not churchgoers? If we secretly video-
taped them for a week, would the tape show any behavior that would
identify them as theists? Of course if they talked about theology they
might say things atheists would not say, but religious topics are seldom
discussed these days even by churchgoers, so let's assume that our theists have no occasion to speak about God. Would anything on their
tapes distinguish them from atheists?

It would be folly to suppose we could deduce their theism from any
display of unusual happiness or well-being, or from any special efforts
to be good and self-sacrificing. Other things being equal, it may be that
a person of faith is slightly happier than an atheist, or works a trifle
harder at being good, but if so (and I am not sure it is so) we have no

ways to measure kinds of happiness and goodness with enough precision to distinguish between the two mind-sets.

There is, however, one thing we might observe on a secretly made videotape that would enable us to guess we were watching a theist. That one thing is occasional prayer. Of course there are exceptions. Some theists, in or out of organized religions, have weak impulses to pray, and for many the impulse takes the form of silent thoughts unaccompanied by any special body posture. C. S. Lewis's demon, writing to his nephew about prayer in *The Screwtape Letters*, quotes approvingly a remark by Samuel Taylor Coleridge that he never prayed "with moving lips and bended knees," preferring instead a silent "sense of supplication."[1] Perhaps this was Coleridge acting under the influence of his mentor, Immanuel Kant. But most theists, when they talk silently to God, find it desirable at times to combine their thoughts with some sort of body change, even if no more than a bowed head or a closing of eyes.

Just as I cannot imagine belief in a personal God that is not accompanied by belief in an afterlife, I cannot imagine belief in God unaccompanied by prayer. An atheist of course has no desire to pray. (Have you heard about the atheist's dial-a-prayer telephone service? You call a certain number and nobody answers.) Although a pantheist can and sometimes does pray after a fashion, the impulse is surely rare. What point is there in talking to Nature? "Infinitude, hadst Thou no face/ That I might look on Thee?" asked Emily Dickinson in a plaintive poem about a time when she tried vainly to pray to a "curious Friend" who kept himself invisible.[2] John Burroughs spoke, I think, for most pantheists when he wrote:

> Prayer is practically a belief in miracles or special providences—a belief that the world is governed, not by immutable law, but by a being whose favor may be won, whose anger may be appeased, or whose purpose may be changed, like that of a great monarch or king. . . . The wisest man cannot pray, has no need of prayer, because his whole life is an aspiration toward, and a desire for, the supreme good of the world.[3]

Kant would have agreed. A good person seeks the *summum bonum*, and (as we have seen) Kant maintained that this seeking is vain unless one posits an afterlife and a God to provide it. Yet, curiously, Kant had nothing to say about prayer in his three great *Critiques*, and in his

Religion Within the Limits of Reason Alone he mounts a vigorous attack on petitionary prayer. To ask God for anything that requires intervention in the causal structure of the world is both absurd and presumptuous, a form of "madness" which Kant likens to the habit some people have of talking aloud to themselves. To pray for anything is a "superstitious illusion." It does no more than express our desires to a Being "who needs no such information" because he already knows what we want. (See Matthew 6:8.) Friedrich Schleiermacher would later take the same hard line and exert an enormous influence over German Protestant theologians who leaned toward pantheism.

When I first encountered these views of Kant I was saddened and perplexed; saddened because they suggest that Kant, like William James, had no strong sense of a personal relationship with the God of his philosophy; perplexed because I could see no reason why Kant, given his own conceptions of God, time, and causality, would find it necessary to disparage petitionary prayer. Is it true that all such prayer, as Burroughs put it, is like praying for a change in the moon's motions, or in the tides and seasons? Or can a person of faith distinguish between praying earnestly for the possible and praying foolishly for the impossible?

Prayers of adoration and praise, prayers of thanks,[4] and prayers for forgiveness offer no stumbling blocks to a philosophical theist, but prayers of request are a different matter. Are we not, as Kant and Burroughs made so clear, asking God to change his mind and intervene in the causal structure of history? Is not this what I have called the "superstition of the finger," of hoping that the Supreme Being, hearing our petty wishes, will stretch out a finger and tinker with the universe in such a way that our desires are gratified?

Let me say at once that the overwhelming majority of theists—ordinary men and women who find prayers of supplication as natural as breathing—such men and women do not worry their heads or their hearts about the metaphysical difficulties involved.[5] If God is the creator and upholder of the universe, for whom every wave and particle dances in obedience to his will, surely there is no limit to his power. Because their relation to God is one of I-Thou, rather than the I-It relation of the atheist or pantheist, it is as natural for them to talk to God about their desires as it is for children to talk about their desires to a parent. By faith they believe that somehow, by a technique they never think about, their prayers will make a difference. Here is how James expresses it in *The Varieties of Religious Experience:*

If it be not effective; if it be not a give and take relation; if nothing be really transacted while it lasts; if the world is in no whit different for its having taken place; then prayer, taken in this wide meaning of a sense that *something is transacting*, is of course a feeling of what is illusory, and religion must on the whole be classed, not simply as containing elements of delusion,—these undoubtedly everywhere exist,—but as being rooted in delusion altogether, just as materialists and atheists have always said it was. At most there might remain, when the direct experiences of prayer were ruled out as false witnesses, some inferential belief that the whole order of existence must have a divine cause. But this way of contemplating nature, pleasing as it would doubtless be to persons of a pious taste, would leave to them but the spectators' part at a play, whereas in experimental religion and the prayerful life, we seem ourselves to be actors, and not in a play, but in a very serious reality.

The genuineness of religion is thus indissolubly bound up with the question whether the prayerful consciousness be or be not deceitful. The conviction that something is genuinely transacted in this consciousness is the very core of living religion. As to what is transacted, great differences of opinion have prevailed.

I do not think it desirable or even possible to go much beyond the sentiments expressed above. "He observed," Boswell says of Samuel Johnson, "that to reason philosophically on the nature of prayer, was very unprofitable."[6] Nevertheless there are those who are cursed by a need to speculate about such matters. Let us see what can be said in defense of petitionary prayer by a fideist who, like myself, wishes to combine faith with the utmost respect for science and unbroken natural laws.

We can all agree that certain kinds of petitionary prayers should never be made. It would be foolish, for example, to ask God to alter the Pythagorean theorem to make the square of the hypotenuse always equal to the *cubes* of the other two sides. God cannot be expected, said Aquinas, to do what is logically contradictory. God cannot make two plus one equal five, because the assertion would be as nonsensical as saying there are five feet in a yard. Nor can we expect God to do something which we know from ordinary experience, or the refined experience of science, to have such a low degree of possibility that it is practically indistinguishable from zero. Yes, Jesus said that sufficiently strong faith could move mountains (Mark 11: 23–24), but Jesus was fond of hyperboles, such as swallowing a camel, and I do not think he meant this literally. Surely only a demented theist would deem it worthwhile to ask God to teleport a mountain for him. By the same token, no intelligent theist can muster up a sincere request that God suspend the laws of gravity for a week, or give him the power to become invisible or to walk through walls. We pray only for what we believe is possible.

Beliefs about what is possible vary, admittedly, from person to person, culture to culture, age to age. Bertrand Russell somewhere speaks of the medieval practice, during a plague, of crowding into churches to pray, thereby transmitting the disease more rapidly. The impulse to pray may have been admirable, since knowledge of microbes was not then available, but God obviously did not see fit to alter laws about the spread of microorganisms.

Does God *ever* see fit to alter natural laws? This is the stupendous problem we have to face. How can a modern fideist, who does not believe in miracles, harmonize this skepticism with a belief in petitionary prayer? We are, I must make clear, not concerned here with the psychological effects of prayer. Even an atheist does not doubt that for many people an earnest prayer can have a marked effect on their will or ability to do something, to resist a temptation, to be courageous, to overcome an illness, to control an anger, and so on. Nobody denies the huge role of belief, the generalized placebo effect, in bringing about cures that seem miraculous. The psychological effects of prayer present no problem. We are concerned here only with the belief, of those who pray for something they think is possible, that their prayers can make a difference that is more than just an alteration inside their head.

Let us take the prayer for rain as a paradigm of all such requests. No one can sincerely pray for rain, during a time of great drought, without believing that God hears the prayer and that the prayer can make a difference. If such a prayer for rain is never justified, neither is any other prayer that asks God to intervene. I cannot agree with those who say it is always foolish to pray for rain, but not foolish to pray that God will keep safe a soldier who has been assigned to combat. If a prayer of supplication is justified in any situation, then in my opinion, scandalous though it may at first appear, it is also sometimes justified when one prays for rain.

The view I hold will strike any atheist or pantheist as a childish way of evading the central problem by taking a position that never can be confirmed or falsified. To this I at once plead guilty. I shall indeed argue that it is impossible in principle to devise any sort of experiment, or make any kind of observation, that will be relevant to the hypothesis that asking God for something can make a difference. (Remember, we are not speaking about psychological or physiological effects on the person who prays.) At the same time, and paradoxically, I shall argue that petitionary prayers are an essential accompaniment of faith.

In *The Screwtape Letters*, Lewis's demon speaks of the atheist's "heads I win, tails you lose" argument: "If the thing he [the theist] prays for doesn't happen, then that is one more proof that petitionary prayers don't work; if it does happen, he will, of course, be able to see some of the physical causes which led up to it, and 'therefore it would have happened anyway,' and thus a granted prayer becomes just as good a proof as a denied one that prayers are ineffective."

I know of no way to counter this except by giving the theist's "heads I win, tails you lose" argument, one that is equally incapable of being confirmed or disconfirmed. If you pray sincerely for something possible and it occurs, your prayer may have contributed to God's answer. If it does not occur, then God has heard the prayer but in his infinite wisdom has decided not to grant it. There is an old joke about a man who complained that God does not answer prayer because he had prayed for a million dollars and didn't get it. "But God did answer your prayer," said a friend. "The answer was no."

Both coin-flip arguments are impregnable, but why should a believer be disturbed? If there were ways to prove the efficacy of prayer, there would be ways to prove the existence of God, and faith would no longer be faith. It would be compelled belief.

I recall Thornton Wilder, in a classroom at the University of Chicago, heaping scorn on an episode in some current play or movie (perhaps it was *Seventh Heaven*) in which the heroine decides that God does not exist because she thinks her lover has died. When she learns he is alive, her faith in God is instantly restored. Millions die every year of famine, Wilder reminded us, or are killed in absurd accidents, yet this woman is so narcissistic that she lets her faith in God depend on what happens to *her*. I have thought of Wilder's remarks many times since. In that marvelous old movie *The Scoundrel*, Julie Haydon sees a newspaper headline reporting that Noël Coward, a book publisher she despises, has been killed in an airplane crash. She breaks into hysterical laughter. When someone asks if she is all right she replies, "I've just discovered there is a God." I thought of Wilder again when I read in *The New York Times* Muhammad Ali's declaration, "There's gotta be a God. I made $14 million last year."

Faith is not much of a faith if, like Huckleberry Finn, you give it up as soon as you discover you don't get everything you pray for. Life obviously would be total chaos if all prayers were answered. The ancient Greeks and Romans were well aware that their gods were perpetually bombarded by foolish prayers, not to mention such contradictory prayers as both sides praying for victory in a battle. "Leave it to the gods," wrote Juvenal, "to decide what is best for us." If there is anything on which great theologians have agreed, it is that every petitionary prayer, springing from a genuine faith in God or the gods, should be in the spirit of Jesus' appeal (Luke 22:42): "Nevertheless, not my will, but thine be done."

What distinguishes the attitude of a theist, convinced that "In His will is our peace" (as Dante's beautiful line has it), from that of an atheist or pantheist who stoically accepts "whatever will be will be"? The answer should be obvious. The theist believes by faith that God's will actually will be done; that God, in some unfathomable way, is assisted by our prayers. Because God is wise and good, the theist accepts what happens with peace and resignation. The atheist or pantheist has no basis for hoping justice will prevail because there is nothing behind impersonal nature to guarantee it. Why pray to Zeus, Lucian asks, if Zeus is in turn controlled by the three Fates? It is one thing to accept a calamity with peace, or a blessing with gratitude, because you believe it is the will of a loving God. It is an altogether different thing to accept such events because they are caused by a universe that gives not a damn what happens to you or anybody else.

With respect to prayer, the theist is in the same quixotic dilemma he is in with respect to faith in God. The absence of evidence for the efficacy of prayer does suggest—why should a theist deny it?—the absence of God and the futility of faith. Nevertheless, by faith the fideist believes. How can such madness be justified?

There is no way to justify it by any argument that will impress an atheist. Nor can it be justified by empirical evidence. Not only would such evidence dilute the uncompelled quality of faith, but (as C. S. Lewis puts it in *Miracles*): "A man who knew empirically that an event had been caused by his prayer would feel like a magician. His head would turn and his heart would be corrupted."[7] There is an amusing and cynical story by H. G. Wells called "Answer to Prayer." A bishop prays during a personal crisis. When a voice answers "Yes. What is it?" the bishop dies of terror.[8]

So what *can* we say to justify prayer? The most we can do is build a crude model of how prayer might work. If the model is consistent, and not in conflict with science, it has at least the merit of making faith in prayer seem less futile. I shall devote the rest of this chapter to two such models. Each has been defended by numerous theologians of the past. I present them less seriously than in a spirit of play. I do not know if either model is true, or even if it embodies a portion of truth. Indeed, I hold that the problem of prayer, like that of free will, forces us into paradox and total darkness. By faith and faith alone one believes that petitionary prayer can make a difference. I agree with Benjamin Franklin, a deist, that if God cannot alter the future, with respect to our experience of time, then "He has tied up his hands and has now no greater power than an idol of wood or stone."

For me the problem of prayer is bound up with the dark mysteries of time, of our wills, and of the will of God. Like the dilemma of defining *will* in a way that escapes both chance and fate, we face a comparable dilemma with respect to prayer. If God responds to our petitions, are we not forced to think of God as changing his mind? On the other hand, if God is unchanging, as most models of God represent him, is it not as useless to ask God for something as to ask a Zeus who is ruled by the Fates? In the first case we attribute free will to God. In the second case fate rules supreme. I think that for most believers in God both horns of this dilemma exert a perpetual tension in opposite directions. They pray in the hope of changing God's mind, and at the same time they recognize the absurdity of this hope by adding, "Thy will be done."

Our first model may be regarded as an extremely subtle version of the superstition of the finger. Let us think of God as capable of intervening in history in ways that lie on a continuum with respect to observability. At one extreme are the wild miracles that decorate the sacred literature of all religions. In the Old Testament, Jehovah talks directly to his prophets. He sends a great flood to drown almost everybody. He divides the Red Sea. He stops the sun. He turns a woman to salt. In the New Testament, the same God, incarnate in Jesus, also suspends natural laws in dramatic ways. He walks on the sea. He turns water to wine. He multiplies loaves and fishes. He revives the dead. He himself rises bodily from the tomb and later floats off into space.

From time to time efforts are made to explain the great miracles of the Bible in terms of natural laws not yet understood by science, but these explanations are so improbable, as well as so contrary to the plain intent of the narratives, that it is hard to imagine how anyone—orthodox Jew or Christian—could take them seriously. In recent years, for example, we have Immanuel Velikovsky invoking absurd hypotheses about the influence on earth of a great comet that erupted from Jupiter and eventually became the planet Venus. And we have among us many occultists and parapsychologists who are suggesting that unknown forces, as natural as gravity and electromagnetism, can account for many Biblical miracles. Jesus was a superpsychic with vast powers of PK that enabled him to levitate, to perform psychic healing, to calm the wind and waves. From this point of view God never had to suspend natural laws to meet the needs of his chosen people, or the needs of Jesus and his followers. He simply made use of laws science has not yet discovered. If a psychic like Nina Kulagina in Russia can levitate a Ping-Pong ball, if transcendental meditators can float in the air while meditating, what is "supernatural" about a superpsychic such as Jesus walking on the sea?

If I were an orthodox Jew or Christian, I would find such attempts to explain biblical miracles to be both preposterous and an insult to God. The Bible clearly depicts God as suspending the laws of the universe, not behaving like someone who knows more science than we do. Since I am not writing now to attack any religious orthodoxy, I will say no more about miracles except that my own attitude toward them is the same as David Hume's. There are no logical reasons why miracles cannot occur. But the evidence for them is so feeble that the hypothesis that the biblical accounts are myths, not historical facts, seems to me, as it does to almost all philosophical theists, to have a probability close to certainty.

What does all this have to do with petitionary prayer? Just this. Although one need not believe that God intervenes in history in such grotesque ways as changing a woman to salt or reviving a corpse, is it possible that God answers some prayers by intervening in a manner so deeply hidden that it is impossible to observe any breaks in causal chains? One thinks of Lewis Carroll's White Knight, who dyed his whiskers green, then used so large a fan that no one could observe the greenness. Perhaps God alters history on the microlevel where the changes introduced are so infinitesimal that the result seems always to be as natural as the falling of a raindrop.

William James was not a praying man. Yet in his *Varieties of Religious Experience* he expressed a belief that the act of prayer might produce changes in the mind of the person praying that are more than just a placebo effect. Through the unconscious mind, James believed, forces could enter from some higher realm. As for God answering prayer by altering events in the material world, James was skeptical but open-minded. A footnote to his "Dilemma of Determinism" reads as follows:

> And this of course means "miraculous" interposition, but not necessarily of the gross sort our fathers took such delight in representing, and which has so lost its magic for us. Emerson quotes some Eastern sage as saying that if evil were really done under the sun, the sky would incontinently shrivel to a snakeskin and cast it out in spasms. But, says Emerson, the spasms of Nature are years and centuries; and it will tax man's patience to wait so long. We may think of the reserved possibilities God keeps in his own hand, under as invisible and molecular and slowly self-summating a form as we please. We may think of them as counteracting human agencies which he inspires *ad hoc*. In short, signs and wonders and convulsions of the earth and sky are not the only neutralizers of obstruction to a god's plans of which it is possible to think.

The significant clause is "as invisible and molecular and slowly self-summating a form as we please." Let us frame this starkly. There is a great drought and a child is dying of thirst. The child's parents pray earnestly for rain. God hears, considers all the consequences of intervention, then in his infinite wisdom decides to answer the prayer. Because he wishes to remain hidden, he does not miraculously conjure a rain cloud from nowhere. Instead, he operates on an invisible microlevel, speeding up molecules here, slowing them down there, until the eventual outcome is a macroalteration of weather that results in rain.

This notion that God answers some prayers by an intervention that "takes place secretly, in the inmost heart of things" (as C. F. D'Arcy puts it in his article on Christian prayer in the *Encyclopedia of Religion and Ethics*),[9] has received an unexpected new defense in the theory of quantum mechanics (QM). QM presents a picture of the material world in which every microsecond, in all regions of the universe, billions upon billions of quantum events are taking place, events that have no antecedent causes. They are the outcome of pure chance. They occur perpetually and silently within every bit of matter, including of course our brains. There are even quantum fluctuations in vacuums, in what physicists had previously supposed to be completely empty space. Could it be that on *this* level, the submolecular level of elementary particles, the level of the photon and electron, God intervenes when he answers prayer?

On the QM level there is no need for God to alter the path or speed of anything so gross as a molecule or an atom. It is only necessary to alter probabilities whenever there is a collapse of a wave function. Here there is nothing even in principle that could be observed as a violation of natural laws. If you flip a penny and get ten heads in a row, the result may be startling but no natural laws have been suspended. By a clever alteration in the probabilities that determine the properties of quantum systems, perhaps God is altering events on the microlevel. One may even suppose in this wild vision that God is deciding *every* outcome of every wave-function collapse. His control is so complete that events never violate the statistical laws of QM. Yet at the same time every seemingly chance quantum event is carefully planned in the light of God's unimaginably vast intentions.

There is a fantastic approach to QM known as the "many-worlds interpretation." In this incredible picture the universe is splitting every microsecond into parallel worlds, billions upon billions of them, that have no further interaction with one another. They represent all possible states of the universe that could follow from every possible outcome of what in standard QM is called a wave-function collapse or, in the language of Hilbert space, a rotation of the state vector. We are aware of none of these splits, in which endless copies of ourselves spin off to live in other worlds, because we each ride along in the one sequence of events that carries us. Perhaps at every microsecond, basing his choice in part on prayers, God chooses the state of the world he wishes to preserve, and instantly causes all the other countless states to vanish. Better, he sees to it that the unwanted states never come into being. Thus at every instant God is shaping the future, but at no time violating a natural law, not even a statistical law. Actually, this is to say nothing different from what was said in the previous paragraph. It merely says the same thing in the colorful language of the many-worlds interpretation.

So much for our first model. Is it true? Don't ask *me*. How could I possibly know? I put it forth whimsically, as a useful model no one can prove false.

A central feature of our first model is that God answers prayer by intervening in history at precise moments of time. Our second model is altogether different. It is based on the notion, introduced in the chapter on free will, that God is wholly outside of time. He sees the entire history of our universe in an eternal, timeless way. This is how Aquinas and other theologians sought to harmonize free will with God's knowledge of what to us is still an undetermined future. From this viewpoint it is not hard to construct another model in which petitionary prayers made a difference, yet at the same time it is impossible in principle to detect breaks in causal chains.

One way to approach this model is through one of Unamuno's favorite metaphors. You and I are in the mind of God in a manner analogous to the way fictional characters are in the mind of a novelist. Although the novel's episodes occur (usually) in causal time sequences, the author sees all these events from a level above the novel's space-time. Because the novel is the author's creation he can adjust the plot any way he likes without destroying its causal consistency. Lewis plays with this idea in Appendix B of his book *Miracles*. In Hamlet, he reminds us, a branch on which Ophelia has climbed breaks and she falls into a river and drowns. "Did Ophelia die because Shakespeare for poetic reasons wanted her to die at that moment—or because the branch broke?" Both reasons are valid. "Every event in the play happens as a result of other events in the play, but also every event happens because the poet wants it to happen."

In a similar way, Unamuno and Lewis reason, human history may be conceived of as one of God's novels. In a manner utterly beyond our understanding, God has given us a reality far greater than Cervantes could confer on poor Don Quixote and Sancho Panza, and he has endowed us with the mysterious ability to act freely. Some of us have the strange habit of making petitionary prayers to the Author. Is it possible that God takes all such prayers into account and, in his infinite wisdom, adjusts the vast plot accordingly? Since God is responsible for the entire story, from beginning to end, these adjustments can be made from a timeless perspective in such a way that the plot, as it unrolls in our space-time, never departs from natural causal chains. In his timeless Now, God knows how every person acts and prays, not how he or she "will" act or pray, because for God there is no before and after. The acts and prayers are genuinely free when they occur in our time. It is as such free events that God sees them from his timeless frame of reference.

This point of view even allows for backward causality, or rather what seems to us, imprisoned in time, to be backward causality. "As time does not exist for God," the French Catholic writer Léon Bloy said, "the inexplicable victory of the Marne may have been decided by the very humble prayer of a little girl who will not be born for another two centuries." Here is Lewis making the same point in Appendix B of *Miracles*, from which I quoted earlier:

> When we are praying about the result, say, of a battle or a medical consultation the thought will often cross our minds that (if only we knew it) the event is already decided one way or the other. I believe this to be no good reason for ceasing our prayers. The event certainly has been decided—in a sense it was decided "before all worlds." But one of the things taken into account in deciding it, and therefore one of the things that really cause it to happen, may be this very prayer that we are now offering. Thus, shocking as it may sound, I conclude that we can at noon become part causes of an event occurring at ten o'clock. (Some scientists would find this easier than popular thought does.) The imagination will, no doubt, try to play all sorts of tricks on us at this point. It will ask, "Then if I stop praying can God go back and alter what has already happened?" No. The event has already happened and one of its causes has been the fact that you are asking such questions instead of praying. It will ask, "Then if I begin to pray can God go back and alter what has already happened?" No. The event has already happened and one of its causes is your present prayer. Thus something does really depend on my choice. My free act contributes to the cosmic shape. That contribution is made in eternity or "before all worlds"; but my consciousness of contributing reaches me at a particular point in the time-series.[10]

Suppose a loved one is killed. Is it reasonable to pray that the event not have taken place? No, replies Lewis, because the model certainly does not permit alteration of the past. He agrees with Aquinas and other Schoolmen that God cannot change the past, for it would be a contradiction to say that an event both did and did not occur. To know a past event is to know it has irrevocably happened. "It is psychologically impossible to pray for what we know to be unobtainable; and if it were possible the prayer would sin against the duty of submission to God's known will." But prayer for a past event about which we are ignorant could be one of the things God takes into account when he writes his Divine Comedy.

I cannot buy the above reasoning. It seems to me to carry the timeless model to a needless extreme, but I present it because it is both logically consistent and interesting. I do not know who first suggested the backward-causality possibility, but the timeless model, apart from this elaboration, is an ancient one.[11] In *The Screwtape Letters* Lewis credits Boethius, a Roman philosopher of the sixth century (who may or may not have been a Christian) with having "let the secret out." It has since been the model of choice for theologians who emphasize God's providence, including such Continental Protestant giants as Karl Barth. Because Lewis has defended it with such clarity and skill, I must give one final quotation, this from one of Screwtape's letters. (*The Enemy* is Screwtape's term for God, the *he* is his nephew's "patient" in whom the nephew is trying to instill doubts about prayer):

If you tried to explain to him that men's prayers today are one of the innumerable co-ordinates with which the Enemy harmonises the weather of tomorrow, he would reply that then the Enemy always knew men were going to make those prayers and, if so, they did not pray freely but were predestined to do so. And he would add that the weather on a given day can be traced back through its causes to the original creation of matter itself—so that the whole thing, both on the human and on the material side, is given "from the word go." What he ought to say, of course, is obvious to us; that the problem of adapting the particular weather to the particular prayers is merely the appearance, at two points in his temporal mode of perception, of the total problem of adapting the whole spiritual universe to the whole corporeal universe; that creation in its entirety operates at every point of space and time, or rather that their kind of consciousness forces them to encounter the whole, self-consistent creative act as a series of successive events. *Why* that creative act leaves room for their free will is the problem of problems, the secret behind the Enemy's nonsense about "Love." *How* it does so is no problem at all; for the Enemy does not *foresee* the humans making their free contributions in a future, but *sees* them doing so in His unbounded Now. And obviously to watch a man doing something is not to make him do it.

So much for our second model. Is it true? Do not ask *me*. How could I possibly know? I put it forth whimsically, as a useful model that no one can prove false.

Although we have no way of knowing whether either model, or a combination of the two, or some completely different model, is true or partly true, the making of such models serves, as I keep repeating, a valuable purpose. They show that there is nothing logically wrong about what theists choose to believe with their hearts. Jesus himself often made petitionary prayers (some of them not answered!) and he recommended that everyone pray for daily bread. I am always astounded when I meet Christians so progressive that they deem prayer for food quite acceptable, but prayer for rain, even if one is dying like the Ancient Mariner from lack of water, is somehow not justified. It goes without saying that under most circumstances praying for rain would be as foolish as praying that a certain basketball team win a game. Mature theists do not indulge in immature prayers. I insist only that the mariner's prayer for rain was not only justified, but impossible for any theist, under similar straits, not to make. It is one thing to say that prayers of this sort should not be made casually or selfishly. It is an altogether different thing to insist they should never be made.

I see no objection to empirical studies of how prayer can influence the mind, body, and behavior of those who pray. With respect to the healing of mental and physical ills I would expect the results to be positive but indistinguishable from a placebo effect. It could be that the effects of prayer are stronger than the effects of belief in the power of a drug or the skill of a physician. It depends, I suppose, on how firmly the person who prays believes. Without belief a prayer is obviously a useless ritual, like praying to an empty sky. In such cases I would expect placebo effects to vanish or at least diminish.

I also see no objection to parapsychologists continuing to look for correlations between prayer and what they interpret as the effect of psychokinesis on the physical world. I would expect all such tests to be negative, and I know of no positive results based on experiments I consider adequately controlled. It is possible that paranormal forces not yet established may allow prayers to influence the material world, and I certainly am not saying this possibility should be ruled out a priori. In science nothing should be ruled out a priori. If such forces exist they would provide the way, or one of the ways, that God has arranged for prayers to make a difference.[12]

Suppose it is true that natural laws, unknown to science, play a role in the efficacy of prayer. Must we then say that the indifferent universe, quite apart from conscious willing on God's part, answers prayers? The question is hopeless because we have not the slightest notion of what it means to say God wills something. Does every electron vibrate in response to God's will or only in response to laws God has willed? How can we understand what such a question means? Whatever be the truth of the matter, the theist prays to God rather than to the universe, and for a very simple reason. A prayer to the universe is not a prayer.

As for empirical tests of the power of God to answer prayer, I am among those theists who, in the spirit of Jesus' remark that only the faithless look for signs, consider such tests both futile and blasphemous. It is the essence of fideism that God chooses not to reveal himself in either a rational or an empirical way. If it were otherwise, faith would not be faith. Let us not tempt God. Let us not lower God to the level of a stage conjuror who floats ladies in the air, vanishes elephants, and produces pigeons from silk scarves. Let us model God's power in ways more consistent with his invisibility, more commensurate with his transcendence. Steve Allen, commenting in his autobiography on an idiotic book called *The Power of Prayer on Plants*, said it this way: "It appears unlikely that God would go out of His way to add an inch to a petunia while leaving innocent children to burn to death while they kneel in the very act of prayer."[13]

Do not ask me, therefore, how petitionary prayer can make a difference. I do not know. I can no more answer this question than I can explain how our wills escape the twin traps of fate and chance, or why children die of cancer, or whether God is in or out of time, or if an action is good because God wills it or God wills it because it is good.[14] I cannot understand how my will can be free. How much less can I understand how God's will can be free? I do not know how our personalities can survive death. I do not know why there is something rather than nothing, or why that something is made the way it is. Nor do I worry about such questions. Trying to play God is too much of a strain.

For me these questions, and others like them, are not just questions that cannot now be answered. They are questions I cannot imagine ever being answered by any mortal on this side of eternity, perhaps not even on the other side. The most we can do is build our dilapidated little models, stammer our flimsy metaphors, always recognizing how crude they are and never taking them seriously. We see all things through a glass darkly. In many spots the glass is so opaque that we cannot see through it at all.

As a theist outside all traditional religions, I cannot believe that a prayer to one deity is more likely to make a difference than an equally heartfelt prayer to another deity. For every unlovely myth about Allah that you can find in the Koran, I will match it with an equally unlovely myth about the God of the Bible. "It may be that the prayers we offer to Yarni Zai," writes Lord Dunsany at the close of a story, "may roll upwards from his image as do the mists at dawn, and somewhere find at last the other gods or that God who sits behind the others of whom our prophets know not."[15]

15

EVIL:
Why?

A bird sings now;
Merrily sings he

Of his mate on the bough,
Of her eggs in the tree:

But yonder a hawk
Swings out of the blue,

And the sweet song is finished
—Is this story true?

God now have mercy
On me, and on you!

—JAMES STEPHENS

My notes on philosophy and on literature are on file cards arranged in rough chronological order. Over the decades I have followed the practice of attaching tiny metal flags of six colors to cards that relate to six metaphysical topics: God, immortality, free will, evil, altruism, and the mystery of being. In going through my file cabinets for philosophy and literature, before writing this chapter, I was surprised to note that the number of flags for evil diminished steadily with time. There were many such flags for the ancient and medieval periods. They started to thin out during the Renaissance, and when the cards reached modern times the flags were few and far between. The problem of evil is not one that interests many twentieth-century writers.

I speak of the theological problem, not descriptions of evil. (Obviously there has been no falling off of descriptions.) How can the fact of evil be reconciled with models of a personal God? This is the dreadful difficulty with which I intend to grapple in this and the next chapter. To say I shall give no new arguments is to say nothing new because I have already confessed that there are no new arguments anywhere in this book. There is no way to say anything new about the problem of evil. It has all been said thousands of times before, in enormous detail, and often with great eloquence. The best I can do is repeat rusty, unsatisfying arguments, all older than Christianity. Not one of these arguments, if it tries to explain why God or the gods permit evil, carries any persuasion for an atheist. At the most they serve only to show that theism is not logically inconsistent, perhaps comfort a believer slightly, perhaps make the immensity of evil a bit easier to bear.

It is customary to distinguish moral evil or sin from what is usually called physical or natural evil, but unless I say otherwise, or the context implies it, I shall use the word to mean every kind of pain and suffering regardless of the cause. A baby who drowns accidentally in a flood is just as incomprehensibly dead as a baby tossed by someone into the sea. If a madman fires a gun at a crowd, killing ten people at random, they are just as needlessly dead as if they had been killed by an earthquake. It is this kind of senseless, irrational evil that is such a monstrous stumbling block for a theist. My little flags for evil diminished with the centuries not because evil diminished, or because theists found better ways to explain it, but because theism, among secular thinkers and writers, has diminished. To the atheist, or to the pantheist who is almost an atheist, there is no problem of evil. Evil is just part of how things are.

Occasionally one encounters the notion that an atheist faces an equally difficult problem in explaining goodness. It is a foolish notion because the atheist has no need to explain either good or evil. Of course if one could muster up a belief that God is supremely evil, then a problem of good might arise. It could be justified (as atheists sometimes do in jest) by asserting that all the good we experience is necessary to make possible greater pain. What better means could a Supreme Devil use for maximizing evil than allowing his creatures to enjoy life for a brief time, even to live with hope for another life, only to meet with final annihilation or perpetual torment in hell? But for the atheist or pantheist there is no problem of good or evil. The world is simply the absurd mixture that it is.

Evil is not even a problem for polytheism unless the gods form a hierarchy with a deity of supreme power and goodness at the top. In

Greek mythology the gods who have power over human lives are themselves mixtures of good and evil impulses, but even in ancient Greece the problem of evil arose whenever the power of Zeus was emphasized. Epicurus seems to have been the first philosopher to state clearly the atheist's most formidable argument. Either Zeus is unable to prevent suffering, in which case he is not powerful enough to be called a supreme God, or Zeus has the power to prevent suffering but doesn't wish to exercise it, in which case he is not moral enough to be worshiped as a supreme deity. Here is how Philo, in David Hume's *Dialogues Concerning Natural Religion*, phrases the argument: "Is he [God] willing to prevent evil, but not able? Then is he impotent. Is he able, but not willing? Then is he malevolent. Is he both able and willing? Whence then is evil?"

This argument, deadly and incisive, has been repeated endlessly by philosophers of all persuasions. I suspect that in every age and place, if you asked an ordinary atheist why he or she did not believe in God you would get some version of Epicurus's argument. If suffering were only a minor aspect of the human scene, the argument might have less force, but the plain truth is that the amount of needless, irrational misery inflicted on humanity passes all comprehension. No one has expressed this with more painful honesty than John Stuart Mill in his essay "Nature." The paragraph is too long to quote in full, but here is how it begins:

> In sober truth, nearly all the things which men are hanged or imprisoned for doing to one another are nature's everyday performances. Killing, the most criminal act recognized by human laws, nature does once to every being that lives, and in a large proportion of cases after protracted tortures such as only the greatest monsters whom we read of ever purposely inflicted on their living fellow creatures. If by an arbitrary reservation we refuse to account anything murder but what abridges a certain term supposed to be allotted to human life, nature also does this to all but a small percentage of lives, and does it in all the modes, violent or insidious, in which the worst human beings take the lives of one another. Nature impales men, breaks them as if on the wheel, casts them to be devoured by wild beasts, burns them to death, crushes them with stones like the first Christian martyr, starves them with hunger, freezes them with cold, poisons them by the

quick or slow venom of her exhalations, and has hundreds of
other hideous deaths in reserve such as the ingenious cruelty of a
Nabis or a Domitian never surpassed. All this nature does with
the most supercilious disregard both of mercy and of justice . .

Emily Dickinson said it ironically:

> Apparently with no surprise
> To any happy flower
> The frost beheads it at its play—
> In accidental power—
> The blonde assassin passes on—
> The sun proceeds unmoved
> To measure off another day
> For an approving God. [1]

Most people seldom worry about any metaphysical problem, and for
that reason an awareness of the full horror of irrational evil comes
upon them rarely, usually at times of personal tragedy. At one end of
the cheerfulness spectrum are the optimists, those whom William
James called the "healthy-minded." They seldom brood over the mystery of pain, accepting whatever comes their way and making the best
of it. Except for those rare moments of extreme despair, there is no
evidence that atheists are less healthy-minded than theists, that they go
about with sadder faces, or are more prone to mental depression. At
the other end of the cheerfulness spectrum are the pessimists, James's
"sick souls," who, regardless of their metaphysical beliefs, constantly
dwell on the extent of misery in the world and in their lives.

Pessimism obviously is a fuzzy word, but for my crude purposes
there is no need to define it precisely. I use it here to mean a philosophical emphasis, not a symptom of mental depression. Whatever the
causes of depression, chemical or environmental, theists can be
stricken by it like everyone else. James, Unamuno, Samuel Johnson,
John Bunyan, Tolstoy . . . these are only a few of many famous theists
who suffered severe attacks of melancholia. A large literature deals
with what Christians sometimes call the "dark night of the soul"—
periods of anguish so intense that only their faith seems to restrain
them from suicide. It is not with such illness I am here concerned. I
am concerned only with the arguments and literary expressions of
those who stress the enormity of evil and the futility of justifying it by
faith in God. The universe would be better off, they sometimes de-

clare, if no human life existed. Better off for whom? For humanity! In *The Tropic of Cancer*, Henry Miller wonders why some compassionate soul doesn't "put a bomb up the asshole of creation" (this before the atom bomb) and give the world the coup de grâce it so sorely needs.

Nontheist philosophers vary in the stress they put on such moods. You will find the tone occasionally sounded satirically in the writings of Bertrand Russell and mournfully in the books of George Santayana, but if Aristotle or Dewey were ever troubled enough by evil to suggest that the human race not try to perpetuate itself, I cannot recall the passage. Is life worth living in spite of evil? Charles Fort, in *Wild Talents*, observes that one usually asks that question only at times of personal travail, and therefore usually answers it negatively. One day, in what Fort calls "one of my frequent, and probably incurable, scientific moments," he decided to make an experiment. For a month, at the end of each day, he recorded a plus or minus sign to indicate whether he thought that on the whole that day had been worth living. "At the end of the month, I totaled up, and I can't say that I was altogether pleased to learn that the plusses had won the game. It is not dignified to be optimistic."[2]

It was especially not dignified among some German philosophers of the nineteenth century. For Arthur Schopenhauer, the greatest of pessimists, pain is not the absence of pleasure, or evil the absence of good. Like one of those optical illusions that reverse figure and ground when you gaze at it, the world under Schopenhauer's gaze became a world in which good is the absence of evil, pleasure the absence of pain. We need not waste time on the interesting biographical question of how much of Schopenhauer's pessimism was a literary pose, how much the projection of a misanthropic temperament, or how much an honestly reasoned view. At least he gave cogent arguments. Consider, he said, one animal devouring another. Is not the pain of the eaten greater than the pleasure of the eater? For every desire satisfied, a multitude are denied. The great symbols of human existence are Tantalus trying vainly to assuage his thirst, Sisyphus forever laboring to roll back the stone. "We have not to rejoice but rather to mourn at the existence of the world; that its nonexistence would be preferable to its existence; that it is something which ought not to be."

For Schopenhauer, ours is the worst of possible worlds. The other great German pessimist of the same century, Eduard von Hartmann (whose work on the unconscious anticipated so much of Freud), took a different tack. He agreed with Leibniz that this is indeed the best of

possible worlds but, as an old jest has it, alas it is too true. Like
Schopenhauer he thought human life ought not to exist: "As the life of
a fish is more enviable than that of a horse, so is the life of an oyster
than that of a fish, and the life of a plant than that of an oyster."[3]

Later in the nineteenth century this fashionable German pessimism
degenerated into the *fin de siècle* mood and those Russian and European trends that group loosely into what has been called nihilism.
Among recent philosophers, the French and German existentialists
have made the most of the irrationality of evil, though like Von Hartmann and Nietzsche they recommended opposing evil rather than doing nothing or jumping off a cliff, in saying what Nietzsche called the
Yea to life rather than the Nay, even though the Yea, in their metaphysics, is meaningless and absurd.

Theists also vary widely in the degree to which they dwell on irrational evil. Can you imagine a positive thinker like Norman Vincent
Peale preaching a sermon about starved and dying bodies on the streets
of Calcutta? At the other end of the spectrum are those religious leaders who like to stress the irrationality of evil in order to contrast the
pessimism of a Schopenhauer with the escape provided by faith. Unamuno called his masterwork *The Tragic Sense of Life*. There is a
strange sense in which those who manage the somersault of faith find
the literature of pessimism more worth reading than the literature of
optimism, especially the optimism of those humanists who ignore the
absurdity of evil, who substitute for God and immortality the hope for
a better human society on earth even though it is a society in which
they cannot participate. More than that, the secular humanist is
doomed never to know whether the human race will ever achieve a
more just social order or whether it will go the way of the dinosaurs.

It is not surprising, when you think about it, to find in the literature
of theism many references to irrational evil, and quotations from the
great pessimists. The dark side of existence, the forces that make for
despair, are precisely those forces that motivate the leap of faith. "We
are perplexed," writes Saint Paul (2 Corinthians 4:8), "but not in despair." To a person of faith it is the atheist pessimist who sees life the
way it is. It is the atheist optimist who seems shallow and half-blind.

Where can you find a more passionate account of the irrationality of
life than the book of Ecclesiastes? It is not relieved by even a hint of
faith, yet it remains in the Bible. And there is that great fantasy about
God, Satan, and Job in which the riddle of evil is never answered.[4]
Shakespeare probably believed in God, yet he produced immortal pas-

sages of despair. Life is "a tale told by an idiot, full of sound and fury, signifying nothing." "As flies to wanton boys, are we to the gods: they kill us for their sport." The writings of Herman Melville and Nathaniel Hawthorne, saturated with an awareness of irrational evil, are popular readings in Christian seminaries.

Even the great expressions of pessimism by atheist poets are, I suspect, savored more by theists than by most atheists. The theist is perplexed, but not unto despair. The atheist is more likely to be perplexed unto despair. I am thinking of Omar's *Rubáiyát*, of James Thomson's *City of Dreadful Night*, of some of the lyrics of A. E. Housman and Thomas Hardy. There are the novels of the French anti-Semite Louis-Ferdinand Céline, for whom *merde* is the great symbol of being. There is Mark Twain's incomparable *The Mysterious Stranger*, the finest blend of bitter humor and ironic pessimism to be written since Voltaire's *Candide*. I have a 1916 edition by Harper and Brothers with handsome color plates by N. C. Wyeth, Andrew's father. Apparently the publisher thought of it as a book for children![5]

Theists can enjoy books like *The Mysterious Stranger* more thoroughly than most atheists precisely because they have a way of escaping the book's grim implications. Theists know as well as any atheist that we are all living on the Magic Mountain, or in the Tropic of Cancer, stricken with that terminal disease called life. They know that we are all undergoing Kafka's Trial, sentenced for something we know not what, tried by mysterious officials who conceal their identities and motives, and are certain to execute us in the end. In his *Varieties of Religious Experience*, James used still another metaphor:

> For naturalism, fed on recent cosmological speculations, mankind is in a position similar to that of a set of people living on a frozen lake, surrounded by cliffs over which there is no escape, yet knowing that little by little the ice is melting, and the inevitable day drawing near when the last film of it will disappear, and to be drowned ignominiously will be the human creature's portion. The merrier the skating, the warmer and more sparkling the sun by day, and the ruddier the bonfires at night, the more poignant the sadness with which one must take in the meaning of the total situation.

I must stress again that this tragic sense of life, this perpetual awareness of evil and death, may have little or no connection with a person's sense of well-being, regardless of his or her beliefs. I do believe that, all other things equal, a person of faith is happier than one who lacks it; but whether this is true or not, we still have the problem that crouches like Blake's tiger at the center of this chapter. How can a person of faith, who believes in a supremely good and powerful God, justify nature's insane recklessness?

Of course there is no problem if God is fundamentally evil. I know of no major religion that has claimed this, or any healthy person who seriously believed it, though pessimists now and then feign such a belief to intensify their rhetoric. God is the Vast Imbecility in Thomas Hardy's poem "Nature's Questing" who is "Mighty to build and blend,/But impotent to tend," who has "Framed us in jest, and left us now to hazardry." God is the "cold mad feary father" on the last page of *Finnegans Wake*.

The God of Moses is not an idiot, but he is pictured in the Bible as capable of such extreme cruelty that anyone who believes these accounts to be accurate comes very close to believing in an evil God. Because most Jews and Christians today read only select passages in the Old Testament, such as the twenty-third psalm, and because the books of Robert G. Ingersoll and other Bible debunkers are now hard to come by, let me cite just a few episodes from the life of Moses.

When Moses' nephews Nadab and Abihu failed to mix the incense properly for a burnt offering, Jehovah was so furious that he sent down a fire that "devoured" them (Leviticus 10). There is no indication that the nephews made a deliberate mistake or were intoxicated. They were just careless. Was Moses consumed with grief? If so, we are not told. We are told only that he ordered the boys buried and asked Aaron, their father, not to mourn, "lest ye die, and lest wrath come upon all the people."

When the son of an Israelite mother and an Egyptian father blasphemed the name of God, Jehovah commanded Moses to have him stoned to death, and decreed *ex post facto* that henceforth anyone guilty of this crime must meet the same fate (Leviticus 24).

When a group of 250 "princes of the assembly, famous in the congregation, men of renown," rebelled against Moses and Aaron, Jehovah caused an earthquake to "swallow" the leaders, followed by a fire that consumed all 250. After the unhappy Israelites complained to Moses that he had "killed the people of the Lord," Jehovah sent a plague that murdered 14,700 more of the chosen people (Numbers 16).

When the Israelites objected to the taste of manna ("our soul loatheth this light bread") Jehovah was so annoyed that he sent "fiery serpents" to bite and kill them (Numbers 21). We are not told how many were bitten, only that "much people of Israel died."

When some Israelite men "began to commit whoredom" with some Moabite women, and to worship Moab gods, Jehovah ordered Moses to hang all the men. This apparently had little effect, because an Israelite prince took into his tent a Midianite woman. Jehovah's punishment was a plague that killed 24,000 Israelites. More would have perished had not the offending couple been murdered by Phinehas, the son of a priest. "Phinehas . . . hath turned my wrath away from the children of Israel," the Lord told Moses, "while he was zealous for my sake among them, that I consumed not the children of Israel in my jealousy" (Numbers 25:11).

Numbers 31 is not only the most infamous chapter of the Bible; it is hard to find its equal in any other sacred book. Moses was ordered by Jehovah to attack the Midianites. The army killed all the male Midianites, burned down their cities, and brought back all the women and children, and all the cattle, sheep, donkeys, and goods. Moses was dumbfounded when he learned that the women had been spared. He told his soldiers to kill all the nonvirgin women and all the male children, but to keep the 32,000 virgin girls for themselves.

After this was done, Jehovah carefully instructed Moses on how to divide the spoils among the 12,000 soldiers (apparently not a single soldier had lost his life) and those who stayed at home. Did God actually approve of all this? "If there be a God," commented Ingersoll, "I pray him to write in his book, opposite my name, that I denied this lie for him."

It won't do to say that these horror tales are exceptions, or that there are reasonable ways of finding behind them a just, compassionate God. The atrocities are not exceptions. There are hundreds of similar ones. You can find them in the Old Testament for yourself, if you want to take the time, or you can read about them in such books as Robert G. Ingersoll's *Some Mistakes of Moses*, and Joseph Wheless's *Is It God's Word?* Exodus 20:5 is the first of many passages in which Jehovah declared his intention to visit the iniquity of fathers (typically, mothers don't count) upon their children and their children's children, even "unto the third and fourth generation of them that hate me."

> Well, then, I hate Thee, unrighteous picture;
> Wicked image, I hate Thee;

> So, strike with Thy vengeance
> The heads of those little men
> Who come blindly.
> It will be a brave thing.[6]

I know of no philosophical theist who does not agree with Ingersoll that the God of the Pentateuch is "a false friend, an unjust judge, a braggart, hypocrite, and tyrant, sincere in hatred, jealous, vain, and revengeful, false in promise, honest in curse, suspicious, ignorant, and changeable, infamous and hideous. . . ."[7]

More believable than demon monotheism is the model in which two gods of equal or almost equal power, one wholly good, one wholly bad, are engaged in a mighty conflict with human history as the field of battle. Perhaps the outcome is in doubt, but in most great religions that have used this model, such as Zoroastrianism and Manicheanism, the good side is predetermined to win. Traditional Christianity reflects a milder form of this dualism, differing mainly in the belief that Satan, the souce of all earthly evil, was originally one of God's creatures and therefore on a much lower scale than the Creator. "It must be remembered," Samuel Butler says somewhere, "that we have heard only one side of the case. God has written all the books." In India, Shiva the destroyer is as essential to the universe as Vishnu the preserver, though both are part of Brahman, the impersonal, unknowable ground of being.

A curious way to justify evil and at the same time preserve a pure monotheism is to regard God as fundamentally good, but troubled by evil impulses. The model is closely related to the God of Moses, except there is no Satan prowling about to do things of which God does not approve. The evil we find in nature and in ourselves reflects a conflict within the mind of God. Modern writers of science fiction and fantasy often play with this notion. Among Western philosophers, Jakob Boehme went further than most in exploring this model.

The model has many variants. God, for example, may be growing more admirable over the millennia. You find something close to this in the contemporary movement known as "process theology," which stems from the views of Samuel Alexander and Alfred North Whitehead. God is indeed as good as it is possible now for any deity to be, but he is still improving and has not yet managed to eliminate all evil, if indeed such a triumph can ever be completed. As we struggle against evil we assist God in his own development.

In this model of a "finite God," growing in time, God remembers all the past but he can guess the future only with probabilities. He can never be absolutely certain how all the details of history will turn out, partly because of a randomness built into nature and partly because his creatures have unpredictable free wills. Because God is in time, not eternity, he suffers and rejoices with us. We and God are thus partners in the great cooperative task of reducing the amount of evil in the universe.

No one has defended this vision with more skill than Charles Hartshorne, one of my fondly recalled teachers at the University of Chicago. Only this model, he passionately believes, will solve the problem of evil for a theist. Hartshorne's writings are stimulating to read and seldom opaque, but I am always made uncomfortable by the fact that he seems to know so much more about God than I do. Is God, for instance, really in time or beyond time? Hartshorne is certain that God is in time. Since I do not know what time is, how can I answer such a question? For me, time is not only a terrible mystery; I agree with Unamuno that it is "the most terrible of all mysteries, the father of them all."[8]

Perhaps God is infinitely good and powerful but not very intelligent, as Jurgen discovers Koshchei (who made all things as they are) to be. "I manage affairs as best I can, Jurgen. But they get in a fearful muddle sometimes."[9]

Perhaps God is supremely intelligent but absent-minded. Maybe he occasionally goes to sleep, and when he does things do not fare so well on earth. Paul Erdös, one of today's top mathematicians, uses the initials SF for God. It stands for the Supreme Fascist, whose two principal traits are that he is all-powerful and enormously lazy.

There is another approach to the problem of evil that should be mentioned before we go on to more serious models. The problem is "solved" by semantic sleight-of-hand, by denying that evil exists at all. Evil is an illusion, or maya, as the Hindus call it. In the United States this is a central dogma of Christian Science.

I do not wish to belittle the emotions behind this point of view. It has a long, respectable history that goes back to Plato, Plotinus, and the Stoics, and you find it in the writings of innumerable Christian thinkers and German pantheists. You find it in Emerson. Evil is merely the absence of good. Just as the light of the sun dims with distance, so does the finite world dim in goodness as its distance from God increases. Evil is that which is not God. Sometimes it is identified with matter, sometimes with all of nature. Sometimes it is equated with nothingness or nonbeing.

Christian thinkers have been fond of pointing out that without a background of evil, good would not be recognizable. If everything were blue, how could we know what blue is? Shadows are necessary in painting; villains are necessary in plays and novels. Could we appreciate musical harmony if we could not also hear discords? Evil is the foil that defines the good. Without it there would be no genuine battles, no heroism, no sacrifices, no saints. One thinks of that marvelous mosaic by M. C. Escher in which angels of light alternate with devils of blackness. Each shape is needed to define the contours of the other.

There is much to be said for these ways of viewing evil as a necessary contrast to the good, but to say that therefore evil doesn't "exist" is like saying that a deep hole in the ground doesn't exist. There is a sense in which the hole is nothing, but one can fall into it all the same and be killed. We are not here dealing with any substantive issue, only with a verbal riddle on the level of asking whether a zebra is white with black stripes or black with white stripes. It does not solve the problem of evil. As Protestant theologian John Hick once put it, it merely "redescribes the problem." Evil may be an illusion, but now we have to ask why the illusion causes so much suffering. "If I sit on a pin and it punctures my skin," as an old limerick goes, "I dislike what I fancy I feel." After all, only a small amount of contrast is needed to define something. A small hole defines a doughnut as well as a large hole. Occasional bouts of pain are enough to make anyone appreciate health. Evil may be maya, but why so much maya? The problem remains as enigmatic as it was before the terminology altered.

How can a theist who believes by faith in a personal God, a God who is all-powerful and all-good, justify the horrors of irrational evil? There is only one way. One must believe, again by faith, that in some unfathomable manner which we cannot now understand, perhaps will never understand, the existence of evil is necessary for ultimately bringing about the greatest good.

No one has expressed this obvious argument more simply or more starkly than C. S. Lewis, writing about the suffering of his wife, Joy, when she was dying of cancer:

But is it credible that such extremities of torture should be necessary for us? Well, take your choice. The tortures occur. If they are unnecessary, then there is no God or a bad one. If there is a good God, then these tortures are necessary. For no even moderately good Being could possibly inflict or permit them if they weren't.[10]

This, of course, is no solution. It leaves the problem of evil, as we left the problems of free will and petitionary prayer, an impenetrable mystery.[11] To any atheist it is a shameful evasion. Nevertheless, clumsy models can be built in defense of this view. They have at least the merit, as I have said, of showing that a view is not logically inconsistent. We will take a look at these models in the next chapter.

16

EVIL:
Why We Don't Know Why

It might be
The final test of man, the narrow way
Proving him worthy of immortal life,
That he should face this darkness and
this death
Worthily and renounce all easy hope,
All consolation, all but the wintry smile
Upon the face of Truth. . . .

—T. H. HUXLEY, AS HE SPEAKS
IN *The Torch-Bearers*, BY ALFRED NOYES

In no way will this chapter solve the enigma of evil. As a theist I believe by faith, and by faith alone, that there is an answer. But I do not know the answer. At the end of the chapter I will defend the view, also supported only by faith, that God does not want us to know the answer.

Let us build some models. One, the model of choice for most of those today who believe in an afterlife, is that the evils that befall us are punishments for sins in previous lives. The doctrines of reincarnation and karma, which this model presupposes, are suggested in Plato (is there anything Plato does not suggest?), defended by Pythagoras and Plotinus, and by some Greek and Roman mystery religions. The model is taken for granted in almost every Hindu sect and in most forms of Buddhism. Today in the United States it is a fundamental dogma of such cults as theosophy, Rosicrucianism, and Scientology.[1]

It is popular among many who belong to no organized church or cult, but who are caught up in current enthusiasms for Eastern religions and the paranormal.

Although the doctrine can be found in some minor strands of old Judaism (parts of the Talmud, the Kabbala, the writings of Philo), even in some early Christian heresies such as Gnosticism and Manicheanism, it has played almost no role in Christian theology. The reason surely is that Jesus did not teach it. It is as unsupported by the New Testament as it is omnipresent in Hindu sacred literature.

The model is logically flawless, incapable of empirical refutation, and like the hypothesis of life after death it could be confirmed by experiments. There is now a considerable literature about individuals who claim to recall details of their past lives. In recent decades experimenters such as Ian Stevenson have reported such recall by persons who have been "regressed" under hypnosis and hypnotic drugs. This is not the place to examine such extraordinary claims. I will say only that I find the evidence as shaky, and the experiments as poorly controlled, as the "evidential" claims of Spiritualism.

The often encountered argument from moments of *déjà vu* is valueless because there are adequate explanations that do not assume previous lives, and because *déjà vu* is counterbalanced by the less common but equally eerie experience of *jamais vu*—a peculiar strangeness about a familiar scene. I recall a startling occasion a few years ago when my wife and I were driving home late at night along a New York parkway we had traversed a hundred times, yet both of us suddenly felt as if we had taken a wrong turn and were on a road we had never traveled before. The feeling lasted several minutes. No doubt something in the environment of which we were unconscious was affecting us, but we never found out what it was.

Occasionally it is argued that our sufferings cannot result from bad karma because we have no recall of past sins and therefore the punishment is useless. It is a poor argument. Believers can reply that lack of memory is essential for the punishment, and that a time will come when our recall will be complete. Perhaps our souls remember past cycles in the intervals between earthly reincarnations. In any case, at some future date we may be able to see the entire pattern, to appreciate the impeccable justice behind it all.

I cannot say this model is wrong. In spite of its singular beauty, and the grandeur it adds to the spectacle of evolution (if one believes that our souls began their pilgrimage in lowly forms of life), in spite of the simple solution it offers for the problem of evil, I cannot say I find the model satisfying. Because I have no memory of a previous life, I tend to rule it out by the principle of Occam's razor. I readily confess that my having been brought up a Christian may play a strong role in this sentiment. Had I spent my childhood in India, with Hindu parents, perhaps I would now find the doctrine more attractive. Another reason I am not now attracted to reincarnation is that in cultures where it is widely believed, it is constantly invoked to condone extreme intolerance. In India, for example, the misery of the untouchables has repeatedly been justified by other castes on the grounds that the unclean are being punished for their sins in a previous life. In any case, my heart has no need for the doctrine. I do not know if it is false. I only feel it is false.

The mathematician I. J. Good, in his entertaining anthology of "partly-baked" ideas, *The Scientist Speculates*, proposes a curious variant of the reincarnation model. Good calls it "a theory which is impossible to believe if true." We are on earth as punishment for crimes committed in heaven, and part of the punishment is that we cannot believe the theory. "For if we did, the punishment would not be effective." Good makes clear that he himself does not believe this. How could he if it were true?[2] And there are other curious models that justify irrational evil on grounds less fantastic to Eastern minds than ours. You'll find some choice examples in Raymond Smullyan's book *5000 B.C. and Other Philosophical Fantasies*.

The models that have dominated theism in the West, in or out of the Judaic-Christian tradition, all have one central and incredible idea in common. They assert that, in some fashion we can now comprehend only dimly (if at all), the evils we suffer are permitted by God because they contribute, in the long run, to the highest obtainable good.

The model is suggested in Plato, by some of Plato's followers, by the Stoics, and by other pre-Christian thinkers. But it was Saint Augustine who placed the greatest stress on it, who stamped it indelibly with its orthodox Christian form.

In Augustine's model, moral evil is the price we and the angels must pay for having been given the gift of free will, and natural evil, in a less direct way, is also a consequence of this freedom. Although God could make angels and human beings incapable of choosing evil, they would not then be fully conscious creatures who are in some respect images of himself. There is a paradox here, for if God has free will but never chooses to do evil, could he not create images of himself that also would always choose to do good? At any rate, so goes the argument, the nature of an angel includes the freedom to do evil, and although most angels remained loyal to their creator, a few, led by Satan, chose to rebel. Since God is outside of time, he knew this would occur. Why then did he permit it? Because only by doing so could he achieve the greater good that comes from letting evil have its hour, of allowing it to display for all time the hideous consequences of rebellion against God.

This rebellion, on a lower plane of creation, is still taking place on earth. Adam and Eve were given free wills like the angels, but, tempted by Satan, they, too, used their freedom to defy their creator. Had they not done so, according to Augustine, they would have lived in a Paradise free of death, aging, disease, and all other natural evils. This, too, was foreseen by God. He permitted the Fall of humanity for the same reason he permitted the fall of Satan. It was all part of the same vast plan in which human history, alongside the ultimate fate of Satan and his followers, would become the great lesson-book of the universe.

Although there are complicated side issues and many subtle variations, it is astonishing how closely later Christian theologians, including the leaders of the Protestant Reformation, adhered to Augustine's model. One can easily see why, for clearly it is the model that best conforms to biblical mythology. Today it is still the accepted model for Catholics and for all traditional Protestants who believe in Satan and original sin. It is a model on which the Pope and Billy Graham can agree.

Jump to the early eighteenth century. The queen of Prussia is distressed by the writings of the French fideist Pierre Bayle. Faith, said Bayle (as Unamuno would later say) is not only unsupported by reason and experience, it is contrary to reason and experience. The unnecessary evil we see around us is so immense that it strongly implies a world that is not under the control of an all-powerful, all-good deity. Could Leibniz, the queen wanted to know, ease her mind on this point? Leibniz responded with his famous *Théodicée*, the only important book he published in his lifetime. Written in French, printed in Amsterdam in 1710, and later translated into Latin, it became enormously popular and influential.

Leibniz's model is essentially Augustinian, but elaborated so as to bring out more clearly that evil cannot be justified by theists unless they recognize that the power of God is severely limited by logic. As we have seen, this notion was familiar to the Schoolmen. Thomas Aquinas readily admitted that omnipotence cannot include the ability to do logically absurd things. Rather than say there are things God cannot do, said Saint Thomas, it is best to say there are things that cannot be done. For example, it is not possible for a creature to be completely a horse and at the same time be completely a human being.

Let us make the point mathematically. If we define a triangle as a polygon of three sides, it makes no sense to say God could create a triangle with four sides. This does not limit God's power. It only limits our ability to find meaning in a meaningless sentence. A four-sided triangle is as meaningless as a married bachelor. To say that God could do something that can be expressed in our syntax only as a self-contradictory string of symbols is simply to utter nonsense.

This applies to the physical world as well as to our mental concepts. We use what Rudolf Carnap called correspondence rules to establish isomorphisms between purely mathematical ideas and physical things. A bead on an abacus, for example, is not made of putty. It is a wooden object that keeps its size and shape as it slides back and forth along a rod. We take each bead as a model of the number one, and posit a one-to-one correspondence between the laws of arithmetic and the way the sliding beads group themselves into sets. To ask if God could slide two beads up a rod, then two more beads up the same rod, and (without creating another bead) produce five beads at the top of the rod, is to ask for something that is logically impossible. This is not a limitation on God's power. It is a limitation on our ability to make sense of what it would mean to say that two beads plus two beads equal five beads. As long as the beads remain what we mean by beads, "four beads" is another name for "two beads plus two beads," just as "yard" is another name for "three feet." Can God make a valley that is not between two mountains? No, because our language defines a valley as something between two mountains. To expect God to do impossible things is to expect something that cannot be done.

In creating a physical universe, said Leibniz, and covering its planets with intelligent creatures, God's power, though infinitely great, is limited (as the Schoolmen had perceived) by laws of logic and mathematics. The universe must be *possible*. We have a dim understanding of trivial ways in which a universe would be impossible because of logical contradictions, but from God's transcendent perspective there are infinitely many other ways we cannot comprehend. Leibniz used the term *compossible* for those elements of a universe that can go together without contradiction. From our finite point of view there is a distinction between logically impossible and what our experience tells us is physically impossible. We cannot conceive of a world in which the number of pigs in a pen depends on our choice of the pig where we first start our count. We *can* conceive of a world in which pigs fly. However, from God's point of view there are higher laws of logic and mathematics, unknown to us, which severely restrict the structure of any universe capable of existing.

Imagine, said Leibniz, an immense pyramid in which God has piled the abstract models of all possible worlds—worlds that contain no contradictions. There are infinitely many such models. God has arranged them so that as you go down the pyramid you encounter structures with less and less total goodness for its creatures—hence with more evil—than the models above. At the apex of the pyramid is the structure that maximizes good and minimizes evil. In his infinite wisdom God perceives that no better world is possible. Being also infinitely good, he selects this as the model for the universe he conjures into existence.

How does this vision justify evil? Moral evil is explained along Augustinian lines. It is the inevitable consequence of free will. God could have created angels and human beings unable to sin, but they would not then have been angels or human beings. They would have been automata of the sort that Thomas Huxley, in a careless moment, said he would like to be. The question is obviously intertwined with the mystery of human will and how it differs from the will of God.

As a Christian, Leibniz believed in the rewards and punishments of an afterlife, and the reality of hell, though his hell was considerably less populous than Augustine's. Leibniz objected vigorously to the belief that hell contains the souls of unbaptized infants, or adults who had no way of knowing about Jesus. Nevertheless he argued (in a passage so offensive to William James that he quotes it at length in *Pragmatism*) that even if a majority of human beings were destined for eternal torment it would be only a minute fraction of the intelligent creatures in the universe who had chosen to obey God. Our universe has many suns, said Leibniz, and presumably many planets, all of which may be inhabited by happy, sinless creatures. And beyond our universe may be a vaster region "replete with happiness and glory." Thus the number of earthlings who are damned are but an infinitesimal part of the number of intelligent beings in the universe who are not. Perhaps only on earth was the Fall necessary to display the terrible consequences of rebellion.

Leibniz's justification of natural evils, such as diseases and earthquakes, follows a similar line. It is not possible for human beings with free wills to exist except in a physical world with an environment structured by natural laws. The price we pay for our structured world is precisely those physical evils we see around us. Besides, these natural evils contribute in numerous ways to higher goods, especially in light of the rewards that await the saved in heaven. Without natural evils there would be less compassion, less opportunity for doing good, less incentive to improve the lot of mankind, and so on.

The reaction to Leibniz's vision, with its central dogma that this is the best of all possible worlds, was understandably mixed. One admirer, Alexander Pope, though himself crippled by nature, summed up the vision in these oft-quoted lines from his *Essay on Man:*

> *All nature is but art, unknown to thee;*
> *All chance, direction, which thou canst not see;*
> *All discord, harmony not understood;*
> *All partial evil, universal good:*
> *And, spite of pride, in erring reason's spite,*
> *One truth is clear,* WHATEVER IS, IS RIGHT.

To a skeptic like Voltaire, Leibniz's *Theodicy* seemed so outrageous that he mercilessly caricatured it through the simpleminded remarks of Dr. Pangloss in *Candide.*[3] For a modern theist who is not a Christian there are indeed aspects of the *Theodicy*, and of Augustine's earlier efforts to justify evil, that are ugly and offensive. The belief in Satan, the doctrine of the Fall of man, the need for preserving the unsaved in perpetual torment—none of these doctrines press themselves on modern theists unless they believe that the Bible contains a special Revelation from the Creator. Augustine's belief that natural evils, like famines and floods, would not have existed on earth had Satan not rebelled, seems incredibly naïve to a philosophical theist.

In preparation for this chapter I read for the first time C. S. Lewis's much-admired book *The Problem of Pain.* As always in reading Lewis I found many estimable things, but I read with acute embarrassment for the author the chapter in which he imagines a possible scenario for what happened at the Fall. Although Lewis makes clear that his account is only a "myth," nevertheless he presents it seriously as a "not unlikely tale" of what actually may have happened. Let me summarize:

For millions of years God used evolution to shape the animal form that would become the image of himself. When the right moment arrived he "caused to descend upon this organism" a new kind of consciousness. The bestial form became human. Lewis does not tell us whether the first human beings were a single pair or many men and women, nor does he mention the odd fact that these first humans would have been brought up and nurtured by parents who were beasts. In any case, the first men and women were sinless and had such marvelous control over their bodies' functions that they experienced no pain. They did not grow old and die. Like the inhabitants of Oz, they could live as long as they pleased. All animals, even the fiercest, were obedient to them.

Enter Satan. Actually, as Lewis suggests in a later chapter on animal pain, Satan had long been "at work for ill on the material universe, or the solar system, or, at least, the planet Earth, before ever man came on the scene. . . ." Lewis believes that this malevolent angel may have corrupted the animal world in the early stages of evolution. As a result, animals became carnivorous and began to eat one another. Disease-producing microbes became part of earth's life-forms. Lewis reminds us that Jesus (Luke 13:16) attributed a woman's infirmity explicitly to her having been "bound by Satan" for eighteen years. Thus does Lewis follow his mentor Augustine in tracing all natural evil, as well as moral evil, back to the machinations of fallen angels.

The paradise God had planned for humanity was shattered when the first humans were tempted by Satan. Like the Evil One, they exercised their free wills to commit the sin of pride, the sin of thinking they knew better than God what was good for them. "For all I can see," writes Lewis in a sentence I had to read several times before I believed it was there, "it might have concerned the literal eating of a fruit. . . ." Fruit or not, the Fall brought into being a new species, not the spotless creatures God had intended but a fallen race that had "sinned itself into existence." This new condition "was transmitted by heredity to all later generations." Of course God, being outside of time, saw the Fall and the Atonement in his timeless Now, allowing it all to happen as part of his unfathomable Plan. The plan may well be confined to Earth. Lewis agrees with Leibniz that if there are rational creatures on other planets there is no reason to assume they too have fallen.

I can find nothing in Lewis's scenario with which Augustine would have taken issue except for those passages that reflect an acceptance of the evolution of life and of man's body, but we certainly can't fault Augustine for not knowing what Darwin knew. The only chapter in *The Problem of Pain* that I found sadder than the chapter on "The Fall of Man" is the chapter on "Hell." But of course Lewis, being an orthodox believer in the Church of England, had no alternative except to defend these monstrous doctrines. To have denied them would have entailed finding fault with the teachings of Jesus, and Lewis was too honest to suppose that he could give up such doctrines and still call himself a Christian.

For the philosophical theist who does not believe in hell, Satan, or the Fall, is there anything in the Augustine-Leibniz way of justifying evil that can be preserved and made more credible? I think there is. Let us call it the revised version of Leibniz's model. You will find it defended by some very early fathers of the Church who were influenced by Greek philosophy, by large numbers of liberal Protestant theologians of recent times, and by many theists outside of Christianity altogether.

Charles Peirce, for instance, regarded the revised version as an "obvious solution," adding that "Columbus's egg was not simpler."[4] For Peirce, evil is necessary because God is "perpetually creating us." The struggle against evil, on the part of both individuals and the race, is essential to the process of what Christians have called "soul-making." Evil exists to be overcome, to make life a genuine battle. As to whether ours is the best possible world, Peirce took the sensible Thomist view. Although we believe God to be omnipotent and omniscient and infinitely good, these words are used vaguely because we cannot know what any human trait is like when raised to God's level. We have no clear notion of what omniscience means, Peirce wrote: "Not the faintest! The question is gabble." Perhaps this is the best possible universe. Perhaps it is the *only* possible universe (as Arthur Stanley Eddington would later speculate). "Perhaps others do exist. But we only wildly gabble about such things."[5]

Peirce often referred to a book called *Substance and Shadow*, by Henry James, Sr., the father of his good friend William, for having clearly presented the "obvious solution." The book is hard to read today, saturated as it is with misty Swedenborgian theology. Perhaps the best expression of the elder James's view of evil is in one of his letters, part of which reads as follows:

> Think of a spiritual existence so wan, so colourless, so miserably dreary and lifeless as this; an existence presided over by a sentimental deity, a deity so narrow-hearted, so brittle-brained, and putty-fingered as to be unable to make godlike men with hands and feet to do their own work and go their own errands, and content himself, therefore, with making spiritual animals with no functions but those of deglutition, digestation, assimilation. . . . These creatures could have no *life*. At the very most they would barely *exist*. Life means individuality or character; and individuality or character can never be *conferred*, can never be *communicated* by one to another, but must be inwardly wrought out by the diligent and painful subjugation of evil to good in the sphere of one's proper activity. If God made spiritual sacks, merely, which he might fill out with his own breath to all eternity, why then of course evil might have been left out of the creature's experience. But he abhors sacks, and loves only men, made in his own image of heart, head and hand.[6]

This notion that suffering is required to make life a genuine adventure, to make history an authentic struggle, reverberates through all of William James's writings about evil. In *Pragmatism*, James compares the world to a football game. If the aim of the game is merely to get the ball over a certain goal line, said James, the team "would simply get up on some dark night and place it there." But of course the aim is to get it there according to fixed rules. "The aim of God is not merely . . . to make men and to save them, but rather to get this done through the sole agency of nature's vast machinery. Without nature's stupendous laws and counter-forces, man's creation and perfection, we might suppose, would be too insipid achievements for God to have proposed them."

One essential condition of the game, according to James, is that human beings have free wills that are unpredictable even by God. "I want a world of anarchy" was how he put it in a letter. This use of anarchism as a metaphor for free will so appealed to G. K. Chesterton that it became the theme of his greatest novel, *The Man Who Was Thursday*.[7] The huge figure of Sunday is Chesterton's symbol of God.[8]

From the back, Sunday resembles an evil beast. From the front he looks like an archangel. The mystery of Sunday, says Thursday, is also the mystery of the world. "When I see the horrible back, I am sure the noble face is but a mask. When I see the face but for an instant, I know the back is only a jest. Bad is so bad, that we cannot but think good an accident; good is so good, that we feel certain that evil could be explained."

Thursday speaks of an occasion when he was racing down a street behind Sunday. He imagined that "the blind, blank back of his head really was his face—an awful, eyeless face staring at me! And I fancied that the figure running in front of me was really a figure running backwards, and dancing as he ran."

Then comes a passage that I have always considered one of the finest capsule descriptions of Platonism I know: "Shall I tell you the secret of the whole world!" shouts Thursday. "It is that we have only known the back of the world. We see everything from behind, and it looks brutal. That is not a tree, but the back of a tree. That is not a cloud, but the back of a cloud. Cannot you see that everything is stooping and hiding a face? If we could only get round in front—"

We cannot, alas, or perhaps happily, get round in front. There is that startling passage in Exodus 33 in which God, after explaining that no person can see his face and live, allows Moses a momentary glimpse of his back. It is this back of the world that we see as a mixture of good and evil. We can guess but we cannot fully know the reason for evil, because if we did know we might become indifferent to it. In Chesterton's fantasy (he subtitled it "a nightmare") Sunday heads an anarchist group that is plotting to destroy humanity. The seven members of its ruling council are known by the seven days of the week. A secret police group is organized to infiltrate the council as spies. It finally turns out that six members of the council are spies, and it was Sunday himself who hired them. God is on both sides of the crazy conflict.

But why a conflict at all? So that every person, by exercising his freedom to rebel, "may have the glory and isolation of the anarchist. So that each man fighting for order may be as brave and good a man as the dynamiter. So that the real lie of Satan may be flung back in the face of this blasphemer [the book's real anarchist], so that by tears and torture we may earn the right to say to this man, 'You lie!' "

Josiah Royce was another distinguished upholder of the revised version. The world, he wrote, is like a beautiful marble statue. Examine it under a microscope and you see nothing but a rough surface covered with blemishes. The world is like a beautiful piece of music. Listen carefully and you hear its discords. Only God, from his timeless perspective, sees all human history the way we see a statue. Only God hears all history the way we hear a symphony. Both metaphors go far back in the literature of speculations about the why of evil.[9] The ugly aspects of any great work of art are ugly only when considered in isolation from the whole. They are those terrible moments in our lives when, to return to GK's allegory, Sunday's "great bright eyes go quite blind," and for hours he seems to forget you are there.

Clearly it is a poor answer to the problem of evil just to proclaim, without any evidence, that life's discords somehow contribute to a final harmony. George Santayana summed up Royce's views with his usual accuracy: ". . . it was really right that things should be wrong, but that it was really wrong not to strive to right them." But how evil contributes to good is something we are not permitted to know, because if we did know, we would not take the battle seriously. "The true solution . . . is that no solution can ever be found."[10]

One of the best statements of the revised version is in *Philosophical Theology*, by the Cambridge University theologian Frederick Robert Tennant. His arguments are the same as those we have been examining, but Tennant expresses them crisply and in a form free of those peculiarly Christian doctrines which in my opinion weaken the model. Evil is the price we pay for existing. Moral evil is the necessary accompaniment of free will. Physical evil is the necessary accompaniment of a structured world.

Let me introduce Tennant's model by way of modern cosmology. It is now widely agreed, as I have mentioned before, that a big bang could in principle create a universe in which fundamental physical constants were not the same as those we find. In Leibniz's language, there are endlessly many kinds of universes, each with compossible constants, that could result from the primeval fireball. Only some of these universes would permit the formation of suns and planets, and consequently the evolution of intelligent life. Higher laws of logic and mathematics, in ways we do not understand, may impose severe limits on possible universes that allow life to evolve. The entire process could be God's only way of creating such a universe. If so, physical evil may be an inescapable aspect of the process. I now quote Tennant:

That painful events occur in the causal chain is a fact; but, that there could be a determinate evolutionary world of unalloyed comfort, yet adapted by its law-abidingness to the development of rationality and morality, is a proposition the burden of proving which must be allotted to the opponent of theism.

One can only add that, in so far as experience in this world enables us to judge, such proof seems impossible. . . . if water is to have the various properties in virtue of which it plays its beneficial part in the economy of the physical world and the life of mankind, it cannot at the same time lack its obnoxious capacity to drown us . And as it was found absurd to suppose that God could make developing beings at the same time morally free and temptationless, so it involves absurdity to suppose that the world could be a moral order without being a physical cosmos. To save mankind from the painful consequences which flow from a determinate world-order, such as the earthquake and the pestilence, would involve renunciation of a world-order, and therefore of a moral order, and the substitution of a chaos of incalculable miracle.[11]

Pope rhymed it this way in his *Essay on Man:*

Think we, like some weak prince, the Eternal Cause,
Prone for his favourites to reverse his laws?
Shall burning Etna, if a sage requires,
Forget to thunder, and recall her fires?
On air or sea new motions be imprest,
O blameless Bethel, to relieve thy breast?
When the loose mountain trembles from on high,
Shall gravitation cease, if you go by?
Or some old temple, nodding to its fall,
For Chartres' head reserve the hanging wall?

The price we pay for gravity is the possibility of being killed if we walk off a cliff, or of being killed by falling masonry. But we can learn not to walk off cliffs. We can learn to build more secure buildings. Only in the context of a structured environment can there be a process of growth for individuals and for humanity.

In his *Philosophy of Religion*, John Hick enlarged on a *reductio ad absurdum* argument by suggesting that we try to imagine a world in which physical evils are impossible:

The consequences would be very far-reaching. For example, no one could ever injure anyone else: the murderer's knife would turn to paper or his bullets to thin air; the bank safe, robbed of a million dollars, would miraculously become filled with another million dollars (without this device, on however large a scale, proving inflationary); fraud, deceit, conspiracy, and treason would somehow always leave the fabric of society undamaged. Again, no one would ever be injured by accident: the mountain-climber, steeplejack, or playing child falling from a height would float unharmed to the ground; the reckless driver would never meet with disaster. There would be no need to work, since no harm could result from avoiding work; there would be no call to be concerned for others in time of need or danger, for in such a world there could be no real needs or dangers.

To make possible this continual series of individual adjustments, nature would have to work by "special providences" instead of running according to general laws which men must learn to respect on penalty of pain or death. The laws of nature would have to be extremely flexible: sometimes gravity would operate, sometimes not; sometimes an object would be hard and solid, sometimes soft. There could be no sciences, for there would be no enduring world structure to investigate. In eliminating the problems and hardships of an objective environment, with its own laws, life would become like a dream in which, delightfully but aimlessly, we would float and drift at ease.

One can at least begin to imagine such a world. It is evident that our present ethical concepts would have no meaning in it. If, for example, the notion of harming someone is an essential element in the concept of a wrong action, in our hedonistic paradise there could be no wrong actions—nor any right actions in distinction from wrong. Courage and fortitude would have no point in an environment in which there is, by definition, no danger or difficulty. Generosity, kindness, the *agape* aspect of love, prudence, unselfishness, and all other ethical notions which presuppose life in a stable environment, could not even be formed. Consequently, such a world, however well it might promote pleasure, would be very ill adapted for the development of the moral qualities of human personality. In relation to this purpose it would be the worst of all possible worlds.[12]

No death or decay mars the scene on Keats's Grecian urn. Spring never ends. The bride and groom are forever young. But of course it is a world without time, and therefore without life. "Try to exclude the possibility of suffering which the order of nature and the existence of free wills involve," wrote C. S. Lewis in *The Problem of Pain*, "and you find that you have excluded life itself."

It is clear that this model imposes severe logical restraints on God. Does this mean one must speak of a "finite God"? Here, I think, we move into a language dispute which I find profitless. My own preference is to speak of God as infinite, as did Aquinas and Leibniz, never forgetting that we have no conception, none whatever, of what words like *infinite* and *omniscient* mean when applied to God. It seems to me that the differences between Leibniz's model in its revised version and similar models that have been put forth in more recent times by non-Christian theists who use the term *finite God* are differences mainly of language and emphasis.

The modern notion of a God whose attributes are finite is usually credited to David Hume, who was probably an atheist, although the first detailed defense was made later by John Stuart Mill. Mill did not think it necessary to combine his theism with belief in an afterlife, though he was open to the possibility. Since Mill, the concept of a finite God, with or without an afterlife, has been set forth by William James, F.C.S. Schiller, Alfred North Whitehead, William Pepperell Montague, Samuel Alexander, Edgar Sheffield Brightman, Charles Hartshorne, and many others. H. G. Wells, of all people, went through a brief phase of interest in the finite-God idea. He even wrote a book about it—the first ever devoted to the topic, *God the Invisible King*—before he concluded he was really an atheist.

Like most concepts, the finite-God idea is on various continua, a fact that leads to all sorts of curious and obscure debates among finite-God philosophers over the best way to talk about justifying evil. In the previous chapter we considered briefly the "process" theologians who like to think of God as developing in time as he struggles to remove defects from the human scene. My own view, to repeat, is that I do not know what it means to say God is in or out of time. But I do not like a language that speaks of God as undergoing growth, because it reduces God's transcendence, because it suggests a deity who is more like a demigod or a superhumanoid than the God of traditional theism. It is one thing to say that God is limited in certain ways, quite another thing to say that God is finite. A circle cannot be a triangle, and its length is finite, but it contains an uncountable infinity of points. Because I do not know what it means to say that God is finite, and because I feel uncomfortable in applying this adjective to God, I find the debates among finite-God theologians over the precise degrees of God's powers to be unproductive wrangling—gabbling, as Peirce would say—over words that have only the cloudiest meaning when applied to God. To me the topic is too dreary to pursue further.

As for the notion of "best of all possible worlds," the phrase seems to me as useless as the adjective *finite*. How can we know whether there is one possible universe, or seven, or a countable infinity, or an uncountable infinity, or perhaps even a higher aleph number? And what does "best" mean? For all I know there could be an infinity of existing worlds, no two alike, all as real as ours, all equally good. To speak of the best possible world may be as absurd as speaking of the best possible bird. Leibniz strikes me as naïve in this respect. As a mathematician who invented the calculus he should have remembered that equations can have no solution, one solution, any finite number, or an infinite number. If two cities, with widely differing customs, can be equally good in maximizing the happiness of their citizens (whatever that means), why not two universes? We gabble nonsense when we talk about such things.

Although a theist can justify evil by making it an inescapable aspect of any physical world capable of sustaining such fantastic creatures as you and I, without a belief in an afterlife the justification surely fails to counter the argument of Epicurus. A God capable of creating a universe that is in turn capable of producing you and me is certainly capable of providing another life for us. And if there is no such afterlife, we are back to the terrible questions that tormented Job, and to the arguments of Immanuel Kant's *Critique of Practical Reason*. We live in a world in which children die of cancer, or are born insane, while wicked persons prosper. Every theist I have cited as a defender of the revised version of Leibniz's model, even some of the finite theists, recognized that their model gives no satisfying answer to the riddle of evil unless it is accompanied (as it was not for Job) by belief in a future life.

Such belief is, of course, part of the irrational leap of faith. From our perspective we obviously cannot see God's final pattern in which injustices are remedied. Thornton Wilder's Brother Juniper charted the relative goodness and badness of fifteen people who died in a pestilence with those of fifteen who survived, and found that the dead were "five times more worth saving." His study of the five who perished when the bridge in Peru collapsed comes to no firm conclusion, and Wilder, who knows so much more about the five than Brother Juniper, ends his novel by recognizing the futility of such investigations.[13] When a tower in Siloam collapsed and killed eighteen people (Luke: 13:4–5), were they killed because they were great sinners? Jesus' answer was: "I tell you, Nay." In his last novel, *The Eighth Day*, Wilder compares history to a vast tapestry. We think we see dim designs in tiny portions, but the Grand Design is known only to God.

Believers in Revelation claim to trace certain features of the Grand Design. Although Judas's betrayal of Jesus was an act of moral evil, Leibniz tells us, it made possible the crucifixion that redeems us all. The betrayal was a *felix culpa*—a happy sin, as an old medieval hymn has it. But even to orthodox Christians such details as the needless suffering of a child are as incomprehensible as they are for any non-Christian theist. Lewis Carroll, a devout Anglican, in a letter to an invalid tried to justify the suffering of children by asking: "May it not be to raise to *higher* glory the soul that is already glorious? To make the good yet better, the pure *more* pure, the saint *more* saintly?"[14] Carroll repeats the words of Jesus (John 15:2), "and every branch that beareth fruit, He purgeth it, that it may bring forth more fruit." Guesses, guesses! But believers have to guess, even though they know they cannot know the answer.

Why cannot we know the answer? I have already mentioned one hypothesis—that if we could see clearly how evils contribute to higher goods, we would become indifferent toward them. Evil, said Royce, is the dirt we must wash out of the universe. This is the symbolic meaning behind the myth of Satan and his angels, behind the devils and lesser demons of other faiths. Evil must somehow be hated by God, even though he permits and uses it. In itself no evil is good. In a sense it is something apart from God, something God is trying to expunge. "Evil is as real as the good . . ." said James in a letter. "It must be accepted and hated and resisted. . . ." Obviosities! As Batman put it on a poster I saw in the mid-sixties, "It is well to remember that evil is a pretty bad thing!" If it is true that evil contributes to ultimate good, it may be part of God's mercy that he has hidden the details from us, that we are in no better position today to answer the enigma of evil than long-suffering Job, or his bitter wife, or his long-winded friends.

There is a still deeper reason, fideists believe, or at least I so believe, why we cannot solve the problem of evil. "Verily thou art a God that hidest thyself, O God of Israel, the Saviour" (Isaiah 45:15). The mystery of evil is part of the larger mystery of why God chooses to remain concealed. The only answer a fideist can give is that God wants uncompelled love, love that springs from a free turning of the heart. If God could be proved by reason, every rational person would believe. If God could be established empirically, every person with respect for science would believe. To formulate a convincing answer to the riddle of evil would require knowing things we cannot know, that we may not have the capacity to know. If we could understand the reason for suffering, God would no longer be hidden. And only if God remains concealed, remains a *deus abscondus*, can faith escape contamination by coercion.[15]

No one has said this more eloquently than Blaise Pascal in his *Pensées*:

> It was not then right that He should appear in a manner manifestly divine, and completely capable of convincing all men; but it was also not right that He should come in so hidden a manner that He could not be known by those who should sincerely seek Him. He has willed to make Himself quite recognizable by those; and thus, willing to appear openly to those who seek Him with all their heart, and to be hidden from those who flee from Him with all their heart. He so regulates the knowledge of Himself that He has given signs of Himself, visible to those who seek Him, and not to those who seek Him not. There is enough light for those who only desire to see, and enough obscurity for those who have a contrary disposition.

Pascal is speaking of God's appearance on earth as Jesus, and he is making the point that even with respect to the Incarnation the Creator concealed himself sufficiently so that no one would be forced to believe. Did not Jesus even thank God that the truths of faith were hidden from the wise and prudent, and revealed only to babes? Innumerable theologians before and after Pascal have sounded this theme. For Sören Kierkegaard, Jesus was God's "Incognito." Not even Jesus' contemporaries who witnessed his miracles could be certain of who he was, for cannot miracles be counterfeited by fallen angels?

A non-Christian fideist may find it hard to believe that anyone could witness, say, the raising of Lazarus and remain in a state of neutrality with respect to Jesus' claim of divinity, but Pascal's point can be applied to evidence for God's existence quite apart from belief in the Incarnation. Indeed, Pascal himself so applied it. Here is another passage from the *Pensées*:

> This is what I see and what troubles me. I look on all sides, and see nothing but obscurity, nature offers me nothing but matter for doubt and disquiet. Did I see nothing there which marked a Divinity I should decide not to believe in him. Did I see every where the marks of a Creator, I should rest peacefully in faith. But seeing too much to deny, and too little to affirm, my state is pitiful, and I have a hundred times wished that if God upheld nature, he would mark the fact unequivocally, but that if the signs which she gives of a God are fallacious, she would wholly suppress them, that she would either say all or say nothing, that I might see what part I should take. While in my present state, ignorant of what I am, and of what I ought to do, I know neither my condition nor my duty, my heart is wholly bent to know where is the true good in order to follow it, nothing would seem to me too costly for eternity.

The view that God must hide himself to make faith genuine is central to Kant's theology. Suppose God were not hidden, Kant asks near the end of his *Critique of Practical Reason*; what would be the consequences? "God and eternity in their awful majesty would stand unceasingly before our eyes." We would believe in God, we would obey his commands, but not of our free wills. We would believe because we could not do otherwise. We would obey out of fear.

> The moral worth of actions, on which alone the worth of the person and even of the world depends in the eyes of supreme wisdom, would not exist at all. The conduct of man, so long as his nature remained as it now is, would be changed into mere mechanism, where, as in a puppet show, everything would gesticulate well but no life would be found in the figures.

God conceals himself so we can be what we are, persons, not robots. For this reason, Kant continues, the

> Governor of the world allows us only to conjecture His existence

and majesty, not to behold or clearly prove them; the moral law in us, without promising or threatening us with anything certain, demands of us a disinterested respect. . . . Thus only can there be a truly moral character . . . worthy of participating in the highest good corresponding to the moral worth of his person and not merely to his actions. . . . The inscrutable wisdom through which we exist is not less worthy of veneration in respect to what it denies us than in what it has granted.

It was Kant's view—perhaps it is also the view of most fideists—that faith is unsupported by reason but not contrary to it. As I have said before, some fideists, of whom Miguel de Unamuno is the last great representative, have gone a step beyond this by granting to atheists the better of the argument. Look at the world honestly, they say. Does not the extent of irrational evil, coupled with God's total invisibility, have as its simplest, most reasonable explanation that God is either cruel or nonexistent? Does not the dependence of mind upon the brain, and the utter silence of the dead, suggest strongly that the dead are truly and forever dead, that there is no hope for life beyond the body's corruption?

When Don Quixote questioned Sancho Panza (Book 1, Chapter 31) about his supposed delivery of a letter to Dulcinea, the knight assumed that when Sancho was near the lady he surely perceived her aromatic fragrance. On the contrary, said Sancho, she had a strong odor of perspiration, no doubt arising from her heavy labors at winnowing wheat. "Impossible!" cried the Don. "That smell must have proceeded from thyself."

Comments Unamuno:

Those for whom the world smells only of matter, smell themselves only; those who see nothing but passing phenomena, see themselves and no deeper. Not in contemplation of the stars that wheel across the sky shall we discover Thee, O God, Thou who didst enrich with madness Don Quixote! The discovery comes by watching, from the depths of our hearts, the soaring of love's aspirations.[16]

Don Quixote's madness was his refusal to accept the world as it appears to those who see only the world's back, who smell only the world's perspiration. Men and women of faith, in their madness, affirm both a compassionate God and a life after death in spite of evidence which suggests (though of course it does not prove) that both affirmations are delusions. They believe, not because it is absurd but even though it is absurd—not because they see evidence that supports their faith but because their hearts tell them that the truth is not what the spectacle of an indifferent nature makes it seem to be.

When the atheist charges that the theist is wearing a blindfold that prevents seeing the obvious, the only honest response is that this is in a way true. Unamuno's one-act play *La venda* is about a blind woman, Maria, whose sight is restored by an operation. She cannot find her way home, to the house where her father is dying, until she covers her eyes with a handkerchief and uses a cane. When her rational sister, Marta, tears off the blindfold, Maria watches in agony her father's death. God is not visible to the eyes of reason and science. For many people, perhaps most, only by closing their eyes can they find their way home, can they avoid seeing the death of God and thereby see God with the blind eyes of faith. Those who are able to see with their hearts, even when their eyes are open, must experience in agony the eternal conflict between faith and reason.

As Don Quixote nears death he suddenly recovers his sanity and admits, even to himself, that his adventures were all dependent on a foolish dream. It is Sancho who tries to persuade him otherwise, Sancho who saw the world as it is, Sancho who still sees it as it is but who now has become infected by his master's madness. It is Sancho who, at the close of Cervantes's sequel, becomes for Unamuno the symbol of a higher quixotism. Blessed are they who see clearly the back of the world and who yet believe.

Obviously there is no way an atheist can counter this kind of madness. Fideists who regard faith as quixotic have already granted the strength of atheism's best arguments. Rudolf Carnap, in his *Logical Structure of the World*, contrasts those who refuse to believe anything unsupported by reason or science with those who accept the nonrational beliefs of faith. The two groups live, said Carnap, on different continents. There is a road that joins the empirical knowledge of science with the formal knowledge of logic and mathematics. No road connects rational knowledge with the affirmations of the heart.

On this point fideists are in complete agreement. It is one of the reasons why a fideist, Christian or otherwise, can admire the writings of logical empiricists more than the writings of philosophers who struggle to defend spurious metaphysical arguments. It is precisely this impregnability of fideism that made Bertrand Russell so furious. His strongest attack on faith is in his chapter on Jean Jacques Rousseau in *The History of Western Philosophy*, where he holds up to ridicule "The Confession of Faith of a Savoyard Vicar" in Rousseau's *Emile*. Although Russell belonged to the emotive school of ethics—a school that rests all morality on posits of the heart—Russell had no patience with any religious faith that rests on similar posits.

> However ardently I, or all mankind, may desire something, however necessary it may be to human happiness, that is no ground for supposing this something to exist. There is no law of nature guaranteeing that mankind should be happy. Everybody can see that this is true of our life here on earth, but by a curious twist our very sufferings in this life are made into an argument for a better life hereafter. We should not employ such an argument in any other connection. If you had bought ten dozen eggs from a man, and the first dozen were all rotten, you would not infer that the remaining nine dozen must be of surpassing excellence; yet that is the kind of reasoning that "the heart" encourages as a consolation for our sufferings here below.
>
> For my part, I prefer the ontological argument, the cosmological argument, and the rest of the old stock-in-trade, to the sentimental illogicality that has sprung from Rousseau. The old arguments at least were honest: if valid, they proved their point; if invalid, it was open to any critic to prove them so. But the new theology of the heart dispenses with argument; it cannot be refuted, because it does not profess to prove its points. At bottom, the only reason offered for its acceptance is that it allows us to indulge in pleasant dreams. This is an unworthy reason, and if I had to choose between Thomas Aquinas and Rousseau, I should unhesitatingly choose the Saint.[17]

Fideists are undismayed by such sentiments. They understand them only too well. "Spiritual agony is the door to substantial truth," wrote Unamuno in his commentary on *Don Quixote* from which I quoted earlier.

> Suffer, in order that you may believe; and believe, in order that you may live. Facing all the negations of *logic*, which governs the

apparent relations of things, stands the affirmation of *cardic*, which rules their substantial values. Though your head tells you that some day your consciousness will flicker and go out, your heart, startled and lighted up by a vast dismay, will teach you that there is a world in which reason is not the guide. The truth is that which makes one live, not what makes one think.

How Russell would have snorted over such a passage! There is no way he could have put marks on paper, combined and manipulated them in accord with rules of logic and syntax, and produced a string of well-formed words and sentences that would have shaken Unamuno's faith. Nor was there anything Unamuno could have said that would have altered Russell's atheism. Both men lived in the same world, saw the same sad spectacle, experienced the same pleasures and pains. So far as I know, neither man ever read the other. Had they done so, each would have thought the other a fool. Russell would have considered Unamuno a fool because he did not follow the cues provided by his eyes and head. Unamuno would have considered Russell a fool because he did not close his eyes and listen to his heart. They lived on separate continents.[18]

17

IMMORTALITY:
Why I Am Not Resigned

> *Down, down, down into the darkness of the grave*
> *Gently they go, the beautiful, the tender, the kind;*
> *Quietly they go, the intelligent, the witty, the brave.*
> *I know. But I do not approve. And I am not resigned.*

—EDNA ST. VINCENT MILLAY,
"DIRGE WITHOUT MUSIC"

We now come to the most scandalous, the most shocking, chapter of my confessions. I, who am widely regarded as a skeptic and an atheist, who am an unabashed disbeliever in ESP, PK, precognition, and all things paranormal, am actually going to defend the hope and belief in a life after death! Let it not be said that this signals senility. I have believed in an afterlife since my boyhood, when I first began to believe in God.

I bear no proofs. There are none to bear. I agree with Miguel de Unamuno that the evidence of our senses strongly suggests the permanent extinction of consciousness at death. "If a man die, shall he live again?" (Job 14:14) That the answer is *no* is the burden of Ecclesiastes. You will look in vain for a *yes* in the oldest writings of Judaism. Moses has nothing to say about an afterlife. Sometimes it is said that modern sciences, especially biology and psychology, have made a *yes* more difficult. This may be true. In other ways, perhaps, physics has made the hope easier, but on the whole I agree with G. K. Chesterton that the advances of science have no bearing on the question. The proportion of disbelievers in ancient times was probably much the same as now. "The materialism of things is on the face of things," said GK; "it does not require any science to find it out. A man who has lived and loved falls down dead and the worms eat him. . . . If mankind has believed in spite of that, it can believe in spite of anything."[1]

To believe in spite of anything! That is the essence of quixotic fideism. One desires not to die. From passionate longing springs that mysterious turning of the will which the fideist believes to be a response to God's own longing. And with this rotation of the heart comes belief; not knowledge in the sense of science and mathematics, but belief all the same.

I am aware that many eminent atheists have expressed a desire *not* to live again. You hear it frequently today, as in all ages, from those who do not even want to make the leap of faith. I suppose if one thinks of immortality as a monotonous continuation of life as we know it, with all its pains and frustrations, unbroken by periods of rest and regeneration, then eternal existence can indeed be terrifying to contemplate. A classic expression of this emotion, Chapter 10 of *Gulliver's Travels*, by Jonathan Swift, tells of the ghastly melancholy of the immortal struldbrugs, and how Gulliver wishes he could send a few of them to England to help banish the fear of death.

Jorge Luis Borges, who greatly admired Unamuno's poetry and fiction but could not tolerate his thirst for immortality, has on many occasions voiced a desire not to live again. Like Groucho Marx, who refused to join any club willing to have him as a member, Borges once said he could not believe in a God willing to be perpetually encumbered by Borges.[2] Borges's struldbrugs live in a city built by insane gods, a city "so horrible that its mere existence . . . contaminates the past and the future and in some way even jeopardizes the stars. As long as it lasts, no one in the world can be strong and happy."[3]

I will not say that all those who believe they do not want to live again are deceiving themselves. I can only say I cannot understand them. "I do not want to die—" wrote Unamuno, "no; I neither want to die nor do I want to want to die; I want to live for ever and ever and ever. I want this 'I' to live—this poor 'I' that I am and that I feel myself to be here and now, and therefore the problem of the duration of my soul, of my own soul, tortures me."[4]

Egoism? Certainly!—though not an ignoble egoism, because it is bound up with a passionate love for others who, too, must perish like the beasts. Here is Morris Raphael Cohen, a philosopher who did not believe in a personal God or an afterlife, writing in his Diary:

> I cannot agree with Spinoza that the free man thinks of nothing less often than of death (which is nothing in itself). The thought of death—or rather of the annihilation of the life of those that are most vivid in my memory, my mother especially—is ever present in my mind. This life that meant most to me—indeed my own past life and that of Felix who is now a man of thirty—is it all of such an evanescent sort? [5]

Going through my files on immortality, I found a folded sheet of yellow paper that I had completely forgotten. It was dated April 1961 and on it I had typed the following minifantasy:

> A great physicist was dying. Beside him sat Rosalie, his mistress, who loved him very much. The physicist loved her only slightly because he loved science more. They were arguing about immortality.
>
> "I know we will meet again, somewhere, sometime," Rosalie whispered.
>
> The physicist snorted. It was a weak snort because he was sinking fast. "Balderdash! If you understood science you would know that."
>
> Rosalie knew nothing about science. "But surely you must *hope* we will meet again?"
>
> The physicist shook his head slowly. "One life is enough. It ends things simply and elegantly. The universe would be too messy otherwise."
>
> He died.
>
> A few million earth-years whirled into the past; then suddenly the physicist found himself standing in the presence of God. He was overcome with confusion. "I cannot understand! How by all the laws of science could I exist again?"
>
> "How by all the laws of science," God replied, "could there be laws of science?"
>
> "But," said the physicist, "I did not even want to live again. I died content. Why am I here?"

"You are here," sighed God, "for one reason only. Rosalie requested it."

Before looking at some of the faded arguments for personal immortality, all nonrational because they rest on posits that have no support except passionate desires—let us dispose of those shabby pseudoimmortalities that atheists and pantheists are forever proffering as substitutes for the real thing. By "personal immortality" I mean what everybody has meant in the past, what everybody means today, when they speak of an afterlife. It is a life in which you retain consciousness of your identity and your memories of the past (the two are the same). Although its nature is transcendent and therefore beyond comprehension, it must be modeled in the only way we can model it: as a body alive in space and time. You cannot conceive of "living" in any reasonable sense of the word if you are something like smoke, or like a marble statue. We are forced to model immortality with something analogous to living flesh and bone because otherwise it will be no model at all.

Personal immortality, the only kind with which faith is concerned, has nothing whatever to do with living on through descendants and friends, or living in future records of the past. It has nothing to do with surviving through achievements in science, literature, music, or art. It has nothing to do with being mentioned in history books, or having your name on a building, a street, a museum, or a city. Lenin did not achieve personal immortality when Leningrad was named. It has nothing to do with one's future influence on society. Joe Hill is not still alive, as the old Wobbly song has it, because workers in the United States still go out on strike. A person does not acquire immortality by identifying himself or herself with the human race, even if one makes the dubious assumption that the race will never become extinct.

Personal immortality has nothing to do with reabsorption, whether it be reabsorption of the soul by the All, as in some Eastern religions and in the philosophy of many pantheists, or in the reabsorption of the body by nature. John Keats did not continue to live, as Shelley's "Adonais" has it, because

He is made one with Nature: there is heard
His voice in all her music, from the moan
Of thunder, to the song of night's sweet bird;

He is a presence to be felt and known
In darkness and in light, from herb and stone,
Spreading itself where'er that Power may move
Which has withdrawn his being to its own;
Which wields the world with never wearied love,
Sustains it from beneath, and kindles it above.

What difference can it make to you and me if the mass-energies of our body's particles will be conserved, or if the atoms of our brain will continue to vibrate somewhere in the cosmos? In that sense of immortality, every blade of grass, every pebble, every snowflake is immortal. To say it in plainer language, nothing is immortal except perhaps mass-energy, and for all we know, it too may eventually vanish into a black hole if the universe stops expanding and goes the other way.

Nor does it make a whit of difference to you and me if at some far future date our descendants find a way to prolong their lives for as long as they desire. It is a common science-fiction ploy. One wild variation, explored by Philip José Farmer in his Riverworld books, is that science may even find a way to confer immortality on those mortals who died in earlier ages!

Of all the forms of pseudoimmortality set forth by philosophers, usually in pompous, pious tones, the most shameless is the notion that one is immortal in the sense that throughout eternity one will be exactly what one has been. From the perspective of a timeless, static Now, a person is always what that person is. Miss Rose is Miss Rose is Miss Rose. As a pantheist might put it, all of us are immortal because our total life experiences are indestructible in the memory of God. Here again the meaning is so broad that it makes everything immortal. From this viewpoint, our *afterlife* is a poetic, Pickwickian term for what ordinary people mean by *death* and *annihilation*.

Spinoza, the greatest of pantheists, defended immortality with just such verbal prestidigitation. Similar arguments are in the writings of Alfred North Whitehead and George Santayana, though Santayana was honest enough to say that in spite of its stoic compensations the view has beneath it an "incurable sorrow." [6] Eminent Protestant theologians, too liberated to need a personal God, also have been addicted to such lofty obfuscations—Paul Tillich, to name one, though (like Hegel) it is hard to be sure what Tillich meant when he wrote and preached about immortality. [7]

> *It fortifies my soul to know*
> *That, though I perish, Truth is so—*

Thank you, Arthur Hugh Clough, for this vapid thought. It does not fortify *my* soul in the least to know that after I die all unmarried men will still be bachelors, that 37 will still be a prime number, that the stars will continue to shine, and that forever I will have been just what I am now. Away with these fake immortalities! They mean nothing to the heart. Better to say with Bertrand Russell: "I believe that when I die I shall rot, and nothing of my ego will survive."[8]

With equal impatience let us dispose of a quaint controversy that once entertained members of the Vienna Circle and other empiricists. Is Job's question "If a man die, shall he live again?" meaningful or is it nonsense? Most of the philosophers who debated this question sensibly concluded that not only is it meaningful, but it is meaningful in more than one way. It is meaningful in the sense that we all know what it means. It is empirically meaningful because, even though it cannot be disconfirmed if false, it is capable in principle of empirical confirmation. Indeed, Spiritualists believe it *has* been confirmed.[9] Moreover, if we die and find ourselves alive again, we will have confirmed it in the strongest possible way. Finally, it is pragmatically meaningful because how we answer it with our heart can make a difference in how we live. When Dorothy and her friends were on the Yellow Brick Road, it made a difference to them whether they believed the road led to the Emerald City or whether they believed it went nowhere.

Just how much difference does faith in another life make to a person traveling the winding road from birth to death? I have already given my opinion that, other parameters being equal, it adds to one's happiness. To repeat, atheists obviously can be happy and well-adjusted; saints can be afflicted with anxiety and depression. Faith doesn't make you happy; it just makes you happier.

I have also expressed my opinion that, other things equal, faith adds to one's incentive to be good. Although it sounds dull to say it, I believe that the added incentive is small in proportion to other forces that influence conduct. In an earlier chapter I argued that belief in God is not necessary for justifying a moral code. Moreover, in the absence of a Revelation in which ethical laws are explicitly commanded by God, theists and atheists alike are in the same boat, under the same sullen sky. A theist believes God is behind the sky, but if there is no voice

from the clouds giving detailed instructions, theism is not much help
in deciding complicated ethical issues. Even for a person who believes
in a sacred Book, or a Church that is divinely guided, modern life
swarms with moral dilemmas for which Books and Churches provide
little or no guidance. Jean-Paul Sartre was right, in my opinion, when
he said that if God exists, the fact solves no important ethical or political problem.

There is a famous statement by Augustine: If you love God you may
do as you please. Alas, it is not so simple. The Spanish inquisitors loved
God. The Christians who burned witches loved God. Promoters of the
Children's Crusade loved God. John Calvin loved God when he allowed Servetus to be burned at the stake. Martin Luther loved God
when he proposed driving Jews out of Germany. Jephthah loved God
when he killed his daughter. Abraham loved God when he was willing
to murder his son. Moses loved God when he ordered his soldiers to kill
the older women and the male children of the Midianites, but to keep
the virgin girls for themselves. In the bloody wars between Christians
and Muslims, between Protestants and Catholics, all sides loved God.

Out of tens of thousands of horror stories about atrocities committed
by those who loved God, I select one small example from fifth-century
Christianity. The world's first great woman mathematician, and the
last great Neoplatonist, was Hypatia. She was said to have been as
beautiful as she was intelligent. Because she refused to become a
Christian, a fanatical mob, inflamed by the Bishop of Alexandria (later
canonized as Saint Cyril), seized her as she left a carriage, stripped her
naked, scraped off her flesh with sharpened oyster shells, and burned
her body. Charles Kingsley's novel *Hypatia* retells the grim story. One
longs to be able to read Hypatia's many treatises on mathematics and
philosophy, but they were all destroyed by Allah-loving Muslims when
they burned the library at Alexandria. Why did they do this? Because,
they said, if the books contained anything in the Koran they were not
needed, and if they contained anything not in the Koran they should
not be read.

Christian historians still delight in repeating the wildly exaggerated
accounts of believers martyred by Roman rulers in the first three centuries after Christ. For a saner perspective, read the memorable six-
teenth chapter of Edward Gibbon's *Decline and Fall of the Roman
Empire*. It concludes with the "melancholy truth" that even if one
accepts the questionable statistics of Christian historians, the number

of believers killed by other Christians in later centuries far exceeds the number killed by non-Christians. In the Netherlands alone, more Protestants were executed by Catholics in a single province, during a single reign, than there were Christians martyred during three centuries of Roman rule.

Huckleberry Finn, who believed in God, considered it "right" to turn in runaway slaves. Should he therefore turn in Jim? Huck tried to pray for strength to do what his culture and his religion had taught him was the will of God:

> So I kneeled down. But the words wouldn't come. Why wouldn't they? It warn't no use to try and hide it from Him. Nor from *me*, neither. I knowed very well why they wouldn't come. It was because my heart warn't right; it was because I warn't square; it was because I was playing double. I was letting *on* to give up sin, but away inside of me I was holding on to the biggest one of all. I was trying to make my mouth *say* I would do the right thing and the clean thing, and go and write to that nigger's owner and tell where he was; but deep down in me I knowed it was a lie—and He knowed it. You can't pray a lie—I found that out. [10]

Huck listened to his heart. Unfortunately, the moral law within, even when strengthened by faith in God and immortality, is a useless guide in endless agonizing decisions. A Roman Catholic doctrine called "equiprobabilism" (it grew out of a much-debated sixteenth-century Jesuit doctrine called "probabilism") says that if arguments for both sides of a difficult moral decision seem equally persuasive, one may choose either side with a clear conscience. In one of Somerset Maugham's war espionage tales, a British spy, Ashenden, has to make a decision that may involve the deaths of many innocent people in a Polish factory. The situation is complicated, and Ashenden has no way of estimating the relevant probabilities. The story ends when he flips a coin. [11] Dilemmas such as this are common enough in ordinary times, but in time of war they can involve the lives of millions. Should the bomb have been dropped on Hiroshima and Nagasaki? Under what circumstances should the President push the button that will obliterate a metropolis, perhaps an entire nation? Theists are as divided as atheists over such questions, and it is hard to see how belief in God and an afterlife would even enter into evaluating the outcomes of alternate actions.

Samuel Johnson once described an acquaintance by saying, "Sir, if it were not for the notion of immortality, he would cut a throat to fill his pockets." To which a friend replied, "He would cut a throat to fill his pockets, if it were not for fear of being hanged."[12]

Who would defend Dostoevsky's Raskolnikov when he argued that if God does not exist there is nothing wrong in killing a useless old woman? Nevertheless, I do think it makes a pragmatic difference, albeit small, whether one looks upon morality as a construction by humans in a godless universe, or believes in God and life after death. Oddly enough, even some atheists incline to agree. Here is how Dwight Macdonald once worried over the matter.

> Discussing the basis of one's moral code is like taking apart one of those wooden Russian eggs, each of which encloses a still smaller one: "I believe it is wrong to kill people." "Why?" "Because I have respect for humanity." "Why?" "Because I am human and recognize my brother's kinship." "Why?" etc., etc. If one believes in God, one finally gets down to an ultimate egg that is solid and so ends the taking-apart (analytical) process. God is simply and logically an absolute, an end and not a means, unique in our— that is, some of us—experience. But an unbeliever gets down to an egg that is hollow like the rest, but that contains no further egg. One's belief turns out to rest, ultimately, on air— "I just feel it to be so." This doesn't bother me too much emotionally, but it is undeniably awkward from a logical point of view.[13]

If faith plays a role in the behavior of some of us, it is surely bound up with a belief that God sees all our acts, and that we will somehow be rewarded or punished accordingly. In Plato's *Republic*, the situation was dramatized by Socrates in his discussion of the Ring of Gyges—a magic ring that makes its wearer invisible. Would you, if you had such a ring, be more likely to commit certain crimes? If you could nod your head, asked Rousseau, and obtain instant wealth at the price of the death of a Mandarin in China, would you nod? I do not know to what extent faith in God and an afterlife provides checks on such behavior. I do believe it makes a difference.

Let us turn now to some of the traditional arguments for life after death. I will not go into those "logical proofs" given by Plato and later by the Schoolmen, because I find them as fragile and unconvincing as the traditional proofs of God. I have already expressed my total disbelief in the claims of Spiritualism. I am even less impressed by recent potboilers defending immortality on the basis of what some persons say at their moment of death, or what they recall when they are revived after a temporary stilling of the heart. I have made clear my agreement with Unamuno and other fideists that the close association of mind and body lends powerful support to the denial of an afterlife. As for whether there is a genetic predisposition to believe in an afterlife, who can say? I suspect not. Even if so, it would prove no more than that such a predisposition had survival value for the species.

There are, however, pragmatic arguments for life after death. Like the pragmatic arguments for God, they are compelling only if one accepts certain posits that spring from almost universal human desires. We have already considered one such argument—it is the core of Immanuel Kant's *Critique of Practical Reason*—that if justice is ultimately to prevail you must assume an afterlife and a God to provide it. And we have briefly considered another argument, also stressed by Kant (and by innumerable theists before and since) that follows from a recogition of life's sad incompleteness.

The second argument takes many forms. Just as we are learning to live well, either our powers decline with old age and finally cease altogether or we are cut down prematurely by illness or accident. If there is a God who truly loves us—this is the necessary emotional posit— would it not be foolish for him to throw us away after taking such pains to bring us into existence by the incredibly long, slow, tortuous process of evolution? Would it not be, as theists have endlessly repeated, like someone devoting a lifetime to a great novel, then when it is finally finished, burning the manuscript? When William James was asked why he believed in personal immortality he replied simply, "Because I am just getting fit to live." [14]

If death ends all, is not God the loser? In Byron's "Cain," when Lucifer assures Cain that the beauty of his sister Adah is doomed to vanish forever, Cain replies:

> *I'm sorry for it; but*
> *Cannot conceive my love for her the less.*
> *And when her beauty disappears, methinks*
> *He who creates all beauty will lose more*
> *Than me in seeing perish such a work.*

Ralph Waldo Emerson, lecturing on immortality, said:

Our passions, our endeavors, have something ridiculous and mocking, if we come to so hasty an end. If not to *be*, how like the bells of a fool is the trump of fame! Nature does not, like the Empress Anne of Russia, call together all the architectural genius of the Empire to build and finish and furnish a palace of snow, to melt again to water in the first thaw. Will you, with vast cost and pains, educate your children to be adepts in their several arts, and, as soon as they are ready to produce a masterpiece, call out a file of soldiers to shoot them down? We must infer our destiny from the preparation.[15]

Jurgen, debating with Pan in Chapter 19 of James Branch Cabell's novel, pursues a similar line, and later sums up his opinion as follows:

As it is, plain reasoning assures me I am not indispensible to the universe: but with this reasoning, somehow, does not travel my belief. . . . No, I cannot believe in nothingness being the destined end of all: that would be too futile a climax to content a dramatist clever enough to have invented Jurgen. No, it is just as I said to the brown man: I cannot believe in the annihilation of Jurgen by any really thrifty overlords. . . .[16]

The rage of the passengers, in Stephen Crane's great metaphorical story "The Open Boat," is several times expressed by the following lines: "If I am going to be drowned—if I am going to be drowned—if I am to be drowned, why, in the name of the seven mad gods who rule the sea, was I allowed to come thus far and contemplate sand and trees?" After one repetition of the passage Crane adds:

If this old ninny woman, fate, cannot do better than this, she should be deprived of the management of men's fortunes. She is an old hen who knows not her intention. If she has decided to drown me, why did she not do it in the beginning and save me all this trouble? The whole affair is absurd. . . . But no, she cannot mean to drown me. She dare not drown me. She cannot drown me. Not after all this work.

So far I have stressed only the incompleteness of individual lives. What about the incompleteness of history? Plainly the epic is just beginning. Science is in its babyhood. We are only starting to learn how to cure our major ills, maybe even find a way of getting along with one

288 • The WHYS of a Philosophical Scrivener

another without destroying the human race. What about the dream of steady progress toward a better world, the Open Conspiracy of H. G. Wells? If there is no afterlife, then individuals who work hard for Utopia, perhaps even sacrifice their lives for it, not only will never enjoy Utopia, they will not even know whether the dream succeeds. History becomes a long drama that can be enjoyed only by a god who sees how it ends.

There is a well-known haiku to which Raymond Smullyan devotes a stimulating chapter in his book *The Tao Is Silent:* [17]

> *The evening cool*
> *Knowing the bell*
> *Is tolling our life away.*

It is the sad tolling of this bell that sounds softly but incessantly between the sentences of all the great secular humanists who are Open Conspirators. Like Old Moses, they are destined never to see the Promised Land. In Wells's finest Utopia novel, *Men Like Gods*, Mr. Barnstaple thinks of a friend who had sacrificed himself for his vision of the future. "He had worked for Utopia all his days. Were there hundreds or thousands of such Utopians yet on earth? What magic upheld them?" [18]

What magic indeed? I am not suggesting that there are not countless numbers of good atheists who find enormous personal satisfaction in working for Utopia. They are capable, in times of war and other crises, of giving their lives for the Cause. I am only suggesting that there is an element of tragedy in their realization—it must come upon them at times in the middle of the night—that they will not even know what degree of success the struggle will bring. It was to Jean-Paul Sartre's credit—in my opinion it was his one major contribution to philosophy—that more than any other Open Conspirator, he saw clearly, and was willing to say so, the ultimate absurdity of the enterprise.

In contrast, Wells seldom recognized the comic and tragic aspects of his boundless enthusiasm for the future. Let us see how he tried (in his lengthy novel of ideas, seldom read today, *The World of William Clissold*) to escape the bell's tolling:

"But why," asks Clementina, "should you care for a World Republic you will never see? Why should the thought that men will never get to the World Republic make you unhappy when it does not seem to trouble you in the least that presently you must die?"

"That is a fair question," Clissold replies. "Why should I have become almost miserly with my days and hours in order to work for ends I can never live to see? Why do these things occupy and compel me so that I forget myself? Why do I not simply take the means of pleasure that I possess now so abundantly and 'enjoy myself'?"

Speaking through his narrator, Clissold, Wells gives the only answer a humanist can give. He has "grown up," matured to the point where his "self" has expanded to include the entire race. "That complete preoccupation with the feelings and deeds and pride and prospects of William Clissold . . . has been modified by and has gradually given place to the wider demands of the racial adventure. That now grips me and possesses me. William Clissold dwindles to relative unimportance in my mind and 'Man' arises and increases."

And though William Clissold, my narrow self, will surely die before any great portion of this present revolution can be achieved, yet just as surely will man, that greater self in which my narrow self is no more than a thought and a phase, survive. Insensibly I have come to think, to desire and act as man, using the body and the powers of William Clissold that were once my whole self, as a medium. And while all that I do expressly and particularly for the pleasure, delight and profit of William Clissold ends, I perceive, and will presently be forgotten and its refuse put away in some grave, all that I think and attempt and do as man goes on towards a future that has no certain and definable end and that need not be defeated by death.

I pass over some paragraphs to the chapter's ending:

That is my philosophy of conduct, my mysticism, if you will, my religion. That is my answer to Clementina's question. This is my final conception of my life as I live it, set in the frame of my world. To this fully adult state men and women are, I believe, finding their way through the glares and threats, the misstatements and absurdities, the violence, cruelties, tumults, and perplexities of the present time. A few come to it now, doubtfully and each one alone, as I have done, but presently more will be coming to it. As they do, the path to the World Republic will open out and this new phase of human life become the common phase throughout our mounting race.

We shall put away childish things, childish extravagances of passion and nightmare fears. Our minds will live in a living world literature and exercise in living art; our science will grow incessantly and our power increase. Our planet will become like a workshop in a pleasant garden, and from it we shall look out with ever diminishing fear upon our heritage of space and time amidst the stars.

We shall be man in common and immortal in common, and each one of us will develop his individuality to the utmost, no longer as a separated and conflicting being but as a part and contribution to one continuing whole.[19]

We is a word Wells liked to use whenever he extolled future glories. But of course it is not *we* in the sense of Wells and his readers, in the sense of you and me. It is *we* in the symbolic sense of the human race. In Wells's repetition of that word, in its repetition in the rhetoric of Marxism, in the political writings of John Dewey and Sartre and other humanists, do you not hear the sobbing of the evening bell? *We* is a way of evading the haiku as I quoted it, of subtly changing it to its other traditional form:

> *The evening cool*
> *Not knowing the bell*
> *Is tolling our life away.*

We are alone among animals in our ability to hear the bell. By identifying oneself with the species, the secular humanist puts his hands over his ears. Not hearing the bell, the humanist can imagine that somehow he or she is *there*, living in that bright future, enjoying the fruits of the great struggle. It is the humanist's magic substitute for personal immortality. But of course it is only an illusion, an ersatz immortality, for the humanist will *not* be there. He will not be anywhere.

Shortly after the Second World War, when Wells was nearing death, his optimism turned to pessimism and he wrote his last book, *Mind at the End of Its Tether*. Here is an excerpt from a letter he wrote to Bertrand Russell during this period:

> I have been ill and I keep ill. I am President of the Diabetic Soc'y and diabetes keeps one in and out, in and out of bed every two hours or so. This exhausts, and this vast return to chaos which is

called the peace, the infinite meanness of great masses of my fellow creatures, the wickedness of organized religion give me a longing for a sleep that will have no awakening. There is a long history of heart failure on my paternal side but modern palliatives are very effective holding back that moment of release. Sodium bicarbonate keeps me in a grunting state of protesting endurance. But while I live I *have* to live and I owe a lot to a decaying civilization which has anyhow kept alive enough of the spirit of scientific devotion to stimulate my curiosity [and] make me its debtor.

Forgive this desolation.[20]

Wells was vanishing. The bell was tolling for him in the sunset.

I remember an old movie in which Jimmy Durante remarked that the show must go on. Someone asked why. After a moment of stunned silence, Jimmy replied, "I guess it don't." Why must the Open Conspiracy go on? Why must the human race go on?

It was August Comte who invented the phrase "egoism versus altruism," and Herbert Spencer who popularized it. Spencer tried to solve the conflict in the way that Dewey and Wells and other humanists later took over, by pointing out that every person is a "social self," combining both egoistic and altruistic impulses. As the social self grows, its capacity for love enlarges beyond the boundaries of family, friends, and country until it includes not only all living persons but also those yet unborn. At this point, Spencer assures us, egoism and altruism merge. The Open Conspirator acts out of enlightened self-interest, the self-interest of his inflated superego.[21]

Does this really end the conflict? To the extent that it does, does it not turn a person into a kind of bee who lives robotlike for the glory of the hive, who has no hesitation in giving its life for the good of the species? No one doubts that atheists can and do lay down their lives nobly on occasion for the "immortal soul of the race," but do they do this rationally, or are they unconsciously moving with the momentum of past ages of faith? How long will this momentum last in Russia? In China? If religious faith is reduced to almost nothing in these countries (which seems unlikely), will the atheist conspirators be able to sustain their altruism, or will it slowly dissipate as they begin to hear in their hearts the tolling of the evening bell? I do not know. My guess is it will fade. I suspect that even now in Communist countries the Utopian vision of Karl Marx is rapidly becoming fusty and irrelevant mythology.

Please do not suppose I am saying that a society cannot be just without faith in God and immortality on the part of most of its members. I agree with Pierre Bayle's famous argument, which so shocked his contemporaries, that such widespread faith is not a necessary ingredient of a moral society or of Open Conspiratorial zeal. But I do believe, unlike most upholders of a naturalistic ethics, that it contributes something to the zeal. By faith one can hope to know the outcome, perhaps even to participate somehow in it. Here is the way William James said it, with his usual eloquence:

> In a merely human world without a God, the appeal to our moral energy falls short of its maximal stimulating power. Life, to be sure, is even in such a world a genuinely ethical symphony; but it is played in the compass of a couple of poor octaves, and the infinite scale of values fails to open up. . . . We do not love these men of the future keenly enough; and we love them perhaps the less the more we hear of their evolutionized perfection, their high average longevity and education, their freedom from war and crime, their relative immunity from pain and zymotic disease, and all their other negative superiorities. This is all too finite, we say; we see too well the vacuum beyond. . . . No need of agonizing ourselves or making others agonize for these good creatures just at present.
>
> When, however, we believe that a God is there, and that he is one of the claimants, the infinite perspective opens out. The scale of the symphony is incalculably prolonged. The more imperative ideals now begin to speak with an altogether new objectivity and significance, and to utter the penetrating, shattering, tragically challenging note of appeal. . . .
>
> Our attitude towards concrete evils is entirely different in a world where we believe there are none but finite demanders, from what it is in one where we joyously face tragedy for an infinite demander's sake. Every sort of energy and endurance, of courage and capacity for handling life's evils, is set free in those who have religious faith. [22]

James's central point, with which I concur, is similar to what I previously said about the influence of faith on happiness and ethics. I believe that, other things equal, faith in God and another life makes it a trifle easier for Open Conspirators to make sacrifices for the future of humanity. As Kant saw so clearly, only if God exists can there be a final, genuine merging of egoism and altruism. Alexander Pope said it this way in his *Essay on Man*:

> *Thus God and Nature link'd the general frame,*
> *And bade self-love and social be the same.*

If there is another life, why has God so carefully concealed the evidence? Of course for Christians who believe in the Resurrection of Jesus, and the other revivals of the dead described in the New Testament, and for Spiritualists convinced they have talked with the departed, God has not concealed the evidence. But for the fideist who has no rational or empirical reason for believing in life after death—who, in fact, finds all the evidence on the other side—the afterlife is as hidden as God himself, as dark a mystery as time and evil and free will.

By faith the fideist believes that evidence for another life would destroy faith. It would destroy the emotional conviction that one's life on earth, and the history of humanity on earth, are adventures with beginnings and ends. History, as well as individual lives, requires rounding with a sleep. "With our weak spirits," said Chesterton, "we should grow old in eternity if we were not kept young by death. Providence has to cut immortality into lengths for us, as nurses cut the bread and butter into fingers."[23] If we knew that the celestial Emerald City were around the bend of death, and knew it with the kind of certainty that we know the existence of London or Paris, our lives would be disrupted by our impatience to get there. You must travel a road to reach the end of it, but jumping out a window will get you off the earth in just a few minutes.

To attribute the hiddenness of heaven to God's mercy is—no fideist would deny it—an argument at which an atheist has every right to scoff. The atheist has a right to scoff at any attempt to justify the ways of God toward man. And not only the atheist! Who are we to tell God how to run his creation? (This is the burden of the book of Job.) All we can do is believe by faith that if heaven were not hidden, faith would not be the uncompelled leap it is.

If I were writing a hundred years ago, I would not quote so often from Pope's *Essay on Man* because its lines would be too familiar. Today I suspect many readers of my confessions will be surprised by passages like the following:

> *Heaven from all creatures hides the book of fate,*
> *All but the page prescribed, their present state:*
> *From brutes what men, from men what spirits know:*
> *Or who could suffer being here below?*
> *The lamb thy riot dooms to bleed to-day,*
> *Had he thy reason, would he skip and play?*
> *Pleased to the last, he crops the flowery food,*
> *And licks the hand just raised to shed his blood.*
> *Oh blindness to the future! kindly given,*
> *That each may fill the circle mark'd by Heaven:*
> *Who sees with equal eye, as God of all,*
> *A hero perish, or a sparrow fall,*
> *Atoms or systems into ruin hurled,*
> *And now a bubble burst, and now a world.*
> *Hope humbly then; with trembling pinions soar;*
> *Wait the great teacher Death; and God adore.*
> *What future bliss, he gives not thee to know,*
> *But gives that hope to be thy blessing now.*

Faith is the substance of things humbly hoped for. We hope for what we desire. With hope travels faith and with faith travels belief. But because it is a belief of the heart, backed by no evidence, it is never free of doubt. I share with Unamuno the persuasion that if we could know whether there is or is not another life with the certainty that we know the sun will rise tomorrow, either belief would make life difficult if not impossible. How free faith is from doubt depends on the strength of faith, but how could it ever be completely free? Just as there are moments when every atheist wonders if he or she will live again, there are moments when every theist wonders if he or she will not. Let us listen again to Unamuno:

> "Is there?" "Is there not?"—these are the bases of our inner life. There may be a rationalist who has never wavered in his conviction of the mortality of the soul, and there may be a vitalist who has never wavered in his faith in immortality; but at the most this would only prove that just as there are natural monstrosities, so there are those who are stupid as regards heart and feeling, however great their intelligence, and those who are stupid intellectually, however great their virtue. But, in normal cases, I cannot believe those who assure me that never, not in a fleeting moment,

not in the hours of direst loneliness and grief, has this murmur of uncertainty breathed upon their consciousness. I do not understand those men who tell me that the prospect of the yonder side of death has never tormented them, that the thought of their own annihilation never disquiets them. For my part I do not wish to make peace between my heart and my head, between my faith and my reason—I wish rather that there should be war between them![24]

18

IMMORTALITY:
Why I Do Not Think It Strange

Still seems it strange that thou shouldst live forever?
Is it less strange that thou shouldst live at all?
This is a miracle, and that no more.
Who gave beginning, can exclude an end.

—EDWARD YOUNG, *Night Thoughts on Life,*
Death, and Immortality

The above lines by Edward Young, from his once-admired book of Christian poetry, express a thought that has been repeated over and over again by theists of all persuasions. It conveys, of course, only an emotion; an emotion that is a variant—or perhaps it is the same—on the sensation of overwhelming awe that comes upon certain people at times when they reflect on the fact that anything exists at all. Why should there be something rather than nothing?

Obviously we have no way to answer. It is no help to say that God created something, because the question can be asked again: Why does God exist rather than nothing? Leibniz, Schopenhauer, Heidegger, and many other philosophers have agonized over this curious question. For some people the emotion—fortunately it is usually short-lived—can arouse an intense anguish. William James called it an "ontological wonder sickness." In Jean-Paul Sartre's novel *Nausea*, the narrator lives in Bouville, the French equivalent of Mudville where our Mighty Casey struck out. Matter is a kind of mud. It really ought not to exist, but obviously it does, and wondering why it does arouses in the novel's narrator a sensation of nausea. Writing on "Why" in the *Encyclopedia of Philosophy*, Paul Edwards calls it the super-ultimate question. Milton K. Munitz produced an entire book about it, *The Mystery of Existence*, in which he argues that the question is not meaningless, but that its meaning lies solely in the absolute impossibility of answering it.

The most incredible fact about existence is that you and I exist. That the universe exists is awful enough, but even more astonishing, we are part of that universe, a part capable of wondering why the whole thing exists and why we ourselves exist. Do you not feel oppressed by this mystery? Most people, I suppose, go through life without ever asking the superultimate question. If you spring it on them they either cannot understand it or they think you mad. Others experience it periodically like the stab of a dagger. They are sometimes amazed to learn they are not alone in having such emotions.

That nothing at all should exist is certainly conceivable, even though you must imagine yourself existing in order to imagine it. William James suggested that you shut yourself up in a closet, and in the darkness meditate on the fact that you are there at that particular spot, rather than somewhere else, alive at that very moment instead of in some other century. Think of your "queer bodily shape." Think of your "fantastic character." Perhaps a strange sense of wonder will steal over you. It is not only terrifying that *anything* should be, said James, "but that *this* very thing," namely *you*, should be! "Philosophy stares, but brings no reasoned solution, for from nothing to being there is no logical bridge." [1]

Vladimir Nabokov, opening his autobiography, *Speak, Memory*, recalls a moment of ontological panic that he experienced as a child when he first saw some homemade movies taken a few weeks before he was born:

> He saw a world that was practically unchanged—the same house, the same people—and then realized that he did not exist there at all and that nobody mourned his absence. He caught a glimpse of his mother waving from an upstairs window, and that unfamiliar gesture disturbed him, as if it were some mysterious farewell. But

what particularly frightened him was the sight of a brand-new baby carriage standing there on the porch, with the smug, encroaching air of a coffin; even that was empty, as if, in the reverse course of events, his very bones had disintegrated.[2]

If you have ever felt the anguish of this darkest of metaphysical mysteries, the superultimate mystery, perhaps you can feel the emotion behind Young's lines. That you exist now is so incredible that your continued existence after death pales in comparison. "Life is a great surprise," says Nabokov's fictional poet John Shade. "I do not see why death should not be an even greater one."[3]

If you are a theist you can look at it this way. God had the power to bring you into being. Surely he does not lack the power to preserve your being. "I trouble not myself about the manner of future existence," wrote Thomas Paine in his celebrated *Age of Reason*. "I content myself with believing, even to positive conviction, that the Power that gave me existence is able to continue it, in any form and manner he pleases, either with or without this body; and it appears more probable to me that I shall continue to exist hereafter, than that I should have had existence, as I now have, before that existence began."

If you believe in life after death it is wise to follow Paine's example and not trouble yourself much about how God can provide another life or what that life will be like. As in the case of God's own existence we are obviously dealing with something that transcends our understanding of space and time, and about which we can speak only in broken metaphors. Let us not take these metaphors seriously. If we must ask questions about the afterlife, let us ask them in a spirit of fantasy and play. How old will children be? Will they grow up in heaven? Will *anyone* age in heaven? Will cripples be made whole? Will the blind see and the deaf hear? Will the insane become sane? Will the aged become young? Will some or all of earth's animals be there? What about material things that we occasionally love: a house, a ship, a city? The fields you roamed as a child?

Will there be rewards and punishments? The fideist is surely entitled to believe there will be; otherwise one of the strongest pragmatic arguments for immortality, Immanuel Kant's argument that rewards and punishments are necessary to satisfy the heart's desire for justice, goes by the board. But the nature of the rewards and punishments must remain a total mystery for all theists who cannot accept the authenticity of those sacred books that describe, in such sickening detail, the torments of the damned and the pleasures of the saved. I do not believe in eternal punishment. I cannot imagine how anyone could believe in it unless compelled by the doctrines of a church that claims a direct Revelation from God.

It is possible, by ingenious linguistic dodges, to reinterpret Jesus' remarks about hell and suppose he really meant to say that the wicked will be annihilated. This has been a popular doctrine throughout the history of Christendom among believers outside the mainstreams, and it has been held by numerous Christian sects, of which the two largest in contemporary America are the Seventh Day Adventists and Jehovah's Witnesses. In both instances the doctrine is associated, as it so often is, with the doctrines of conditional immortality and soul sleeping. Annihilationism has also appealed to many philosophers, starting with Chrysippus, a Stoic, and including such thinkers as Jean Jacques Rousseau, Thomas Hobbes, and John Locke. In recent U.S. philosophy it has been defended by William Hocking, Edgar S. Brightman, William P. Montague and others. Endless books have argued for the annihilation of the unsaved, of which *Man and the Attainment of Immortality* by James Young Simpson, a Presbyterian at the University of Edinburgh, is as good a reference as any.[4]

Among Protestant fundamentalists the doctrine is usually linked with the bodily resurrection of everyone at the day of judgment, followed by Christ's division of humanity into sheep and goats, and finally by the permanent destruction of the unsaved. For other annihilationists, the wicked who die will stay permanently nonexistent. As the atheist believes will happen to us all, the unsaved simply drop feet-foremost at death, like Oscar Wilde's prisoner in Reading Gaol, "into an empty space," a state of eternal nonbeing from which there is no return.

A correspondingly immense literature exists on the contrary doctrine, also unorthodox, of universalism. By equally clever interpretations of biblical passages, universalist Christians maintain that the Bible teaches the eventual salvation of everybody, including (perhaps) even Satan and the other fallen angels. They allow, however, for some sort of punishments, unimaginable to us now, for the wicked. I know of no theists, outside traditional religions in which eternal hell is part of the creed, who are not universalists. Even the Roman Church, though it does not permit denying hell, allows Catholics to *hope* for the eventual salvation of the lost.

As often said, the population of hell for both Catholics and traditional Protestants has been steadily declining since the Middle Ages. *U.S. Catholic* magazine reported (November 1977) the results of a survey in which only a third of the Catholics who responded said they believed in hell. As Father James Breig told the press, for American Catholics hell has become "a sort of whimsical place, more of a joke than an eschatological reality. It is a fictional domain, created from one part Dante and one part Milton with a dash of religious art thrown in."[5]

I find this trend all to the good. To me there is no sadder aspect of the literature of Christianity than that which describes the eternal—the eternal!—torments of the unsaved. I am thinking of passages in Augustine and Aquinas and Dante, in Martin Luther, John Calvin, John Wesley, and Jonathan Edwards, the final note in John Henry Newman's *Grammar of Assent*, the terrible Chapter 8 of C. S. Lewis's *Problem of Pain*. It is hard to believe, but in past ages millions of good Christian souls have not only believed in the endless—the endless!—suffering of the unsaved, they have defined *unsaved* to mean not the wicked but those who do not believe that Jesus was God. Some have even defined *unsaved* to mean a failure to be baptized into a particular church! There were instruments in medieval times for baptizing a child in the womb lest the unborn embryo die unbaptized and thus fail to make it to Paradise. The torture and execution of heretics would never have been possible without widespread belief that it was better a few should die than that their false teachings would send millions to everlasting pain.

Here is how Francis Bacon begins his little essay on "Superstition," with nary a hint of its obvious application to his professed faith in the Church of England:

> It were better to have no opinion of God at all, than such an opinion as is unworthy of him. For the one is unbelief, the other is contumely: and certainly superstition is the reproach of the Deity. Plutarch saith well to that purpose: *Surely*, saith he, *I had rather a great deal men should say there was no such a man at all as Plutarch, than that they should say there was one Plutarch that would eat his children as soon as they were born*; as the poets speak of Saturn.

For a splendid defense of universalism, as it has been held by millions of devout Christians since the time of Origen, look up Lewis

Carroll's essay on "Eternal Punishment."[6] The doctrine of hell seems to me, as it did to Carroll, the supreme disgrace of Christendom. It makes God out to be a monster of cruelty, less merciful than mortals whose admirable attributes God is supposed to possess in an infinite degree. I do not know how justice will be served in the afterlife that I believe by faith will be our destiny. I only know I cannot model it with everlasting misery for the wicked, certainly not for those whose only sin is their inability to believe in the Incarnation.[7] If Jesus did indeed teach such a damnable doctrine, it is the strongest possible reason for not believing him to have been God in human flesh.

Robert Ingersoll was not a deep thinker, but he saw many things with a simple clarity that few liberal Christians have been willing to admit. Above all he saw how impossible it was for a God who, through Jesus, could tell his disciples to love their enemies and turn the other cheek, to say also, through that same Jesus, "Depart from me, ye cursed, into everlasting fire, prepared for the devil and his angels" (Matthew: 25:41). I agree with Ingersoll that the doctrine of hell "like a venomous serpent crawls and coils and hisses in every orthodox creed."

> It makes man an eternal victim and God an eternal fiend. It is the one infinite horror. Every church in which it is taught is a public curse. Every preacher who teaches it is an enemy of mankind. Below this Christian dogma, savagery can not go. It is the infinite of malice, hatred and revenge. Nothing could add to the horror of Hell, except the presence of its creator, God. While I have life, as long as I draw breath, I shall deny with all my strength, and hate with every drop of my blood, this infinite lie.
>
> Nothing gives me greater joy than to know that this belief in eternal pain is growing weaker every day—that thousands of ministers are ashamed of it. It gives me joy to know that Christians are becoming merciful, so merciful that the fires of Hell are burning low—flickering, choked with ashes, destined in a few years to die out forever.[8]

Although there may be rewards and punishments in the afterlife, who are we to know what forms they will take? And there are many other questions involving space and time in the life to come that it is wise not to try to answer. Does immortality really mean forever or just a very very very long period? Will there be a sequence of new lives, each ending in something like what we know as death, so that (to recall G. K. Chesterton's metaphor) eternity is cut up for us into finite strips? Here is Chesterton again on the matter:

> The divisions of time which men have adopted are in a sort of way a mild mortality. When we see the Old Year out, we do what many eminent men have done, and what all men desire to do; we die temporarily. Whenever we admit that it is Tuesday we fulfil St. Paul, and die daily. I doubt if the strongest stoic that ever existed on earth could endure the idea of a Tuesday following on a Tuesday, and a Tuesday on that, and a Tuesday on that, and all the days being Tuesdays till the Day of Judgment, which might be (by some strange an special mercy) a Wednesday.[9]

If Life is indeed eternal (whatever that means), do we ever reach perfection, or is perfection an unobtainable limit, as Joseph Addison suggested, like the way the arms of a hyperbola approach but never touch their asymptotes? Perhaps the punishment of the wicked consists, as some religions have maintained, in forever lagging behind the good while everyone progresses toward higher and higher states of being. Will there be *news* in heaven, as William James liked to say? Will mathematicians in heaven, as Lewis Carroll hoped, find fresh problems to work on? Will Wolfgang Pauli, as in a joke that physicists like to tell, read through God's explanation of why the fine structure constant is so close to $1/137$, then look up and exclaim, "But this is wrong!"? Will Isaac Asimov, to his vast amazement, discover thousands of new topics to think and write about, even to write limericks about?

Will there be sex in heaven? "Yes!" shouts the Koran. The Christian "No" is based almost solely on how Jesus answered the Sadducees when they tried to trap him with a story about a woman who survived seven husbands. Whose wife would she be in the life to come? Jesus replied (Matthew 22:30) that in heaven there is neither marriage nor giving in marriage. Aquinas, following Augustine, believed that after judgment day, when we receive our celestial bodies, we will keep our sexual organs, but only to restore the perfection of our former identities as male and female. The organs will otherwise be functionless.[10]

C. S. Lewis handles the topic circumspectly:

> The letter and spirit of scripture, and of all Christianity, forbid us to suppose that life in the New Creation will be a sexual life; and

this reduces our imagination to the withering alternative either of bodies which are hardly recognisable as human bodies at all or else of a perpetual fast. As regards the fast, I think our present outlook might be like that of a small boy who, on being told that the sexual act was the highest bodily pleasure, should immediately ask whether you ate chocolates at the same time. On receiving the answer "No," he might regard absence of chocolates as the chief characteristic of sexuality. In vain would you tell him that the reason why lovers in their carnal raptures don't bother about chocolates is that they have something better to think of. The boy knows chocolate: he does not know the positive thing that excludes it. We are in the same position. We know the sexual life; we do not know, except in glimpses, the other thing which, in Heaven, will leave no room for it. Hence where fulness awaits us we anticipate fasting. In denying that sexual life, as we now understand it, makes any part of the final beatitude, it is not of course necessary to suppose that the distinction of sexes will disappear. What is no longer needed for biological purposes may be expected to survive for splendour. Sexuality is the instrument both of virginity and of conjugal virtue; neither men nor women will be asked to throw away weapons they have used victoriously. It is the beaten and the fugitives who throw away their swords. The conquerors sheathe theirs and retain them. "Trans-sexual" would be a better word than "sexless" for the heavenly life.[11]

Such quaint speculations seem to me harmless provided they are recognized as frivolous guesses about details God has wisely concealed. On the other hand, we cannot leave the nature of the afterlife a total blank. If we make no guesses at all, how can it satisfy those longings that impel the leap of faith?

I think we have a right to say—or, rather, it is impossible for a theist not to say—that certain features about the other world must be assumed for the simple reason that if we don't assume them we will be unable to imagine what it means to "live." We do not want to live again in some vacuous disembodied state. We want to live again in a manner that somehow resembles life on earth. Just as we are forced to think of God as having certain personal traits that are the highest we know (simultaneously recognizing that we do not know how those traits apply to God), so there are aspects of the afterlife we are forced to affirm with the same kind of vague analogical predication.

We cannot, at least I cannot, imagine how I can "live" unless I am in some sort of time and space, retaining my consciousness of self, which means retaining my memories. For a person "to be," Nabokov writes in the long section on time in his novel *Ada*, means to know one "has been." Tell me I will live again, but without memory of my life here, and I will be as much impressed as if you told me that only my left foot will be alive in heaven.

> *I'm ready to become a floweret*
> *Or a fat fly, but never, to forget,*

writes Nabokov in Canto 3 of "Pale Fire," the poem in his novel of the same name. He will turn down heaven, the poem continues, unless he can remember the "melancholy and the tenderness," the "passion and the pain," of his life on earth. The entire canto is a remarkable reflection on what Rabelais called the "great perhaps," or as Nabokov calls it, punning on the French *peut-être*, the "grand potato."

Nor can I conceive of living again unless there are others there whom I have liked and loved, and others yet to like and love. "O thou soul of my soul! I shall clasp thee again, and with God be the rest!"—if I may quote once-familiar lines from "Prospice" at a time when no one seems to read Robert Browning anymore. I cannot imagine living unless there are things to do, challenges to be met, struggles and adventures to undergo. All this is, of course, said analogically.

It goes without saying that, as a theist who accepts no Revelation, I believe we can learn nothing about life after death from such all-too-human visions as we find in John Bunyan or Dante, in the writings of eccentric seers like Emanuel Swedenborg, in the descriptions of Paradise in the Koran, or in the turgid vision that concludes the Christian Bible. I do not believe that the departed speak to us through mediums. Nothing bores me more than the idiotic descriptions of life "behind the veil" that drivel from the lips of men and women who claim to be transmitting the voices of discarnates.

I believe by faith, by faith alone, that I will continue to exist after death in a state now completely beyond my understanding. God's house, said Jesus, has many mansions. The writer of I Corinthians (2:9), referring to Isaiah 64:4, tells us—forgive me, readers, for quoting a passage so well known to those who have read the Bible—"But as it is written, Eye hath not seen, nor ear heard, neither have entered into the heart of man, the things which God hath prepared for them that love him."

We may draw our dim sketches of heaven any way we like, wrote Karl Barth, provided we "make it very clear to ourselves that we, who must do our thinking from this time that is known to us, have not the slightest idea what we are saying when we talk either positively or negatively about the time of that God with Whom we shall live in unbroken peace in eternal life." [12] If our childish guesses are all wrong, Lewis says somewhere, the reality will be better.

> *It isn't that we dream too wild a dream:*
> *The trouble is we do not make it seem*
> *Sufficiently unlikely; for the most*
> *We can think up is a domestic ghost.* [13]

Barth was fond of quoting Sören Kierkegaard's famous remark that there is an infinite qualitative difference between our time and God's time, between human history and God's history. There is no harm in dreaming wild dreams about transcendental realms. Nor is there any harm in believing that, if we are to be something like what we are now, we must live in a world that in some fashion resembles the only world we know. The New Testament speaks of a new heaven and a new earth, as though there may even be a time—Teilhard de Chardin called it the Omega Point—when earth's history and the Kingdom of God will merge to become one.

> *. . . though what if Earth*
> *Be but the shadow of Heav'n, and things therein*
> *Each to other like, more than on earth is thought?* [14]

Of course Barth is right. We know nothing—nothing whatever—about heaven. At the same time let us not be ashamed, when we dream our crazy dreams of hope, to model heaven in the only way we can: as life that deserves to be called life, not something it would be more honest to call death. Listen once more to one of Miguel de Unamuno's passionate cries:

> And the soul, my soul at least, longs for something else, not absorption, not quietude, not peace, not appeasement, it longs ever to approach and never to arrive, it longs for a never-ending longing, for an eternal hope which is eternally renewed but never

wholly fulfilled. And together with all this, it longs for an eternal lack of something and an eternal suffering. A suffering, a pain, thanks to which it grows without ceasing in consciousness and in longing. Do not write upon the gate of heaven that sentence which Dante placed over the threshold of hell, *Lasciate ogni speranza!* Do not destroy time! Our life is a hope which is continually converting itself into memory and memory in its turn begets hope. Give us leave to live! The eternity that is like an eternal present, without memory and without hope, is death. Thus do ideas exist, but not thus do men live. Thus do ideas exist in the God-idea, but not thus can men live in the living God, in the God-Man.

An eternal purgatory, then, rather than a heaven of glory; an eternal ascent. If there is an end of all suffering, however pure and spiritualized we may suppose it to be, if there is an end of all desire, what is it that makes the blessed in paradise go on living? If in paradise they do not suffer for want of God, how shall they love Him? And if even there, in the heaven of glory, while they behold God little by little and closer and closer, yet without ever wholly attaining to Him, there does not always remain something more for them to know and desire, if there does not always remain a substratum of doubt, how shall they not fall asleep? [15]

19

IMMORTALITY:
Why I Do Not Think It Impossible

And he said unto Jesus, Lord, remember me when
thou comest into thy kingdom.
And Jesus said unto him, Verily I say unto thee,
Today shalt thou be with me in paradise.

—LUKE 23:42–43

Lord, remember me! If God is the creator and sustainer of the universe, if every wave and particle is what it is, does what it does, because God remembers it, then we exist now because God remembers us. And if God remembers us after we die, we may continue to exist. That is all a theist need say to establish in his or her heart the possibility of immortality.

Nevertheless, there is a compulsion to build models even though we do not know, cannot possibly know, to what extent a model conforms to a transcendent reality. As I have said, such models serve two purposes. They establish the possibility that something can be true without logical contradiction, and they can play a role, at least in the minds of some believers, in strengthening faith.

The oldest model for immortality—the model preferred by all the major religions that affirm life after death—is that the body is inhabited by an immortal soul. The soul is capable of existing apart from the body. It uses the body, including of course the brain, the way one uses a car. In Gilbert Ryle's pejorative phrase, it is the "ghost in the machine."

Because the soul is not observable by the senses, or by scientific instruments, we must suppose it to consist of a spiritual substance, incorporeal, utterly unlike what we know as matter. Although for a time it uses the physical body, the soul is what a person truly is. In Eastern religions it is this soul that survives death and is reincarnated in a succession of other bodies. In Christianity it is this soul that, after death, either unites with a glorified body or remains disembodied until the day of Resurrection.

Is the soul immortal, in the sense that it cannot be destroyed, or is its immortality contingent on a decision by God? This is largely a verbal question because for a theist everything is contingent on God. Even the Schoolmen, who believed the soul to be intrinsically immortal, took for granted that God could annihilate a soul if he liked. In Western philosophy, Plato's Socrates was the first important thinker to defend this model with systematic "proofs" that souls cannot, by their very nature, die. Today only a small number of extremely traditional theologians take Plato's proofs seriously. Nevertheless, the view that every person has an immortal soul, distinct from the body, continues to be the view of most believers in an afterlife.

To say that Plato's model cannot be proved is not, of course, to say the model is inconsistent or even wrong. Indeed, I can conceive of no rational way to establish or refute the model. It is true that believers often report seeing spirits of the departed, or talking to them, and some Spiritualists have claimed to have photographed them, but (as I have said before) I find this evidence so soaked with fraud and self-deception that I consider it a drain of energy to write about it.

My attitude is the same toward OOBEs, or out-of-body experiences. There is no question that such experiences occur. I myself have had dreams or half-dreams of leaving my sleeping body and wandering about with vivid sensations of being in real places and retaining my will to move about as I pleased, sometimes floating through the sky, sometimes moving through walls. Although they are dreams of a peculiar sort, not like normal dreams, I have not for a moment believed they were anything but dreams.

Is Plato's two-substance model of the soul and body true or false? Do not ask *me*! It is quite possible there are incorporeal substances undetectable by instruments made of ordinary matter. In quantum physics the basic particles are far removed from what the word *corporeal* means in ordinary language. They are discrete packets of energy only when you measure them in certain ways. Measure them in other ways and they are complicated probability waves of nothing, described in abstract, artificially constructed spaces of many dimensions. Is anything more ghostly than a neutrino? Well, the other particles are just as spooky, and if some are made of quarks, the quarks are more mysterious still. If matter consists of particles known only by properties that are given by mathematical formulas, and if no one knows what is behind the formulas, who are we to say there cannot be other substances based on formulas not yet known, as undetectable by instruments of earthly matter as the neutrino is undetectable by a finger and a thumb. I do not know if Plato's model is true or false. I offer it only as a logically possible model. You may believe it if you like, reject it if you like.

Suppose we reject it. Can we build another model that will support—support, not prove—the possibility of life after death? Yes, there are other models. Let me proceed at once to the most radical before I describe a third model that mediates between the two extremes.

Our second model derives from Aristotle's view that the soul is merely a name for the body's form. I know that Aristotle's treatises are not consistent on the nature of the soul, but this view is the one given in *De Anima* (*On the Soul*), which most historians take to be Aristotle's mature thoughts on the topic. Put in modern terms, the soul is the pattern, the total set of relations, that obtains between the billions upon billions of molecules that make up the brain. In Aristotle's language, it is the form of the body, as inseparable from the body as the form of a wax seal is inseparable from the wax, or as sight is inseparable from a living eye. There is no seeing, said Aristotle, without an eye, and if an eye does not see, it is no more a real eye than the eye of a statue. Of course we can think of the form of a chair apart from a chair, but the form does not exist the way the chair does. And to imagine that a human soul could transmigrate, say, to the body of an animal is as absurd as finding the form of a chair in the structure of a flute. (We can ignore Aristotle's obscure view that there is a rational element in the soul that is part of the universe or God. If Aristotle were alive today, I think he would say that the world has a logical structure that is also a part of the operation of the mind.)

Aristotle's one-substance view of the living person, with the soul as the body's pattern, is of course the so-called functional view of consciousness that has dominated psychology since William James. The soul or self is a function, a pattern, of the brain. We must not, of course, succumb to the reductionist fallacy of supposing that the self is "nothing more" than an assemblage of molecules. When molecules unite in complicated structures, startling properties obviously emerge which are qualitatively unlike the properties of simpler structures. To use the most hackneyed example, water has properties not possessed by hydrogen or oxygen. The human brain is the most complicated structure we know. From this structure, so goes the functional view, emerges the self, with its strange awareness of its own existence, its free will, its ability to reason and feel emotions, to laugh and cry, to love and hate, to create and destroy, to imagine God, and to long for immortality. As Douglas Hofstadter says in *The Mind's I* (combining two puns with a spoonerism), the soul is greater than the hum of its parts. Wondrous though the soul may be, from this point of view it is a pattern that requires a living body to exist. Without a body the pattern can, of course, exist in a sense, the way an abstract dodecahedron exists, but this is not an existence that deserves to be called a living person.

Like the two-substance view of Plato, the one-substance view is also as old as humanity. Although Aristotle in *De Anima* rejects an older and popular theory that the soul is a "harmony" of the body, like a melody played on a lyre, his rejection is based on pressing the analogy with music too far. If we do not press it far, the analogy is not a bad one. A melody is a pattern that cannot be heard and enjoyed unless it is produced by vocal cords or musical instruments. The soul is a pattern, inconceivably more intricate, that requires a body in order to live. If this is true, how can a believer in an afterlife reply to Simmias when he argues (in Plato's *Phaedo*) that we should no more expect a soul to survive the death of its body than we should expect the music of a lyre to exist after the lyre is destroyed?

The answer is obvious. The melody can be played again on another lyre. But now we run into profound difficulties that are best brought out by a series of shocking thought experiments, most of which go back to ancient times. As a starter, imagine that your body is utterly destroyed by fire. Now suppose that material particles are put together in exactly the same pattern your body had before its destruction. Would not this be your resurrection? Would it not be you, brought back to life again?

I cannot blame you if you are uneasy in thinking the new body is *really* you. Is it not just a duplicate, a clever copy; a living person, yes, possessing all your habits and memories, looking exactly like you, behaving like you, but actually someone else?

Let me increase your uneasiness by another thought experiment. Suppose an exact duplicate of you has been constructed, atom by atom, while you are still alive. Each of the pair naturally thinks he or she is the original. Now you are told you are to be killed. Would you be impressed by the argument that you will not really die because standing over there is this other person, perhaps smiling, who will be allowed to live? Obviously you would not take kindly to this notion. You would protest your death as vigorously as if your replica were not there. Nor would your copy wish to die after being told that he or she would survive in you. To be a person is to be unique, irreplaceable, unduplicatable. We touch here on problems that are not trivial. Many philosophers and theologians have agonized over whether an exact duplicate of a person would be the same person or someone else, and it seems to matter not at all whether the copy is made while the original is still alive or after the individual is dead.[1]

The travel of persons from place to place at the speed of light is commonplace in modern science fiction. This is often accomplished by a machine that scans a person's body, particle by particle, disintegrating the body while simultaneously sending the body's pattern by electromagnetic radiation to another spot where another machine reassembles the body with duplicate molecules. Perhaps a receiving machine is unnecessary. That is how officers of the USS *Enterprise*, in *Star Trek*, "beam down" from their spaceship to the surface of a planet. The ship's machine can also beam them up again.

We now ask the same disconcerting question. If you are transmitted by such a process, is the person at the other end really you? Or were you annihilated at one end and a duplicate fabricated at the other? A pioneering science-fiction yarn by Robert Locke, "Dark Nuptial," tells how a man's wife dies in an accident.[2] He is reminded that he and his wife once made a long trip together by beam transmission and that the matrix of his wife's transmission is still available. He uses it to have her duplicated. But is she really his wife, or a soulless copy? Come to think of it, were he and his wife really themselves after the trip they made by beam transmission?

Arthur C. Clarke has long been fascinated by this kind of matter transmission. In *Profiles of the Future* he cites one of Sir Arthur Conan

Doyle's Professor Challenger stories, "The Disintegration Machine," as an early example of transporting people this way in science fiction.[3] In *The Challenge of the Spaceship*, Clarke reminds us how much we are like a candle flame, in that atoms of our body are constantly being replaced by other atoms. Only the pattern stays the same. No man steps twice into the same river, said Heraclitus. "No man ever looks at his face twice in the mirror," writes Clarke. "The flow of flesh may be slower than the movement of water to the sea, but it is no less inexorable."

Clarke sees no reason why persons cannot someday be stored on tape and later reconstituted. In the book version of his movie *2001: A Space Odyssey*, David Bowman is reborn by just such a transfer of information from his adult brain to the brain of a baby. Perhaps I should add that the problem we are dealing with here has nothing in common with cloning. A cloned person would simply be one who grew from a cell with the same genetic components as those of another person. Clones raise no metaphysical problems not raised by normally born identical twins.

I do not know how long it takes for all the atoms of a human body to be replaced by others, or whether there are parts of the body (the brain, the DNA molecules, and other spots) where they are never replaced. It is probably safe to say that over 90 percent of the brain's atoms are replaced over a period of a few years. In any case the speed and percentage do not matter. We "wander about earth," said James Branch Cabell in *Beyond Life*, "like a wind-whirl over a roadway, in a vortex of ever-changing dust." Here is how Richard P. Feynman, the physicist, says the same thing with different images:

> So what is this mind, what are these atoms with consciousness? Last week's potatoes! That is what now can *remember* what was going on in my mind a year ago—a mind which has long ago been replaced.
>
> That is what it means when one discovers how long it takes for the atoms of the brain to be replaced by other atoms, to note that the thing which I call my individuality is only a pattern or dance. The atoms come into my brain, dance a dance, then go out; always new atoms but always doing the same dance, remembering what the dance was yesterday.[4]

Thomas Aquinas was much concerned with the question of whether the immortal soul, after receiving its new body on the day of Resurrection, would be made of the same material substances that composed it before, or whether it would be made of new substances. Because Aquinas opted for the first opinion, many curious problems arose. Bertrand Russell considered one of them:

> St. Thomas Aquinas, the official philosopher of the Catholic church, discussed lengthily and seriously a very grave problem, which, I fear, modern theologians unduly neglect. He imagines a cannibal who has never eaten anything but human flesh, and whose father and mother before him had like propensities. Every particle of his body belongs rightfully to someone else. We cannot suppose that those who have been eaten by cannibals are to go short through all eternity. But, if not, what is left for the cannibal? How is he to be properly roasted in hell, if all his body is restored to its original owners? This is a puzzling question, as the Saint rightly perceives.[5]

For Lewis Carroll, as for most post-medieval Christians, the cannibal argument alone is sufficient to prove that the resurrected body will consist of entirely new substances:

> *My* conclusion was to give up the *literal* meaning of the *material* body altogether. *Identity*, in some mysterious way, there evidently is; but there is no resisting the scientific fact that the actual *material* usable for *physical* bodies has been used over and over again—so that each atom would have several owners. The mere solitary fact of the existence of *cannibalism* is to my mind a sufficient *reductio ad absurdum* of the theory that the particular set of atoms I shall happen to own at death (changed every seven years, they say) will be mine in the next life—and all the other insuperable difficulties (such as people born with bodily defects) are swept away at once if we accept St. Paul's "spiritual body," and his simile of the grain of corn.[6]

Imagine a future when, as cells of a human brain wear out, they are replaced by miniature electronic components until the original brain has been entirely transformed into a computer. Will it be the same person? Raymond Smullyan, in *The Chess Mysteries of Sherlock Holmes*, gives what he calls "An Unsolved Problem" that bears on the topic. White's pawn has captured a black rook on that rook's starting square, and White has called for its replacement by a black rook—a bizarre move not forbidden under old chess rules. The solution of Smullyan's problem depends on whether Black can legally castle, which in turn depends on whether the black rook has "moved." It has moved in the sense that White has taken it from the board. However, Black has replaced the same rook on its original square, or perhaps replaced it with another black rook. "Is it really the same rook?" Holmes asks.[7]

Of course this is a trivial question easily settled by making chess rules, and our terminology, more precise. But do you see how the chess problem applies to our reconstitution model? God retains a person's pattern in his mind. When that person dies, God removes the pattern from the board (the universe), and replaces it, then or later, by putting a person with the same pattern on another board (heaven). Is it the *same* person? I maintain that we don't really know what this question means because we don't know enough about the nature and the rules of God's game. In a final ontological sense we have no clear notion of what "identity" means when applied to anything. Is an electron or a photon the same particle after it has moved from here to there? Is it like asking if a water wave is the same wave after it has traveled a few kilometers? No, it is far more mysterious. Quantum waves are not "real" waves like water and sound waves. They are waves of probabilities, waves of nothing. A quantum physicist is likely to find these questions as nonsensical as Holmes's question about the rook.

L. Frank Baum's Tin Woodman poses the problem of personal identity in an acute and amusing way. Nick Chopper was originally a Munchkin woodman in love with a girl named Nimmie Amee. But Nimmie Amee was also loved by a wicked witch, the same witch destined to be destroyed when Dorothy's house, blown to Oz by a cyclone, falls on top of her. Jealous of Nick Chopper, the old witch enchanted his ax, causing it periodically to chop off portions of his body. As parts were cut off, a local tinsmith, Ku-Klip, made new parts of tin which he attached to Chopper's body with magic glue. Eventually the woodman was made entirely of tin. Is he now the same man he was before?

In *The Tin Woodman of Oz* the tin man returns to his Munchkin home, where he has a bewildering conversation with his former head. To complicate matters even more, after the Tin Woodman had abandoned Nimmie Amee, believing he had no heart and therefore could not marry her, she had fallen in love with Captain Fyter. Jealous as before, the wicked witch enchanted the captain's sword and soon he, too, with the help of Ku-Klip, became a man of tin. The two tin men meet. Together they go in search of their former sweetheart. They find her happily married to Chopfyte, a composite man wearing the Tin Soldier's original head, and with a body that is a patchwork of parts of the "meat" bodies of her two earlier lovers.

Baum played similar games with personal identity in other fantasies. In *John Dough and the Cherub* there is a general who consists entirely of artificial replacements for bodily parts lost in combat, including his head. In *The Road to Oz*, Jack Pumpkinhead, whose head is a carved pumpkin, raises new heads to replace old ones that spoil. Princess Langwidere, in *Ozma of Oz*, owns thirty beautiful heads, no two alike. Each morning "she" puts on a new one. In *Sky Island* the wicked Boolooroo of the Blues punishes his subjects in pairs by a process called "patching." Each victim is sliced vertically in half; then they are put together again with sides exchanged.

The problem of what it means to say that a thing preserves its identity is one of the most curious and persistent problems of philosophy. Ancient thinkers imagined a ship that slowly loses parts. The lost pieces are replaced until eventually nothing of the original ship remains. Is it the same ship? Suppose the lost parts are carefully preserved and eventually put together just as they were before. Two ships now exist. Which is the original?

There are amusing geometrical paradoxes in which you rotate a cardboard disk, or exchange parts of a rectangle, and thirteen Chinese warriors become twelve, or fifteen leprechauns become fourteen. Which leprechaun vanished? Where did he go? Switch the parts back again. Which leprechaun returned? Where did he come from? No one seems upset by these paradoxes, in which parts of pictures are simply rearranged, when they are pictures of straight lines, or even inanimate objects such as pencils or hats. But when pictures of animals or people are involved, personal identity slips into the paradox and the transformations become confusing and disturbing.[8]

John Locke raises a number of strange questions about personal identity in his *Essay Concerning Human Understanding* (Book 2, Chapter 27). He sensibly concludes that "the difficulty or obscurity that has been about this matter rather arises from the names ill-used than from any obscurity in things themselves." In other words, they are verbal riddles. He quotes a whimsical passage from Sir William Temple's *Memoirs* about an old parrot in Brazil that was said to converse with people more rationally than any of today's talking apes. The point of the story is that everybody considered it an intelligent bird, not a person in a bird's body. Similarly, Locke contends, if a man is as stupid as a parrot or a cat, we would still call him a man. On the other hand, if a prince and a cobbler exchanged souls, we would not hesitate to say that the prince occupied the cobbler's body and vice versa. Agree, says Locke, on exactly what is meant by such terms as *man*, *spirit*, *person*, and such conundrums are easily resolved.

For Locke, persistence of memory is the basis for persistence in time of a person's identity, and this is independent of whatever material substances make up the body.[9] If he could recall Noah's ark and the Flood as vividly as he recalls having seen the Thames overflow its banks last summer, Locke writes, he would assume it was he himself who had once occupied a body in Noah's time. Locke has no difficulty assuming it will be he himself in a resurrected body, even though it be made of an entirely different substance.

Locke says he can easily imagine two souls inhabiting the same body, one by day, the other by night. If they retain separate memories, he would consider the souls as distinct as Plato and Socrates. Similarly, he can imagine one soul operating, at different times, in two bodies. In this case he would consider it comparable to one person wearing two different suits of clothing.

These are strange thought experiments, Locke concedes, but they are "pardonable" in the light of how little we know about

> that thinking thing that is in us and which we look on as our *selves*. Did we know what it was or how it was tied to a certain system of fleeting animal spirits, or whether it could or could not perform its operations of thinking and memory out of a body organized as ours is, and whether it has pleased God that no one such spirit shall ever be united to any but one such body, upon the right constitution of whose organs its memory should depend, we might see the absurdity of some of those suppositions I have made.

Wise words! Because we know nothing about the nature of consciousness, let us leave to God the question of whether our fantastic thought experiments could actually be made.

In his *Treatise on Human Nature* (Book 1, Part 4, Section 6) David Hume considers a variety of simple puzzles involving the sameness of objects: the slowly altered ship, a ruined church that is rebuilt with completely different architecture, a flowing river, an acorn that grows into an oak tree, a baby that becomes an adult, and a nation that alters radically as centuries pass. In all such cases, Hume agrees with Locke that the question of whether something is the same or different is not ontological, but only a problem about how we use words. In every case "identity" is tied to the persistence of a set of relations—what I have been calling a pattern—and ordinary language varies in the pattern it singles out when it calls something the "same." A church rebuilt with different architecture is not the same material building, but it is the same church with respect to relations involving church members. And so on.

When objects like ships and churches and trees are involved in such riddles, it is easy to see that the issues are mainly linguistic. Only when living animals or persons are involved does the nature of the self introduce special perplexities. If by *self* one means an immaterial soul existing independently of the brain, then the exchange of souls of the prince and cobbler indeed raises formidable and perhaps unanswerable questions. But if the soul is the pattern of the brain, what does it matter whether we say the brain patterns exchanged bodies or the bodies exchanged brain patterns? If by *cobbler* we mean the cobbler's body, then the cobbler acquired a different self. If by *cobbler* we mean the cobbler's brain pattern, then the cobbler acquired a different body. Since we do not yet know how memories are stored in the brain, or what makes us conscious of our identity, it is impossible to know how such a transfer could be made even in principle. If memory is stored chemically, the transfer might require the transfer of entire brains. If memory is stored electrically, it is conceivable that the electrical patterns could be switched without switching brains. If memory is stored both chemically and electrically, the task becomes more complicated.[10]

In quantum mechanics, Werner Heisenberg's uncertainty principle makes it impossible to say where an electron is until its position is measured. Most physicists believe that an electron has no precise location, that it does not even exist as a particle, until it is measured. An atom is more like a tune than a table. Since a table is made of atoms, is it not just a more complicated tune? Are *we*, as Plato's Simmias argued, no more than complicated tunes?

There are respectable modern theories of space and time, anticipated by Maimonides, Descartes, and other thinkers, in which space-time is not continuous. Space consists of discrete points separated from one another by an extremely small distance, and time is a sequence of discrete ticks called chronons. Maybe the points of space-time form a regular lattice, as Werner Heisenberg proposed; maybe they form a complex, spongy "foam," as John Wheeler suggests. In any case, when an object goes from here to there, when we go from here to there, the motion is an illusion, like the movements produced by flashing bulbs in an advertising sign, like the changes in color of cells on a television screen, or the movement of "life-forms" in John Conway's cellular automata game of Life. Nothing really goes from here to there, because between the points of space-time nothing exists. Every microsecond the moving object is being repeatedly created and destroyed. Our identity is nothing more than the preservation of a pattern as the points of space-time fluctuate in their states. In his essay "A New Refutation of Time," Jorge Luis Borges refers to an old Buddhist text which says that the entire universe, like the rapid succession of still pictures on a movie screen, annihilates itself and reappears, slightly altered to give the illusion of continuous change, 6.5 billion times a day.

In the light of these possibilities, perhaps your anxiety is lessening about the reconstitution model of immortality. At some moment after a person's death, perhaps billions of years later, God recreates a body's pattern and lo, there stands the same person as before! If at every microsecond our soul, our pattern of particles in the brain, is jumping points in a discrete space, could it not jump after death to a new set of points in another space without any break in continuity? Perhaps human history is a three-dimensional motion picture that God likes to rerun from time to time. After seeing the show for, say, the billionth time, God is so moved by human longings for immortality that as each person on the screen dies he plucks the body's pattern from the film and allows it to live again.

In Christianity this reconstitution model is closely related to a doctrine that goes under such names as mortalism, conditional immortality, and conditionalism. The words imply that we are not intrinsically immortal. When we die we truly cease to exist. We live again only if and when God chooses to give a new body to our original pattern. Conditionalism is often combined with a belief in the annihilation of the wicked. As I mentioned earlier, God either does not give new bodies to the wicked, which means they never exist again, or he reconstitutes them on judgment day so there can be a ceremonial division into sheep and goats. The goats are then permanently annihilated. This is the view of Seventh Day Adventists, a view with a long history painstakingly documented in the two-volume work by L. E. Froom that I cited in the previous chapter.[11]

To relieve the anxiety that inevitably arises over whether a reconstituted person is the same person or someone else, the doctrine has often been combined (as in Seventh Day Adventism) with a view known as "soul sleeping." This doctrine, necessarily fuzzy, supposes there is a "spirit" of some sort behind the pattern. It is not a soul in the Platonic sense, with consciousness and memories, but something more ethereal that "sleeps" in God and so preserves a direct continuity between the body that dies and the body God later re-creates. The New Testament, both in the gospels and later, often speaks of death as a sleep. "The damsel is not dead, but sleepeth," said Jesus (Mark 5:39) before raising from the dead the twelve-year-old daughter of Jairus. For one who sleeps what Raymond Chandler called the Big Sleep, there is no awareness of time passing. If Resurrection Day is a billion years from now, measured by earth time, it will seem to the Big Sleeper that an instant after death he or she is alive again.

The difference between the concept of a sleeping soul and the concept of God retaining a memory of a person's pattern seems to me entirely verbal.[12] What could be more "real" than God's memory? Does not such a memory serve just as well as soul-sleeping to eliminate from the reconstitution model the sense of discontinuity which so many theists find troubling? It is God's memory of our pattern that supports our existence now. The pattern is eternal because God's memory is eternal. If and when God chooses to give the pattern a new body, there will be no break in the continuation of that which is most truly us. There is only a break in the material substance that embodies the pattern. Of course I am only playing with ideas about realities of which we know nothing.

Like the doctrine of annihilation of the wicked, the doctrine of soul-sleep has been held by many eminent Christian thinkers for the simple reason that Paul's writings clearly suggest it. It is true that mainstream Christianity has preferred to believe that souls with an incorporeal body go directly at death to some kind of intermediate state where they are conscious of their existence while they await the Resurrection of the flesh. Nevertheless the doctrine of conditional immortality has always had its adherents. Before Christianity it was favored by some Stoics, notably Chrysippus. Among the early church fathers, Arnobius vigorously defended it. It dropped out of medieval Catholicism (no Schoolman supported it), but later resurfaced with explosive force in the writings of Thomas Hobbes, John Locke, Jean Jacques Rousseau, Sir Thomas Browne, Richard Overton, Goethe, Johann Fichte, Rudolf Lotze, Pierre Bayle, and many others. Among scientists, Joseph Priestley favored it. John Milton strongly held the view.

Milton's opinions, given most explicitly in his *Treatise on Christian Doctrine* (Chapter 13), closely parallel the opinions of many modern fundamentalist sects. He cites as evidence for soul-sleep the fact that Jesus called his friend Lazarus back from the grave. Can anyone seriously believe, asked Milton, that Lazarus left heaven to reenter his decaying corpse? Milton considers Jesus' dramatic reply to the good thief on the cross beside him, the reply that provides the epigraph for this chapter. Is it a case of a misplaced comma, as Seventh Day Adventists affirm? Does the original Greek really mean: "Verily I say unto thee today, thou shalt be with me in paradise"? Milton does not buy this. He favors the view that *paradise* is here used allegorically to refer to the state of soul-sleeping. [13]

Conditionalism versus immortal-soulism was actively debated by British Christians of the seventeenth and eighteenth centuries. Hundreds of books and thousands of articles argued the two sides. There were even periodicals devoted entirely to the topic. Henry Layton, a lawyer, wrote a dozen books defending conditionalism. William Coward, a medical doctor, was another widely read proponent. He vigorously attacked the Roman Church for having corrupted Paul's views by accepting the Platonic model of certain early church fathers, and by inventing purgatory. Henry Dodwell produced in 1706 the most systematic work. It was titled: *Epistolary Discourse, proving from the Scriptures and First Fathers, that the soul is a principle naturally mortal, but immortalized, actually by the pleasure of God, to punishment, or to reward, by its union with the divine baptismal Spirit*. Dodwell's treatise was bitterly attacked, mainly because he insisted that God confers immortality only on those who are properly baptized into the Church of England!

William Hocking, Edgar S. Brightman, and William P. Montague were among recent American philosophers who favored mortalism. Of this century's Protestant theologians who held similar views we can list Karl Barth, Emil Brunner, Rudolf Bultmann, Reinhold Niebuhr, Anders T. S. Nygren, Robert McAfee Brown, and many others. Barth was particularly scornful of the Platonic model in which, as Barth put it in his *Dogmatics in Outline*, "a tiny soul, like a butterfly, flutters away above the grave and is still preserved somewhere, in order to live on immortally." That, Barth continues, is not the Christian hope, based on a Resurrection of the body, but the way the heathen looked upon life after death.

The British mathematician H. Martyn Cundy, who considers himself a conservative Anglican (he is known to recreational mathematicians as co-author of *Mathematical Models*), defends mortalism in his book *The Faith of a Christian*. The largest Christian sects in the United States that now preach mortalism are the Seventh Day Adventists, Jehovah's Witnesses, and Herbert Armstrong's hilarious one-man denomination, The Worldwide Church of God. Armstrong purloined the doctrine, along with others, from the Adventists with whom he was associated in his youth. His excommunicated son, Garner Ted, is preaching mortalism from his radio headquarters in Tyler, Texas, but who can take Garner Ted seriously?

As I have said, mortalism has often been combined with a belief in the annihilation of the unsaved (a combination strongly favored by Brunner), but clearly it combines just as easily with universalism. At a person's death or later, God simply reconstitutes everybody.

It is worth observing that many objections against immortal-soulism have almost no relevance to the reconstitution model. At what moment after conception does the immortal soul enter the embryo? At precisely what moment does it detach itself from the dying body? At what time in the geological past did beasts acquire immortality? Did God infuse an immortal substance into animal bodies when a certain mutation threshold was crossed? These are difficult questions for an immortal-soulist, but to the mortalist they are easily sidestepped.

Among philosophers who are not Roman Catholics, I suppose the leading defender of the neo-Thomist view—that at a precise time in the past apelike beasts gave birth to children with immortal human souls—is Mortimer J. Adler, whose views about proofs of God we examined in an earlier chapter. In a book titled *The Difference of Man and the Difference It Makes*, Adler argues that humans differ from apes in kind, not degree, but he distinguishes a superficial difference in kind from a radical difference. By *superficial* he means that the human brain is merely a more powerful animal brain. By *radical* he means that humans have a non-animal soul. [14]

Adler wrote his book when there was a big flap (now subsided) over the possibility that porpoises could learn to speak a humanlike language, and before a similar flap started about talking apes. In an essay in *The Great Ideas Today* series, Adler explains why he believes that the talking-ape results in no way affect his former arguments. [15] Although I dislike Adler's pejorative use of the word *animalists* to describe those who oppose what he calls his "humanist" views, I agree with him that most talking-ape researchers have greatly exaggerated the ability of apes to think conceptually and to understand syntax. But I find Adler's distinction between difference in degree and superficial difference in kind too fuzzy to be of much use.

To me the funniest aspect of Adler's essay is the photographs that accompany it. One shows a woman proudly displaying a patterned quilt; another shows a small boy playing chess. As if we didn't know that apes can't embroider or play chess! All the many ape/human differences in kind that Adler catalogs are obvious, and all of them apply equally well to differences between a newborn baby and an adult. It may be that talking apes have only the dimmest understanding of syntax, if any, but neither does a month-old human baby. If a baby can grow into an adult by sliding along continua, by imperceptible changes, what is to prevent an animal species from evolving into a human species by imperceptible changes?

The current controversy between the gradualists, who stress the slowness of evolutionary change, and the punctuationists, who believe in periodic jumps, is as irrelevant to our concerns as the work with talking apes. For the advocates of rapid transitions, a jump is measured in many tens of thousands of years. That there occurred a macromutation so huge that in one generation it changed the beasts that perish utterly to human beings with immortal souls cannot, of course, be ruled out as impossible, but it seems too unlikely to be seriously entertained. Nor is there any need to invoke paranormal acts of creation if you believe in a God who upholds every wave, every particle, and every natural law of the universe. To invoke special acts of God to explain transitions in the evolutionary process is as unnecessary as invoking special acts of God to explain eclipses of the sun and moon.

Saint Francis believed that some animals were immortal, but the

Roman Church's dominant teaching has been that no animals are. It seems foolish to suppose that every wasp is immortal, not to mention amoebas, polyps, and microbes.[16] How about dogs and cats? It has often been remarked that some dogs are more deserving of another life than some men and women. I do not know if any dog will live again—I do not even "know" if you and I will live again. As for my hope, I hope that some animals will live again, though I do not hope it with great passion.[17] I can only say that, from the standpoint of the reconstitution model, God is free to make anything immortal, organic or inorganic. Perhaps a better way to put it is that God is free to restore material existence to anything that has not ceased to exist as a pattern in his mind.

William James, in his little book *Human Immortality*, said that as far as he was concerned every leaf on every tree could be immortal. Maybe, but the remark leaves me more bemused than cheering. How about strands of hair snipped off by a barber, or clipped fingernails? But James had a point. God can make anything immortal. On the scale of evolution, from lower to higher forms of life, God can draw lines wherever he pleases. If I am not bothered by colors that are halfway between blue and green, why should I lose sleep over whether God will confer immortality on gorillas or on our apelike ancestors? We deal here with transcendent issues about which we can make only the most childish guesses. Is the reconstitution model true? I do not know. Do not ask *me*. I offer it only as a possible model, free of inconsistencies.

There is a third model—one that may be viewed as an elaboration of the reconstitution model because it assumes also that the soul is just a name for the total pattern of the brain. But it adds something new. It posits that in some manner unknown to us, perhaps unknowable, our brain constantly transmits its changing patterns to another "self" in a higher space-time continuum. What kind of self? If the higher self is no more than God's memory of our patterns, this model reduces to the previous one. However, we can think of the higher self in more mundane terms.

Imagine that our true self is in another world, and that our body here is only a shadow projection, something like the way our mind in a dream is a pale shadow of our mind when awake. Our life seems real to us now, but actually it is a kind of dream. In this dream we have genuine experiences, acquire genuine memories, but our earth brain is always transmitting this information to our truer self in the other world. When life is over here, we wake up there with all our memories of the earth-dream intact.[18]

This is the model William James defended so adroitly in *Human Immortality*. He called it a "transmission theory" or a "filtration theory." It allows one to accept completely that thought is a function of the brain. At the same time it permits personal immortality. As James wrote in a preface to his book's second edition, one can say in the afterlife, "I am the same personal being who in old times upon the earth had those experiences."

James compares our brain to Shelley's dome of many-colored glass that stains the white radiance of eternity. The brain stains and shapes our transcendent consciousness, restricts it, so to speak, throughout its life on earth. James finds this view essentially the same as Kant's. There is no need for God to re-create us, because our higher, transcendent self, to which our earth brain transmits its experience, is always there.[19]

Let us fantasize. My eye is not part of my brain. It is a cellular automaton that observes the outside world and transmits information by electrical impulses to the computer inside my skull. Think of our earth-brain as a kind of eye. It is connected—how we cannot know—with the supercomputer that is the brain of our higher self. As our body experiences events here, the information is recorded there.

Nineteenth-century theists who were fascinated by the extension of Euclidean geometry to higher dimensions often defended a geometrical model which can be viewed either as a model of a Platonic soul or of a transmission-theory soul. Imagine Flatlanders, living on a plane, who actually are three-dimensional without knowing it. Their flat minds cannot visualize three-space, yet all their memories are being stored in a solid brain that extends along a third coordinate of space in a direction they cannot comprehend. Death is the detachment of the planar surface of their body from their true three-dimensional self. In an analogous way, our solid brain is a three-space "surface" of our higher four-space body. Death is the shuffling off of our three-space mortal coil. This is the model defended by two Scottish physicists, Balfour Stewart and Peter Guthrie Tait, in a book called *The Unseen Universe: or Physical Speculations on a Future State*. The book went through innumerable editions near the end of the last century.

Is the transmission model, in the form given by James or the geometrical form given it by Stewart and Tait, true? I do not know. For my part, I believe that none of the models presented in this chapter is true. I am persuaded that the truth about immortality is as far beyond our grasp as the ideas in this book are beyond the grasp of a glowworm. I believe that no model we can frame does justice to the truth.[20] Let us leave these details to our Creator. As John Hick has said, "We must each wait and see—or, it may be, wait and not see!" By faith, I hope and believe that you and I will not disappear forever when we die; that we will find ourselves "alive" in a way that will be superior to anything we can now imagine.

Was your taste consulted in the peopling of this globe? How, then, should it be consulted as to the peopling of the vast City of God? Let us put our hand over our mouth, like Job, and be thankful that in our personal littleness we ourselves are here at all. The Deity that suffers us, we may be sure, can suffer many another queer and wondrous and only half-delightful thing.[21]

20

SURPRISE:
Why I Cannot Take
the World for Granted

We glibly talk
of nature's laws
but do things have
a natural cause?

Black earth turned into
yellow crocus
is undiluted
hocus-pocus.

—PIET HEIN

Will science someday discover everything? The question is hopelessly blurry, so let's try to sharpen it. If living organisms are no more than complex arrangements of molecules, it is conceivable that biology and psychology will eventually be reduced to physics. And if waves and particles dissolve into mathematical equations, it is conceivable that physics may eventually become a single deductive system. If this ever occurs, will all the laws of physics, and hence all the laws of the universe, become discoverable in principle?

This notion of physics as a formal system is carried to an ultimate extreme in David Hume's *Dialogues Concerning Natural Religion*. In Part IX, Cleanthes is attacking the ontological argument. If God is necessarily existent, he says, may not the universe itself be necessarily existent? "We dare not affirm that we know all the qualities of matter; and for aught we can determine, it may contain some qualities, which, were they known, would make its non-existence appear as great a contradiction as that twice two is five."

In other words, total nothingness is impossible. I have no idea what this could mean. Indeed, if we could know something about matter that would render its nonexistence absurd, that knowledge would solve the superultimate question. I can, however, imagine that, given a small set of axioms (about space, time, matter, logic, and mathematics), all the laws of the universe will follow in the way a theorem follows from the axioms of Euclidean geometry.

Physics seems to me a long long way from this goal, though occasionally an eminent physicist will voice contrary sentiments. In an 1894 speech Albert A. Michelson made the following notorious statement: "The more important fundamental laws and facts of physical science have all been discovered, and these are now so firmly established that the possibility of their ever being supplanted in consequence of new discoveries is exceedingly remote. . . . Future discoveries must be looked for in the sixth place of decimals."[1]

Other famous physicists have made similar remarks. I find in my files a 1931 assertion by Arthur H. Compton that there are only three basic things in the physical universe: protons, electrons, and photons.[2] That was a year before the neutron was discovered. In 1959, in his *Principles of Modern Physics*, Robert B. Leighton wrote: "With the rapid advances that are being made in particle physics, perhaps it is not too much to expect that in a few more decades *all* physical phenomena will be equally well understood."[3] George Gamow once compared the growth of scientific knowledge with a circle that was rapidly expanding on the surface of a sphere. Beyond a certain point the circle begins to shrink.[4] As late as 1971, Werner Heisenberg was talking about the near approach of the day when there would be no more "surprises" in particle physics.[5]

In 1965, Richard P. Feynman expressed the opinion that ours is an age in which the fundamental laws of nature are being discovered, and that this day, like the discovery of America, "will never come again." Of course there will be other tasks, such as exploring the solar system and investigating the way fundamental laws operate on levels such as biology, but the "perpetual novelty" of finding new structural levels cannot go on "say for a thousand years." To this view he gave the following twist:

> It seems to me that what can happen in the future is either that all the laws become known—that is, if you had enough laws you could compute consequences and they would always agree with

experiment, which would be the end of the line—or it may happen that the experiments get harder and harder to make, more and more expensive, so you get 99.9 percent of the phenomena, but there is always some phenomenon which has just been discovered, which is very hard to measure, and which disagrees; and as soon as you have the explanation of that one there is always another one, and it gets slower and slower and more and more uninteresting. That is another way it may end. But I think it has to end in one way or another.[6]

Most physicists, I suspect, hold contrary views. For them nature is infinitely inexhaustible, and there will always be wheels within wheels, and wheels outside wheels. Murray Gell-Mann once compared physics to the task of perpetually cleaning out a cluttered basement. No sooner is the basement's outline seen than somebody finds a cleverly hidden trapdoor leading to a vast subbasement.[7] David Bohm and Stanislaw Ulam are among those who believe that the universe has infinitely many levels of structure in both directions, toward the large and toward the small.

"Perhaps the pattern will be summed up," said Philip Morrison; "perhaps it will become lost in an endless regress of intricacy. I do not know. But I would bet right now that matter, like logic, is destined to remain forever in part within, and in part without, the reach of any closed form."[8]

In an admirable essay on "The Art of Teaching Science," Lewis Thomas proposes that the best way to interest young people in science is to teach not only what is known, but also what is unknown. There should be "courses dealing systematically with ignorance," with "informed bewilderment." To see science as a great adventure, young minds should be told that "every important scientific advance that has come in looking like an answer has turned, sooner or later—usually sooner—into a question. And the game is just beginning."

On any Tuesday morning, if asked, a good working scientist will tell you with some self-satisfaction that the affairs of his field are nicely in order, that things are finally looking clear and making sense, and all is well. But come back again on another Tuesday, and the roof may have just fallen in on his life's work. All the old ideas—last week's ideas in some cases—are no longer good ideas. The hard facts have softened, melted away and vanished under the pressure of new hard facts. Something strange has happened. And it is this very strangeness of nature that makes science engrossing, that keeps bright people at it, and that ought to be at the center of science teaching.[9]

Suppose for argument's sake that someday physics will indeed reach the closed form of an axiomatic system. There will still be severe limitations on what science can tell us. For one thing, we could never be absolutely sure that the axioms are permanent. We do not know if they were the same in the far distant past, especially before the big bang, if indeed there was a "before." We do not know if they will be the same in the far future, or if they hold in parallel universes, if there are parallel universes. It may be, as John Wheeler and other physicists have suggested, that many of our basic laws are the result of pure chance events that occurred during the first few seconds of the primeval explosion; that if those events had been slightly different, as they might well have been, some of the fundamental constants of nature would have been different.

For another thing, in a formal system such as Euclidean geometry there is an infinity of theorems to discover, even though they are, in a sense, given by the system's finite axioms and rules. If physics is ever formalized, an infinity of laws could follow, many of which—perhaps an infinity of which—will be beyond the reach of the human species, even though in principle they may be discoverable on the unlikely assumption that the human race has an endless future. The decimal expansion of pi, to give a simple analog, follows inexorably from the axioms of number theory, but no one will ever calculate pi to the last decimal digit because pi *has* no last digit.

Since the discoveries of Kurt Gödel, the situation has become even more hopeless. If physics turns out to be a formal system, or at least describable by one, there will be undecidable laws that can be expressed in the system's language but established only by adopting a new system with new axioms. Physicists may find themselves burdened with an infinite hierarchy of formal systems similar to the infinite hierarchy of such systems in logic and mathematics.

It is hard for me to imagine how any mathematician could be distressed by Gödel's incompleteness theorem. In his marvelous book, *Infinity and the Mind*, Rudy Rucker speaks of how an understanding of Gödel's theorem can hit one like a religious conversion, bringing with it a great feeling of liberation from anxiety. Rucker describes Gödel's laughter as frequent, rhythmic, and hypnotic.[10] I sometimes fancy that God invaded Gödel's mind (note the "God" in his name) for the purpose of letting us mortals in on one of Heaven's transcendent jokes; that even in elementary number theory there are truths we will never know with certainty to be true.

A still deeper limitation of science is built into the nature of all formal systems. At any stage of the game one may ask: Why this particular system? Obviously there is no way to answer if the question is asked about the ultimate system. The only way science can explain a law is to subsume it under a more general law. Suppose that physicists eventually discover one monstrous equation that describes how space-time gets itself tied into all those fantastic little knots called particles. We could then ask: Why *that* equation? Clearly physics, regardless of how close it gets to bedrock axioms, has to accept the ultimate structure of the universe as something given. It is the nature of the scientific enterprise that it cannot in principle ever answer the superultimate question of why there is something rather than nothing, or even the lesser question of why the something that is our universe has the basic structure it has. The statement that science can in principle discover everything is defensible only when reduced to the trivial tautology that science can discover everything science is capable of discovering.

Anyone who has read this far surely realizes that I believe there are truths totally beyond the reach of science and reason, even assuming an infinite time for the human mind to evolve. I do not mean anything so trivial as whether the cosmos will stop expanding, or whether there are black holes, or if gravity and electromagnetism can be unified, or if there are intelligent creatures on other planets, or whether Fermat's last theorem and Goldbach's conjecture are true. I mean questions that are in principle beyond the capacity of any mind (other than God's) to formulate; truths that lie beyond the farthest rim science is capable of reaching.

Georg Cantor was criticized by some of his unworthy opponents for implying that God did not exist, because in Cantor's transfinite set theory, one can prove there is no highest transfinite number. Cantor not only did not imply this, he did not even believe it. He was a deeply religious man who placed God in a region that transcends all finite and infinite sets. It is because I, too, believe in this "wholly other" realm, a realm in which our universe is an infinitesimal island, that I can call myself a mystic in the Platonic sense.

I am, of course, not arguing a case but only expressing an emotion. It has no agreed-upon name. There is no way you can talk someone into feeling it, any more than you can talk someone into falling in love or liking a piece of music or a type of cheese. Rudolf Otto, the German Protestant theologian, coined the word *numinous* (from the Latin *numen*, meaning divine power) to express this emotion. (The word should not be confused with Immanuel Kant's *noumena*, which refers to the unknowable realities behind the *phenomena* of our experience.) For Otto, the essence of the emotion is an awareness of what he called the *mysterium tremendum*, the tremendous mystery of the wholly other. Otto did not invent the phrase "wholly other." It is a translation of what Saint Augustine called the *aliud valde*. Two thousand years earlier, the Hindus called it the *anyad eva*, applying it to Brahman, their ultimate God.

For Otto, the sense of the numinous is compounded of feelings expressed by such words as awe, terror, dread, mystery, fascination, astonishment, wonder. If one is a theist, the emotion combines with strong feelings of humility, of the littleness of one's self, of holiness, of gratitude for the privilege of existing. I believe that the degree to which a person feels such emotions is roughly proportional to the strength of that person's faith in God. I know of no great theologians, in or out of any organized religion, who did not have a profound sense of the numinous. It is the secret of the book of Job. It is the emotion that engenders and sustains all the religious faiths of history.

Pantheists vary widely in the degree to which they are moved by the numinous. The emotion is understandably weak among those for whom all existence is no more than a dreary repetition of the fields we know. It is strong among pantheists who see the universe as a shadow of some vaster realm, as a world of illusion, the maya of the Hindus. It is strong in Taoism, for the Tao is as far beyond our comprehension as Brahman. It is strong in Spinoza, who, although he had no personal God to whom he could pray, thought of Being as having an infinite number of attributes that transcend human comprehension. The emotion was strong in Albert Einstein, who considered himself a Spinozist.

"The most beautiful experience we can have is the mysterious," Einstein wrote in a passage that is often quoted.

It is the fundamental emotion which stands at the cradle of true art and true science. Whoever does not know it and can no longer wonder, no longer marvel, is as good as dead, and his eyes are dimmed. It was the experience of mystery—even if mixed with fear—that engendered religion. A knowledge of the existence of something we cannot penetrate, our perceptions of the profoundest reason and the most radiant beauty, which only in their most primitive forms are accessible to our minds—it is this knowledge and this emotion that constitute true religiosity; in this sense, and in this alone, I am a deeply religious man. [11]

The last sentence could almost have been lifted out of Otto's best-known work, *The Idea of the Holy.*

We all know the statement by Sir Isaac Newton, about how he thought of himself as a boy playing on the seashore and diverting himself by now and then finding "a smoother pebble or a prettier shell than ordinary, whilst the great ocean of truth lay all undiscovered before me." Using a less familiar metaphor, Einstein once said to an interviewer:

We are in the position of a little child, entering a huge library whose walls are covered to the ceiling with books in many different tongues. The child knows that someone must have written those books. It does not know who or how. It does not understand the languages in which they are written. The child notes a definite plan in the arrangement of the books, a mysterious order, which it does not comprehend, but only dimly suspects. That, it seems to me, is the attitude of the human mind, even the greatest and most cultured, toward God. [12]

"Madam," said Dr. Lao, "the role of skeptic becomes you not; there are things in the world not even the experience of a whole life spent in Abalone, Arizona, could conceive of." "Human knowledge," Jean Henri Fabre somewhere wrote, "will be erased from the world's archives before we possess the last word that a gnat has to say to us." Substitute *stone* for *gnat* and I think the statement is still true. Jorge Luis Borges recalls an old Buddhist text that says: "If there were as many Ganges Rivers as there are grains of sand in the Ganges and again as many Ganges Rivers as grains of sand in those new Ganges Rivers, the number of grains of sand would be smaller than the number of things *not known* by the Buddha." [13]

One of Hamlet's familiar remarks is that "there are more things in heaven and earth, Horatio, than are dreamt of in your philosophy." It is quoted less often these days than a similar remark by J.B.S. Haldane. "Now, my own suspicion is that the universe is not only queerer than we suppose, but queerer than we *can* suppose."[14] Change *we* to *you* and Haldane's statement is a good summary of what God shouts to Job out of the whirlwind.

Herbert Spencer, more than any other British philosopher who called himself an agnostic or atheist, stressed the mystery of the wholly other. Spencer called it the Unknowable—not the Unknown. It contains all the transcendent truths of Kant's noumena as well as the infinity of other truths totally beyond our grasp. Theodore Dreiser was so taken by the concept of the Unknowable that he closes his novel *The Genius* by reproducing a long passage in which Spencer writes about the mystery of space and the Sartrean "nausea" it arouses in him:

> Beyond the reach of our intelligence as are the mysteries of the objects known by our senses, those presented in this universal matrix are, if we may say so, still further beyond the reach of our intelligence, for whereas, those of the one kind may be, and are, thought of by many as explicable on the hypothesis of creation, and by the rest on the hypothesis of evolution, those of the other kind cannot by either be regarded as thus explicable. Theist and Agnostic must agree in recognizing the properties of Space as inherent, eternal, uncreated—as anteceding all creation, if creation has taken place. Hence, could we penetrate the mysteries of existence, there would still remain more transcendent mysteries. That which can be thought of as neither made nor evolved presents us with facts the origin of which is even more remote from conceivability than is the origin of the facts presented by visible and tangible things. . . . The thought of this blank form of existence which, explored in all directions as far as eye can reach, has, beyond that, an unexplored region compared with which the part imagination has traversed is but infinitesimal—the thought of a space, compared with which our immeasurable sidereal system dwindles to a point, is a thought too overwhelming to be dwelt upon. Of late years the consciousness that without origin or cause, infinite space has ever existed and must ever exist produces in me a feeling from which I shrink.[15]

Here is atheist Bertrand Russell in one of his rare numinous moods: "I want to stand at the rim of the world and peer into the darkness beyond, and see a little more than others have seen of the strange shapes of mystery that inhabit that unknown night. . . ." That was from a letter Russell wrote when he was in prison during the First World War.[16] Later, in a philosophical book, he wrote: "But if there be a world which is not physical, or not in space-time, it may have a structure which we can never hope to express or to know." Russell hastens to add that he has now "lapsed into mystical speculation," and will say no more because by the very nature of the case there is nothing more he can *say*.[17]

George Santayana, another honest atheist, admired Spencer's concept of the Unknowable, and occasionally allowed himself to report on this region. "A really naked spirit," he wrote, "cannot assume that the world is thoroughly intelligible. There may be surds, there may be hard facts, there may be dark abysses before which intelligence must be silent for fear of going mad."[18] Do you not sense, behind that casual remark, Santayana's awareness of the *mysterium tremendum?*

H. G. Wells, another atheist (aside from his momentary flirtation with a finite God), also had occcasional glimpses of the tremendous mystery. His most numinous writing is a section on "Ultimate Truth" in *The Work, Wealth and Happiness of Mankind:*

> It may be that we exist and cease to exist in alternations, like the minute dots in some forms of toned printing or the succession of pictures on a cinema film. It may be that consciousness is an illusion of movement in an eternal, static, multidimensional universe. We may be only a story written on a ground of inconceivable realities, the pattern of a carpet beneath the feet of the incomprehensible. We may be, as Sir James Jeans seems to suggest, part of a vast idea in the meditation of a divine circumambient mathematician. It is wonderful exercise for the mind to peer at such possibilities. It brings us to the realization of the entirely limited nature of our intelligence, such as it is, and of existence as we know it. It leads plainly towards the belief that with minds such as ours the ultimate truth of things is forever inconceivable and unknowable. . . .
>
> It is impossible to dismiss mystery from life. Being is altogether mysterious. Mystery is all about us and in us, the Inconceivable permeates us, it is "closer than breathing and nearer than hands and feet." For all we know, that which we are may rise at death

from living, as an intent player wakes up from his absorption when a game comes to an end, or as a spectator turns his eyes from the stage as the curtain falls, to look at the auditorium he has for a time forgotten. These are pretty metaphors, that have nothing to do with the game or the drama of space and time. Ultimately the mystery may be the only thing that matters, but *within the rules and limits of the game of life*, when you are catching trains or paying bills or earning a living, the mystery does not matter at all.[19]

Commenting on these pages in his autobiography, Wells summarizes:

> I realize that Being is surrounded east, south, north and west, above and below, by wonder. Within that frame, like a little house in strange, cold, vast and beautiful scenery, is life upon this planet, of which life I am a temporary speck and impression. There is interest beyond measure within that house; use for my utmost. Nevertheless at times one finds an urgency to go out and gaze at those enigmatical immensities. But for such a thing as I am, there is nothing conceivable to be done out there. Ultimately those remote metaphysical appearances may mean everything, but so far as my present will and activities go they mean nothing.[20]

Nothing? Observe how quickly Wells, like Russell, dismisses the *mysterium tremendum* as unworthy of worship or prolonged contemplation.

Among recent philosophers John Dewey seems to me the outstanding example of an atheist for whom a sense of the numinous was minimal. I have been unable to find a single passage in all of Dewey's writings that strikes me as a memorable expression of wonder about the mystery of being. Nothing seems ever to have mystified Dewey. Never, so far as I can recall, did he see anything tragic or comic or absurd about the human condition. We are all organisms interacting with our environment, and that's that. I suggest it is this almost total absence of a sense of mystery in Dewey, and a sense of the comic, that makes his writing so incredibly dull. Who can read him anymore?

I find in my files a reference to a letter in *The New Leader* in which someone complains of Dewey's lack of a sense of wonder. I have saved only the published reply, a letter from Corliss Lamont. On the contrary, says Lamont, Dewey had a "keen awareness of the awesome and grand totality of the cosmos." To prove it, Lamont quotes the following passage from Dewey's A Common Faith:

> The community of causes and consequences in which we, together with those not born, are enmeshed is the widest and deepest symbol of the mysterious totality of being the imagination calls the universe. It is the embodiment for sense and thought of that encompassing scope of existence the intellect cannot grasp. It is the matrix within which our ideal aspirations are born and bred. It is the source of the values that the moral imagination projects as directive criteria and as shaping purposes. [21]

I rest my case. If this is the most numinous statement Lamont can find in Dewey's books (and I have not found a better one), it testifies to Dewey's remarkable uninterest in the wholly other. Indeed, as Lamont recognizes, the purpose of A Common Faith was to redefine religion and faith so that all feeling for the supernatural would be eliminated. In this respect Dewey is a type of the practical down-to-earth person who finds metaphysical speculation a waste of time. I do not mean someone who recognizes there are no rational or empirical ways to solve metaphysical puzzles, but one who seems never to be troubled by the puzzles. Greatly as I admire Rudolf Carnap for his contributions to the philosophy of science, I find him akin to Dewey in this respect. Both men recognized the mystery that envelops all scientific knowledge, yes, but emotionally they were low in metaphysical awe. In Richard Burgin's Conversations with Jorge Luis Borges, Borges recalls a highly intelligent woman he once knew who was incapable of getting anything out of the books by Bishop Berkeley and William James that he gave her:

> She didn't see why people should be poring over things that seemed very simple to her. So I said, "Yes, but are you sure that time is simple, are you sure that space is simple, are you sure that consciousness is simple?" "Yes," she said. "Well, but could you define them?" She said, "No, I don't think I could, but I don't feel puzzled by them."

Unlike most atheists and agnostics, Borges is perpetually astonished by the world, even though he is not sure there is a God, even though he professes no desire to live again. The majority of men and women, and especially women, he told Burgin (I do not go along with Borges in distinguishing between the sexes here), take the universe for granted:

> They never wonder at anything, no? They don't think it's strange that they should be living. I remember the first time I felt that was when my father said to me, "What a queer thing," he said, "that I should be living, as they say, behind my eyes, inside my head, I wonder if that makes sense?" And then, it was the first time I felt that, and then instantly I pounced upon that because I knew what he was saying. But many people can hardly understand that. And they say, "Well, but where else could you live?"[22]

No modern writer lived with a more pervasive sense of ontological wonder, of surprise to find himself alive, than Gilbert Chesterton. Surely it is one reason why Borges was so fond of GK's poetry and fiction. In his autobiography Chesterton accurately calls it "the chief idea of my life" and defines it as not taking the world for granted, but taking it with humility and gratitude. It is to see everything, even the most common thing, as something both unexpected and undeserved. "The only way to enjoy a weed is to feel unworthy even of a weed."[23] All the evils of the world are a small price to pay for the privilege of existing.

One could assemble a large volume of excerpts from GK's books in which he plays beautiful and amusing variations on this theme of enjoying the world the way a happy child enjoys it, as something miraculous. It would include Chesterton's preface to an edition of Job. It would include that refreshing rhapsody to order in the opening chapter of *The Man Who Was Thursday*. An anarchist poet maintains that order is dull, that disorder is the soul of poetry. Why do the riders on the London subway look so sad and tired? "It is because they know that the train is going right. . . . It is because after they have passed Sloane Square they know that the next station must be Victoria, and nothing but Victoria. Oh, their wild rapture! oh, their eyes like stars and their souls again in Eden, if the next station were unaccountably Baker Street!"

Nonsense, replies Gabriel Syme. "The rare, strange thing is to hit the mark; the gross, obvious thing is to miss it. We feel it is epical when man with one wild arrow strikes a distant bird. Is it not also epical when man with one wild engine strikes a distant station? Chaos is dull; because in chaos the train might indeed go anywhere, to Baker Street or to Bagdad. But man is a magician, and his whole magic is in this, that he does say Victoria, and lo! it is Victoria."

My anthology would include many of Chesterton's short stories, such as "The Unthinkable Theory of Professor Green" in which an astronomer, stricken suddenly by a sense of awe toward ordinary things, delivers a solemn lecture on his discovery of a new planet. As he talks on, it slowly dawns on his learned listeners that he is talking about the earth.[24]

My anthology would include at least two of GK's poems. One of them, "The Sword of Surprise," is short enough to quote in full:

> *Sunder me from my bones, O sword of God,*
> *Till they stand stark and strange as do the trees;*
> *That I whose heart goes up with the soaring woods*
> *May marvel as much at these.*
>
> *Sunder me from my blood that in the dark*
> *I hear that red ancestral river run,*
> *Like branching buried floods that find the sea*
> *But never see the sun.*
>
> *Give me miraculous eyes to see my eyes,*
> *Those rolling mirrors made alive in me,*
> *Terrible crystal more incredible*
> *Than all the things they see.*
>
> *Sunder me from my soul, that I may see*
> *The sins like streaming wounds, the life's brave beat;*
> *Till I shall save myself, as I would save*
> *A stranger in the street.*

The other poem, "A Second Childhood," is so much longer that I shall quote only the first two stanzas. If you don't know this poem, I urge you to look it up in *The Collected Poems of G. K. Chesterton*.[25] I think it is one of the greatest religious lyrics ever written:

> *When all my days are ending*
> *And I have no song to sing,*
> *I think I shall not be too old*
> *To stare at everything;*
> *As I stared once at a nursery door*
> *Or a tall tree and a swing.*

Wherein God's ponderous mercy hangs
On all my sins and me,
Because He does not take away
The terror from the tree
And stones still shine along the road
That are and cannot be.

My book of Chestertonian wonder would include many essays and passages in which GK praised the glory and mystery of ordinary things—*Tremendous Trifles*, as he calls them in the title of one of his best books. And there are those passages in which he combines awe with a sense of absurdity, seeing the pelican as one of God's jokes, seeing men and women as four-footed animals balancing precariously on their hind legs. I find in my GK files a clipping (dated 1945) of the comic strip "Blondie." Dagwood has made one of his giant sandwiches, and while eating it he startles Blondie by reflecting aloud: "Eating is a silly thing. In order to get food into your stomach you've got to push it through your face." The sentiment is pure Chesterton. In *The Napoleon of Notting Hill*, GK describes eating as the stuffing of alien substances through a hole in the head, and somewhere else he sees drinking as pouring liquid through an opening the way one fills a bottle. If he hadn't thought it bad taste he could have written hilarious descriptions of the sex act. A great admirer of Edward Lear and Lewis Carroll, GK often called attention to the role of nonsense in arousing an emotion of spiritual wonder toward the world.

My anthology would be incomplete without the chapter on "The Ethics of Elfland" from *Orthodoxy*.[26] In the spirit of Hume, though Hume is never mentioned, Chesterton argues that all natural laws should be looked upon as magic because there is no logical connection between any cause and its effect. Fairy tales, said GK, remind us that the laws of nature have an arbitrary quality in that they could, for all we know, be quite other than what they are. Maybe the regularities of nature, its weird repetitions, as Chesterton called them, are not logically necessary but exist because God, like a small child, is

strong enough to exult in monotony. It is possible that God says every morning "Do it again" to the sun; and every evening, "Do it again" to the moon. It may not be automatic necessity that makes all daisies alike; it may be that God makes every daisy separately, but has never got tired of making them. It may be that He has the eternal appetite of infancy; for we have sinned and grown old, and our Father is younger than we. The repetition in Nature may not be a mere recurrence; it may be a theatrical *encore*. Heaven may *encore* the bird who laid an egg.

This way of viewing Nature as sheer magic, which of course implies a Magician, is surely part of the fascination of watching a great conjuror. The art of prestidigitation has been one of the loves of my life, and like Chesterton I find it intimately connected with a love of fantasy fiction. Science reminds us of the reason behind things. Magic and fantasy remind us of the unreason behind things.

> Reason has moons, but moons not hers
>   Lie mirror'd on her sea,
> Confounding her astronomers,
>   But, O! delighting me.[27]

Conjuring, wrote Max Beerbohm in his novel about a beautiful lady magician, *Zuleika Dobson*, is "an art which, more potently perhaps than any other, touched in mankind the sense of mystery and stirred the faculty of wonder; the most truly romantic of all the arts. . . ." We enjoy seeing a conjuror perform because his counterfeit miracles make us realize that natural laws could easily permit women to float in the air and elephants to disappear. A spectator with a sense of the numinous leaves the theater with heightened surprise that objects fall when dropped, that stars vanish in the daytime only to reappear mysteriously at night.

You can be sure that Chesterton, like Charles Dickens (who actually performed magic on the stage) and Lewis Carroll, enjoyed seeing magic shows. In fact, GK wrote an unusual play called *Magic*, in which a professional conjuror is the main character. I can easily imagine Wells and Einstein and Santayana sitting entranced through a magic show. It is hard to imagine Dewey or Carnap watching a magician without being bored.[28] Both men, although no doubt they would have agreed that natural laws could be other than they are, saw little value in speculating about such nonsense possibilities. They were like the man from Cadiz in an anonymous limerick:

There was a young man of Cadiz
Who inferred that life is what it is,
For he early had learnt,
If it were what it weren't,
It could not be that which it is.

To the atheist and positivist the world is what it is. How could it be otherwise? Where else could we live? There is no point in speculating on why it is what it is, because there is no way reason or science can get a handle on the question. Accept the only universe we know. Find out what you can about its structure. Try to be as happy as possible before you vanish back into the Black Hat from which you popped into existence.

Just as knowing how a magic trick is done spoils all its wonder, so let us be grateful that wherever science and reason turn they plunge finally into stygian darkness. I am not in the least annoyed because I do not understand time and space, or consciousness, or free will, or evil, or why the universe is made the way it is. I am relieved beyond measure that I do not need to comprehend more than dimly the nature of God or an afterlife. I do not want to be blinded by truths beyond the capacity of my eyes and brain and heart. I am as contented as a Carnap with the absence of rational methods for penetrating ultimate mysteries.

Must we conclude, then, that all metaphysical speculation is futile? A metaphysician asks this question in one of Raymond Smullyan's wry dialogs, and a mystic answers as follows:

> Oh, not at all! It is sometimes absolutely necessary to bat one's head against a stone wall trying to use objective methods which cannot possibly work before one sees for oneself the necessity of direct introspective methods. Metaphysics is essentially one giant koan, not for an individual, but for the human race as a whole—a koan whose purpose is to force the realization of the impossibility of metaphysical methods being pushed any further. Stated otherwise, metaphysics is the necessary ripening process of the human race to prepare it for mysticism.[29]

I agree with Smullyan—for the mystic's voice is his. There *are* no metaphysical methods. There is no rational way to approach God—or, as Smullyan would prefer to say, the Tao—except inwardly. As for the heart's leap that leads to theism, I confess again that I do not know why some people are compelled to make it and others find it impossible. I do not even know if a sense of the numinous is essential for such a leap.

In the second Oz book, when Tip brings a wooden sawhorse to life with Mombi's magic powder, the creature is more surprised than Tip. "He rolled his knotty eyes from side to side, taking a first wondering view of the world in which he had now so important an existence." Have none of the quotations in this chapter aroused in you, patient reader, a similar sense of surprise and wonder? Have you never felt amazed to find yourself not only living in an Ozzy world but, more incredibly, aware of the fact that you are alive? Are you capable of identifying with the Sawhorse when he says, in the third Oz book, "A creature like me has no business to live"?

If you are looking puzzled and shaking your head, that small cave-like region in which you are so mysteriously hiding for a time—and for so brief a time!—then my book of *Whys* is not for you. After all, where else could you hide?

21

FAITH AND
THE FUTURE:
A Prologue

> Mr. Coleridge used very frequently to insist upon the
> distinction between belief and faith. He once told me,
> with very great earnestness, that if he were that
> moment convinced—a conviction, the possibility of
> which, indeed, he could not realize to himself—that
> the New Testament was a forgery from beginning to
> end—wide as the desolation in his moral feelings
> would be, he should not abate one jot of his faith in
> God's power and mercy through some manifestation of
> his being towards man, either in time past or future,
> or in the hidden depths where time and space are not.
>
> —H. N. COLERIDGE, IN *Specimens of the
> Table Talk of Samuel Taylor Coleridge*

I am one of those persons Samuel Taylor Coleridge could not imagine
himself to be. Although I do not think the New Testament is a forgery
from beginning to end, I do think it a forgery in the sense that it gives
wildly inaccurate accounts of events in the life of Jesus. For reasons
both rational and empirical, so well summed up by David Hume in his
essay on miracles, I cannot (for example) believe that Jesus had no
human father. Assuming that the gospel accounts of his birth are based
partly on fact, I find it easier to believe that Jesus was an illegitimate
son of Mary, and that Joseph was quite justified in thinking this when
he first learned of his young wife's pregnancy. It would explain why
Joseph faded so completely from the narrative. There is no reason to
suppose Jesus ever heard of the biblical doctrine of the virgin birth, or
the unbiblical doctrines of the immaculate conception and the perpetual virginity of his mother. Paul's silence on all three doctrines
suggests strongly that he hadn't heard of them either.

For similar reasons I cannot believe that Jesus rose bodily from the tomb, or that after his death "the graves were opened; and many bodies of the saints which slept arose, And came out of the graves after his resurrection, and went into the holy city, and appeared unto many" (Matthew 27:52–53). I do not believe the story (told only by John) about how Jesus brought his dear friend Lazarus, the brother of Martha and Mary, back to life after he had been dead for so many days that, as Martha bluntly put it, "he stinketh." (I can say with Spinoza, as Pierre Bayle said Spinoza said, that if I believed the truth of this legend I would at once become a Christian.) I cannot believe that Jesus raised the daughter of Jairus from the dead, or that he brought back to life the only son of the widow of Nain.

Nor can I believe that when Tabitha died at Joppa, and Peter said to the corpse, "Tabitha, arise," she opened her eyes and sat up, as we are told in Acts 9:40. There is some doubt as to whether Paul worked a similar miracle as recounted in the twentieth chapter of Acts. He had been preaching a lengthy sermon, under strong lights, when a young man named Eutychus fell asleep and toppled from the third loft. He was "taken up dead," but after Paul embraced him, his life returned. I hope no reader need be reminded that stories of miraculous revivals of the dead abound in the sacred literature of other great religions, and that believers uniformly discount all such tales except those of their own tradition.

Even less can I believe that God in human flesh would have lowered himself to such droll magical shenanigans as turning water into wine, multiplying loaves and fishes, walking on the water, or causing a fig tree to wither because it bore no fruit even though he knew (as we are told) it was not the time of year for figs. I cannot believe that Jesus commanded a legion of devils to leave a possessed man (or two men if you trust Matthew) and enter a herd of two thousand pigs that rushed into the sea and were drowned. As Bertrand Russell once observed, this certainly was not very kind to the pigs.[1] These are typical miracle tales of the sort no intelligent Christians would believe for a moment if they came upon them in the Koran.

But, you may reply if you are a liberal Christian, there is no need to believe such absurdities. Let us demythologize the Bible. Let us purge it of superstition and preserve only the central doctrine that Jesus was God in flesh and bone, come down from heaven to save us from our sins. It is not an intention of this book to persuade anyone to abandon

Christianity, so I shall be brief and list only two of many reasons why I cannot accept the Incarnation.

One reason, on which I have dwelt in an earlier chapter, is that for me the doctrine of eternal punishment in hell is a blasphemy, and there is no question that Jesus, certainly the Jesus portrayed in the gospels, believed and preached it. Of course it was a doctrine that was part of the culture in which Jesus grew up, and one can argue that Jesus, being truly a man, could not be expected to escape his cultural heritage. I agree. I would no more expect a human Jesus, living when and where he did, not to believe in hell than I would expect him not to believe the earth flat or not to believe that Adam was formed from the dust and Eve created from Adam's rib. I would expect Jesus to accept, as we are told he did, the historical truth of all the Old Testament stories, including Noah's flood and Jonah's travail in the belly of a whale. But on a question so basic to faith as the fate of the wicked, I would expect an incarnated God to rise above his culture.

Jesus once spoke of seeing the mote in a neighbor's eye while overlooking the beam in one's own. It is easy to see motes in the sacred writings of other cultures because alien myths are so unfamiliar that their crudities are readily apparent. It is not so easy to recognize beams in the sacred books one has known from childhood. Exotic doctrines and legends always seem funny, just as everybody else's big toe looks funny. To a devout Muslim who, I assure you, is as ardent in his dedication to God as Billy Graham or the Pope, the very notion that God could have a son is too outrageous to be entertained. Curiously, the Koran defends the virgin birth of Jesus as the promised Jewish messiah, but it also says, "God hath not begotten offspring," and "Far be it from His glory that He should have a son." Muslims find the Atonement, the notion that God required a blood sacrifice of his son to forgive the sin of Adam, an abominable doctrine.

A second reason I cannot believe Jesus was God is that he clearly was mistaken about the time of his Second Coming. I am aware of all the ways that theologians of the past, and adventist cults today, cleverly evade the plain intent of Jesus' words as the gospels record them. He said explicitly that he would return during his own generation (Matthew 24:34, Mark 13:30, Luke 21:32), and that "There be some standing here, which shall not taste of death, till they see the Son of man coming in his kingdom" (Matthew 16:28, Mark 9:1, Luke 9:27). As Albert Schweitzer made so clear in *The Quest of the Historical Jesus*, there is not the slightest reason to doubt that Jesus believed this, or that his apostles and the earliest community of Christians also believed it. C. S. Lewis, in his essay "The World's Last Night" (in a book of the same title), does his best to avoid the embarrassing implications of Jesus' mistake. (There is a sense in which the rise of the Christian Church was a consequence of this mistake.) Lewis's best is not good enough. Nevertheless, I agree with Lewis that it is "impossible to retain in any recognizable form our belief in the Divinity of Christ and the truth of the Christian revelation while abandoning, or even persistently neglecting, the promised, and threatened, Return."[2]

There is a remarkable scene at the end of the gospel of John. After Jesus had spoken of his approaching death, he said to Peter, "Follow me." Peter turned and saw John also following. Since John, as we are told in John, was the disciple Jesus especially loved, it is only natural that Peter would ask, "Lord, and what shall this man do?" Jesus answered enigmatically: "If I will that he tarry till I come, what is that to thee? Follow thou me."

"Then went this saying abroad among the brethren, that that disciple should not die: yet Jesus said not unto him, He shall not die; but, If I will that he tarry till I come, what is that to thee?" (John 21:23).

This passage gave rise to two early Christian legends that have long been forgotten, though at one time both were widely believed. One was that John ascended bodily into heaven, and the other was that John was buried at Ephesus in a state of suspended animation, his heart still faintly throbbing, where to this day he awaits his Master's return. Both legends were eclipsed by the more dramatic legend of the Wandering Jew, which in a more colorful way served the same sad purpose—to escape from the admission that Jesus erred about his Father's timetable.

The higher criticism and the rise of liberal Protestantism have been valiant efforts to demythologize the Bible and at the same time preserve an inner core of doctrine that would distinguish Christianity from other Revelations and from philosophical theisms. In my novel *The Flight of Peter Fromm* I tried to explain why I think it more honest to call oneself a non-Christian than to continue to call oneself a Christian after abandoning belief in the historicity of those myths that support the central doctrines of the Church. On this matter I find myself in agreement with G. K. Chesterton and C. S. Lewis, with the Pope, and with conservative Catholics and evangelical Protestants.

Of course I also believe—it is the main theme of this book—that one can drop out of a traditional religion such as Christianity without at the same time abandoning faith in a personal God or in life after death. Indeed, I believe that such a faith, unburdened by strange dogmas, is truer to the heart of what Jesus probably taught than the New Testament records indicate. Many of the doctrines of Paul would have astonished Jesus, just as Paul would have been amazed by some of the myths that became part of the gospels. And Jesus and Paul alike would surely have been bewildered—in my opinion, shocked—by most of the doctrines fabricated later by the Holy Roman Church.

The comedian Lenny Bruce liked to express pleasure at seeing so many people "leaving the Church and going back to God." I do not find this impious. I believe, in a spirit of reverence, that if Jesus were to return to earth today he would not call himself a Christian. I believe that conservative Christians continually commit the sin of pride by learning as little as they can about modern science and contemporary biblical criticism. William James was once asked on a questionnaire if he accepted the Bible as an authority on religious matters. His reply was, "No. No. No. It is so human a book that I don't see how belief in its divine authorship can survive the reading of it."[3] Among my friends who attend conservative churches, both Protestant and Catholic, I do not know a single one who has considered it worthwhile to read the Bible from "In the beginning . . ." to its next to last sentence, "Even so, come, Lord Jesus."

Another major theme of this book is that one can be a theist, with all that faith in a personal God entails, and at the same time combine theism with the utmost respect for reason and science, or, to say the same thing negatively, with utmost freedom from superstition. No philosophical theist of the sort defended here could read Andrew Dickson White's great work, *The History of the Warfare of Science and Theology in Christendom*, and have his or her faith shaken in the slightest by White's incredible disclosures. I cannot imagine a conservative Christian reading this work without being deeply disturbed.

Let me underscore what I am saying by considering two famous writers of Edwardian England who were friends even though they perpetually disagreed with each other. I speak of H. G. Wells and G. K. Chesterton. Both have long been out of fashion among the critics, though their books are avidly collected and each man still has an intensely loyal following. Perhaps at the moment their reputations are on an upswing. At any rate, to me each had enormous merits the other lacked, and I have come to see them as symbols of two seemingly irreconcilable attitudes.

Chesterton had a strong faith in a personal God and in life after death, combined with a vast knowledge of literature and art, but he was abysmally ignorant of science. He was admirable when he wrote about faith in general, or about Dickens or Stevenson or Browning or Chaucer. Whenever he touched on science (as in his essays deriding evolution) he revealed an ignorance exceeded only by that of his faithful friend Hilaire Belloc.

I am also aware of GK's anti-Semitism, of which he was innocently unaware. In this he reflected the culture of England at the time; you will find the same kind of anti-Semitism in the poems of T. S. Eliot. Moreover, as an orthodox Christian there was no way Chesterton (or Eliot) could escape from the anti-Semitism that is built into the foundations of Christianity. If you believe that God prepared the Jews, and no other ethnic group, to allow him to enter human history as Messiah and Savior, there is no way to get around the bizarre fact that when the Messiah finally did appear, he was not accepted by the very people God had so carefully chosen.

Nor do you have to remind me of Chesterton's embarrassing flirtation with Italian fascism. After interviewing Mussolini, GK was so impressed—Mussolini told him how much he had enjoyed *The Man Who Was Thursday!*—that he took the Italian dictator to be a genuine Catholic, and wrote one of his worst books, *The Resurrection of Rome*, in which he praised all the fine things Mussolini was doing. GK made clear that he preferred the English tradition of liberty to fascist discipline, but where, he asks, is English liberty? At least in Italy, Chesterton argued, there is less hypocrisy, because Mussolini "does openly what enlightened and democratic governments do secretly."

As for Wells, he was incapable of believing in a God who was loving and powerful enough to provide for an afterlife. Wells was admirable when he wrote popular books about science and history and politics, about women's rights and our changing sexual mores, and about the Open Conspiracy. He was a pioneer of science fiction, including marvelous visions of better or worse worlds to come. Many of the books by Wells and Chesterton will be deservedly forgotten, but some of them, in my opinion, will not be. I am unashamed to confess my fondness for both authors and to admit that I own some fifty books by each (roughly half of each man's output). I am a charter subscriber to the Canadian quarterly *The Chesterton Review*, and I used to take a British journal called *The Wellsian*. Can you comprehend, as most of my friends cannot, how it is possible to admire and relish the writings of both men? If so, you will understand how it is possible to combine a Chestertonian faith in a personal God with a Wellsian admiration for science, and at the same time ignore each man's areas of blindness.

In the past, when science was only beginning, it was not easy to preserve a faith in God without saturating it with what I have called the superstition of the voice and the superstition of the finger. The first refers to a belief that God speaks directly to humanity, in special and unique ways, through chosen individuals, some of whom write divinely inspired books. The Israelites believed that Jehovah constantly spoke to them directly, through their prophets. Orthodox Christians believe that God spoke both through the Jewish prophets and through Jesus, and through the writers of both Biblical testaments. Orthodox Muslims accept most of this, to which they add the further Revelations of Muhammad.

Roman Catholics, believing as they do in papal infallibility, are persuaded that God still speaks directly, and with unerring accuracy, through the living Church. Mormons—I mean those who are Mormons in more than name only—do not question that God spoke to humanity through Joseph Smith and the curious Bible he wrote. Conservative Seventh Day Adventists do not question the divine inspiration of their prophet Ellen Gould White.[4] Moon's disciples do not question the new Revelation of the Reverend Sun Myung Moon. Followers of Herbert Armstrong have no doubt that God selected Mr. Armstrong to broadcast to all the world the "plain truth" of the gospel which, according to Armstrong, all of Christendom has forgotten for 1,900 years. Christian Scientists read Mary Baker Eddy, Scientologists read L. Ron Hubbard, with a reverence that is not much different from the way Herbert Armstrong and Billy Graham and Jimmy Carter read their Bibles.

I do not mean to suggest that peculiar and short-lived sects, dominated by paranoid leaders, are as worth studying for religious insights as the great religions of the past, with their rich accumulation of literature, theology, and apologetics, much of it written by men and women of the highest intellect. But do not make the provincial mistake of supposing that Thomas Aquinas and Saint Bonaventure and Duns

Scotus were more intelligent or closer to God's truth than, say, Maimonides or Averroes or Avicenna. There is nothing like a sympathetic study of comparative religion to impress on any open mind the pervasiveness of the superstition of the voice. No one who has troubled to explore the histories of Judaism and Islam could have said, as our United Nations ambassador Warren Austin reportedly said in 1948, that Jews and Arabs should sit down at the conference table and resolve their differences "in a true Christian spirit."

By the superstition of the finger I mean, as I have earlier explained, the notion that God periodically thrusts a hand into the universe to break the sequence of natural causes and produce a genuine miracle. It is not even necessary to believe in such interventions, I have argued, to believe in Providence and prayer. It is only necessary to believe, by faith of course, not reason, that everything is miraculous; that every spear of grass, as Walt Whitman wrote, is a miracle. "Every hour of the light and dark is a miracle, every cubic inch of space is a miracle."

A faith free of the superstition of the finger has nothing to fear from science. Faith in God does not require you to believe that at certain times an angel came down from heaven (as we are told in John 5) to trouble the water of the pool of Bethesda, and that whoever first stepped into the water after this event would be cured of any infirmity. Faith in God does not require you to believe that God parted the Red Sea, or that he destroyed Moses' nephews with a burst of fire because they had not properly prepared the sacrificial incense. You can believe in God without having to believe that when you take Communion you are eating the flesh and drinking the blood of a carpenter's son who died two thousand years ago on a wooden cross. Can you imagine what a young Buddhist must think of *that* doctrine when he hears it for the first time?

Nothing is more difficult for those brought up in any religious tradition than to break old rituals and habits. H. L. Mencken wrote a moral fable about this which I consider a masterpiece. In Baltimore around the turn of the century (so the fable goes) a freethinker named Fred Ammermeyer enjoyed irritating the local evangelicals. He would give away copies of the Bible in which embarrassing passages were marked with an indelible red pencil. Several times a year he would mail copies of Thomas Paine's *Age of Reason* to the town's ministers, the packages marked *special delivery* and *urgent*. He hired rabble-rousers to stand on soapboxes and bombard passersby with attacks on the doctrine of hell.

In those days the town's Salvation Army and other missions got together every Christmas to throw a big feast for Baltimore's outcasts, but before the poor bums could eat, they were forced to listen for hours to sermonizing and hymn singing. Fred decided to beat the missions at their own game by giving a "Christmas party for bums to end all Christmas parties for bums." He hired the largest hall on the waterfront, arranged for a bountiful supply of food, booze, and fine cigars. He even hired a band and a burlesque company to provide continuous raunchy entertainment. At no time were any sermons, prayers, or hymns to be inflicted on the joyful guests.

The feast began on Christmas Day at eleven in the morning. At ten in the evening, Fred announced from the stage that the burlesque performers needed a rest before continuing with the midnight show. In the interval, if anyone wanted to come onstage and sing he could do so. The first four volunteers formed a quartet that started off with "Sweet Adeline"; then, after a few more numbers, to Fred's horror they broke into "Are You Ready for the Judgment Day?" The entire audience now joined in. With tears trickling down their noses, and beating time on the tables with their beer glasses, the bums were soon bellowing such rousing hymns as "Showers of Blessings," "Throw Out the Lifeline," "Where Shall We Spend Eternity?" and "Wash Me, and I Shall Be Whiter Than Snow."

Since the band knew none of the hymns, its accompaniment steadily diminished and finally ceased altogether. In the silence, a bum stood up to speak in a quavery, boozy voice:

> Friends, I just want to tell you what these good people have done for me—how their prayers have saved a sinner who seemed past all redemption. Friends, I had a good mother, and I was brought up under the influence of the Word. But in my young manhood my sainted mother was called to heaven, my poor father took to rum and opium, and I was led by the devil into the hands of wicked men—yes, and wicked women, too. Oh, what a shameful story I have to tell! It would shock you to hear it, even if I told you only half of it. I let myself be . . .

Crushed and speechless, Fred fled into what Mencken calls "the cold, stinging, corpse-reviving air of a Baltimore winter night."[5]

I hope I am not as naïve as Fred Ammermeyer. If any conservative Protestants or Catholics read my book and find their religious reflexes wavering, I would not know whether to be dismayed or pleased. In any case, this book was not intended to shake anyone's faith, nor have I written it to convert any atheist or pantheist to my brand of theism. Since I do not believe in hell, I find no urgency in persuading anyone of anything.

Why *have* I written this book? Partly, of course, to get my own beliefs sorted out and down on paper, to find out what I myself, as I approach the end of my life, truly believe. But mainly I think I have written it for those who, like me, find themselves unchurched but still praying, still trusting in God, still hoping for another life. I suspect there may be more of us around than we realize, but since we attend no church for the unchurched we have no way of recognizing one another. The Unitarian Church was once a haven for some of us, but, alas, most Unitarians are now humanists who are not interested in God, and attending a Unitarian service is too often like attending a secular lecture.

There are liberal Protestant churches whose ministers and members hold views not much different from those defended in this book, but I find myself (I speak for no one else) repelled by their services because they are as unable to break away from traditional rituals, hymns, and Scripture readings as Mencken's outcasts were unable to break away from evangelical reflexes. Self-deception hangs over their congregations like a Los Angeles smog.

Many years ago, having heard of a "progressive" Methodist minister whose church was not far from where I then lived, I attended his service one morning to see if it was one with which I might affiliate. (I was brought up a Methodist in Tulsa.) During the service everyone stood up and solemnly recited the Apostle's Creed! I would have staked a sizable bet that more than 80 percent of those present considered the creed sheer nonsense. Young people in particular are sensitive to this kind of hypocrisy. It is one reason they are leaving the liberal churches in droves to go nowhere, or into Eastern religions, or occult movements, or to evangelical churches where they can belt out songs with moving melodies and lyrics that tell of the cross and the blood.

I do not care to attend a church in which I am asked to sing dreary, tuneless hymns, and profess creeds I cannot believe. I do not want to take Communion, even symbolically interpreted, if I no longer think that Christ was God's son who died for my sins. On the other hand, neither do I care to attend a church just to hear good music and listen to speeches that have nothing to say about God or a life to come.

Yes, we philosophical theists are a lonely, fragmented breed. We are the closet theists. We can work for years alongside someone who will never suspect that we believe in God. We can even have wives or husbands, children and parents, who do not know what we believe. When we pray, we pray in secret, as Jesus himself (remember? Matthew 6:6) recommended.

Do not assume that Mr. Smith, who attends church regularly, believes in God. He may have affiliated with the church for any of a dozen reasons that have nothing to do with what he believes. Indeed, even his minister or priest may be a pantheist or atheist (see Miguel de Unamuno's greatest story, "Saint Manuel Bueno, Martyr"). And what about Mrs. Jones, whom you have known for years and always supposed to be an atheist because she never went to church? Have you ever asked her what she believes?

I recall an occasion during World War II when, as a sailor, I was striking up an acquaintance with a shore-based WAVE. Somehow I happened to mention, perhaps in answer to a question, that, yes, I believed in God. Ah, was I a Catholic? (She herself was.) No. Was I a Protestant? No. But you don't look Jewish, she said. No, I said, I'm not Jewish. Then what was I? I tried to explain. She had never heard of Plato or Immanuel Kant or William James or Unamuno. In her eyes I suddenly became an oddball. That anyone could believe in God and not belong to an established church was totally outside her experience.

We closet theists are close cousins to another group, how large I cannot say, that I call nominal atheists. These are the sophisticated unchurched who became atheists in their youth and have not thought about the matter since. Ask them if they believe in God and the automatic response is a smile and a headshake. But during moments of extreme agony a strange thing happens. They are startled to hear themselves pray. Secretly, subliminally, they suspect and hope that God exists and that they and others may actually live again. Yet it is as difficult to tell themselves they believe in God as it is for so many fallaway Christians to tell themselves they have lost their faith.

One reason I have written this book is to assure closet theists they are not alone. Perhaps my confessions will strengthen their faith to some extent, as well as my own. Perhaps I have also written it with the hope that here and there someone who imagines he or she is an atheist, surprised by the notion that faith in God does not require believing that God once walked the earth with human feet, like a pagan deity, will look up from my pages to consider the wild possibility that God may exist after all.

Are you one of those dabblers in Eastern religions who likes to sit in a lotus position and meditate on a mantra, or on *om*, or on nothing? Let me recommend a more ancient practice. Try meditating about God. Say something to God. Give thanks for something. Ask forgiveness for something. Ask for something you desire, remembering that God knows better than you whether you should have it or not. What can you lose? You might discover that at the heart of those old religious traditions, buried under the blood and balderdash, was something that gave them vitality, that held and still holds the allegiance of millions. You might discover that you have something in common with these believers after all. In brief you might, you just might, entertain the fantastic notion that God is more than an old wives' tale.

It remains to say a few words about what I think the future holds for religion. Here my crystal ball is murky. It is surely possible for any great religion to fade and disappear. Who today worships the gods of Homer and Virgil? When Christianity arrived, Great Pan did indeed die. On the other hand, Zoroaster's Ahura Mazda is still alive and well among the wealthy Parsees of Bombay. I would guess that Christianity—not the simple doctrines Jesus preached but those expounded by Paul and elaborated by the Roman Church and the Reformers—will eventually expire, though not for centuries. At present its many branches are growing and altering in ways difficult to predict. Liberal Protestantism seems to me drifting toward its own dissolution, as Reformed Judaism, liberal Muslimism, and liberal Hinduism are similarly drifting toward pallid views that have little resemblance except in terminology to the robust doctrines they once were.

The Catholic Church obviously is changing more slowly, and I expect that the current crop of radical Catholic theologians (such as Hans Küng and Edward Schillebeeckx) will soon go the way of those Catholic modernists who flourished for a brief time after the turn of the last century. There is even a revival of conservative sentiment now sweeping the Catholic Church, as there is a revival of evangelical and fundamentalist Protestantism (the two are not easily distinguished!) taking place in the United States, and a revival of conservative Muslimism in Islamic countries.

As the year 2000 approaches, I would expect that just as the millennial year 1000 set off a great hue and cry about the imminence of the Second Coming, the adventist sects will grow in noise and hysteria until 2000 passes, as it surely will, with no signs of the Parousia. I would expect that until the century gets safely past 2000, the top fundamentalist preachers will be increasingly emphasizing the Second Coming.

On September 12, 1976, I listened with vast amusement to Billy Graham's stirring sermon on "The Antichrist" as it came over television. It was as naïve and primitive as a sermon by Dwight L. Moody. The Antichrist, Dr. Graham informed us, would be the incarnation of Satan, a politically powerful leader permitted by God to rule the entire world for a short time. Billy said he agreed with those biblical "scholars" who figure that the Antichrist will control the world for about three and one-half years. He did not say just when this period would start (as Jesus made clear, only God knows the day and hour), but he left no doubt in the minds of his listeners that the time would be *very* soon.

What about the tens of thousands of preachers in past centuries who were just as persuaded that the signs of the times pointed to the Second Coming in *their* lifetimes? Billy waved them all away. Does not the Bible tell us that when the Antichrist speaks, all the world will listen? That could not have been the case, said Billy, before the invention of radio and television! The number of the Beast—666—said Billy, may refer to a falling short of 777, a number associated with the true Christ, but he allowed there was a mystery about 666 not yet revealed.

The world will not be destroyed, Billy assured us. After the Antichrist's reign of terror, during which many Christians will be killed for their faith, Jesus will return, the Battle of Armageddon will be fought, and Satan and his demons will be cast into the lake of everlasting fire. The Millennium will then begin with Jesus reigning on earth as the King of Kings. Billy closed by saying that he had a "reserved seat" for the Battle of Armageddon. Where will *your* seat be? This led to the altar call, and hundreds filed forward as usual to the haunting, plaintive singing of "Just As I Am Without One Plea. . . ." I will spare you a report on a later sermon by Dr. Graham, "Matthew 24 Is Knocking at the Door," based on a line in a song about the Second Coming written by the born-again country singer Johnny Cash.

After 2000 I would expect the adventist fanfare slowly to abate. After all, there must be a limit to how many times the "scholars" of Biblical prophecy can keep revising their interpretations of key passages in Daniel and Revelation. There is a story (how authentic I do not know) about George Rapp, the tall, muscular, white-bearded leader of a German adventist sect that first settled in Harmony, Pennsylvania, then in

1814 migrated west to Harmony, Indiana. As Rapp lay dying he announced that, were he not certain that God had chosen him to present his followers to Christ at the time of the Second Advent, he would think his last hour had come. The Rappites also did not long survive. They were so convinced of the nearness of the Second Coming that marriage, sex, and children were forbidden. In 1825 the dwindling colony moved back to Pennsylvania after selling Harmony to Robert Owen, the Welsh-born British socialist. Owen changed the town's name to New Harmony, and there established a socialist colony that lasted several years. If you visit New Harmony, Indiana, today, you can walk through the reconstructed hedge maze, grown by the Rappites to symbolize the serpentine paths of sin. You will see the limestone tablet bearing footprints of the angel Gabriel where he stood when he delivered a message to Father Rapp.[6]

If the world's great traditional faiths continue to disintegrate throughout the next few centuries, in spite of temporary upswings, who can guess what strange new Revelations will take their place? Perhaps an understanding of science will become so widespread among the masses that new religious movements will be relatively free of superstition. On the other hand, it is possible that science will remain understood and admired by only a small minority, and the new religions will be as scientifically absurd as Scientology. If present trends continue, twenty-first-century religions may be linked in curious ways to outer space, extraterrestrial intelligences, UFOs, ESP, PK, electronic technology, and quantum mechanics. Perhaps the diversity of such cults will be so great that no single one will dominate. Perhaps philosophical theism will come back into vogue among the educated, as deism was once fashionable among the elite of the eighteenth century. Perhaps the unchurched theists will remain a small, secret group, bound by no creed or organization. False messiahs and prophets, as Jesus correctly predicted, have come and gone, and it is safe to say that many more will be coming and going. Only God does not come and go.[7]

In an earlier chapter I spoke of the leap of faith that played such an essential role in Whittaker Chambers's break with communism. I find his *Witness* intensely moving, beautifully written, with a ring of biographical truth that every communist, ex-communist, and ex-fellow-traveler will instantly recognize. Having said this (yes, I know it is still chic in some liberal circles to suppose Hiss innocent and Chambers a psychopathic liar), let me single out what I think are the two main flaws in Chambers's apocalyptic vision. I mention them not to revive bitter controversies, but to come to grips with a trend that I find far more dangerous than the growing expectation among Protestant evangelicals of the Second Coming. I refer to the belief that this country and the Soviet Union are fated to fight a nuclear war that could end civilization.

A friend once told Chambers that he, Chambers, saw everything in black and white. The friend was right. For Chambers, communism is only one expression of a deeper malignancy, the Satanic sin of pride, the evil of trying to live without God. "Economics is not the central problem of this century," Chambers wrote in a passage that President Reagan loves to recite. "It is a relative problem which can be solved in relative ways. Faith is the central problem of this age. The Western world does not know it, but it already possesses the answer to this problem—but only provided that its faith in God and the freedom He enjoins is as great as Communism's faith in Man."[8]

In place of God, secular humanism puts humanity. In place of immortality for individuals, it puts the immortality of the race. In Chambers's vision this secular faith, spearheaded by communism, can be defeated only by an equally robust religious faith. For Chambers, as for Aleksandr Solzhenitsyn and so many others today who are both Christians and political conservatives, the only viable opposing faith is, of course, Christianity. It has always been typical of true believers to assume that their own religious tradition is essential to any just state. When Chesterton visited the United States and wrote about it in a book, What I Saw in America, he concluded on his last page but one: "So far as that democracy becomes or remains Catholic and Christian, that democracy will remain democratic. In so far as it does not, it will become wildly and wickedly undemocratic."[9]

The most powerful of Christian nations, perhaps I should say of so-called Christian nations, is the United States. The most powerful state that is officially atheist is the Soviet Union. Chambers saw the two nations as "two jet planes whose political destiny could be fulfilled only when one destroyed the other."[10] If this is true, if the U.S. and the U.S.S.R. are on a collision course, there are, Chambers tells us, just three possible scenarios:

Communism will soon dominate the world.

The United States will soon dominate the world.

The two nations will soon destroy each other.

Chambers could be right; but I think he is not, and that his vision of the future rests on two mistaken posits. First, he assumes that any major secular effort to build a better world would inevitably take the form of Marxist totalitarianism. There are no kind words anywhere in Chambers's book for democratic socialism. No reference to Wells, to Bertrand Russell's early socialist attack on the Soviet system, to influential books by anti-communist socialists who told all those willing to listen about Stalin's hallucinations. There are no references to any of the democratic socialist economic systems around the world. Names such as Gunnar Myrdal, Norman Thomas, John Kenneth Galbraith, Robert Heilbroner, Wassily Leontief, are totally absent. You will look in vain for even a mention of such democratic socialist periodicals in the United States as *The New Leader* or *Dissent*, which constantly disclosed the truth about Stalinism.

In his years as a Columbia University student Chambers found "no life" in the democratic socialist books he read. "I brushed them aside. Socialism was not the answer."[11] Even after he became an anti-communist, the non-communist left held no appeal for him. An uninformed reader of *Witness* might suppose democratic socialism to be nowhere a force in the world. Chambers saw everything in black and white. For him democracy, unmotivated by capitalist freedoms and Christian dogma, is too flabby to withstand the ruthlessness of the Soviet onslaught. Secular socialism in the broad sense (democratic as well as totalitarian) was for Chambers the great evil which "in the name of liberalism, spasmodically, incompletely, somewhat formlessly, but always in the same direction, has been inching its ice cap over the nation. . . ."[12]

The second flaw in *Witness*, in my opinion, is the assumption, more implicit than explicit, that religious faith means Christian faith. Chambers had almost no interest in Islam, Judaism, Buddhism, Taoism, Hinduism, or any other non-Christian religion. His book's index lists no philosophical theists except Unamuno, and I suspect Unamuno is there because Chambers considered him a Christian. For Chambers, even a private belief was not enough to sustain theism. "My need was to be a practicing Christian in the same sense that I had been a practicing Communist. I was seeking a community of worship in which a daily mysticism (for I hold that God cannot be known in any other way) would be disciplined and fortified by an orderly, and even practical spirit and habit of life and the mind."[13] For Chambers it was the Quaker Church that met this need.

Chesterton's entertaining fantasy *The Ball and the Cross* is about an atheist and a Catholic who periodically cross swords with one another. "I myself believe," wrote William Buckley, Jr., in the foreword to his first book, *God and Man at Yale*, "that the duel between Christianity and atheism is the most important in the world. I further believe that the struggle between individualism and collectivism is the same struggle reproduced on another level." The passage is a key to all of Buckley's writings. It is behind the apocalyptic vision Buckley shares with Chambers. In their eyes, as in the eyes of so many politically conservative Christians, Chesterton's duel has now taken the form of a battle to the death between "Christian" America and "atheist" Russia.

Obviously I cannot accept this vision. I do not believe it inevitable that either Soviet communism or U.S. democracy, or both, will be obliterated by war or even vanquished by peaceful means. Nor do I believe that Christianity or any other religion is indispensable for restraining the spread of communism. We all know how a vigorous theism can readily combine with totalitarianism and massive violations of human liberties. Stalin's purges had their precursors in the tortures and executions of millions of heretics and witches in the name of a Christian God. Better a large number of such persons should perish than that their evil teachings send even larger numbers of souls to the eternal flames! It may be that the ideals of democracy are strengthened to some degree by faith in God, but when those ideals congeal in a Church, which in its monstrous pride considers itself the unique conduit of God's will, the Church can be as savage and merciless as communism.

Michael Servetus was burned at the stake in John Calvin's Geneva because, though a devout Christian, he disagreed with Calvin about infant baptism and the Trinity. French Catholics, who wanted him burned with a "slow fire," burned him in effigy, but the Calvinists burned him in the flesh. (Calvin had opposed this on the grounds that he preferred to have Servetus decapitated.)[14] Bloody wars have been fought between rival monotheistic cultures, each side firmly believing it was killing infidels. Protestants and Catholics have not hesitated in the past to massacre one another. On a smaller scale they are doing so today in Northern Ireland.

Open Conspirators who believe in democratic freedoms obviously

can be atheists, theists, pantheists, or members of almost any organized religion. They also can and do wildly disagree about economic
theories. But Chambers never stopped seeing things in black and
white. He never ceased to be stirred by those lines in a song he loved to
sing in his youth, the French *Internationale:*

> 'Tis the final conflict.
> Let each stand in his place.

Chambers just substituted "International Christendom" (in the next
line) for the "International Soviet." It was Chambers who, at the urging of pious Protestant Henry Luce, wrote a famous *Life* essay on "The
Devil." Slowly, with terrible agony, Chambers climbed out of what he
came to see as the Devil's abyss. Like so many others who wander in
and out of communism, he never reached that summit described by
Stephen Crane:

> When the prophet, a complacent fat man,
> Arrived at the mountain-top,
> He cried: "Woe to my knowledge!
> I intended to see good white lands
> And bad black lands,
> But the scene is grey."[15]

Do not suppose that because I quote this poem I see no significant
difference between the political systems of Western democracies and
the Soviet Union. Quite the opposite, as I surely made clear in a previous chapter. I believe that the Soviet Union has been and is the most
repressive tyranny in world history, with China and other Marxist dictatorships not far behind.

With vast sadness, colored by amusement, I have watched American liberals and radicals of many persuasions, having become finally
convinced of the evils of Stalin (after all, it was Nikita Khrushchev
himself who convinced them), turn their visionary eyes toward China
and make the same innocent mistakes all over again. Mao's policy
toward dissent was as horrendous in its persecutions, especially of intellectuals, as Stalin's. Yes, the analog is not perfect—after all, Russia
and China are vastly different cultures. And we do not yet know how
many dissidents were murdered by Mao, or how many are presently in
Chinese labor camps. The first number may be larger than the num-

ber killed by Stalin, and the second is surely larger than the corresponding number of political prisoners in the Soviet Union now.

The childish double standard that American liberals and assorted
leftists apply to Moscow and Peking reached some sort of zenith in
Shirley MacLaine's documentary film about China, and the book she
wrote about it, *You Can Get There From Here.*[16] It is this double
standard (Vietnam and Cuba can be substituted for China to provide
other examples) that makes it so difficult today for democratic socialists
to talk to so many "liberals" and self-styled Marxists. Of course one
may hope otherwise, but as of now it seems to me improbable that
Russia, China, or Cuba will move significantly toward democratic
freedoms in the next few decades. On the other hand, I consider it
highly probable that Western democracies will continue to make
steady progress toward such freedoms.

There are indeed good and bad persons; good and bad religious beliefs; above all, good and bad political systems. There are few good
white lands and bad black lands. If the United States and the Soviet
Union are on a collision course, God forbid, it is their political systems
that threaten to collide, not angelic Christianity and demonic atheism.
I would hesitate even to say there is now more heartfelt love of God
among ordinary people in the United States than among ordinary people in the Soviet Union. It could be so, but I suspect that from God's
eternal summit the scene looks gray.

Let me close this book, as I began, with some lines from the always
quotable Chesterton. After all, what GK called the central idea of his
life is also the central idea of mine, and although I regret that Chesterton became a Catholic as much as I regret that Wells became an atheist, I feel closer to the heart of GK than to the heart of HG. Chesterton
was fond of colors, every color. In his essay, "The Glory of Grey," he
insists that grey is a splendid color, and that its chief glory is that
against a grey background every color appears unusually beautiful. A
blue sky can kill the brightness of blue flowers. "But on a grey day the
larkspur looks like fallen heaven; the red daisies are really the red lost
eyes of day; and the sunflower is the vice-regent of the sun."

Lastly, there is this value about the color that men call colorless;
that it suggests in some way the mixed and troubled average of
existence, especially in its quality of strife and expectation and
promise. Grey is a color that always seems on the eve of changing

to some other colour; of brightening into blue or blanching into white or bursting into green and gold. So we may be perpetually reminded of the indefinite hope that is in doubt itself; and when there is grey weather in our hills or grey hairs in our heads, perhaps they may still remind us of the morning. 17

NOTES

CHAPTER 1

1. I cannot recall where I read this. Of the many other anecdotes and jokes about solipsism, I particularly like one that Raymond Smullyan gives in his book *5000 B.C. and Other Philosophical Fantasies* (1983). The logician Melvin Fitting once said to Smullyan: "Of course I believe that solipsism is the correct philosophy, but that's only one man's opinion." The book contains fascinating speculations on many aspects of the egocentric predicament.

2. Miguel de Unamuno, *The Tragic Sense of Life* (1913), Chapter 11.

3. Raymond Smullyan provides a delightful example of just such a game in his book *This Book Needs No Title* (1980).

> Wouldn't it be funny if things were really such that physical objects existed only when they were *not* perceived! That is, while they were not seen, felt, heard, etc., they existed perfectly well, but the minute one perceived them, they went out of existence; they would then *appear* to exist, but the appearance would be only an illusion.
>
> The funniest thing of all is that such a universe is logically possible!

4. John Stuart Mill, *An Examination of Sir William Hamilton's Philosophy* (1865), Chapter 11.

5. *The Letters of William James* (1926), edited by his son Henry, Vol. 2. Throughout *The Meaning of Truth* (1909) James expresses similar amazement that anyone could suppose he denied a reality independent of minds. Here is a passage from his preface:

> Having previously written that truth means "agreement with reality," and insisted that the chief part of the expediency of any one opinion is its agreement with the rest of acknowledged truth, I apprehended no exclusively subjectivistic reading of my meaning. My mind was so filled with the notion of objective reference that I never dreamed that my hearers would let go of it; and the very last accusation I expected was that in speaking of ideas and their satisfactions, I was denying realities outside. My only wonder now is that critics should have found so silly a personage as I must have seemed in their eyes, worthy of explicit refutation.

But exactly how external is this reality? James never gives a clear answer. Sometimes he writes as if it is "out there," independent of all human life. At other times he adopts the Millian view that it is no more than the regularities of our phaneron.

There is an old myth about how the earth rests on an elephant that stands on a turtle that stands on another turtle, and (as an old joke goes) it is "turtles all the way down." James recalls this myth in Chapter 3, then asks, "Must not something end by supporting itself?" Why not make experience the final support? There may be, he writes, an "extra-experiential 'ding an sich' that keeps the ball rolling," but why trouble yourself about the existence of such a "black inane"? It is an unnecessary posit. "Experience as a whole is self-containing and leans on nothing. . . . the knower and the object known must both be portions of experience." Again (Chapter 13): "The 'experience' which the pragmatic definition postulates *is* the independent something which the antipragmatist accuses him of ignoring."

In Chapter 8, James lists eight common misunderstandings of pragmatism. Commenting on charges 3, 4, 6, and 8, he repeatedly states that correspondence with an external reality is precisely what makes a belief "true." "Realities are not *true*, they *are*; and beliefs are true *of* them." Although pragmatism is compatible with solipsism, he writes, it has no special affinity for it, or with any other ontology. As for himself, "I remain an epistemological realist."

> One word more, ere I end this preface. A distinction is sometimes made between Dewey, Schiller and myself, as if I, in supposing the object's existence, made a concession to popular prejudice which they, as more radical pragmatists, refuse to make. As I myself understand these authors, we all three absolutely agree in admitting the transcendency of the object (provided it be an experienceable object) to the subject, in the truth-relation. Dewey in particular has insisted almost ad nauseam that the whole meaning of our cognitive states and processes lies in the way they intervene in the control and revaluation of independent existences or facts. His account of knowledge is not only absurd, but meaningless, unless independent existences be there of which our ideas take account, and for the transformation of which they work. But because he and Schiller refuse to discuss objects and relations "transcendent" in the sense of being *altogether trans-experiential*, their critics pounce on sentences in their writings to that effect to show that they deny the existence *within the realm of experience* of objects external to the ideas that declare their presence there. It seems incredible that educated and apparently sincere critics should so fail to catch their adversary's point of view.

I must confess that I find it more incredible that James could not understand why his opponents were mystified. He admits that his previous writings on pragmatism were often "slipshod" and "elliptical," but the new book fails to make his ontology any clearer. If objects are external to any one person's mind, but not transcendent in the sense of being outside human experience, we are back with John Stuart Mill in denying the need to posit a reality behind the phaneron. We are still trapped in a kind of collective, humanistic solipsism that certainly clashes with James's theism. Did James believe that if all minds in the universe were wiped out of existence, and hence all human experience, planets never seen by living eyes would continue on their journeys? I am convinced he did, but how he managed (or how Dewey would later manage) to believe this without positing a reality independent of all human experience still eludes my comprehension.

6. John Dewey, *Logic: The Theory of Inquiry* (1938), Chapter 25.

7. *The Philosophy of John Dewey*, edited by Paul Schilpp, Tudor Publishing, New York (1939), page 542 fn.

8. Rudolf Carnap, who considered his *Der logische Aufbau der Welt* (1928) no more than a tentative sketch of a program, early recognized its flaws. In a preface to the second edition (1961) he said his main error was basing the *Aufbau* program on a single primitive relation rather than many, but he remained persuaded that his thesis of the "reducibility of thing concepts to autopsychological concepts remains valid."

A strenuous effort to repair the *Aufbau* program was made by Nelson Goodman in *The Structure of Appearance* (1951). See also Goodman's paper on the significance of the *Aufbau* program in *The Philosophy of Rudolf Carnap* (1963), and Carnap's comments in the same volume.

Philosophers continue to disagree over whether it is possible to reduce the entire empirical content of a physical language to a phenomenal one, or vice versa. Everyone agrees that no attempt at either reduction has been successful, though almost everyone thinks the attempts have been worthwhile. My guess is that there are portions of each language that cannot be reduced to the other.

Father Frederick Copleston, in the chapter on Mill in his marvelous *History of Philosophy* (Volume 8, Part I) summarizes the situation well:

> Solipsism has proved the haunting spectre of phenomenalism. It is not that phenomenalists have actually embraced solipsism. For they have done nothing of the kind. The difficulty has been rather that of stating phenomenalism in such a way that it leads neither to a solipsistic conclusion on the one hand nor to an implicit

abandonment of phenomenalism on the other. Perhaps the most successful attempt to state the phenomenalist position has been the modern linguistic version [e.g., Carnap's]. . . . But this can easily appear as an evasion of critical problems. At the same time, if we once start looking for hidden substrates, we shall find ourselves in other difficulties. And one can sympathize with the down-to-earth common-sense approach of some recent devotees of the cult of ordinary language. The trouble is, however, that once we have brought things back to ordinary language, the familiar philosophical problems tend to start up all over again.

9. For attacks on the view that all mathematics is a human construction see my "Mathematics and the Folkways" and my review of *The Mathematical Experience*, by Philip Davis and Reuben Hersh, both reprinted with additional commentary in my *Order and Surprise* (1983).

10. Alfred North Whitehead, *Science and the Modern World* (1925), Chapter 3.

11. *The Philosophy of Rudolf Carnap*, op. cit.

12. Bertrand Russell, "William James's Conception of Truth," in *Philosophical Essays* (1910).

13. The literature on the philosophy of quantum mechanics is too vast to permit citing more than two references. Max Jammer's *The Philosophy of Quantum Mechanics* (1974) is indispensable. For a light-hearted discussion of QM and reality see the chapter on "Quantum Weirdness" in my *Order and Surprise* (1983).

14. G. K. Chesterton, "The Crime of Gabriel Gale," in *The Poet and the Lunatics* (1929).

CHAPTER 2

1. See for instance Plato's *Sophist*, lines 262–263.

2. An amusing example of how James was forced to use such cumbersome counterfactuals can be found in his "Dialogue" that closes

The Meaning of Truth. The antipragmatist maintains that one may regard statements as true or false even when they concern past events that can never be tested. James agrees, but only if he is allowed to say it in his own language:

> The truth of an event, past, present, or future, is for me only another name for the fact that *if* the event ever *does* get known, the nature of the knowledge is already to some degree predetermined. The truth which precedes actual knowledge of a fact means only what any possible knower of the fact will eventually find himself necessitated to believe about it. He must believe something that will bring him into satisfactory relations with it, that will prove a decent mental substitute for it.

3. Readers who care to examine in detail the Dewey–Russell controversy should take the following references in chronological order:

(1) "A Short Catechism Concerning Truth," in Dewey's *The Influence of Darwin on Philosophy* (1910). This early paper is not about Russell, but in it Dewey (like William James before him in Chapter 8 of *The Meaning of Truth*) replies to all the major charges that had been hurled at pragmatism.

(2) Bertrand Russell, "Dewey's New Logic," in *The Philosophy of John Dewey*, edited by Paul Arthur Schilpp (1939).

(3) Dewey's reply to Russell, *ibid*, pages 544–549.

(4) Chapter 23 of Russell's *Inquiry into Meaning and Truth* (1940), in which Russell responds to Dewey's reply.

(5) The chapter on Dewey in Russell's *History of Western Philosophy* (1945).

(6) "Propositions, Warranted Assertibility, and Truth," in Dewey's *Problems of Men* (1946). Dewey's rebuttal.

(7) Chapter 3 of Russell's *Impact of Science on Society* (1951).

On Russell's earlier controversy with William James see:

(1) Russell, "William James's Conception of Truth" (1908), and "Pragmatism" (1909), both reprinted in *Philosophical Essays* (1910).

(2) James's reply to these two papers, in which he calls Russell's views "diseased abstractionism," is reprinted as Chapter 14 of James's *The Meaning of Truth*, op. cit.

4. Charles S. Peirce, *Collected Papers*, Vol. 5, Section 211 (1934).

5. The Strong–James correspondence is in Volume 2, Chapter 82, of *The Thought and Character of William James* (1935), by Ralph Barton Perry.

6. Paul Edwards, "Kierkegaard and the 'Truth' of Christianity," in *Philosophy*, Vol. 46, April 1971, pages 89–108. The paper attacks Kierkegaard for his James-like effort to redefine truth as that which a person passionately believes.

7. John Stuart Mill, *A System of Logic*, Book 4, Chapter 4, Section 6. The section is headed: "Evil Consequences of Casting Off Any Portion of the Customary Connotation of Words."

Bishop Berkeley, who had earlier redefined *matter* in an unusual way (for Berkeley it was the mind of God), was equally aware of the importance of keeping the customary meaning of words unless there are strong reasons not to. Here is how his disputants put the matter in the second of his *Three Dialogues Between Hylas and Philonous, in Opposition to Skeptics and Atheists:*

> PHILONOUS: Tell me, Hylas, hath every one a liberty to change the current proper signification attached to a common name in any language? For example, suppose a traveller should tell you that in a certain country men pass unhurt through the fire; and, upon explaining himself, you found he meant by the word *fire* that which others call *water*: or, if he should assert that there are trees that walk upon two legs, meaning men by the term *trees*. Would you think this reasonable?
>
> HYLAS: No, I should think it very absurd. Common custom is the standard of propriety in language. And for any man to affect speaking improperly is to pervert the use of speech, and can never serve to a better purpose than to protract and multiply disputes where there is no difference in opinion.

8. Tarski's original paper is in many anthologies, including Tarski's *Logic, Semantics, Metamathematics* (1956), where it appears as Chapter 8, "The Concept of Truth in Formalized Languages." For a less technical account, see his "Truth and Proof," in *Scientific American*, June 1963.

9. A recent example of the verbal difficulties that arise whenever someone tries to do away with the correspondence theory of truth is provided by the curious history of Thomas Kuhn. His *Structure of Scientific Revolution* (1962) has been enormously influential, especially among sociologists of science. Its thesis is simple. Science usually proceeds by normal growth in which a scientific community engages in puzzle solving within a commonly accepted theory which Kuhn called a paradigm. (Kuhn singles out crossword puzzles and jigsaw puzzles for metaphors, unfortunate choices because in both cases there are unique solutions known in advance.) These periods of "normal science" are punctuated by revolutionary breaks that occur when "anomalies" arise, puzzles that cannot be solved within the accepted paradigm. Slowly, painfully, against the opposition of many scientists (especially the elderly), a "gestalt shift" takes place and the old paradigm gives way to a new one. In this respect the history of science resembles the history of music, painting, and other fine arts.

Now, paradigm shifts certainly occur, though most historians of science find Kuhn's schema exaggerated and simplistic. His use of "incommensurable" to describe competing paradigms led many to suppose that he considered the choice between paradigms irrational. If so, one would find it difficult to say that science makes genuine progress when it changes paradigms. Writing in his postscript to the second (1970) edition of his book, Kuhn denied this vigorously. New paradigms, he insisted, are *not* chosen irrationally. They are adopted on the basis of "accuracy, simplicity, fruitfulness, and the like." Again: "accuracy of prediction, particularly of quantitative prediction; the balance between esoteric and everyday subject matter; and the number of different problems solved" are some of the criteria that are used in choosing.

One would suppose that by "accuracy" Kuhn meant the accuracy with which a theory fits the world; but no, he makes clear that he has no use for the notion that one theory is better than another "because it is somehow a better representation of what nature is really like"; that theories "grow ever closer to, or approximate more and more closely to, the truth . . . to the match, that is, between the entities with which the theory populates nature and what is 'really there.' "

Since writing that postscript, Kuhn has been struggling to defend the above remarks, but in ways that grow increasingly hard to understand. As Harvey Siegel put it (reviewing Kuhn's 1977 book, *The Essential Tension*, in *The British Journal for the Philosophy of Science*, Vol. 31, 1980, pages 359–384), "Kuhn seems to want it both ways: he wants to maintain incommensurability (and so irrationality), yet deny irrationality and allow for communication between proponents of competing paradigms (thus giving up incommensurability). It is clear, I hope, that Kuhn cannot have it both ways. His maintenance of incommensurability vitiates his denial of the irrationality thesis "

Consider the ways in which science, though always fallible, has made undisputed progress. It has advanced in its ability to explain, solving millions of puzzles the ancient Greeks could not solve. It has advanced in its ability to predict; it can make millions of predictions the Greeks could not make. It has developed marvelous instruments for better observing nature (telescopes, microscopes, cyclotrons, and so on). Its application to nature has given rise to a technology of awesome power in its ability to control nature and use it for human ends. More than anything else, this technology would stagger Plato and Aristotle if they could return and see it.

Why has science been so fantastically successful? There is a simple, obvious answer that a child can understand. It has been successful for the same reason a bird is successful in finding food and building nests. It is successful because human brains have learned more than birds about the structure of the world—yes, a world "out there," independent of you and me and our cultural biases. If Kuhn could ever bring himself to admit the strength of this simple, ancient hypothesis, it would dispel all his difficulties.

CHAPTER 3

1. It is hard to believe, but just such a chaos is recommended by Paul Karl Feyerabend, a Vienna-born philosopher of science who has taught at the University of California, Berkeley, since 1958. Feyerabend believes there is no scientific method (in the sense that there are no rules that cannot be violated), and that competing theories are as incommensurable as different cultures. Because he recommends that state-supported schools be allowed to teach anything taxpayers want, including astrology, parapsychology, Hopi cosmology, creationism, voodoo, and ceremonial rain dances, he has become the favorite philosopher for believers in the paranormal who read and can understand him. For my opinion of Feyerabend's "epistemological anarchism,"

see my 1982 article "Science and Feyerabend," reprinted in *Order and Surprise* (1983).

2. Samuel Goudsmit, *ALSOS* (1947).

3. Sociologists William Sims Bainbridge and Rodney Stark, writing on "Superstitions: Old and New" in *The Skeptical Inquirer* (Volume 4, Summer 1980), reported on their surveys of how beliefs in certain aspects of the current occult mania correlated with religious faith. They found that persons with no professed religion were the most inclined to believe in ESP and extraterrestrial UFOs. Paranormal cults were strongest in areas where traditional churches were weakest.

4. *Fads and Fallacies in the Name of Science* (1952).

5. *Science: Good, Bad and Bogus* (1981).

6. The following list of papers and books dealing with parascience in general may be helpful to some readers. In each category I have arranged the items chronologically. First the articles:

Laurence J. Lafleur, "Cranks and Scientists," *The Scientific Monthly*, Vol. 73, November 1951, pages 284–290. Edwin G. Boring, "The Validation of Scientific Belief," *Proceedings of the American Philosophical Society*, Vol. 96, October 1952, pages 535–539. I. Bernard Cohen, "Orthodoxy and Scientific Progress," *ibid*, pages 505–512. L. Sprague de Camp, "Orthodoxy in Science," *Astounding Science-Fiction*, May 1954, pages 116–129. Ernest Nagel, "Stigmata of Pseudoscience," in *Logic Without Metaphysics* (1956). Fred J. Gruenberger, "A Measure for Crackpots," *Science*, Vol. 145, September 25, 1964, pages 1413–1415. Wesley C. Salmon, "Inquiries into the Foundations of Science," in *Vistas of Science* (1968). L. Sprague de Camp, "The Way of the Charlatan," *Science Digest*, March 1975, pages 51–57. Philip H. Abelson, "Pseudoscience," *Science*, Vol. 184, June 21, 1974, page 1233. Bill Harvey, "Cranks—and Others," *New Scientist*, March 16, 1978, pages 739–741. James S. Trefil, "A Consumer's Guide to Pseudoscience," *Saturday Review*, April 29, 1978, pages 16–21. Carl Sagan, five chapters on "The Paradoxers" in *Broca's Brain* (1979). Lyell D. Henry, Jr., "Unorthodox Science as a Popular Activity," *Journal of American Culture*, Vol. 4, Summer 1981, pages 1–22. Kendrick Frazier, "Will the Real Science Please Stand Up," *Sciquest*, September 1981, pages 11–15. Douglas R. Hofstadter,

"Metamagical Themas," *Scientific American*, February 1982. Jeremy Bernstein, "Scientific Cranks: How to Recognize One and What to Do Until the Doctor Arrives," in *Science Observed* (1982). Steven I. Dutch, "Notes on the Nature of Fringe Science," *Journal of Geological Education*, Vol. 30, 1982, pages 6–13.

Books on parascience in general, published since 1950, include: D. H. Rawcliffe, *Illusions and Delusions of the Supernatural and the Occult* (1959). Christopher Evans, *Cults of Unreason* (1973). John T. Sladek, *The New Apocrypha* (1973). Charles Fair, *The New Nonsense* (1974). R. Laurence Moore, *In Search of White Crows* (1977). Roy Wallis, ed., *On the Margins of Science* (1979). Marsha P. Hanen, Margaret J. Osler, and Robert G. Weyant, eds., *Science, Pseudoscience and Society* (1980). Kendrick Frazier, ed., *Paranormal Borderlands of Science* (1981). George O. Abell and Barry Singer, eds., *Science and the Paranormal* (1981). Martin Gardner, *Science: Good, Bad and Bogus* (1981). Daisie and Michael Radner, *Science and Unreason* (1982).

See also numerous books by Daniel Cohen, starting with *Myths of the Space Age* (1967), and all issues of *The Skeptical Inquirer*. The magazine is edited by Kendrick Frazier, whose book listed above is an anthology of articles from the magazine. For the baleful influence of crank science on science fiction, consult Peter Nicholls's article "Psuedoscience," in *The Science Fiction Encyclopedia* (1979), edited by Nicholls.

7. *Fads and Fallacies*, op. cit.

8. Joseph Banks Rhine, *The Reach of the Mind* (1947), Chapter 11.

9. Schmidt's cockroach experiment is described in "PK Experiments with Animals as Subjects," *The Journal of Parapsychology*, Vol. 34, 1970, pages 255–261. For some unintended humor, see the accounts of Schmidt's animal PK tests in *Psi—What Is It?* (1975), by Louisa E. Rhine, and the chapter on "ESP and Animals," in *What's New in ESP* (1976), by Martin Ebon.

When Walter J. Levy, Jr., was working for Rhine, he discovered that live chicken eggs could influence a randomizer so that it kept them warmer than chance would have otherwise permitted. Schmidt had earlier reported on similar experiments with his cat. For Levy's work on fertilized eggs see "Possible PK by Young Chickens to Obtain

Warmth," by Levy and E. André, in *The Journal of Parapsychology*, Vol. 34, 1970, page 303. Because Levy was later caught cheating while testing the ability of rats to influence a randomizer (see Note 13 below), references to his pioneering work on egg PK have dropped out of psi literature.

10. The quotation is from Flew's article "Parapsychology Revisited," in *The Humanist*, May 1976.

11. These claims, by the psychic Scientologist Ingo Swann, have been "confirmed" by Harold Puthoff and Russell Targ in experiments reported in Chapter 2 of their book *Mind-Reach* (1977).

12. This marvelous technique for winning at roulette by amplifying the precognition of a group of players was explained by Puthoff and Targ in the bound galleys of *Mind-Reach* that were mailed to reviewers by Delacorte Press/Eleanor Friede. After reporting fantastic success with the method they added:

> Such casino exploits have, in fact, stood up to scientific investigation and have resulted in published papers. For those interested, we include here the description of a proven and published strategy. Although somewhat complicated, it has provided a number of individuals known to us an opportunity to succeed at the casino and come away with money in their pockets as testimony to their psychic prowess.

I commented on this system in a review of *Mind-Reach* reprinted in *Science: Good, Bad and Bogus* (1981). To my surprise, when *Mind-Reach* was published, its pages on the roulette system had vanished. See my book for details.

13. The Levy scandal was reported by Boyce Rensberger in *The New York Times* (August 20, 1974). Other reports appeared in *Time* (August 26, 1974), and the *APA Monitor* (November 1974). Rhine himself discussed the affair (without mentioning Levy's name) in "A New Case of Experimenter Unreliability," in his *Journal of Parapsychology* (June 1974).

14. In spite of numerous accusations of fraud by C. E. M. Hansel and other skeptics, leading parapsychologists refused to believe the charges until Betty Markwick published her sensational findings in the

Proceedings of the Society for Psychical Research (Vol. 56, May 1978, pages 250–277). For a summary of her evidence, and J. G. Pratt's incredible way of rationalizing it, see *Science: Good, Bad and Bogus*, op. cit., Chapter 19. The Rhine statement about Soal appears in Chapter 10 of Rhine's *Reach of the Mind* (1947).

CHAPTER 4

1. This is the second stanza of poem 812 in *The Complete Poems of Emily Dickinson*, edited by Thomas H. Johnson (1960).

2. From *Nude Descending a Staircase* by X. J. Kennedy (1961).

3. The second stanza of poem 566 in the book cited in Note 1 above.

4. One of the widest swings in the history of U.S. painting and sculpture occurred around the turn of the nineteen seventies to the eighties, a swing from abstraction back to academic realism. I have long found the art criticism of *The New York Times* to be almost as funny as Russell Baker's columns, but nothing in this area has struck me as funnier than Hilton Kramer's article (Sunday, October 25, 1981) on "The Return of the Realists."

For decades Kramer had been lyrically boosting the most extreme forms of abstract expressionism. Consider, for instance, Jasper Johns's painting "The Barber's Tree." It consists entirely of a jumble of pink parallel lines. Here is how Kramer rhapsodized about it on February 1, 1976: "Johns aims at a most delicate coherence, playing off one range of pinks against another, never chopping the all-over rhythm of the picture, and setting up (as between his brush and our eye) the equivalent of a lover's luncheon."

That same year Kramer was unmercifully blasting realism. Andrew Wyeth, said Kramer on October 16, is dull, boring, repetitious, depressing, drained of feeling, and shamelessly sentimental. The trouble with Wyeth is that his realism is "utterly false." The "excremental brown" with which he douses his landscapes suggests to Kramer a "hidden scatalogical obsession." The Maine countryside, Kramer wrote, swarms with bright flowers. Where are the bright flowers in Wyeth's pictures?

"Emerging from this phony atmosphere [Kramer had been covering a Wyeth show at the Metropolitan Museum of Art], how grateful one was for the sun and the crowds on Fifth Avenue! Even the polluted air of Manhattan smelled a little sweeter after the visual murk of Mr. Wyeth's . . . evocations, and the bright yellow taxis looked as if Matisse had put them there."

Now confronting a trend of monumental momentum—even top critics and museums are hopping on the bandwagon—Kramer is compelled to think of good things to say about realism in his October 1981 piece or else run the risk of appearing to be an old fogy. The best he can do is express amazement at the trend, point out that it is not unified (as if any art movement was ever unified!), and to acknowledge that "it has succeeded in reestablishing something fundamental to the art life of our time—a way of thinking about art that binds its forms, its imagery and the very process of its creation to the act of individual perception, to the self as it negotiates its difficult progress in the world of experience." I assume what Kramer means is that artists have gone back to painting things the way they look.

Kramer's latest enthusiasm is, of all people, a near-forgotten American artist, Milton Avery, whose works are (as I write) enjoying a retrospective at the Whitney Museum in Manhattan. Kramer wrote a book about Avery back in 1962, and his cover story on him (*The New York Times Magazine*, August 29, 1982), praises him as an American master who "had the finest eye for color in the entire history of American painting," and whose landscapes and seascapes have a "lyric intensity . . . unlike anything else in the art of our time."

Avery's pictures are too abstract to make him a "realist," yet sufficiently representational to enable Kramer to write: "The orthodoxy that made abstraction the sole touchstone of achievement has now pretty much collapsed. Abstraction is now seen to be but one of the many artistic options open to a serious painter, and not always the most fertile." So what else is new?

In my opinion, Avery is the worst of the two worlds—neither a great abstractionist nor a great realist. We shall have to wait a few decades and see whether the influence of the Whitney and *The New York Times* is sufficiently strong to boost Avery to the master level, or whether his reputation will soon drift back into the obscurity it had thirty years ago.

Also at the moment, a movement called neo-expressionism is struggling to capture the eyes and wallets of wealthy collectors. Julian

Schnabel, the best known American neo-expressionist, likes to glue broken plates on his canvas. One German neo-expressionist, George Baselitz, has discovered another new way to express himself. He paints all his images upside down. Writing on "Art's Wild Young Turks" in an essay boxed inside his longer article, "The Revival of Realism" (*Newsweek*'s cover story, June 7, 1982), Mark Stevens finds Baselitz's inverted art "oddly affecting." It affects me oddly, all right. It makes me want to bend over and look back at it through my legs.

I hope no reader supposes that I dislike abstract art. On the contrary, I believe that nonobjective painting, like objective painting, can range from excellent (Klee, Miró, Matisse . . .) to worthless (Ad Reinhardt). At the worthless end I would also put most of the abstract expressionists and action painters who acquired vast reputations (Pollock, Rothko, Kline, Still, Motherwell, De Kooning . . .) by inventing gimmicks that generated the publicity that got their bogus work reproduced in *Time* and *Life*, put their monstrosities into the big museums, and hornswoggled everybody whose taste in art is no more than a reflection of the latest fashion.

5. For a startling selection of low opinions by eminent critics and writers of such poets as Shakespeare and Milton, along with high praise of poets now totally forgotten, see the entry "Criticism, Curiosities of," in William S. Walsh, *Handy-Book of Literary Curiosities* (1892).

6. This interview appeared in *The New York Times Book Review*, July 22, 1979. "Sandburg is the poet of Chicago," Borges said, "but what is he? He's just noisy—he got it all from Whitman. Whitman was great, Sandburg is nothing."

7. Forgive me, but (as any admirer of Williams would at once have realized) I switched the two poems—a dirty trick I learned from Max Eastman when I heard him lecture at the University of Chicago on the low quality of most modern poetry. The lines I said were parody are the opening lines of Williams's short poem "Portrait of a Lady." Sorrentino, in the review mentioned (it ran in *The New York Times Book Review*, November 22, 1981), calls this the "first *absolutely* modern American poem."

"This miraculous poem, *in toto*," Sorrentino continues, "is a paradigm of Williams's technical concerns. We note a perfectly balanced iambic hexameter, distributed over two lines, suddenly mocked and broken; an elegant alexandrine pulled up short; and a recurrent aborting of causality and logical development. Nothing like it had been seen before in English or American poetry. . . ."

Lest you think my low opinion of Williams idiosyncratic, let me add that as many critics share my view as agree with those who elevate Williams above Eliot, Pound, and Wallace Stevens. Marius Bewley, reviewing J. Hillis Miller's *Poets of Reality* for *The New York Review of Books* (January 20, 1966) calls Williams "the dullest poet of any importance America has produced in this century. . . . Mr. Miller submits poem after poem to sustained technical analysis the effect of which, for me at least, is only perversely to reveal the nullity of the work he is examining."

8. Chesterton's essay about this book, "On Bad Poetry," is worth looking up if only for its comments on the awful limericks of the father of the Brontë sisters. You'll find it in *All I Survey* (1933).

9. See Burton Egbert Stevenson, *Famous Single Poems* (1923), revised edition (1935).

10. To this day the only essay ever written about Langdon Smith and his ballad is my "When You Were a Tadpole and I Was a Fish," reprinted in *Order and Surprise* (1983). No one even knows the date of the Manhattan newspaper in which Smith's only known poem first appeared.

CHAPTER 5

1. Russell's first major defense of emotive ethics was Chapter 19 of *Religion and Science* (1935); his last major defense, *Human Society in Ethics and Politics* (1954). See also the preface he wrote for a privately printed edition of his most famous essay, *A Free Man's Worship* (published in Portland, Maine, by Thomas Bird Mosher in 1923), where what he has to say about ethics could have been written by Dewey: ". . . people do not differ much as to what is ultimately desirable on its own account, but only as to the means of obtaining it. Everybody is agreed that happiness is better than unhappiness, love than hate, and knowledge than ignorance."

2. Carnap wrote little about ethics. For his final views on the topic, see *The Philosophy of Rudolf Carnap*, edited by Paul Arthur Schilpp (Open Court, La Salle, Ill., 1963), especially Abraham Kaplan's paper, "Logical Empiricism and Value Judgments," and Carnap's comments on pages 999–1,013. A good summary of the emotive ethics of Carnap and his friends is in A. J. Ayer, *Language, Truth and Logic* (1935)

3. Reichenbach's defense of emotive ethics will be found in the last two chapters of his *Rise of Scientific Philosophy* (1951). For Santayana's similar views, see his section on ethics in "The Philosophy of Mr. Bertrand Russell," Chapter 4 of *Winds of Doctrine* (1914). Russell actually changed his opinion about ethical values as a result of Santayana's criticism! It is one of the few examples I know of one philosopher altering his beliefs as a result of criticism by another.

4. Dewey's 1938 essay is reprinted in *Problems of Men* (1946). Compare his position with that taken by Bronislaw Malinowski in a chapter on " What is Human Nature?" in *A Scientific Theory of Culture and Other Essays* (1944). Malinowski lists the following needs which all humans have in common: breathing, eating, drinking, sex, rest, activity, sleep, micturation, defecation, escape from danger, and avoidance of pain. The list is notable for failing to distinguish a human being from a hippopotamus.

5. Franz Boas, "An Anthropologist's Credo," in *The Nation*, August 27, 1938.

6. *The Autobiography of Mark Twain* (1959), edited by Charles Neider, Chapter 7. I take the passage from Note 12, Chapter 22, of *The Annotated Huckleberry Finn* (1981), by Michael Hearn.

7. C. S. Lewis, *The Case for Christianity* (1947), Part I.

8. Melville J. Herskovits, *Man and His Works: The Science of Cultural Anthropology* (1948).

CHAPTER 6

1. James Boswell, *The Life of Samuel Johnson*, 1769 section. See also Boswell's discussion (1778 section) with Johnson on the problem of reconciling free will with God's foreknowledge.

2. The quotation is from a surprisingly good account of the free-will problem in the second chapter of Mencken's *Treatise on Right and Wrong* (1934). Writing these pages, he said in a letter, took him two weeks and reduced him to a "frazzle."

Robert Nozick reports similar frustration over the question. In his ponderous *Philosophical Explanations* (1981) almost a hundred pages are devoted to free will. There is lots of what Nozick calls "thrashing about," all of which, to borrow a witticism from Whitehead, "leaves the darkness of the subject unobscured." Nozick confesses that he spent more time "banging" his head on the topic than any other topic in his book except the foundations of ethics. Unfortunately he never takes the ultimate step of recognizing that there is no intelligible way to avoid what he aptly calls the "quicksand" of indeterminism and the "frozen ground" of determinism.

3. The literature on prediction paradoxes is growing rapidly. The one I gave is a variant of one I devised for Chapter 11 of my *New Mathematical Diversions from Scientific American* (1966). On the notorious paradox of the unexpected hanging, see the first chapter of my *Unexpected Hanging and Other Mathematical Diversions* (1969). The more recent Newcomb's paradox was the topic of my *Scientific American* column for July 1973, a guest column by Robert Nozick (March 1974), and Chapter 31 of my *Science Fiction Puzzle Tales* (1981), where I give a selected list of major references. Karl Popper has written about prediction paradoxes, especially in relation to quantum mechanics and idealized computers.

4. William James, "The Dilemma of Determinism," in *The Will to Believe* (1903).

5. Darrow's debate, with G. B. Foster, is in *Little Blue Book, No. 1286*, published by Haldeman-Julius in 1928.

6. See Peirce's *Collected Papers*, Volume 5, section 565. This is the section in which Peirce gives his famous definition of pragmatic truth as the ideal limit of belief. Kant was equally contemptuous of the view—"wretched subterfuge," he called it—that free will is somehow

saved by making it a matter of interior psychological causation rather than a mystery of the transcendent, timeless, noumenal self.

7. *The Autobiography of G. K. Chesterton* (1936), Chapter 7. Bertrand Russell, writing on ethics and free will (*Philosophical Essays*, 1910) said the same thing this way:

> But if determinism is true, there is a sense in which no action is possible except the one actually performed. Hence, if the two senses of possibility are the same, the action actually performed is always objectively right; for it is the only possible action, and therefore there is no other possible action which would have had better results. There is here, I think, a real difficulty.

Russell goes on to defend determinism, but without in any way clearing up the difficulty.

8. Kant's view can be compressed as follows: In the space-time world of our experience, the world investigated by science, causal determinism must be assumed; in this sense the will is not free. But morality is meaningless unless the will *is* somehow free. For practical reasons, therefore, we must assume that the human soul, considered as a noumenon, a thing in itself, belongs to a transcendent, timeless realm, and in this realm it is truly free. How empirical determinism and noumenal freedom can be reconciled, however, is a mystery utterly beyond our finite minds. When I say I follow Kant in my attitude toward free will, I do not mean that I buy all of his metaphysics, but only that I buy his conviction that the free-will problem is unsolvable.

In *Religion within the Limits of Reason Alone* (in a footnote for the final section of Book 3), Kant wrote: "Hence we understand perfectly well what freedom is, practically (when it is a question of duty), whereas we cannot without contradiction even think of wishing to understand theoretically the causality of freedom (or its nature)."

9. From the reference cited in Note 6 above.

10. William James, *Pragmatism* (1907).

11. For a good defense of Bohr's complementarity approach to human actions see Clarence Shute, "The Dilemma of Determinism after Seventy-five Years," in *Mind*, Volume 70, July 1961, pages 331–350. I agree with all that Professor Shute says, regretting only his failure to

recognize that he was restating Kant's view, and that he did not follow Kant in declaring the antinomy unsolvable.

12. Paine's essay, "Predestination," is in Volume 7 of *The Writings of Thomas Paine* (1908), edited and annotated by Daniel Edwin Wheeler.

13. René Descartes, *Principles of Philosophy*, Part 1, 41.

14. Charles S. Peirce, *Collected Papers*, Volume 4, section 67.

15. C. S. Lewis, *Beyond Personality* (1945).

16. James Boswell, *The Life of Samuel Johnson*, 1778 section.

17. Raymond Smullyan, "Is God a Taoist?" in *The Tao Is Silent* (1977). Rousseau's Savoyard vicar, in the fourth book of *Émile*, puts it this way: If you try to convince me that I have no free will, he says, "you might as well convince me I do not exist."

That free will is part of the mystery of what it means to be a person is, of course, much older than Descartes, Rousseau, and Kant. Few Catholic theologians emphasized it more effectively than William of Occam, the fourteenth-century English fideist. On the question of how free will can be harmonized with God's foreknowledge, Occam was not happy with Aquinas's casual answer that God, from an eternal vantage point, sees exactly how each person will freely decide. Occam saw more clearly than Aquinas that the problem is an unsolvable paradox. "It is impossible," he wrote in his *Commentary on the Sentences* (of Peter Lombard), "for any intellect, in this life, to explain or evidently know how God knows all future contingent events." I quote from Ernest Moody's excellent article on Occam in *The Encyclopedia of Philosophy* (1967).

Occam, Moody tells us, presented an interesting paradox involving the wills of God and created minds. Can God will that a person disobey him? Because God wills that all creatures love and obey him, such a command seems impossible to fulfill. It would require a person simultaneously to both obey and disobey. (One thinks of Abraham and Isaac.) Must we conclude, then, that it is logically impossible for God to issue such a command?

18. From Huxley's essay on Descartes, in *Methods and Results* (1893).

CHAPTER 7

1. Garry Wills, *Confessions of a Conservative* (1979).

2. "Milton Friedman," by Robert Edward Brown, in *Human Behavior*, November 1978.

3. Rusher's remark appears in Deirdre Carmody's feature story, "*National Review*, at 25, Celebrates Dual Victory," *The New York Times*, December 1, 1980. "Dual Victory" refers to the magazine's celebration of its twenty-fifth anniversary and also the election of Ronald Reagan. "Do you realize what that means?" said Rusher, continuing his comments on the death of liberalism. "We're like an old married couple who has fought every day of their lives and now one of the team has passed away."

4. George Gilder, *Wealth and Poverty* (1981).

5. William F. Buckley, Jr., *The National Review*, July 24, 1981, page 860.

6. William James, *Memories and Studies* (1911), Chapter 13.

7. Herbert Spencer, *The Study of Sociology* (1873). Spencer gives some colorful examples of the unintended consequences of government action. The United States could have profited from one of them. In 1617, Scotland tried to combat drunkenness by forbidding the sale of liquor. The unexpected result was an *increase* in the consumption of gin. I first encountered Spencer's iron-plate metaphor in, of all places, Havelock Ellis's *Sex in Relation to Society*, where he applies it to futile efforts to suppress prostitution by making it a crime.

8. Irving Howe's chapter on the 1960s in his autobiography, *A Margin of Hope* (1982), is an excellent analysis of why the New Left was such a short-lived phenomenon. It may not last long, but today's college students are revolting less, and are less revolting than they used to be. They are bored with political action, interested mainly in religion, money, marriage, job training, physical fitness, local football and basketball teams, and their sex and social lives. See "Why It's All Quiet on the Campus Front," *U.S. News & World Report*, January 31, 1983, pages 44–47.

9. The technical question of whether an extreme socialist state can

set prices as rationally as an ideal free market is now resolved. According to Mises, government agencies would have to handle such a torrent of relevant information, to solve quickly so many horrendous simultaneous equations, that a rational allocation of prices is impossible in principle. Indeed, Mises insisted that "economics" loses all meaning in an ideal socialist state. Hayek softened this view a bit. He thought socialist price allocation to be possible in principle though not in practice.

Since the development of modern computers, linear programming, and sophisticated statistical methods, this argument has become as obsolete as the arguments of those astronomers who earlier in the century wrote about the impossibility of ever traveling to Mars. One can even make a case for the view that a socialist regime can now obtain more accurate data about a given sector of the economy than private business managers who have no access to information kept secret by competitors.

It is not so much the solving of equations as it is the setting of tentative prices that are raised or lowered on the basis of fast feedback of information about supply and demand. Setting aside the snarls produced by bureaucratic inefficiency and corruption, some economists now believe that an enlightened socialist regime could, if it wanted to and tried hard enough, allocate prices on basic goods as rationally, if not better, than a capitalist economy.

10. Do not be sidetracked by libertarians who try to convince you that children in nineteenth-century factories were healthier and better off than those down on the farm. (See *Capitalism and the Historians*, 1953, edited and with an introduction by Friedrich von Hayek.) First, you don't have to believe it. Second, even if true, so what?

11. For a convenient summary of the fourteen planks in the 1928 Socialist Party platform, with comments on how they have been absorbed into the American economy, see Appendix A of the Friedmans' *Free to Choose* (1979). There is now a large literature on why democratic socialism, as a political movement of the Debs-Thomas variety, faded away in the United States. Daniel Bell's justly admired essay "The Failure of American Socialism" is reprinted in his collection, *The End of Ideology* (1960).

12. Both statements are from "Harvard's Nozick: Philosopher of the

New Right," by Jonathan Lieberson, *The New York Times Magazine*, December 17, 1978. Nozick's belief that volunteer contributions to charity, uncoerced by tax laws, could replace federal efforts to alleviate large-scale human misery, passeth all understanding. Studies have shown that individuals in our culture simply do not find it rational to make private contributions that they are quite willing to make if federally enforced, not to mention the fact that voluntary charitable organizations often spend 80 to 90 percent of the funds collected to pay for the costs of collecting.

In 1981, business would have had to multiply its voluntary contributions some twentyfold to fill the gap produced by Reagan's cuts in social spending. George Gilder's statement (in *Wealth and Poverty*) that "in order to succeed the poor need most of all the spur of their poverty" may make partial sense in boom times, but in times of high unemployment it is a cruel remark. To expect the poor to suffer patiently through severe economic slumps in the hope that money will trickle down to them if an untested Smithian program succeeds eventually, is to exhibit an indifference toward the poor that is characteristic of only the most fanatical Smithians.

Keynes's remark that in the long run we will all be dead is quoted more often than the sentence that follows it: "Economists set themselves too easy, too useless a task if in tempestuous seasons they can only tell us that when the storm is long past the ocean is flat again."

13. Samuel Scheffler, "Natural Rights, Equality, and the Minimal State," in *Reading Nozick: Essays on Anarchy, State, and Utopia* (1981), edited by Jeffrey Paul.

14. William F. Buckley, Jr., "Ayn Rand RIP [rest in peace]," *The National Review*, April 2, 1982, pages 380–381.

Rand's influence on Nozick was considerable, even though he has gone to some lengths to fault her reasoning. In the anthology cited above in Note 13, Nozick has a paper "On the Randian Argument" in which he tries to show that her way of justifying the moral superiority of free-market capitalism is unsound even though he accepts her conclusion. The next paper in this curious volume is by two Randians who insist that Nozick completely misunderstood Rand's argument.

Nozick writes in his first footnote:

Since I shall be quite critical of Miss Rand's argument in the remainder of this essay, I should here note (especially since she has been given a largely vituperative and abusive hearing in print) that I have found her two major novels exciting, powerful, illuminating, and thought-provoking. These virtues, even combined with a "sense of life" that is worthy of man do not, of course, guarantee that her conclusions are true, and even if we suppose they are true, all this does not, of course, guarantee that the actual *arguments* offered will be cogent, that they will prove their conclusions. Nothing I say in this essay is meant to deny that Miss Rand is an interesting thinker, worthy of attention.

CHAPTER 8

1. Although Reagan believed the supply-side arguments, his understanding of economics is not much above the level of his understanding of the physical and biological sciences, and it is now recognized that Reagonomics is a weird mixture of incompatible ideas. James Tobin (interviewed by *U.S. News & World Report*, February 1, 1982) compared Reagonomics with a train at New Haven that has a locomotive at both ends. "The stationmaster announces that the train will leave for both Boston and New York. But, under the circumstances, it's doubtful the train will reach either destination."

At the time I write (1982), Reagan's popularity continues to be high, mainly because the public still perceives him as a conservative—upright, patriotic, a good Christian (even though he believes in astrology), friendly, smiling, skilled at telling jokes, brave in the face of danger, and (not least) an actor with a glamorous Hollywood background. Voters have not yet realized that Reagan is not so much a practical, flexible politician, like his four predecessors in office, as a hard-nosed radical of the right who is doing his best to turn the country around 180 degrees from the direction given to it by Roosevelt. Of course Reagan has for thirty years been declaring this intention, but most Americans either weren't listening or they didn't take him seriously until they woke up one morning to find that the old showman had conned his way into the White House.

For a sympathetic account of Reagan's attempted rollback, see *The Reagan Revolution* (1981) by Rowland Evans and Robert Novak. For a slashing attack by an economist and democratic socialist, see *Greed Is*

Not Enough: Reagonomics (1982) by Robert Lekachman. Here is Lekachman's crisp summary of the Reagan program:

> The Reagan manner clothes a political initiative unique in our national history: a quite deliberate redirection of income and wealth from the poor to the rich; blacks and Hispanics to whites; women to men; the elderly to the young; old, declining regions to booming Sun Belt cities; and social services to the Pentagon.

2. Like his friend Jude Wanniski, mentioned later in this chapter, George Gilder is both a journalist and a disenchanted liberal. In fact, at one time Gilder even edited *The New Leader*, a democratic socialist journal. In 1973 he got himself into a bind with the feminists when his book *Sexual Suicide* explained how women "socialize" men by persuading them to marry and support them. The book was followed by *Naked Nomads: Unmarried Men in America* (1974). David Stockman, Reagan's blabbermouth budget director, found Gilder's *Wealth and Poverty* "Promethean in its intellectual power and insights. It shatters once and for all the Keynesian and welfare state illusions that burden the failed conventional wisdom of our era." That was before Stockman became a turncoat who advocated increasing taxes and cutting defense spending.

Gilder made another lurch to the right in 1980 by giving a speech in which he announced that although he owed much to the neoconservatives, especially to Midge Decter, who edited two of his books for Basic Books, he now must abandon them for being too evasive. All their insights, said Gilder, add up to less than you can find in William Buckley's first book, *God and Man at Yale*. For one thing, neoconservatives ignore God. Phyllis Schlafly, said Gilder, knows more about foreign policy than Pat Moynihan, Anita Bryant knows more about gays than the American Association of Psychiatrists, and the Moral Majority is more responsible than the Democratic Party.

Gilder reiterates his central dogma: Capitalism is not based on greed, as Adam Smith perversely assumed, but on altruism and old-fashioned moral values. It must be combined with religious faith, although Gilder doesn't specify which kind. Buckley reprinted this adolescent speech in *The National Review*, March 5, 1982, with a response by Ben Wattenberg, a neoconservative, and a rebuttal by

Gilder. For reader comments see the April 2, 1982 issue, pages 360–361.

3. Irving Kristol, "Ideology & Supply-Side Economics," *Commentary*, April 1981, pages 48–54.

4. For a satirical account of the Laffer curve, as the supply-sider's simple-minded answer to the "cruel dilemma" posed by the Phillips curve (which graphs the apparent impossibility of maintaining low inflation and high employment), and an attempt to construct a neo-Laffer curve more in harmony with the snarls of modern technology, see my Mathematical Games column in *Scientific American*, December 1981. I first sketched this marvelous curve on toilet paper while sitting in the men's room of the Library of Congress.

5. Kevin Phillips, *Post-Conservative America* (1982).

6. See Paul Blustein's front-page article on supply-side history, *The Wall Street Journal*, October 8, 1981.

7. "No Shrinking Supply-Sider: Economist Arthur Laffer Keeps the Faith," *Barron's*, December 21, 1981.

8. Jude Wanniski, *The Way the World Works* (1978). In *The New York Times* business section (Sunday, July 26, 1981) Wanniski's attack on Friedman was vitriolic. Although Friedman is "barely five feet tall," said Wanniski, he weighs so much that he is now a "deadweight burden" on the backs of Menachem Begin, Margaret Thatcher, Ronald Reagan, and the entire U.S. economy.

Interviewed by Louis Rukeyser on his TV show *Wall Street Week* (November 13, 1981), Wanniski called Friedman a demand-sider, and said he agreed with Galbraith that Reagan's big mistake was trying to walk in two directions at once. One direction is toward supply-side tax cutting, the other is toward Friedman's monetary policy which hopes to stop inflation by permitting a deep recession. The only way to stabilize the dollar, according to Wanniski, is by returning to the gold standard. He declared this to be inevitable, and predicted it would occur before the end of Reagan's first term. "I don't expect that a gold standard would last more than a hundred years," said Wanniski, "but I'm willing to take even fifty."

Friedman has a low opinion of the views of supply-side goldbugs: Laffer, Wanniski, Gilder, Jack Kemp, and starry-eyed former Reagan aide Jeffrey Bell, to name five. It is customary to call this group the radical supply-siders to distinguish them from conservative supply-siders with less extreme views. The radicals actually were convinced that Reagan's tax cuts would increase government revenue so rapidly that budget cutting, especially defense cutting, would not be necessary!

9. Was the anarchist longing to escape from the complexities of industrialization, to return to agrarian simplicities, unconsciously reflected in their fondness for single-word periodical titles: *Now, Why, Man, Blast, Politics, Revolt, Vengeance, The Torch, The Word, The Whip,* and many others? Even the state-hating Thoreau called his greatest book *Walden.*

10. Simons's pamphlet is reprinted in his posthumous collection of papers, *Economic Policy in a Free Society* (1948). Although an opponent of Keynes, Simons favored vigorous government action to eliminate all private monopoly, including labor unions. He also favored monetary and tax reforms, and the elimination of all tariffs, but it was his extreme opposition to monopoly that led to his being labeled a "radical conservative." Wage and price controls, even antitrust policies, are no more than stopgap measures, Simons believed, that accomplish little and are easily corrupted by bureaucracies. Only when monopolies are eliminated altogether can the free market function as it should.

Another University of Chicago economist widely hailed as a conservative is the Nobel Prize winner (1982) George Stigler. Conservative journalists like to praise Stigler's attacks on government efforts to regulate big business, but they seldom tell you why he opposes such efforts. It is because he believes that the regulations are usually in the interests of the regulated; indeed, are often requested by the regulated. They benefit not consumers but the megacorporations.

In the fifties Stigler was as down on oligopoly as Simons. In "The Case Against Big Business" (*Fortune,* May 1952) he argued that oligopolies compete only in superficial and socially undesirable ways (for example, the competition among the big four tobacco companies). Moreover, they stimulate the growth of big government and big labor, both of which Stigler deplores. Instead of taking over the giants or trying to control them, Stigler then wanted the government to dissolve them, leaving the field to genuine competition among smaller firms. It was the only way, he was convinced, that private enterprise can counter the drift toward socialism. Stigler wanted stronger antitrust action, a weakening of patent laws that stifle competition, and the elimination of all restrictive tariffs. "The obvious and economical solution . . . is to break up the giant companies. This . . . is the minimum program and it is essentially a conservative program." Conservative? Two decades later Stigler decided that megacorporations compete more than he formerly thought, and administer prices less than he thought. His present views seem to be that government should leave big business alone.

Simons's most famous student, Milton Friedman, has never looked kindly on federal takeovers, federal regulations, or trust busting. It is not big business that causes big labor and big government, he has declared, but the other way around. Big government causes big business and big labor! (See Lekachman's book cited in Note 1). Presumably, if government powe⋅ can be reduced, so will the power of megacorporations to interfere with free markets.

U.S. News & World Report (January 31, 1983) asked six American Nobel Prize economists what they believed the government should do to promote recovery. Their lack of agreement is monumental. Milton Friedman, as usual, writes as if all the other Nobel winners are crazy except for his old friend Stigler, and he is not too sure about Stigler. Stigler in turn makes what I consider the most vacuous statement ever uncorked by a top economist. "The human race existed for several million years," he said, "without governmental rules; now we suddenly need so many of them. That's a little paradoxical to me."

11. See *The Wall Street Journal*, April 2, 1982. If there were a way to do it, American corporations would rearrange the stars to spell the names of products. The back cover of *Time* (October 4, 1982) showed a young couple holding hands and gazing up at an indigo sky. The stars had formed a constellation that spelled TRUE. "You found it," said the caption. "True. In the ultra low tar universe, True outshines them all." On the left is the Surgeon General's warning. When I first saw this advertisement I thought I was looking at the back of *Mad* magazine, but it turned out to be a serious effort by Madison Avenue.

12. Writing on "A Tale of Two Capitalisms" (*The New York Times*, October 4, 1981), political scientist Benjamin Barber drew a striking contrast between the Smithian vision of big businessmen as brave, risk-taking adventurers, and the actual timid, risk-minimizing managers of large corporations. Although our captains of industry like to talk about getting the federal government off their backs, they know that the government is underneath, shoring them up. Their cry is not *laissez-faire*, said Barber, but *gardez nous!* Here is how he summed it up:

> Business may parrot the rhetoric of entrepreneurial capitalism from time to time, but there is little doubt that our multinational corporations look to government to buy their goods, prop up their prices, subsidize their inefficiencies, protect their monopolies, minimize their competition, guarantee their credit, cover their losses, and absorb their bankruptcies.

13. Because economists are always annoyed by the allegation that when ten economists are asked to solve a problem, they produce eleven solutions, it is worthwhile to consider what they mean when they deny this. They mean that, given the same data, they will usually agree on the nature of the problem and what the immediate outcome will be if certain measures are adopted. But there are so many complex parameters that economists, like weathermen, are poor at long-range forecasting. Moreover, they disagree profoundly on moral and political questions; that is, over what the economy *should* be. Since all important economic questions involve long-range forecasts joined to what ought to be, the claim that economists are in substantial agreement reduces to the tautology that they agree on just those trivial technical questions about which it is possible for them to agree.

14. Weintraub makes this statement in his review of *Free to Choose* by Milton and Rose Friedman, in *The New York Times Book Review*, February 24, 1980. It is a pity, Weintraub concludes, that history does not march backward. If it did, it might return to a state in which the Friedmans' book would offer some valuable advice.

15. Reagan followed Heller's advice. It was largely because of Reagan's untiring efforts that Congress passed a large tax-increase bill in August 1982. In his *Newsweek* column of August 23, Friedman called the bill "a monstrosity."

16. Paul Samuelson, *Economics*, 11th revised edition (1980).

17. Norman Thomas, "Dark Day for Liberty," *Christian Century*, July 29, 1942. I quote the passage from Michi Weglyn's richly documented book, *Years of Infamy: The Untold Story of America's Concentration Camps* (1976).

18. The exact number of innocent people executed by Stalin or sent to die in slave labor camps is not known, because the massive data gathered in the inquiry initiated by Krushchev and Mikoyan is still buried in Soviet archives or has been destroyed. The most authoritative figures can be found in *The Time of Stalin* (1981) by Anton Antonov-Ovseyenko, who had partial access to this data. He estimates that 19 million died in the purges of the thirties. Nine million more were executed after the Second World War. If to these deaths you add those resulting from the civil war that followed the Bolshevik appropriation of the Menshevik revolution, deaths from famine that inevitably followed the harsh measures for collectivizing the farms, deaths from the enforcement of other government policies, and needless deaths in World War II that were the direct result of Stalin's blundering, barbaric orders (over 30 million Soviets died in that war, of which the Germans were responsible for about half), you get a total of some 80 million souls who were murdered by Soviet leaders. No tyranny in history has thrown away so many of its own people.

19. From a letter from Corliss Lamont to Sidney Hook. It appears in *Free Inquiry*, Winter 1981/82, page 39.

20. I ended my letter with the following paragraph:

> I will be interested in knowing what Elinor Lipper might have to say about Wallace's contention that because his interpreter was John Hazard, liaison officer of the Division of Soviet supply in lend-lease, it was not possible for him to be fooled by office girls posing as swineherd girls on the hog farm near Magadan. Wallace's long record of being deceived counts heavily against this protest. Perhaps John Hazard could be induced to make a statement about the episode.

John Hazard went on to become one of the country's most respected government advisors on Soviet affairs. His best-known book, *The Soviet System of Government* (1957) has become a standard reference that has had many editions. He is now professor emeritus of law, Columbia University. Hazard certainly knew all about Magadan, and must have known that the young ladies knew nothing about pigs, but as far as I know he has never written about the incident. I hazard the guess that he never will.

CHAPTER 9

1. I would like to see the Electoral College abolished, and our election system changed to one of "approval voting." Good arguments for both changes will be found in *The Presidential Game* by Steven J. Brams (1978), and *Approval Voting* by Brams and Peter Fishburn (1983).

2. In his Labor Day speech of 1981 President Reagan went Kennedy one "jobs" better. The goal of his economic program, said Reagan, is "very clear: jobs, jobs, jobs, and more jobs."

3. H. G. Wells, *Russia in the Shadows* (1920).

4. A weird aspect of the U.S. college scene at the moment (1982) is that while students are moving right, less concerned about political action than in learning how to enjoy life and make a living, the number of self-declared Marxists on the faculties is growing. When the Monopoly-type simulation game Class Struggle went on sale in 1978, I thought it was intended as a joke. But no; its inventor, Bertell Ollman, professor of politics at New York University, is a dedicated Marxist. He doesn't buy the Soviet, Chinese, or Cuban models, and he wants a peaceful democratic revolution, but he really believes that the struggle between capitalists and workers is still just what Marx said it was. Capitalism must go! The proletariat must rise! As to just what should replace capitalism, the new Marxist scholars are almost as hazy as they were in the sixties when some of them were New Left undergraduates.

5. For a merciless drubbing of Harrington's "authentic Marx," see Daniel Bell, "The Once and Future Marx," a paper reprinted in his collection *The Winding Passage* (1980).

6. *The Nation,* February 27, 1982, reprints Sontag's speech, along with convoluted comments by eight listeners, and a rejoinder by Sontag. See also *The Nation's* letters section in its March 27, 1982, issue; *Newsweek,* February 22, 1982; *Time,* March 15, 1982; Richard Gre-

nier, "The Conversion of Susan Sontag," *The New Republic*, April 14, 1982; comments on Grenier's article, with a reply by the author, *ibid.*, May 26, 1982; and Charles Ruas's interview with Sontag, *The New York Times Book Review*, October 24, 1982.

7. One of the most comic aspects of the American business scene is the untiring effort by corporations to make stockholders think they have some voice in company policy. Here is how Galbraith describes the ridiculous ritual in *The New Industrial State* (1967):

> With even greater unction although with less plausibility, corporate ceremony seeks also to give the stockholders an impression of power. When stockholders are (or were) in control of a company, stockholders' meetings are an occasion of scant ceremony. The majority is voted in and the minority is voted out, with such concessions as may seem strategic, and all understand the process involved. As stockholders cease to have influence, however, efforts are made to disguise this nullity. Their convenience is considered in selecting the place of meeting. They are presented with handsomely printed reports, the preparation of which is now a specialized business. Products and even plants are inspected. During the proceedings, as in the report, there are repetitive references to *your* company. Officers listen, with every evidence of attention, to highly irrelevant suggestions of wholly uninformed participants and assure them that these will be considered with the greatest care. Votes of thanks from women stockholders in print dresses owning ten shares "for the excellent skill with which you run *our* company" are received by the management with well-simulated gratitude. All present show stern disapproval of critics. No important stockholders are present. No decisions are taken. The annual meeting of the large American corporation is, perhaps, our most elaborate exercise in popular illusion.

8. "In analogy to sex," Galbraith writes in *The New Industrial State*, "one must imagine that a man of vigorous, lusty and reassuringly heterosexual inclination eschews the lovely, available and even naked women by whom he is intimately surrounded in order to maximize the opportunities of other men whose existence he knows of only by hearsay. Such are the foundations of the maximization doctrine when there is full separation of power from reward."

9. Thurow is quoted in "Change in Mood," *The Wall Street Journal*, July 23, 1981.

10. Ibid. Fraser, by the way, is on the board of Chrysler.

11. In 1981, Ben Sargent, a political cartoonist for United Features, drew a picture of two businessmen reading a sign at the entrance to hell. It said: "A wholly owned subsidiary of the Perdition Industries Division of Hades, Inc., an affiliate of Ever and Ever Corporation, part of the Megalith Group, another Fumarole Industries Company, a subsidiary of Mammon Bank and Trust, another quality service of Omneity Company . . ." If you like to keep up with such money games, Dun & Bradstreet publishes a valuable annual called *Who Owns Whom: North America.*

12. The last two labels are recent. A group of native economists like to call themselves post Keynesian (without a hyphen) to emphasize their distance from Keynesian theory. In 1978 they founded the *Journal of Post Keynesian Economics*, edited by Paul Davidson and Sidney Weintraub. For a good introduction to their views, see Davidson's *Money and the Real World* (1978).

The humanistic economists are so called because they stress all human needs, not just the need for money. Who could object to that? See *The Challenge of Humanistic Economics* (1979) by Mark Lutz and Kenneth Lux. Both movements are broad, eclectic states of mind, well within what I call democratic socialism.

13. A good example of the growing uselessness of traditional labels is provided by the strange case of Daniel Bell. Bell has considered himself a democratic socialist since his youth when he was managing editor of the socialist weekly, *The New Leader*. "I would say quite seriously," he wrote as late as 1978, "that I am a socialist in economics, a liberal in politics, and a conservative in culture." Yet Bell is persistently called a neoconservative, a term he considers meaningless even though his ex-socialist friend Irving Kristol wears the badge proudly.

Bell and Kristol parted politically in 1972 when Kristol supported Nixon for President and Bell favored George McGovern. Bell resigned as coeditor with Kristol of *The Public Interest*, which they had founded seven years earlier when Kristol still called himself a liberal. In *The Neoconservatives: The Men Who Are Changing America's Politics* (a male sexist title if ever there was one, since the book identifies Midge Decter as a leading neoconservative), Peter Steinfels devotes a chapter to Bell in which he does his best to explain why Bell should be considered a conservative. As far as I can make out, it is mainly because Bell has friends who call themselves conservatives.

The tendency to speak for Bell rather than let him speak for himself reminds me of a symposium I once attended in Manhattan. The participants (including Bell, W. H. Auden, and others) sat in a row of chairs on the platform. After the speeches, questions from the floor were handed to Sidney Hook, the moderator. Hook read a question directed to Bell. "I think we can answer that easily," said Hook, or words to that effect. After giving a lengthy reply, Hook turned to the next question. The audience howled when Bell stood up, turned his chair around, and sat with his back to the audience.

Hook is another democratic socialist who is occasionally branded a neoconservative by writers who should know better. Neither Daniel Patrick Moynihan nor Seymour Martin Lipset calls himself a socialist, but they, too, reject the neoconservative label often pinned on them. Norman Podhoretz accepts the label. His slashing attack on Reagan ("The Neo-Conservative Anguish over Reagan's Foreign Policy," *The New York Times Magazine*, May 2, 1982) signaled the massive rebellion of extreme conservatives against Reagan. The resentment exploded in August 1982 when the President, finally recognizing the futility of radical supply-side theory, reversed his earlier tax cutting with a bill that increased taxes, especially on the wealthy. Naturally, Reagan could not say publicly that the supply-side enthusiasts had misled him. He had to talk about the new tax bill as if it did little more than close loopholes to produce "revenue enhancement."

On the depth of conservative resentment, see the special issue of *Conservative Digest* (July 1982) in which leading conservatives express their sorrow over what Podhoretz had called "the slipping away of a precious political opportunity that may never come again." The magazine's cover showed six photographs of Reagan that progressively faded toward blankness. *Time* and *Newsweek* covered the right-wing revolt in their August 16, 1982, issues. It remains to be seen whether the radical right will cool its anger and go back to supporting Reagan, or whether they will shift their allegiance to supply-sider Jack Kemp or some other 1984 presidential hopeful who has kept the faith.

14. These are the last lines of *The People, Yes* (1936), a book by the

democratic socialist, poet, historian, folksinger, and optimist, Carl Sandburg.

15. H. G. Wells, *The Open Conspiracy: Blue Prints for a World Revolution* (1928).

CHAPTER 10

1. G. K. Chesterton, "A Grammar of Shelley," in A *Handful of Authors* (1953), edited by Dorothy Collins.

Perfect vacuums, in the sense of nothing at all, have disappeared from quantum mechanics (QM). "Empty" space is now seen to be a constantly bubbling sea in which virtual particles of every possible type, including those not yet discovered, are coming into being as particle-antiparticle pairs, existing for a fleeting instant before they annihilate one another. (The fluctuations follow from the uncertainty relation governing time and energy.) Under certain conditions these quanta can become actual. It is now fashionable to imagine that the big bang resulted from a monstrous vacuum fluctuation. As physicist Heinz R. Pagels says in his excellent survey of QM, *The Cosmic Code* (1982), "The entire universe is a reexpression of sheer nothingness."

Before the fireball, the vacuum fluctuated into an unstable state which exploded. Of course the probability of such an explosion is extremely minute, but "since no one is waiting for the event to happen," says Pagels, and eternity is long, "it is certain to happen sometime."

When the muon, a peculiar particle (exactly like an electron except heavier), was first discovered, the physicist I. I. Rabi asked a famous question: "Who ordered *that*?" Suppose that someday physicists succeed in constructing GUT (Grand Unified Theory) as a quantum field with a structure such that eventually it will explode into all the quanta that make up our universe. We can still ask: Who ordered *that* field? There will still be the same fundamental division between those who believe the field was always there or just happened, and those who by faith believe that somebody ordered it.

2. Here is an honest statement by Isaac Asimov, than whom no one is more honest in stating his opinions. Asimov is telling philosopher Paul Kurtz (in *Free Inquiry*, Spring 1982, page 9) why, even though technically he is an agnostic, he prefers to call himself an atheist:

I am an atheist, out and out. It took me a long time to say it. I've been an atheist for years and years, but somehow I felt it was intellectually unrespectable to say one was an atheist, because it assumed knowledge that one didn't have. Somehow it was better to say one was a humanist or an agnostic. I finally decided that I'm a creature of emotion as well as of reason. Emotionally I am an atheist. I don't have the evidence to prove that God doesn't exist, but I so strongly suspect he doesn't that I don't want to waste my time.

3. Hundreds of modern novels and tales of science fiction and fantasy play with every conceivable variation of polytheism. A good summary of outstanding examples will be found under the entry "Gods and Demons" in *The Science Fiction Encyclopedia* (1979), edited by Peter Nicholls. It is a sad commentary on the state of professional philosophy that the most interesting metaphysical writing today is to be found in fantasy and science fiction, not in books by academic philosophers.

4. Thomas Aquinas asserts somewhere that "one," in the sense of the first positive integer, is not a predicate of God. Many other theologians, including Martin Luther, have said the same thing. Just as God is beyond our concepts of time and space, so also is God beyond our concepts of numbers; I would add, even beyond Georg Cantor's transfinite numbers, as Cantor himself emphasized. What can it possibly mean to say that God is 1, 2, 3, 7, the square root of 37, pi, *e*, or aleph-10? We cannot even say that God is the highest aleph because in Cantorian set theory there *is* no highest aleph.

5. G. K. Chesterton, *Orthodoxy* (1908), Chapter 8.

6. William James, *The Varieties of Religious Experience* (1902), Postscript.

7. Sören Kierkegaard, *Concluding Unscientific Postscript* (1944), translated by David F. Swenson and Walter Lowrie, Part 2, Chapter 2:

If one who lives in the midst of Christendom goes up to the house of God, the house of the true God, with the true conception of God in his knowledge, and prays, but prays in a false spirit; and one who lives in an idolatrous community prays with the entire passion of the infinite, although his eyes rest upon the image of an idol: where is there most truth? The one prays in truth to God though he worships an idol; the other prays falsely to the true God, and hence worships in fact an idol.

CHAPTER 11

1. John Dewey, *A Common Faith* (1934).

2. Sidney Hook, "Modern Knowledge and the Idea of God," *Commentary*, Volume 29, March 1960, pages 205–216.

3. If God is the universe, and the universe is everything there is, I know of no better summary of this brand of pantheism than the following doggerel by Robert Service (from his *Songs of a Sun-Lover*, 1949):

> *God is the Iz-ness of the Is,*
> *The One-ness of our Cosmic Biz;*
> *The high, the low, the near, the far,*
> *The atom and the evening star;*
> *The lark, the shark, the cloud, the clod,*
> *The whole darned Universe—that's God.*

4. William James saw clearly how this distortion of Christian theism was propelling Protestant theology in the direction of secular humanism. I quote from a footnote to the Postscript of *The Varieties of Religious Experience* (1902):

> It is strange, I have heard a friend say, to see this blind corner into which Christian thought has worked itself at last, with its God who can raise no particular weight whatever, who can help us with no private burden, and who is on the side of our enemies as much as he is on our own. Odd evolution from the God of David's psalms!

5. Today's leading defender of the view that God's relation to the world is best viewed as analogous to our mind's relation to our body is the American philosopher Charles Hartshorne. "Thus God must be the world-soul, but in such fashion that he loves each creature as a cell within his own body. . . ." In the forties Hartshorne called this view

"panentheism," which he sees as mediating between pantheism and traditional theism. The word is as ugly as Peirce's "pragmaticism," which may explain why nobody has adopted it. See Hartshorne's articles on panentheism, pantheism, analogy, God as personal, omnipotence, omniscience, omnipresence, transcendence, perfect, and infinite, in *The Encyclopedia of Religion* (1945), edited by Vergilius Ferm.

6. You'll find this story, which Asimov considers his best, in the collection *Nine Tomorrows* (1959). A listing of other tales with similar themes is given under the entry "Computers" in *The Science Fiction Encyclopedia*, edited by Peter Nicholls (1979).

7. Miguel de Unamuno, *The Tragic Sense of Life*, Chapter 5.

8. Although the dichotomy between I-It and I-Thou was made famous by Martin Buber, it is interesting to find William James putting it in a similar way in his essay "The Will to Believe": "The Universe is no longer a mere *It* to us, but a *Thou*, if we are religious; and any relation that may be possible from person to person might be possible here."

In *The Meaning of Truth* (1909), Chapter 8, James makes the same point with a startling metaphor. He compares the godless universe to a female robot:

> . . . an "automatic sweetheart," meaning a soulless body which should be absolutely indistinguishable from a spiritually animated maiden, laughing, talking, blushing, nursing us, and performing all feminine offices as tactfully and sweetly as if a soul were in her. Would any one regard her as a full equivalent? Certainly not, and why? Because, framed as we are, our egoism craves above all things inward sympathy and recognition, love and admiration. The outward treatment is valued mainly as an expression, as a manifestation of the accompanying consciousness believed in. Pragmatically, then, belief in the automatic sweetheart would not *work*, and in point of fact no one treats it as a serious hypothesis. The godless universe would be exactly similar. Even if matter could do every outward thing that God does, the idea of it would not work as satisfactorily, because the chief call for a God on modern men's part is for a being who will inwardly recognize them and judge them sympathetically. Matter disap-

points this craving of our ego, so God remains for most men the truer hypothesis, and indeed remains so for definite pragmatic reasons.

9. It is often said that when the emphasis on God's immanence is too strong, theism becomes pantheism, and when it is too weak, it becomes deism, the name given to a popular religious movement of the seventeenth and eighteenth centuries. I find this a gross oversimplification arising from a widespread but false belief that all deists maintained that a transcendent God created the universe, then forgot about it because it could get along well enough by itself.

Deists did indeed deny biblical miracles, as well as a special Judaic-Christian Revelation, but most deists thought of God as both transcendent and immanent. The truth is, it is impossible to list a set of theological doctrines that united the so-called deists of France (Voltaire, Rousseau . . .) with the deism of Kant, the views of the now-forgotten British deists, and the deism of Thomas Paine and such founding fathers of the United States as Washington, Jefferson, and Franklin.

What most deists had in common was a belief in a creator-God combined with a disbelief in Christianity as a unique revelation. Paine, for instance, although he wrote one of the world's most persuasive indictments of the Bible, believed in both God and immortality. So did Benjamin Franklin. "The longer I live," Franklin wrote somewhere, "the more proof I see that God governs in the affairs of men." Hardly a creator who winds up the world, then leaves it alone to run down.

For my broad purposes most of the deists were what I call theists. I would call myself a deist if the word were less misleading and had not dropped out of common use. As for whether God created a universe of natural laws, capable of operating by itself, or whether every event is the direct outcome of God's will, I have not the slightest notion. We have no idea what such questions even mean. If I build a machine and it runs when I leave the room, it still runs in obedience to my will, and I am still free to modify it, improve it, or destroy it. The relation of God to natural law obviously is totally outside our grasp. What difference does it make in our lives whether we think of the sun as rising every morning because of natural laws God established, or we think of it as rising because every microsecond God is giving the spinning earth little pushes? What difference does it make whether we think of the solar system as made of quantum waves capable of existing when God is not looking (whatever "looking" means!), or whether the waves and the laws that govern them are all thoughts in the mind of the Creator, as Bishop Berkeley and so many other theologians (using, of course, the scientific language of their day) maintained?

For an excellent account of the diversity of deist opinions, consult Ernest Campbell Mossner's article on deism in the *Encyclopedia of Philosophy* (1967).

10. For example, see Karl Heim's *God Transcendent* (1935), and *Christian Faith and Natural Science* (1953).

11. Peirce's statement, made partly but I suspect not entirely in jest, is on page 487 of his *New Elements of Mathematics*, Volume 2 (1976), edited by Carolyn Eisele.

12. In 1982 when a reporter asked John Bennett Shaw, Santa Fe's distinguished Sherlockian authority, if Holmes were real or fictitious, Shaw gave the best possible answer. He said "Yes."

13. C. S. Lewis, *Miracles* (1947).

14. This and the three preceding quotations from James will be found in the second volume of *The Letters of William James*, edited by his son Henry (1926).

15. From Santayana's chapter on James in *Character and Opinion in the United States* (1920).

16. Among recent attempts to alter the language of Christianity so it does not, as someone put it, "render half the human race invisible," editors of the next edition of the *Revised Standard Version* of the Bible are planning extensive changes that are now hotly debated. Should Jesus be called the "child of God"? Should the Lord's prayer begin: "Our creator who art in heaven"? *The New York Times* reported (September 12, 1980) the formation by Manhattan Episcopalian women, both clergy and laity, of a Mother Thunder Mission. Instead of singing hymns at their nonsexist services, a spokeswoman said jokingly, they will sing "hers."

For an appalling essay in defense of Christianity's inescapable masculinity, see "Priestesses in the Church?" by C. S. Lewis, in *God in the Dock* (1970). I must, however, agree with Lewis when he likens current efforts to allow the ordination of women in the Church of England to sentiments expressed in the following exchange (from *Pride and Prejudice*) about the nature of (how appropriate!) balls:

CAROLYN BINGLEY: "I should like Balls infinitely better if they were carried on in a different manner. . . . It would surely be much more rational if conversation instead of dancing made the order of the day."

CAROLYN'S BROTHER: "Much more rational, I dare say, but it would not be near so much like a Ball."

17. Elaine Pagels, *The Gnostic Gospels* (1979).

18. For an impressive account of Christianity's intolerance of homosexuality from the Middle Ages until now, with Thomas Aquinas as the leading heavy, see John Boswell, *Christianity, Social Tolerance, and Homosexuality* (1980). The question of whether Jesus was a hermaphrodite, by the way, was soberly considered by Aquinas and other Schoolmen.

CHAPTER 12

1. Whittaker Chambers, *Witness* (1952), Foreword.

2. Long before the discovery of molecules and atoms, and before the development of evolutionary cosmology, Francis Bacon expressed the same emotion. In the following passage from his essay "On Atheism," Bacon contrasts Democritus's particle theory of matter with the four-elements theory of Aristotle and the Schoolmen:

> For it is a thousand times more credible that four mutable elements and one immutable fifth essence, duly and eternally placed, need no God, than that an army of infinite small portions or seeds, unplaced, should have produced this order and beauty without a divine marshal.

David Hume considered the design argument at such length that it is not easy to say anything about it that Hume did not say. Even evolution enters the argument in Hume's *Dialogues Concerning Natural Religion* when Philo insists that the universe is more like a growing tree than a watch or a knitting-loom. Because a tree knows nothing about the ordering of its parts, why should we assume a universal mind behind what today we call the "tree" of evolution?

3. Sir Fred Hoyle and N. Chandra Wickramasinghe, *Evolution from Space* (1981).

4. On the anthropic principle see Chapter 8 of Paul Davies, *Other Worlds* (1980), and "The Anthropic Principle," by George Gale, *Scientific American*, December 1981.

5. Arthur Stanley Eddington, *Space, Time and Gravitation* (1920).

6. R. H. Dicke, and P. J. E. Peebles, "The Big Bang Cosmology— Enigmas and Nostrums," in *General Relativity: An Einstein Centenary Survey*, S. W. Hawking and W. Israel, eds. (1979).

7. Sigmund Freud, *Jokes and Their Relation to the Unconscious* (1904).

8. See *Life*, April 20, 1953, for an account of a Los Angeles landscape gardener who built an electrically operated nonsense machine with seven hundred moving parts.

9. This witty poem, with stanzas from A to Z, first appeared in *The Oxford Magazine*, November 30, 1933. I quote from its reprinting in the Fifth Anniversary Issue of *The Bulletin of the New York C. S. Lewis Society*, Vol. 6, No. 1, November 1974.

10. Raymond Smullyan, in *5000 B.C. and Other Philosophical Fantasies* (1982), has great fun playing with the ontological argument and formalizing it in different ways on the basis of certain posits. He recalls the following proof handed in by a freshman as part of her term paper: "God must exist because he wouldn't be so mean as to make me believe he exists if he doesn't." Is this much worse, Smullyan asks, than Anselm's proof? And what should we make of Smullyan's argument that the Devil, defined as the most imperfect being of which we can conceive, cannot exist, because nonexistence is an imperfection; therefore a nonexistent Devil is more imperfect than an existing one.

11. Mortimer J. Adler, *How to Think About God* (1980), Chapter 8.

12. Karl Barth, *Anselm: Fides Quaerens Intellectum* (1931).

13. Updike's review of Barth's book is reprinted in Updike's *Assorted Prose* (1965).

14. Mortimer J. Adler, *Philosopher at Large* (Macmillan, New York, 1977), pages 310–311. To me the most fascinating pages in this autobiography of a man called by Clare Boothe Luce (on the book's jacket) "the world's highest paid philosopher" are pages 314–317, whereon Adler struggles to explain why, as this country's best-known fellow-traveler of Catholicism, he has never become a Catholic. In *How to Think About God* he writes: "There have been moments in my life, during my late thirties and early forties and later in my early sixties, when I contemplated becoming a Christian—in the first instance a Roman Catholic, in the second an Episcopalian. Suffice it to say, I have not done so." His autobiography gives the reason:

I think I now know the answer to that crucial question, though I did not grasp it at the time. It lies in the state of one's will, not in the state of one's mind. The individual who is born a Jew or a Christian, a Catholic or a Protestant, can know himself to be such, however loosely or feebly, without having to live as a truly religious Jew or Christian should live. But the case of the convert to Judaism or Christianity is quite different. The only reason to *adopt* a religion is that one wishes and intends to live henceforth in accordance with its precepts, forswearing conduct and habits that are incompatible. For me to become a Roman Catholic—or, for that matter, an Anglo-Catholic or Episcopalian—would require a radical change in my way of life, a basic alteration in the direction of my day-to-day choices as well as in the ultimate objectives to be sought or hoped for. I have too clear and too detailed an understanding of moral theology to fool myself on that score. The simple truth of the matter is that I did not wish to live up to being a genuinely religious person. I could not bring myself to will what I ought to will for my whole future if I were to resolve my will, at a particular moment, with regard to religious conversion.

Note that Adler not only avoids saying whether he *believes* Christianity to be true—that is, believes with his mind that Jesus was God incarnate—he even evades saying why he evades it. When asked by a reporter, Michiko Kakutani, why he never made the Christian leap of faith, he replied (*The New York Times*, August 15, 1981):

> It's still an open question. I've gotten a great deal of intellectual satisfaction by studying and thinking about theological matters, and I think I understand intellectually what a person of Christian faith affirms. But whatever the reluctance is, I cannot make the affirmation. It may indeed be that if I were less intellectually interested in theology, I might be emotionally more interested in religion. It may be that I'm too intellectual—I don't really know the answer. If I were to confess to any serious fault, it would be the imbalance between my emphasis on the intellectual and my underemphasis on feelings. But you have to take me as I am.

Adler's inability to make the leap with his heart is certainly understandable, but does he believe with his head? Does he half-believe Jesus was the unique Son of God, or does his subjective probability estimate incline more one way than the other? It is a curious blank in Adler's intellectual career. There is something both comic and tragic about a man who has an Aristotelian love of sharp distinctions, who is uncomfortable sitting on things that are neither chairs nor not-chairs, but whose entire life has been a halfway thing. With one foot in Christianity and the other out, he walks around the fringes of the philosophic scene like a man with one foot on the curb and one in the street. Perhaps in this sense he is symbolic of today's Western world.

Hans Küng, Germany's controversial Catholic theologian, is executing a walk that impresses me as equally comic. Although I agree with Küng's approach to the traditional proofs of God as given in his 1978 book *Does God Exist?* (Küng is a fideist in the Kantian tradition, though he seems not to have read Unamuno), I find his unwillingness to walk out of the Roman Church as perplexing as Adler's unwillingness to walk in. And I feel the same way about Karl Rahner, whose "Catholicism" seems to me as bogus as Paul Tillich's "Protestantism."

Back in 1940, Adler gave a speech on "God and the Professors" in which he warned that the "positivistic" philosophy of our teachers was a greater threat to democracy than Hitler. It kicked up an academic ruckus similar to the one kicked up later by William Buckley's *God and Man at Yale*. I sent a tongue-in-cheek letter about it to *The New Republic* which appeared in their December 13, 1940, issue under the heading "The Road to Rome." Now more than forty years later the letter is still timely:

> The text of Mortimer Adler's recent paper, "God and the Professors" (to which Sidney Hook replied in the October 28 issue of your magazine), has just been printed in full in the student newspaper of the University of Chicago, and I have just finished reading it.
>
> As a former graduate student in the positivistic-minded philosophy department of the University, and a present resident of the campus community, I would like to make a plea to the readers of *The New Republic*.
>
> *Pray for the conversion of Mr. Adler.*
>
> Mr. Adler has stated many times that he intellectually accepts the doctrines of the Roman creed, but that he lacks the divine faith necessary for conversion and entrance into the Church. There is strong traditional precedent for such an attitude. Gilbert Chesterton, for example, wrote his *Orthodoxy*, one of the greatest of modern Catholic apologies, almost fifteen years before he joined the Church.
>
> So let us unite in prayer for Mr. Adler. And on the date that he enters Rome, let academic circles proclaim a day of rejoicing and thanksgiving. For Mr. Adler's brilliant and exasperating rhetoric will at last have found a home; and out of the dialectic fog will emerge a shape definite enough to be recognized, and solid enough to be worthy of honorable combat.

In his most recent book, *The Angels and Us* (1982), Adler manages to write an entire monograph on Roman Catholic angelology without revealing whether he believes angels exist or not. Of all Adler's books this is the most grotesque. It is almost as funny as Billy Graham's phenomenal best-seller of 1975, *Angels: God's Secret Agents*, though not nearly as funny as Aquinas's several hundred articles on the topic. Of course Adler must be highly selective of the thousands of subtle questions about angels that were debated by top intellects of the Middle Ages. Nowhere, for example, does he consider that fascinating quodlibet: Can angels, when they assume human form, defecate and break wind?

15. The step would mean shifting allegiance from Saint Thomas to

William of Occam, the greatest of the medieval fideists, and (understandably) Martin Luther's favorite scholastic.

Many distinguished Catholic theologians have been vigorous fideists, but the papacy has usually dealt with them harshly, regardless of how devout their nonrational beliefs in orthodox doctrines were. Occam was imprisoned and excommunicated. His French pupil, Nicolas of Autrecourt, was condemned by Pope Clement VI in 1347, forced to recant, and his books were publicly burned.

The papacy was less harsh on Montaigne's adopted son and disciple, Father Pierre Charron (1541–1603) and Leibniz's Jesuit bishop friend, Pierre Daniel Huet (1630–1721). However, the last of the great French Catholic fideists, Louis Eugene Marie Bautain (1796–1867) was condemned by Pope Gregory XVI and compelled to sign six theses, of which the first stated that reason can prove God's existence with certainty. Similarly condemned by Gregory were the nineteenth-century French traditionalists and fanatical ultramontanists who replaced human reason with a common tradition that began with God's revelation to Adam and Eve, and culminated in the absolute supremacy of the papacy.

It is a measure of the Vatican's increasing tolerance of heresy that a fideist today, like Hans Küng, is in little danger of imprisonment or excommunication. Of course if Adler became an Occamist it would mean turning his back on Thomism, which seems unlikely.

16. The quotation is from Fosdick's "On Being a Real Skeptic," in *Adventurous Religion* (1926).

17. Josiah Royce, *The Religious Aspect of Philosophy* (1885), Chapter 9.

18. Frederick Robert Tennant, *Philosophical Theology* (1928), Volume 1.

CHAPTER 13

1. I suppose it was inevitable that sooner or later someone would apply modern game theory, with its payoff matrices, to the various encounters between God and man in the Old Testament. In any case, Steven J. Brams, professor of politics at New York University, has done

it. His book, *Biblical Games: A Strategic Analysis of Stories in the Old Testament*, was published in 1980 by MIT Press, Cambridge, Massachusetts. Chapter 2, "The Meaning of Faith," deals with the two-person strategies involved in the sacrifice stories of Abraham and Jephthah.

2. The sacrifice of Jephthah's daughter has two colorful parallels in Greek mythology: the intended sacrifice of Agamemnon's daughter, and the sacrifice of Idomeneus's son. In one version of the first legend, Agamemnon vows to Artemis that if she provides him with a child he will sacrifice the dearest possession he acquires within a year. The possession is his baby daughter, Iphigenia. Agamemnon understandably refuses to carry out his foolish vow. Years later, on his way to fight the Trojans, his fleet is stranded by lack of wind. A psychic convinces him that Artemis is angry, and that only the sacrifice of Iphigenia will get the ships moving again.

Agamemnon sends for his daughter, under the pretense of marrying her to Achilles. When she learns the awful truth she consents to the sacrifice, like Jephthah's daughter, out of her deep "love" for her father, for the gods, and for her country. Just before the knife descends, Artemis takes pity on the girl and spirits her away, leaving a wild deer on the altar. Two surviving plays by Euripides deal with the legend, two operas by Gluck, and plays by Goethe, Racine, and others.

The second legend concerns Idomeneus, king of Crete, who vows to Poseidon that if he gets safely home from Troy he will sacrifice whatever living creature he first encounters. That creature is his son. Idomeneus carries out the murder, but the gods punish Crete with a terrible plague, and his countrymen exile him.

Both legends seem to me less blasphemous than the legend of Jephthah's daughter. Artemis was more merciful than Jehovah, the Cretans more just than the Israelites. It should be said that historical Judaism has strongly denounced Jephthah, and tradition has him punished with a horrible death. In the fifth canto of Dante's *Paradiso*, Beatrice likens Jephthah's crime to Agamemnon's and condemns them both. Similar judgments are in numerous tragedies based on the Jephthah story, and in an opera by Handel. A Victorian painting by Sir John Millais shows Jephthah in deep sorrow, being comforted by his simpleminded daughter. I find the picture as preposterous as Byron's poem "Jephthah's Daughter," which ends with the girl saying to her father, "And forget not I smiled as I died!"

One marvels at the mind-set of those Christian commentators who praised Jephthah's "faith," as though somehow his insane trust in Jehovah was more admirable than the trust of Agamemnon and Idomeneus in their gods. Some commentators even regarded Jephthah and his daughter, like Abraham and Isaac, as foreshadowings of the Atonement, with special reference to the prayer of Jesus, anticipating his execution, "Not my will but thine be done."

3. Joseph Butler, in his *Analogy of Religion*, writes:

> Indeed a proof, even a demonstrative one, of a future life, would not be a proof of religion. For that we are to live hereafter is just as reconcilable with the scheme of atheism, and as well to be accounted for by it, as that we are now alive is; and therefore nothing can be more absurd than to argue from that scheme, that there can be no future state.

4. The well-known passage in which Kant speaks of the two things that most fill him with awe, the starry heavens above and the moral law within, came to mind when I encountered in the second volume of Bertrand Russell's autobiography a paragraph that Kant would surely have found mystifying. Russell was near finishing his *Practice and Theory of Bolshevism* (1920), even more incisive an attack on Lenin's government than *Russia in the Shadows*, the book by H. G. Wells from which I quoted in Chapter 8. Russell is trying to decide if he should publish his book:

> To say anything against Bolshevism was, of course, to play into the hands of reaction, and most of my friends took the view that one ought not to say what one thought about Russia unless what one thought was favourable. I had, however, been impervious to similar arguments from patriots during the War, and it seemed to me that in the long run no good purpose would be served by holding one's tongue. The matter was, of course, much complicated for me by the question of my personal relations with Dora. One hot summer night, after she had gone to sleep, I got up and sat on the balcony of our room and contemplated the stars. I tried to see the question without the heat of party passion and imagined myself holding a conversation with Cassiopeia. It seemed to me

that I should be more in harmony with the stars if I published what I thought about Bolshevism than if I did not. So I went on with the work and finished the book on the night before we started for Marseilles.

5. Miguel de Unamuno, *The Tragic Sense of Life*, Chapter 8.

6. The basic argument of Pascal's wager seems to have been first explicitly given by Arnobius, a Christian theologian who lived about A.D. 300 in Africa:

> But Christ himself does not prove what he promises. It is true. For, as I have said, there cannot be any absolute proof of future events. Therefore since it is a condition of future events that they cannot be grasped or comprehended by any efforts of anticipation, is it not more reasonable, out of two alternatives that are uncertain and that are hanging in doubtful expectation, to give credence to the one that gives some hope rather than to the one that offers none at all? For in the former case there is no danger if, as is said to threaten, it becomes empty and void; while in the latter case the danger is greatest, that is, the loss of salvation, if when the time comes it is found that it was not a falsehood.

I quote from Augustus De Morgan's *Budget of Paradoxes*, Vol. 2 (1872), where a footnote supplies a translation of the Latin passage which De Morgan quotes from Pierre Bayle, a seventeenth-century French Protestant of extreme fideist views. "Really Arnobius seems to have got as much out of the notion," comments De Morgan, ". . . as if he had been fourteen centuries later, with the arithmetic of chances to help him."

7. Count Manuel's remarks are almost a paraphrase of the following passage from Cicero's essay "On Old Age":

> And after all, should this my firm persuasion of the soul's immortality, prove to be a mere delusion; it is at least a pleasing delusion; and I will cherish it to my latest breath. I have the satisfaction in the meantime to be assured, that if death should utterly extinguish my existence, as some minute philosophers assert; the groundless hope I entertained of an after-life in some better state,

cannot expose me to the derision of these wonderful sages, when they and I shall be no more.

8. George Santayana, *Character and Opinion in the United States* (1920).

9. Raymond Smullyan, mathematician and magician, has this to say about science and magic in a whimsical essay on astrology in his book *The Tao is Silent* (1977):

> Speaking of magic, I am genuinely open to the possibility that the entire Universe works ultimately by magic rather than by scientific principle. Who knows, perhaps the Universe is a great magician who does not want us to suspect his magical powers and so arranges most of the visible phenomena in a scientific and orderly fashion in order to fool us and prevent us from knowing him as he really is! Yes, this is a genuine possibility, and the more I think about it, the more I like the idea!

Smullyan's suggestion is, of course, not far from the Hindu doctrine that the entire universe is an illusion. Although the medieval Schoolmen thought the universe was real enough, many of them (notably William of Occam) argued that God was quite capable of annihilating, say, a chair or a star, substituting for it the illusion of a chair or a star which we would be unable to distinguish from a real one.

10. Miguel de Unamuno, *The Tragic Sense of Life*. op. cit. Chapter 9.

CHAPTER 14

1. C. S. Lewis, *The Screwtape Letters* (1942).

2. Emily Dickinson, *The Complete Poems of Emily Dickinson*, Thomas H. Johnson, ed. (1960), poem 564.

3. John Burroughs, "An Open Door," in *Indoor Studies* (1889).

4. Atheists occasionally express frustration, sometimes sincerely, sometimes sarcastically, over having no God to thank. I will give an

example of each. In *Our Knowledge of God* (1959), John Baillie quotes from a letter of Katherine Mansfield in which she expresses her delight with a spot in the Alps where she was staying: "If only one could make some small grasshoppery sound of praise to some one, thanks to some one—but who?" *The New York Times* (November 19, 1956) quotes Nikita Khrushchev: "If we could have the revolution over again, we would carry it out more sensibly and with smaller losses. But history does not repeat itself. The situation is favorable for us. If God existed, we would thank him for this."

The impulse to express gratitude to God certainly does not prove God exists, but Baillie is surely correct in seeing this as evidence of a universal desire to model God as a person. You can thank a person for giving you a drink of water. You can't thank a cloud.

5. "Astrée-Luce and the Cardinal," book four of Thornton Wilder's *The Cabala* (1926), is about a pious Catholic lady who was never troubled by the paradoxes of prayer until one day when a learned Italian cardinal, to whom she is devoted, argues with her. The aging cardinal, knowing that Astrée-Luce never thought deeply about her beliefs, foolishly decides that for her own good he should instill some doubts. As a cruel intellectual game, he defends the view that one should never pray for anything because it implies the heresy that God will change his mind. The cardinal does not realize how much he has shaken the poor woman's faith until a later occasion when she fires a revolver at him.

6. James Boswell, *The Life of Samuel Johnson*, 1772 section.

7. For an unusually barbaric account of just such a corrupting experiment, see Chapter 18 of the first book of Kings. It is a time of great drought. Elijah, in conflict with the prophets of Baal, proposes testing the powers of their respective gods. Each side sacrifices a bull and demands a sign. Only Elijah's sacrifice produces results. Elijah then slays the prophets of Baal, all 450 of them, and a great downpour follows.

8. H. G. Wells, "Answer to Prayer," *The New Yorker*, May 1, 1937.

9. *Encyclopedia of Religion and Ethics*, James Hastings, ed. (1908).

10. C. S. Lewis, *Miracles* (1947).

11. Although the timeless model is consistent, it is difficult not to feel in it the age-old tug of war between fate and freedom of will, and be disturbed by the implication that history is frozen on some inscrutable metalevel. In a footnote to his "Dilemma of Determinism" James asks: "Is not the notion of eternity being given at a stroke to omniscience only just another way of whacking upon us the block-universe, and of denying that possibilities exist? . . . To say that time is an illusory appearance is only a roundabout manner of saying there is no real plurality, and that the frame of things is an absolute unit. Admit plurality, and time may be its form."

James preferred the concept of a limited, finite God, bound by time just as we are, but of course James was only letting his imagination juggle questions for which there are no earthly answers. How can we know whether God is in or out of some sort of hypertime when we do not even understand the ordinary time in which we ourselves grow old and die?

12. It is trivially obvious that if certain petitionary prayers are made in a social context, such as a congregation praying for funds to build a new church, or for the recovery of someone ill, such prayers can stimulate the behavior of people in ways that may help answer the prayers. Members of a congregation will be more likely to make donations, visit the sick, and so on. I mention this only because Henry Nelson Wieman, in *An Encyclopedia of Religion* (1945), edited by Vergilius Ferm, contributes a short article on prayer in which he maintains that this is the only way God answers prayer. "This deepening and widening of community wherein we are more responsive to one another is what answers prayer."

Although Wieman was a distinguished professor in the University of Chicago's Divinity School, he did not believe in a personal God; indeed, if there is any difference between Wieman's "theology" and John Dewey's atheism, I have not been able to discern it. I find his article on prayer one of the funniest examples I know of theological language obfuscation.

13. Steve Allen, *Mark it and Strike It* (1960).

14. "The point which I should first wish to understand," says Socrates in Plato's *Euthyphro*, "is whether the pious or holy is beloved by the gods because it is holy, or holy because it is beloved by the gods."

15. Lord Dunsany "The Men of Yarnith," in *Time and the Gods* (1906).

CHAPTER 15

1. *The Complete Poems of Emily Dickinson*, Thomas H. Johnson, ed. (1960), Poem 1624.

2. Charles Fort *Wild · alents* (1932)

3. This quotation and the earlier one from Schopenhauer are from Paul Edwards's excellent essay "Life, Meaning and Value of," in *The Encyclopedia of Philosophy* (1967).

In his major work, *The Philosophy of the Unconscious* (1869), Von Hartmann maintains that although the fundamental reality has no conscious mind, it does have a secret, subliminal, evolutionary plan. (Von Hartmann accepted evolution, but not Darwin's mechanistic theory of how it operates.) The goal of history is neither an afterlife nor a utopia of happy creatures on earth. The latter is as much an illusion as the former because cultural progress inevitably produces greater misery. The goal of the Unconscious is to eliminate the evil it has blindly created, and the only way to do this is by eliminating all life.

In Von Hartmann's incredible pantheism, "God" is originally unconscious, yet somehow possessing what Schopenhauer called Will. By a process we cannot comprehend, it willed into existence a world in which, through us, it became conscious of the evil it had brought about. At some far-off time, humanity will come to realize that the only way to redeem the folly of creating life is to abolish all life. This will allow God to lapse back again into blissful sleep where there is no evil anywhere because there is no living thing to experience pain.

The final suicide will become possible, Von Hartmann believed, through the advancement of science. Of course he had no inkling of how quickly science would provide humanity with this power to self-destruct, but because of its happy possibility he regarded his pessimism as essentially *optimistic*.

Von Hartmann's voluminous writings were enormously popular in his day, and the object of intense controversy. One of the best attacks on his views was actually written by himself. He did not reveal his authorship until his enemies had praised the book and quoted him against himself!

4. For some frightening speculations about God's motive in allowing Job to suffer so irrationally, including the hypothesis that God told Job a false cover story to conceal a truth too terrifying for Job to contemplate, see the lengthy footnote 3, ￭n Chapter 5, in Robert Nozick's *Philosophical Explanations* (1981).

5. The 1916 text of this book is a corrupt version. The true text did not become available until 1969, with the publication of *Mark Twain's Mysterious Stranger Manuscripts*, by William M. Gibson. See also *Mark Twain's Mysterious Stranger: A Study of the Manuscript Texts*, by Sholom J. Kahn (1978).

6. From *The Collected Poems of Stephen Crane* (1930).

7. Robert G. Ingersoll, *Some Mistakes of Moses* (1879), Chapter 23.

8. From an essay of Unamuno's I have not read. The quotation is from *Miguel de Unamuno* (1966), by Julián Marías, Chapter 8.

9. James Branch Cabell, *Jurgen* (1919), Chapter 49.

10. C. S. Lewis, *A Grief Observed* (1963).

11. I never expected to hear Oral Roberts say anything I would find worth quoting, but on one of his 1982 television specials he surprised me. Speaking about irrational tragedies of the sort that seem so unnecessary, Roberts summed up all that a theist can say in one casual sentence: "God knows something you don't know."

CHAPTER 16

1. I did not include the Unity movement, because it professes to have no dogmas. However, both Charles and Myrtle Fillmore, who founded this New Thought cult in Kansas City in the 1890s, were passionate believers in reincarnation, and today most of Unity's ministers and members share that belief.

2. I. J. Good, *The Scientist Speculates* (1962).

3. John Stuart Mill, in his essay "Nature," expresses surprise that

Leibniz's *Theodicy* was "so strangely mistaken for a system of optimism and, as such, satirized by Voltaire on grounds which do not even touch the author's argument." The main point of *Candide* is that at this stage of history we live in what is not the best possible world, a point so obvious that Leibniz took it for granted. It is as trivial as asserting that a teen-ager is not the best possible adult. Leibniz's world is the best possible only in its incomprehensible totality, and in the long run, which of course includes an afterlife.

4. *Collected Papers of Charles Sanders Peirce*, edited by Charles Hartshorne and Paul Weiss, Vol. 6 (1935), paragraph 507.

5. Ibid, paragraphs 508–510.

6. Ralph Barton Perry, *The Thought and Character of William James*, Vol. 1 (1935).

7. G. K. Chesterton, *The Man Who Was Thursday* (1908).

8. When I call Sunday a symbol of God I oversimplify. As Chesterton made clear in his autobiography, Sunday "is not so much God, in the sense of religion or irreligion, but rather Nature as it appears to the pantheist, whose pantheism is struggling out of pessimism." Earlier, in an interview partly reprinted in Maisie Ward's biography *Gilbert Keith Chesterton* (1943), he said:

> People have asked me whom I mean by Sunday. Well, I think, on the whole, and allowing for the fact that he is a person in a tale—I think you can take him to stand for Nature as distinguished from God. Huge, boisterous, full of vitality, dancing with a hundred legs, bright with the glare of the sun, and at first sight, somewhat regardless of us and our desires.
>
> There is a phrase used at the end, spoken by Sunday: "Can ye drink from the cup that I drink of?" which seems to mean that Sunday is God. That is the only serious note in the book, the face of Sunday changes, you tear off the mask of Nature and you find God.

Chesterton wrote his "nightmare" long before he became a Catholic, and he is on record as denying it is a Christian allegory. Well, it certainly turns into one at the end. The book has puzzled lots of readers, and perhaps GK himself did not fully know what he was trying to say. Amory Blaine, in F. Scott Fitzgerald's *This Side of Paradise*, says he liked the novel without understanding it. When the pulp magazine *Famous Fantastic Mysteries* reprinted the entire novel (March 1944), its readers complained in a later issue that they didn't understand it either.

I see it like this: In the sense that all of nature is part of God, then Sunday is God. In the sense that the Creator transcends the universe, Sunday is not God. He is, as Gary Wills puts it in *Chesterton: Man and Mask* (1961), "the God of Whitman." Only at the end of the story, when Sunday's face expands until it covers the sky and all goes black, do we hear the voice of the Creator and understand that behind Sunday is the true Sabbath, the peace of God, in which good and evil have their inscrutable final reconciliation.

Wills has written an excellent introduction to a 1975 edition of *The Man Who Was Thursday*. I hope that someday he will give us *The Annotated Thursday*.

9. Poets have often used musical discord as a metaphor for evil. I think in particular of Robert Browning's "Abt Vogler" ("Why rushed the discords in, but that harmony should be prized?") and George Meredith's sentimental but touching "Martin's Puzzle," in which Martin tries to comprehend why a girl has been cruelly crippled by an accident ("They tell us that discord, though discord alone,/Can be harmony when the notes properly fit:/Am I judging all things from a single false tone?").

10. George Santayana, "Josiah Royce," in *Character and Opinion in the United States* (1920).

11. F. R. Tennant, "The Problem of Evil," in *Philosophical Theology*, Vol. 2 (1930).

12. John Hick, "Grounds for Disbelief in God," in *Philosophy of Religion* (1963).

13. Thornton Wilder, *The Bridge of San Luis Rey* (1927).

14. *The Letters of Lewis Carroll* (1979), edited by Morton N. Cohen, Vol. 2.

15. It is possible to give this argument in a game-theoretic framework. See Steven J. Brams, *Superior Beings: Game-Theoretic Implications of Omniscience, Omnipotence, Immortality, and Incom-*

prehensibility, a forthcoming book. In Chapter 13, Note 1, I referred to Brams's earlier work, *Biblical Games*. I have not yet decided just what to make of these two books. They may be significant contributions to theology, or little more than ingenious attempts to apply game and decision theory in areas where such applications are unproductive. Brams concerns himself exclusively with Old Testament myths, but clearly his approach is just as applicable (or inapplicable) to myths in the New Testament, Homer, the Koran, or the sacred books of any other religious tradition. It is Brams's view that it may be rational for a god who wants to be believed to adopt a mixed strategy in which there is genuinely random behavior of the sort that would appear to us as irrational.

16. Miguel de Unamuno, *Life of Don Quixote and Sancho* (1905).

17. Bertrand Russell, *A History of Western Philosophy* (1945).

18. Russell's refusal to let his heart tell his head anything about God is poignantly revealed in this passage from a letter he wrote in 1918, and which he includes in the second volume of his autobiography:

> Even when one feels nearest to other people, something in one seems obstinately to belong to God and to refuse to enter into any earthly communion—at least that is how I should express it if I thought there was a God. It is odd isn't it? I care passionately for this world, and many things and people in it, and yet . . . what is it all? There *must* be something more important, one feels, though I don't *believe* there is. I am haunted—some ghost, from some extra-mundane region, seems always trying to tell me something that I am to repeat to the world, but I cannot understand the message.

Katherine Tait, Russell's only daughter, became a convert to the Church of England. In the chapter about this in *My Father Bertrand Russell* (1975) she writes movingly about her father's inability to understand the message. "I believe myself that his whole life was a search for God. . . . Somewhere at the back of my father's mind, at the bottom of his heart, in the depths of his soul, there was an empty space that had once been filled by God, and he never found anything else to put in it."

Mrs. Tait ends her chapter this way:

I would have liked to convince my father that I had found what he had been looking for, the ineffable something he had longed for all his life. I would have liked to persuade him that the search for God does not have to be vain. But it was hopeless. He had known too many blind Christians, bleak moralists who sucked the joy from life and persecuted their opponents; he would never have been able to see the truth they were hiding. He should have been a saint; he had the passion, the intemperate longing for truth and justice, the yearning for a world of peace and love. Perhaps he was a saint, even without the faith. God's gadfly, sent to challenge the smugness of the churches with a righteousness greater than their own.

I could not have persuaded him, could not even talk to him about religion. All I could do was trust him to God's care, knowing that God loved him more than I did and would do what was best for him.

CHAPTER 17

1. G. K. Chesterton, *All Things Considered* (1909), Chapter 22.

2. Writing on personal immortality in *First and Last Things* (1908), H. G. Wells said the same thing:

My idea of the unknown scheme is of something so wide and deep that I cannot conceive it encumbered by my egotism perpetually. I shall serve my purpose and pass under the wheel and end. That distresses me not at all. Immortality would distress and perplex me. If I may put this in a mixture of theological and social language, I cannot respect, I cannot believe in a God who is always going about with me.

3. Jorge Luis Borges, "The Immortal," in *Labyrinths: Selected Stories and Other Writings* (1962), edited by Donald Yates and James Irby.

"I think of death as a great hope," said Borges, age eighty-two, to an Associated Press writer in November 1981. "I hope to be wiped out, utterly forgotten, saved by nothingness."

Isaac Asimov voiced a similar hope in an essay on life after death that closes his collection *The Road to Infinity* (1979). Asimov says he prefers "nothingness" to any sort of heaven. After giving his reasons for believing that his "I" will be gone forever when he dies, he adds: "And that suits me fine." Maybe my friend Isaac really believes that this suits him fine, but I wonder.

4. From the chapter on "The Hunger for Immortality" in Unamuno's *Tragic Sense of Life*.

5. Morris Raphael Cohen, *A Dreamer's Journey* (1949), Chapter 28.

6 From "Ideal Immortality," a chapter in Santayana's *Reason in Religion* (1905)

Santayana writes with crystal clarity. In contrast, Whitehead's Ingersoll lecture on immortality (reprinted in *The Philosophy of Alfred North Whitehead*, edited by Paul Schilipp, 1941) is a masterpiece of ambiguity, unintelligibility, and disorganized writing. Whitehead does his best to prevent readers from realizing that he has no expectation of living again

7. For a good summary of Tillich's misty view that immortality consists solely in being remembered by God, not in the continuation of an individual life in time, see John Hick, *Death and Eternal Life* (1976), Chapter 11. Hick also discusses the same fake immortality, though more clearly expressed, in the writings of Charles Hartshorne. Our "book of life" closes at death, Hartshorne believes, but remains perfectly preserved in God's mind. Nothing is added to it, nothing taken away. We exist forever, in the sense that God never forgets, preserved like a motion picture film. Although Hartshorne seems to find this inspiring and comforting, I agree with Hick that it severely distorts ordinary language to call such a frozen memory, of what we "are" from birth to death, an "afterlife."

8. The quotation is from Russell's *What I Believe* (1925).

9. All ancient cultures—Judaic, Egyptian, Greek, Roman, and so on—had their oracles and soothsayers who claimed the power not only to foresee the future but also to communicate with the dead. Plotinus, at the close of his treatise on the immortality of the soul, cites such communication as empirical support for the rational arguments for life after death.

10. Mark Twain, *The Adventures of Huckleberry Finn*, Chapter 30.

11. W. Somerset Maugham, "The Flip of a Coin," in *Ashenden: or, The British Agent* (1927).

12. James Boswell, *The Life of Johnson*, 1775 section.

13. From an article by Dwight MacDonald in *Partisan Review*, May/June 1950.

14. *The Letters of William James* (1920), edited by his son Henry, Vol. 2.

15. Ralph Waldo Emerson, "Immortality," in *The Complete Works of R. W. Emerson* (1903–1904).

16. James Branch Cabell, *Jurgen* (1919), Chapter 23.

17. Raymond Smullyan, *The Tao Is Silent* (1977).

18. H. G. Wells, *Men Like Gods* (1927).

19. Wells, *The World of William Clissold* (1926), Vol. 2.

20. Wells's letter is in the third volume (years 1944–1969) of *The Autobiography of Bertrand Russell* (1969).

21. We are here concerned only with how altruism is justified rationally, not with what causes a person, in rare moments of crisis, to sacrifice his or her life for someone else or for a cause. Sociobiologists maintain that although altruistic behavior is largely a product of conditioning, there is a genetic component which evolved because it has survival value for a species. Unfortunately, the same writers believe, there are also genes for egoistic impulses.

Edward O. Wilson argues (*On Human Nature*, 1978) that our genetic heritage is a mixed bag with respect to these conflicting impulses, and now we are faced with the dilemma of deciding (by free will?) which kind of impulse, egoistic or altruistic, to suppress and which to enlarge. The dilemma will become awesome if and when human evolution can be altered by genetic engineering. At this point Wilson drifts off into Wellsian expressions of vague hope that somehow we will choose wisely, and so create a better world, the nature of which remains unspecified.

Here is an interesting reflection on egoism versus altruism, from a

Christian viewpoint, that I found in a letter Lewis Carroll wrote to his lifelong friend, the actress Ellen Terry:

> And so you have found out that secret—one of the deep secrets of Life—that all, that is really *worth* the doing, is what we do for *others*? Even as the old adage tells us, "What I spent, that I lost; what I gave, that I had." Casuists have tried to twist "doing good" into another form of "doing evil," and have said "you get pleasure yourself by giving this pleasure to another: so it is merely a refined kind of selfishness, as your own pleasure is a motive for what you do." I say "it is *not* selfishness, that my own pleasure should be *a* motive so long as it is not *the* motive that would outweigh the other, if the two came into collision?" The "selfish man" is he who would still do the thing, even if it harmed others, so long as it gave *him* pleasure: the "unselfish man" is he who would still do the thing, even if it gave him no pleasure, so long as it pleased *others*. But, when both motives pull together, the "unselfish man" is *still* the unselfish man, even though his own pleasure *is* one of his motives! I am very sure that God takes real *pleasure* in seeing his children happy! And, when I read such words as "looking unto Jesus, the author and finisher of our faith, who *for the joy that was set before him* endured the cross," I believe them to be *literally true*

I take this from Morton N. Cohen's essay "The Actress and the Don: Ellen Terry and Lewis Carroll," in *Lewis Carroll: A Celebration* (1982), edited by Edward Guiliano.

22. William James, "The Moral Philosopher and the Moral Life," in *The Will to Believe* (1903).

23. G. K. Chesterton, *Manalive* (1912), Part 2, Chapter 1. There are many similar remarks, in Chesterton's writings, on the importance of limits in both life and art. One of the most essential parts of a painting, GK liked to say, is its perimeter.

Robert Nozick considers the same point in the last chapter of *Philosophical Explanations* (1981). He scorns the argument that death is good because it makes life meaningful, but he grants that the fact of death, and our lack of knowledge about a future life does form a boundary that creates, in the words of Victor Frankl, "the imperative of utilizing our lifetimes to the utmost."

"It would appear, then," Nozick writes, "that persons who were or could become immortal should choose to set a temporal limit to their lives in order to escape meaninglessness; scientists who discovered some way to avoid *natural* death should suppress their discoveries . . . perhaps, you do best thinking you are mortal and very long-lived (having no good idea of approximately when the end would come, whether after 200 or 2,000 or 20,000 years), while in fact being immortal. . . . Persons who are immortal need not be limited to the desires and designs of mortals; they might well think up new plans that, in Parkinsonian fashion, expand to fill the available time."

24. Miguel de Unamuno, *The Tragic Sense of Life*, Chapter 6.

CHAPTER 18

1. William James, "The Problem of Being," Chapter 3 of *Some Problems of Philosophy* (1911).

2. Vladimir Nabokov, *Speak, Memory* (1967).

3. Nabokov, *Pale Fire* (1962), Commentary on line 549.

4. James Young Simpson, *Man and the Attainment of Immortality* (1922). Surely one reason why the annihilation of the wicked has always been a popular doctrine in the history of unorthodox Christianity is that, in contrast to the teachings of Jesus, it clearly seems to be the opinion of Saint Paul. It takes a great deal of verbal acrobatics to make Paul's apocalyptic vision anything other than that of a universe finally washed clean of Satan and his angels, and of all evil, with no perpetual hell to remind the saved of God's unrelenting cruelty.

The history of annihilationism, including all the relevant biblical references, is given at great length in the Seventh Day Adventist two-volume study, *The Conditionalist Faith of Our Fathers* (1966) by LeRoy Edwin Froom. It is a valuable reference, though marred by occasional errors, by heavy-handed Adventist rhetoric, and by art of the crudest possible sort. Seventh Day Adventists seem unable to outgrow the practice of saturating their books with pictures that resemble soft-drink advertisements.

5. My quote is from a UPI story in *The New York Times*, Sunday, October 23, 1977.

5. This essay, which Carroll intended as part of a book on religious topics which he never wrote, first appeared in *The Lewis Carroll Picture Book*, edited by his nephew Stuart Dodgson Collingwood (1899), reprinted in 1961 as a Dover paperback entitled *Diversions and Digressions of Lewis Carroll*. See also *The Letters of Lewis Carroll*, Vol. 2, edited by Morton N. Cohen (Oxford University Press, New York, 1979), pages 745–747, 1040–1043.

"If I were forced to believe that the God of Christians was capable of inflicting 'eternal punishment' . . . I should give up Christianity," Carroll wrote to his sister. Over the centuries this has been a leading reason why many persons, including me, have given up Christianity.

7. Although I rarely read Billy Graham's syndicated column in our local newspaper, a passage in his March 13, 1982, reply to someone with the initials J.D.C. caught my eye. J.D.C. had been thinking about accepting Christ, but wanted first "to live it up a little." Billy warned against procrastinating. "Think how tragic it would be if you delayed accepting Christ, and your life was snuffed out in an automobile wreck or other accident. You would be lost eternally because of your delay."

For Billy, *lost* of course means perpetual torment in hell. Can you conceive of a merciful God capable of condemning anyone to eternal flames merely because he or she had not converted to Christianity before a sudden fatal accident? Surely there must be occasions, in moments of prayer or contemplation, when Billy is shaken by the horror of this doctrine. When such evil thoughts come, we all know what Billy does. He orders Satan to get behind him.

8. I do not know where in the thirteen volumes of Robert Ingersoll's collected writings and speeches this passage appears. I found it in Elbert Hubbard's *Little Journey to the Home of Robert Ingersoll* (1902), a fine tribute to a brave and good man. Though he was not a theist, Ingersoll's booming voice was like a great wind that left American Christendom a bit cleaner for having blown through it.

9. G. K. Chesterton, in an essay called "January One," from *Lunacy and Letters* (1958), edited by Dorothy Collins.

10. Thomas Aquinas, *Summa contra Gentiles*, IV, 98. See Volume 4, page 300ff, of the English translation by the Dominican fathers.

11. C. S. Lewis, *Miracles: A Preliminary Study* (1947), Chapter 16.

12. Karl Barth, *Credo*, Chapter 16.

13. Vladimir Nabokov, *Pale Fire*, op. cit., Canto 2 of the poem.

14. John Milton, *Paradise Lost*, Book V, lines 574–576. Ralph Waldo Emerson quotes the passage in his admirable essay "Immortality."

15. Miguel de Unamuno, *The Tragic Sense of Life*, Chapter 10

CHAPTER 19

1. In *Death and Eternal Life* (1976), Chapter 15, John Hick defends the reconstitution model on the grounds that there is no good reason why we cannot extend what we mean by "same person" to an exact replica, created without causal continuity, in another space at some time after a person's death. He considers the following objection: If God can create one replica, it is conceivable he can create two or more who would exist simultaneously. But this is absurd Therefore the reconstitution model is absurd.

Hick agrees that if creations of multiple replicas occurred, "our present system of concepts would be unable to deal with it. . . . Our concept of 'the same person' has not been developed to cope with such a situation. . . . A person is by definition unique. There cannot be two people who are exactly the same in every respect, including their consciousness and memories. That is to say, if there were a situation satisfying this description, our present concept of 'person' would utterly break down under the strain."

However, Hick sensibly maintains, from the fact that we would be "linguistically helpless" if the universe permitted multiple re-creations of a person, it does not follow that the universe does not permit single re-creations.

Dr. J. H. Kellogg, in the 1879 book cited in Note 11 below, said it this way:

> It is very easy to conjure up in the fancy any number of absurd difficulties which might be created, should the Almighty choose to employ his power for such a purpose; but it should be especially

borne in mind that no difficulty of the sort suggested, as a multiple number of identities, could possibly occur without the special exhibition of creative power. In this we should have a still greater difficulty involved, since we should have the strange spectacle of an omnipotent, omniscient, all-wise Creator, exercising his power for the express purpose of involving himself in difficulty.

2. "Dark Nuptial" first appeared in *Startling Stories Magazine* in 1952, and was reprinted in *Startling Stories* (1954), edited by Sam Mines.

3. The earliest known use of a matter transmitter in fiction is in "The Man Without a Body," by Edward Page Mitchell. This comic horror tale originally appeard in the *New York Sun* (1877), and you will find it in Sam Moskowitz's collection of Mitchell's pioneering yarns, *The Crystal Man* (1973). Professor Dummkopf succeeds in transmitting a cat by wire, but when he tries it on himself there is a battery failure and only his head is sent. For a history of matter-transmission machines in science-fiction stories and films, see the entry on "Matter Transmission" in *The Science Fiction Encyclopedia* (1979), edited by Peter Nicholls, and the entry on "Technologies and Artifacts" in *The Visual Encyclopedia of Science Fiction*, edited by Brian Ash (1977).

4. Feynman's remarks are from his essay on "The Value of Science" in *Frontiers in Science* (1958), edited by Edward Hutchings, Jr.

5. From "An Outline of Intellectual Rubbish," reprinted in Bertrand Russell's *Unpopular Essays* (1950).

6. *The Letters of Lewis Carroll*, Vol. 1, edited by Morton N. Cohen (Oxford University Press, New York, 1979), page 604.

7. Raymond Smullyan, *The Chess Mysteries of Sherlock Holmes* (1979).

8. For examples and an analysis of these bewildering geometrical vanishes, see Chapters 7 and 8 of my *Mathematics, Magic and Mystery* (1956), and Mel Stover's article "The Disappearing Man and Other Vanishing Paradoxes" in *Games* magazine, November 1980, pages 14–18.

9. Joseph Butler and some later thinkers maintained that although

memory is an essential aspect of the persistence in time of the same person, it is insufficient to guarantee identity. In an appendix, "Of Personal Immortality," to his *Analogy of Religion*, Bishop Butler attacks what he calls Locke's "wonderful mistake," the error of supposing that memory is sufficient to provide continuity for the self. One must assume, Butler argues, a soul that is either a substance or a property of a substance. To base immortality on a reconstituted body is an "inexpressible absurdity" which can spring only from a "secret corruption of the heart." Butler's appendix is reprinted in *Body, Mind, and Death* (1964), edited by Anthony Flew. On this Locke/Butler conflict, see the article on "Personal Identity," by Terence Penelhum, in *The Encyclopedia of Philosophy* (1967).

10. Additional puzzles involving personal identity (some based on the switching of half brains like the patching process of Baum's Boolooroo of the Blues) are examined in Robert Nozick's *Philosophical Explanations* (1981), Chapter 1, Section 1. See also the essays and fictional pieces, with commentary by the editors, in *The Mind's I* (1981), compiled and edited by Douglas Hofstadter and David Denning.

"Mindswaps," in which bodies exchange minds (or vice versa), have been so fully exploited in science fiction that it is hard to invent a basic plot that hasn't been used. Perhaps the earliest example of a mindswap is Edward Page Mitchell's "Exchanging Their Souls" (1877), in which a prince and wheelwright swap bodies. (The story can be found in *The Crystal Man*, the collection cited in Note 3 above.) There are SF stories in which adult humans swap minds with animals, extraterrestrials, babies, and computers. Plots can get complicated when multiple swaps occur.

Mindswaps have been successfully performed with flatworms, the lowliest form of animal life with brains. After the tiny brains are switched, the cut nerves repair themselves, and in ten days both worms are behaving normally

11. LeRoy Edwin Froom, *The Conditionalist Faith of Our Fathers* (1966). The work has an extensive bibliography. Conspicuously missing from it is a now-rare work, *Harmony of Science and the Bible on the Nature of the Soul and the Doctrine of the Resurrection*, by Dr. John Harvey Kellogg, the founder of a sanitarium at Battle Creek, Michigan, and of Kellogg's breakfast cereals. The book appeared in

1879, when Kellogg was a leader of the Adventist movement, but after disagreements with Ellen Gould White, the Church's prophet, he was excommunicated. For the story of this, as well as a splendid account of the life of Mrs. White and the early history of the Adventist Church, see *Prophetess of Health: A Study of Ellen G. White* (1976), by Ronald L. Numbers.

Kellogg's more mature thoughts on the reconstitution model are given in his book *The Living Temple* (1903). After considering what is meant by the identity of a bushel of wheat, a river, a lake, a community of persons, a rainbow, and a tree, Kellogg sensibly concludes that when we speak of something remaining the same, the identifying principle "depends on the nature of the thing to be identified." For the human being, he argues that the identity is preserved by the body's form, which he likens to a record of music played by the body, and permanently recorded in the mind of God. The form is not the person's consciousness, for that requires a body, but the abstract pattern of that person's individuality as God remembers it. After death, "the singing is no longer heard, but so long as the melody, the tune, is preserved, the song may be reproduced."

Curiously, although Froom does not mention Dr. Kellogg, he discusses with high praise a history of conditionalism by Dudley Marvin Canright, a Seventh Day Adventist minister who later repudiated the Church and wrote a savage attack on Mrs. White. Canright's *History of the Doctrine of the Immortality of the Soul* was first published by the Church in 1871. The second edition (1881), greatly expanded, was titled *History of the Doctrine of the Soul.* His *Life of Mrs. E. G. White: Seventh Day Adventist Prophet, Her False Claims Refuted,* was published in 1919.

On the history of conditionalism, see also Norman T. Burns's valuable monograph *Christian Mortalism from Tyndale to Milton* (1972), and the article on "Conditional Immortality" in James Hastings's *Encyclopedia of Religion and Ethics* (1922).

12. The use in religious languages of words for such transcendental concepts as *God* and *immortal soul* has certain parallels with the use of words for theoretical concepts in the language of science. If two different theoretical terms have the same operational meanings, many philosophers of science believe they are just two ways of saying the same thing. It may be that the concept of an immortal soul made of a divine

430 • The WHYS of a Philosophical Scrivener

substance has the same pragmatic meaning for believers as the concept of God's everlasting memory of a person's pattern.

Philosophers of science have a way of showing that sentences in physics involving theoretical terms can in principle be translated into what is called a "Ramsey sentence," which contains only observational terms, and that the two sentences have the same empirical content. Of course any Ramsey sentence would be enormously long and too cumbersome to be of any use. It has occurred to me there may be a similar way of writing a theological Ramsey sentence in which any statement involving transcendent terms could be replaced by a much longer sentence containing only pragmatic terms describing how a believer felt about transcendental concepts and how they influence his behavior. The fact that a long theological Ramsey sentence with no transcendent terms would have the same pragmatic meaning as a shorter sentence with transcendent terms would, of course, no more show that such entities as God and the soul do not exist than Ramsey sentences in physical theory show that electrons and gravity fields do not exist.

13. Rudy Rucker has pointed out (in conversation) that believers in mortalism can give a simple explanation of Jesus' remark to the good thief by taking "today" as defined within the time frame of the thief. Since he would have no consciousness until he is reconstituted, even though billions of years may intervene between his death and resurrection, even though an infinity of years may intervene, there will be for him no passage of time. In his consciousness, his resurrection will follow instantaneously, "today," after his death on the cross.

14. Mortimer J. Adler, *The Difference of Man and the Difference It Makes* (1967).

15. Adler, "The Confusion of the Animalists," in *The Great Ideas Today, 1975.*

16. Polyps are loosely organized animals, so constituted that if they are cut into small pieces, each piece will grow into a complete polyp. The discovery of this had a strong influence on the rise of French materialism in the eighteenth century, in particular on Julien de La Mettrie, whose book *L'Homme machine (Man a Machine)* defends the now commonplace opinion that the brain is no more than an extremely complicated computer made of protein. See "Trembley's Polyp, La Mettrie, and Eighteenth-Century French Materialism," by

Aram Vartanian, in *Roots of Scientific Thought* (1957), edited by Philip P. Wiener and Aaron Noland.

17. A voluminous world literature wrestles with the question of whether animals survive death, most of it written in the seventeenth and eighteenth centuries in response to Descartes's contention that animals are soulless automatons. For those who believe both in personal immortality and in evolution, the problem of course is where to draw the line. A similar problem concerns human embryos. If a fertilized egg dies a few hours after conception, it certainly cannot be said to have possessed anything resembling a brain with memories. Of course if it had an immortal soul in the Platonic sense, there is no problem.

John Fiske, in his Ingersoll lecture *Life Everlasting* (the book appeared in 1901), recognizes that on these questions the best a theist can do is make a frank confession of ignorance. He points out, quite correctly, that although nature everywhere displays continuity, it also has a propensity for making prodigious leaps of the sort that are analyzed today by catastrophe theory, and in evolution theory by upholders of the punctuationist approach. Fiske gives two good analogies. Water can rise slowly in a tank until suddenly it overflows and starts vast machinery working. Conic sections alter smoothly as you shift the tilt of the plane that cuts a cone. The eccentricity of the ellipse slowly increases until suddenly, "presto! one more little shift, and the finite ellipse becomes an infinite hyperbola mocking our feeble powers of conception as it speeds away on its everlasting career."

> Perhaps in our ignorance such analogies may help us to realize the possibility that steadily developing ephemeral conscious life may reach a critical point where it suddenly puts on immortality. . . . In the course of evolution there is no more philosophical difficulty in man's acquiring immortal life than in his acquiring the erect posture and articulate speech.

I have already indicated that mortalism leaves to God the question of where to draw such lines. Believers in this model simply trust Divine wisdom and justice. C. S. Lewis, in *The Problem of Pain* (1962), speculates on the possibility that our pets may be the only animals to survive death because they alone have close bonds of love with us.

Animal souls offer few problems to believers in transmigration. F. C. S. Schiller, unlike his fellow-pragmatists William James and John

Dewey, preferred this model. In his *Riddles of the Sphinx* (1891) he adds the notion that since personal identity depends on memory, and because the extent of an animal's memory lies on an evolutionary spectrum, we must think of immortality also in terms of degree. An amoeba has so infinitesimal a memory, or none at all, that there is nothing there to survive, not to mention the fact that an amoeba doesn't even die; it just splits into two other animals. As you go higher up the evolutionary scale, memory gradually increases in scope; hence (reasoned Schiller) there is something more and more worth passing on to a higher incarnation.

One of the most curious of all views about animal souls was put forth in 1739 by Father Guillaume Hyacinthe Bougeant, a French Jesuit. He argued (perhaps in jest) against Cartesians that, contrary to the views of Descartes, beasts do indeed have souls, but they are the souls of fallen angels undergoing punishment. Father Bougeant's book, *Philosophical Amusements about the Language of Beasts*, was translated into English in 1740, though I have not seen a copy.

That a belief in the immortality of pets is widespread is evident from the touching inscriptions on gravestones of animals in cemeteries around the world, especially in California. Many poems and stories tell of finding a beloved beast in heaven. I recommend Frederic Brown's "Search," a short-short story in his *Angels and Spaceships* (1954), reprinted as a paperback, *Star Shine* (1956), and Lord Dunsany's poem, "A Heterodoxy," in his *Fifty Poems* (1929).

18. In *The Tao is Silent*, op. cit., Raymond M. Smullyan has an essay titled "Wouldn't It Be Funny If—." Smullyan asks you to imagine that after death you discover you are really an electronic computer, in another space, that has been dreaming it is a human body on earth. Moreover, as a body you were unable to believe in personal immortality on the grounds that thoughts are nothing more than physical events in a brain; therefore when you die you go out like a candle. Now you learn that your body didn't even exist!

A new worry enters your computer mind. You exist only so long as there is energy to supply your electric current. Will you not go out like a candle if the current is turned off, or if the universe runs down until no energy sources are left? "At this point, you *really* wake up, and find to your amazement that you are not a computer at all, nor a human being, nor anything like that, but a totally different kind of being than you or I have ever imagined, which all this time had been merely *dreaming* that he is a computer."

19. James's *Human Immortality* was his Ingersoll lecture on the topic, delivered at Harvard University in 1897, and published the following year. It is worth reading, even though it is marred by an almost unbelievable blemish.

The book is subtitled *Two Supposed Objections to the Doctrine*. The first objection is that if thought is a function of the brain, how can our memories survive death? James disposes of this easily with his transmission model. The second objection is so absurd that it is hard to suppose James would have deemed it necessary to consider it at all. It is that so many people have lived and died, with billions more yet to come, where will God find room for them? The same childish mistake had been made earlier by David Hume, as the following passage from his sarcastic essay "Of the Immortality of the Soul" will prove:

> How to dispose of the infinite number of posthumous existences ought so to embarrass the religious theory. Every planet in every solar system, we are at liberty to imagine peopled with intelligent mortal beings, at least we can fix on no other supposition. For these then a new universe must every generation be created beyond the bounds of the present universe, or one must have been created at first so prodigiously wide as to admit of this continual influx of beings. Ought such bold suppositions to be received by any philosophy, and that merely on the pretext of a bare possibility? When it is asked, whether Agamemnon, Thersites, Hannibal, Varro, and every stupid clown that ever existed in Italy, Scythia, Bactria, or Guinea, are now alive; can any man think, that a scrutiny of nature will furnish arguments strong enough to answer so strange a question in the affirmative?

James Boswell, on a visit to Hume in 1776 when the philosopher was mortally ill, asked him if he thought an afterlife was possible. About as possible, Hume replied, as that a piece of coal on the fire would not burn. The belief was a "most unreasonable fancy," Hume added, because it would entail that "the trash of every age must be preserved," and that would require the creation of new universes to hold so large a number. William James, I am saddened to report, found it necessary to justify the right to live again, not just for the dregs of humanity but for an entire race! I know that he spoke at a time when Americans were aroused by what they called the Yellow Peril. Even so, it is difficult to believe that his Harvard listeners were then so racist that James could say:

> Take for instance, all the Chinamen. Which of you here, my friends, sees any fitness in their eternal perpetuation unreduced in numbers? Surely not one of you. At most, you might deem it well to keep a few chosen specimens alive to represent an interesting and peculiar variety of humanity; but as for the rest, what comes in such surpassing numbers, and what you can only imagine in this abstract summary collective manner, must be something of which the units, you are sure, can have no individual preciousness. God himself, you think, can have no use for them.

When I first read this I could scarcely believe it. It is not how James feels—he takes great pains to explain the supreme worth of every individual and to rebut the crude notion of the "tiresomeness of an over-populated heaven"—but that James imagined his audience would consider this a stumbling block to the idea of immortality is a shocking testimonial either to James's poor perception of his listeners or to their philosophical immaturity and ethnocentrism.

20. A bizarre model of the afterlife, combining elements from all the models discussed in this chapter, underlies the famous Riverworld series of science-fiction novels by Philip José Farmer. All intelligent beings who evolved in our universe had no self-awareness or free will until a scientist, on a planet not the earth, accidently created a "walthan." A walthan is a form of "extraphysical energy" which attaches itself to a zygote. If the life-form is sentient it acquires a "soul," which keeps a permanent record of the creature's life experience. The scientist's machine "spat out" billions of walthans, all uniting instantly with bodies to create the universe's first self-aware sentients.

Believing it their moral duty to confer self-awareness on all other sentients, the Firsts (as they are called) traveled about the cosmos, in spaceships moving faster than light, to seek out planets with life. On these planets they buried machines that generated walthans. Descendants of the Firsts, called the Ethicals, selected a barren moonless planet to be the spot where all human beings who ever lived on earth would be reconstituted, and put through a kind of purgatory ("purgatory is hell with hope"). This is done by transferring their walthans to the new planet, where, on Resurrection Day A.D. 2246), they are all given new bodies. The new bodies copy the old ones, including the brain and all its memories, but are free of all physical and mental defects. Those who were older than twenty-five when they died are given bodies of age twenty-five. Children of under five are reconstituted at the age of their death and allowed to grow to twenty-five. The new bodies, naked and hairless, come to life on the banks of an enormous artificial river, millions of miles long, that snakes its way around the Riverworld, with both mouth and tail at the North Pole.

As in Oz, there are no physical diseases in the Riverworld, and no one grows old, though one can die as a result of accident, murder, execution, war, or suicide. However, at death one's walthan is immediately given a new body at some random spot along the river. After many such reincarnations, if one has advanced far enough in the ability to love, the walthan is capable of breaking completely away from the body, preserving its memories, and "Going On" to some higher region about which nothing is known, not even to the leaders of the Riverworld's Church of the Second Chance. Presumably a Creator God has planned everything, but the actual immortality is conferred on sentients by other sentients who make use of science.

I oversimplify a rich, funny, fast-paced, pulp-style adventure series. Its cast of characters includes Richard Burton (translator of *The Arabian Nights*), Alice Liddell (Lewis Carroll's child-friend), Jesus, Tom Mix, Herman Göring, King John, Mark Twain, Cyrano de Bergerac, and many other unlikely notables. The basic plot line is a quest up the river to a high tower at the North Pole where the Ethicals are believed to live. The saga ends happily when Alice, recalling passages from Carroll's nonsense books, thinks of a clever way to repair the Riverworld's dying protein computer and thereby save billions of human souls from permanent extinction.

The problem of whether a reconstituted body is the original person or just a duplicate is discussed most explicitly in *To Your Scattered Bodies Go* (1971, Chapters 16 and 29), *The Fabulous Riverboat* (1971, Chapter 20), and the final chapter of *The Magic Labyrinth* (1980). What happens if two identical bodies are reconstituted at the same time? The walthan unites with only one of them. (On this see *The Magic Labyrinth*, Chapter 20. Similar notions are in Farmer's earlier and deservedly forgotten novella, *Inside-Outside* [1964], where the walthan is called a "soul quantum.")

No science-fiction writer has ever been more preoccupied with life after death. Raised a Christian Scientist, Farmer was an atheist for a time, then later became a philosophical theist. "It may seem idiotic or naïve to express belief in the attainment of immortality of everybody who's existed or will exist," Farmer says in a short article that appears in *The Visual Encyclopedia of Science Fiction* (1977), edited by Brian Ash. "But, without immortality, there is no meaning in life." Farmer concludes with a statement that could almost have been written by Miguel de Unamuno:

> For me, only those stories concerned with this one vital issue are serious stories. All others, no matter how moving or profound, are mere entertainments. They do not deal with that which is our gravest concern. Without a belief in eternal life for us, the terrestrial existence is something to be gotten through with as little pain and as much pleasure as possible.
>
> If this conclusion is the triumph of irrationality over logic, so be it. After all, irrationality is the monopoly of sentients.

21. William James, *Human Immortality* (1898).

CHAPTER 20

1. The lecture is reprinted in Albert A. Michelson's book *Light Waves and Their Uses* (1903). However, Michelson attributed the remark about the search for new decimal places to an "eminent physicist," and no one seems to know who he had in mind. Robert Millikan, in his *Autobiography* (1950), says he thinks it was Lord Kelvin, and adds: "Later, in conversation with me, he [Michelson] was to upbraid himself roundly for this remark." (See Stephen Brush's letter, "Romance in Six Figures," *Physics Today*, January 1969, page 9.) It was only a few decades after Michelson's speech that the paradoxes of relativity and quantum mechanics introduced depths of previously unimagined richness.

2. Arthur H. Compton's remark is quoted in *The University of Chicago Magazine*, February 1931, page 191.

3. Robert B. Leighton, *Principles of Modern Physics* (1959).

4. I was unable to locate the source of Gamow's statement about the expanding circle, but here is a similar remark from an article of his in *Physics Today* (January 1949) that I found quoted in William H. Whyte, Jr.'s *The Organization Man* (1956):

> It seems to me that our science definitely shows signs of convergence, although this statement can also be easily classified as wishful thinking. We see, nevertheless, from our analysis, that in the field of microphenomena there is only one big region remaining to be explored: the theory of elementary length in its relation to the problem of elementary particles.

5. My source for Werner Heisenberg's remark is an interview by Walter Sullivan in *The New York Times*, December 13, 1971. Heisenberg said he agreed with Plato that the ultimate constituents of matter are ideal mathematical forms. The notion of an infinite complexity of smaller and smaller entities, going on forever, he called an "old-fashioned" and "foolish idea." On these philosophical grounds he expressed skepticism about the reality of quarks, and questioned the advisability of building more powerful atom smashers, because, in Sullivan's phrasing, "the ultimate has probably been reached in probing the innermost sanctum of matter."

6. Richard P. Feynman, *The Character of Physical Laws* (1965).

7. Murray Gell-Mann is quoted in *Time*, January 2, 1960.
"In the village of World's End," writes Lord Dunsany (in his *Book of Wonder*, 1912),

> at the furthest end of Last Street, there is a hole that you take to be a well, close by the garden wall, but if you lower yourself by your hands over the edge of the hole, and feel about with your feet till they find a ledge, that is the top step of a flight of stairs that takes you down over the edge of the World. "For all that men know, those stairs may have a purpose and even a bottom step," said the arch-idolater, "but discussion about the lower flights is idle." Then the teeth of Pompo chattered, for he feared the darkness, but he that made idols of his own explained that those stairs were always lit by the faint blue gloaming in which the World spins.

8. Philip Morrison's remark is in his article "Science May Beggar

Predictions," *The New York Times Annual Educational Review*, January 12, 1970.

9. Lewis Thomas, "The Art of Teaching Science," *The New York Times Magazine*, March 14, 1982.

10. Rudy Rucker, *Infinity and the Mind* (1982).

11. From Albert Einstein's essay "What I Believe," in *Forum and Century*, Vol. 84, 1930, pages 193–194; reprinted in the thirteenth of the *Forum* series, *Living Philosophies* (1931).

12. I copied this from a deteriorating newspaper clipping that I failed to date or identify. Peter Michelmore, in his *Einstein, Profile of the Man* (1962), gives almost the same quotation. He attributes it to an interview by George Sylvester Viereck, published in Viereck's *Glimpses of the Great* (1930).

13. Dr. Lao's statement is in *The Circus of Dr. Lao* (1935), by Charles Finney. I do not know the source of the Fabre quote. The Buddhist text is given by Jorge Luis Borges in a footnote to his essay "From Someone to Nobody," in his *Other Inquisitions: 1937–1952* (1964).

14. From J. B. S. Haldane's essay "Possible Worlds," in his book of the same name (1928).

15. Eugene Witla, the artist and protagonist of Dreiser's novel, reads this passage ("the sanest interpretation of the limits of human thought I have ever read," he says to himself) from Spencer's *Facts and Comments* (1902). For Spencer's fullest discussion of the Unknowable, see the first section of his *First Principles* (1862).

16. I have copied this from a newspaper clipping, but I do not know where the letter was printed.

17. Bertrand Russell, *Some Problems of Philosophy* (1927), retitled *Philosophy* for its United States edition, Chapter 24.

18. From George Santayana's address "Ultimate Religion," published in his *Obiter Scripta* (1936).

19. H. G. Wells, *The Work, Wealth and Happiness of Mankind* (1931).

20. Wells's *Experiment in Autobiography* (1934), Chapter 5, section 2.

21. I failed to date my clipping of Corliss Lamont's letter. The passage he quotes from John Dewey (to which I added the paragraph's final sentence) can be found in the last chapter of *A Common Faith* (1934).

22. Borges's remarks are in the first chapter of Richard Burgin's *Conversations with Jorge Luis Borges* (1969).

23. *The Autobiography of G. K. Chesterton* (Sheed and Ward, New York, 1936), pages 90–91, 132, 341–350.
In his life of Samuel Johnson (April 15, 1778 section), Boswell records an interesting conversation between Johnson and a lady about the fear of annihilation at death. Although a person who does not exist obviously can feel no pain, reasoned Johnson, "It is in the apprehension of it that the horror of annihilation consists." "Mere existence," he said, "is so much better than nothing, that one would rather exist even in pain, than not exist." Miguel de Unamuno often recalled his childhood fears of hell, when he took the doctrine of eternal punishment seriously, and how even then he found the prospect of life in torment preferable to ceasing to exist.

24. The story about Professor Oliver Green is in Chesterton's *Tales of the Long Bow* (1925).

25. *The Collected Poems of G. K. Chesterton* (1932).

26. The chapter derives from an earlier essay, "A Fairy Tale" (1906), that was one of the weekly columns Chesterton wrote for the London *Daily News*. The column is reprinted in Chesterton's posthumous *Lunacy and Letters* (1958), edited by Dorothy Collins. Admirers of "The Ethics of Elfland" will find the column much worth reading.

27. "Reason," a one-stanza poem by the British poet Ralph Hodgson. It is surely in one of his books, but I have not tried to run it down.

28. Perhaps this is unfair to both Dewey and Carnap. Charles W. Morris, a philosopher whose views were close to, and strongly influenced by, Dewey and Carnap, not only loved conjuring but actually performed magic semiprofessionally in his youth. However, Morris's

philosophy had a romantic side, a passionate interest in Maitreyan Buddhism. In temperament he was closer to Charles Peirce (who invented several unusual mathematical card tricks) than to Dewey or Carnap.

29. "When the Time is Ripe—," the last essay in Smullyan's book *The Tao is Silent* (1977). The passage could almost have been written by either of the two German fideists and,opponents of Kant: Johann Georg Hamann and Friedrich Heinrich Jacobi. Both men praised Hume's skepticism as having demonstrated the inability of reason to solve any fundamental metaphysical question, thereby preparing the way for unencumbered faith.

CHAPTER 21

1. Bertrand Russell's remark is in his essay "Why I Am Not a Christian." This courageous lecture, with which I am in almost total sympathy, was delivered in London in 1927, and first published in Girard, Kansas, by E. Haldeman-Julius, as Little Blue Book No. 1372. It is reprinted in *Why I Am Not a Christian, and Other Essays on Religion and Related Topics* (1957), edited by Paul Edwards.

2. C. S. Lewis, *The World's Last Night* (1960).

3. See *The Letters of William James* (1926), edited by his son Henry, Vol. 2.

4 There is now a growing split in the Adventist Church over the question of Ellen G. White's "inspiration." Evidence that she consciously, shamelessly, and extensively plagiarized the writings of others has been mounting steadily since D. M. Canright made the charge in his 1919 biography of Mrs. White (see Chapter 19, Note 11). For the devastating, unanswerable details, see *The White Lie* by former Adventist minister Walter T. Rea, published in 1982 by M & R Publications, Box 2056, Turlock, California 95381.

A front-page story in *The New York Times* (November 6, 1982) reveals that more than one hundred Adventist ministers have resigned over the unwillingness of the sect's leaders to face up to the implications of Mrs. White's plagiarisms. The issue is clearly a major turning point in the history of the "remnant church," because if Mrs. White's divine authority goes down the drain, many of the Church's idiosyncratic doctrines are likely to go down with her.

5. Mencken's great fable was first printed as "Stare Decisis" in *The New Yorker* (December 30, 1944). Two years later Knopf brought it out as a small book titled *The Christmas Story*, with pictures by Bill Crawford. The story is reprinted in H. L. Mencken, *The American Scene* (1965), edited by Huntington Cairns.

On its top metaphorical level Mencken's banquet is a symbol of today's Western world. Fred Ammermeyer is modern science and skepticism. We are the bewildered bums, feasting on the riches of technology, hooked on alcohol, obsessed by porn, and unable to forget our Christian past.

6. On the colorful history of New Harmony, I recommend Marguerite Young's book *Angel in the Forest* (1945). George Rapp turns up in, of all places, Byron's *Don Juan* (Canto 15, stanza 35):

> *When Rapp the Harmonist embargo'd marriage*
> *In his harmonious settlement—(which flourishes*
> *Strangely enough as yet without miscarriage,*
> *Because it breeds no more mouths than it nourishes,*
> *Without those sad expenses which disparage*
> *What Nature naturally most encourages)—*
> *Why call'd he "Harmony" a state sans wedlock?*
> *Now here I have got the preacher at a dead lock.*

7. In Peter Steinfels's *The Neoconservatives* (1979) the most discussed writers who do not share Steinfels's Roman Catholic faith are Daniel Bell, Irving Kristol, and Norman Podhoretz. Yet all three often speak these days of a need for "religion" in any healthy culture. Bell has considered this most explicitly in "The Return of the Sacred," the last chapter of his latest collection of papers, *The Winding Passage* (1980). He observes such current trends as the revival of fundamentalism and the turn toward Eastern cults, but he is as shy as Kristol and Podhoretz in letting us in on what sort of religious faith he would *like* to see revived. I have again the eerie feeling of looking at the back of Bell's head. There is little point in talking about a return to the sacred if nothing more is meant than a vague awe before the mystery of existence and the reality of death, since these emotions are easily felt by any atheist.

Exactly what does Bell mean when he defines religion as "a set of coherent answers to the core existential questions"? Pantheists and atheists alike recognize such questions and give coherent answers, even if they consist in saying there are no answers. We will have to wait and see if Bell has more to say. If by "religion" he means something less than a leap of faith toward transcendent answers, we are back to August Comte's positive church in which humanity is the Great Being to be worshipped in ritual and prayer, and to Dewey's similar efforts in *A Common Faith* to transform secular humanism into a religion by the trick of pilfering a terminology.

8. Whittaker Chambers, *Witness* (Random House, New York, 1952), page 17.

9. G. K. Chesterton, *What I Saw in America* (1922).

10. Chambers, op. cit., pages 500–501.

11. Ibid., page 194.

12. Ibid., page 741.

13. Ibid., page 482.

14. The definitive biography of Servetus is *Hunted Heretic: The Life and Death of Michael Servetus* (1953), by Roland H. Bainton.

15. *The Collected Poems of Stephen Crane* (1922).

16. For a lively exchange of opinions about Shirley MacLaine's film, see Walter Goodman, "The False Art of the Propaganda Film," *The New York Times*, Sunday "Arts and Leisure" section, March 23, 1975, and Miss MacLaine's impassioned rebuttal, same section, April 6, 1975. Two good recent antidotes to Miss MacLaine's rosy picture are Fox Butterfield, *China: Alive in the Bitter Sea* (1982), and Richard Bernstein, *From the Center of the Earth: The Search for the Truth About China* (1982). Both books are favorably reviewed by John K. Fairbank in "China on the Rocks," *The New York Review of Books*, May 27, 1982.

17. G. K. Chesterton's essay on grey is in his *Alarms and Discursions* (1911).

INDEX

DATE DUE

			PRINTED IN U.S.A.